MW01231229

THE GUIDE
TO
RELIGIOUS AND
INSPIRATIONAL
MAGAZINES

PUBLISHED BY WRITER'S RESOURCES

WRITER'S
RESOURCES

53 BRANDON ROAD, MILTON, MA 02186

CONTENTS

ELIZABETH GOULD, PUBLISHER

LIVIA FIORDELISI, EDITOR

BRANDT GOULD, DESIGN EDITOR

EDITORIAL ASSISTANTS: ANDREW KAUFMAN, ANNIE LASKEY, MICHELLE MATHEWS, ROBIN RUSING

THE GUIDE TO RELIGIOUS AND INSPIRATIONAL MAGAZINES

International Standard Serial Number
ISSN 1071-4014

International Standard Book Number
ISBN 0-9637387-0-4

THE GUIDE TO
RELIGIOUS AND INSPIRATIONAL MAGAZINES

"Know that being able to write is a gift from God, whether or not your work is published. May God bless your writing and your ministry through it."
—Christine Dallman, Editor, Sunday Digest

This book is the result of two people sharing a common interest and goal. Our vision was to create a truly inspirational market guide that went beyond a general overview of the market to the specifics that can make the difference between getting published and getting rejected. We wanted to offer you the best freelance opportunities and at the same time encourage new ideas by showcasing the diversity of interests in the religious and inspirational markets. It is our hope that you will find publications suitable for your already written work *and* be inspired to write new articles and stories as a result of reading though the listings.

As religious and inspirational writers, we are led not only to create, but in our creation, inspire others to their purpose. Some of us tell stories that teach children; others compose articles that call on the rest of us to act, to defend our beliefs, and preserve our freedoms; still others can bring the wisdom and inspiration of the ages into a context more easily understood in contemporary society. Whichever kind of writer you are, whatever your purpose is, you will find opportunities to get published within these pages.

Most of the publications we list are based in Christian or Jewish belief and tradition. Some are ecumenical; others focus solely on denominational concerns. We also list inspirational markets including writers magazines, non-religious magazines open to religious writing, and culturally focused publications concerned with issues affecting religion, faith, and freedom. The common thread that runs through all the publications we have chosen is that they inspire, inform, teach, and uplift the reader's mind and spirit in some way.

To acquaint yourself with the scope of the market, turn to the Subject Index (pp.13–36) where both religious and inspirational magazines are indexed under 79 categories and 26 denominations. We encourage you to explore a variety of categories—you may be surprised at what you have to offer, and to whom.

Within these categories, editorial interests are wide and varied. For instance, under Jewish magazines, *Dimensions* welcomes writings on the Holocaust, while *Response* does not. Often inspirational and religious interests will overlap as in the cases of spirituality, fiction, and parenting. Therefore, it is important to read each publication's listing to ascertain its particular slant and needs. Using the Market Listings (pp.11–12) will show you how to get the most out of each listing.

There are many ways to use *The Guide.* If you have a finished piece, you may want to start with the Subject Index to locate publications in line with your ideas and writing style. If, on the other hand, you have ideas but have not yet put pen to paper, use *The Guide* for focus and motivation. Peruse the book—you may find topics or themes that interest you. Your curiosity can develop into an article. You might discover that you possess knowledge, skills, or experience that others are in need of. You may have parenting ideas, prayers, or stories that come to mind as you review each magazine's needs and concerns. The possibilities for creation and publication are endless when you open your mind and let your creativity flow.

You may choose to examine the listings themselves for publications most open to freelance writing, or those that pay within a certain range, and tailor your piece to fit their requirements. While the majority of the publications in our book offer payment, don't ignore those markets that do not pay. Often, these publications are smaller and more open to working with new writers. They can provide important contacts, establish publishing credits, and offer valuable experience with editors and the process of freelance writing.

In addition to the listings, we wanted you to have as much information as possible about the submissions process. Beginning on page 5 you will find tips on manuscript presentation and how to write cover and query letters. The postage chart on page 9 shows you an easy way to calculate first-class postage for your manuscript. On page 10, we have listed proofreaders symbols and examples of their usage. And the Glossary on pages 538–539 will answer any questions you have about terms and abbreviations used in *The Guide.*

We have written this book with you in mind, and in that light, we welcome your suggestions, comments, and questions. You can write to us, Elizabeth Gould and Livia Fiordelisi, at Writer's Resources, 53 Brandon Road, Milton, MA 02186.

HOW TO SUBMIT YOUR WORK

"Your manuscript stands a better chance of acceptance if it is neatly presented, carefully polished, and on a topic of special interest to our readers."
—Rev. Allan Weinert, C.SS.R., Editor-in-Chief, Liguorian

The market listings that follow are tools of the trade. They will help you choose which few among the hundreds of religious publications are best suited to your work. Your options will narrow and focus as you consider each publication's interests, audience, payment policies, and denominational concerns. Using our listings to target appropriate markets can save you hours of research time. They also provide general information on how, when, and to whom you submit your material. They are not, however, a substitute for hands-on knowledge of the magazines you select. It is often impossible to fit the full range of editorial needs and requirements into a one-page analysis. Nor can we convey the magazine's design and style, its look and feel.

Most editors request that perspective writers send for contributor's guidelines and a sample magazine before submitting material. Writer's guidelines will differ greatly in scope and content. Some consist simply of one or two paragraphs of suggested topics; others run several pages and detail very specific editorial and submissions requirements that guarantee rejection if not followed. Many magazines are thematic and will accept writing only on predetermined topics or at particular times of the year. All contain information that will help you present an article, story, or proposal that is well thought out and professional. You are wise to study the guidelines and several samples of all publications you deem viable avenues for your work.

HOW TO WRITE A QUERY LETTER

A query letter is a one page, single-spaced business letter, the purpose of which is to interest an editor in your article idea. Generally, query letters are used to propose a nonfiction piece such as a feature article, interview, news report, or book review. As a rule, editors prefer to review fiction—short stories, drama, monologues—in its entirety.

The goal of your query is to convince an editor that not only is your idea a good one, but that you are the writer to bring it to life. Remember that this is an editor's first impression of you and your work. Therefore, your letter should be well written and edited. If in the query you demonstrate your ability as a writer and a thinker, you are more likely to get an assignment.

Query Format

A query generally consists of four parts:

1. The Lead (1 paragraph). A brief and enticing lead-in that conveys clearly the nature of your article and your ability to write.

2. Article description (1–2 paragraphs). A clear and concise description of your article idea. Explain the focus of your piece, how you will approach the subject, and why your approach is unique or valuable. List any elements you plan to use to supplement your article: interviews, expert opinions, informative sidebars, and/or resource lists. State the availability of photos or artwork that will illustrate your text. Demonstrate your knowledge of the magazine and why your article will appeal to its readers.

3. Experience (1 paragraph). Describe your qualifications. List any relevant experience or expertise such as educational background, lay or professional ministries, or volunteer work that qualifies you to write the article, along with previous publishing credits, if any. If you have not been published, there is no need to mention it. Remember to stress the positive, but do not overdo it. If you have enclosed a resume, clips, writing samples, or other relevant materials, mention them here.

4. Closing (1 paragraph). State the proposed word length and when the finished manuscript can be available. Do not discuss payment. If you have submitted the same manuscript to another magazine, mention it here (many publications accept simultaneous submissions; some wish to be notified). Note that you have enclosed a self-addressed, stamped envelope for a response. End cordially and professionally.

Common Mistakes

The following are common mistakes or oversights that lead to rejection:

1. Lack of research. A query should imply your knowledge of the magazine and its editorial needs. Studying back issues and writer's guidelines will tell you if your idea is appropriate. If the magazine has recently published an article that is similar to what you are proposing,

you may want to consider refocusing your piece or submitting to another publication. Your research will minimize the risk of proposing articles that are overdone or ill-suited to the magazine's needs.

2. Too long or too informal. Editors usually do not have time to weed through pages of irrelevant, wordy material. Keep your query brief and focused. Avoid being too friendly, sentimental, or chatty. A query letter is a business proposal and deserves professional treatment.

3. Careless writing. Poorly written and edited letters do not entice editors. Proofread your letter for spelling errors and typos. Double check the editor's name against the magazine's masthead to be sure it is spelled correctly.

4. Sloppy presentation. Presentation is important. Use quality bond paper, cream or white, and be sure that the type is clean and legible.

It is good practice to include a self-addressed, postage-paid envelope for materials you want returned and/or a self-addressed, stamped postcard for confirmation of receipt. Many editors will not contact you without one. Keep a copy of all query letters for your files. Finally, a positive, confident attitude is an asset. Be yourself, and be professional.

HOW TO WRITE A COVER LETTER

Some publications prefer that writers submit a complete manuscript for review. As mentioned earlier, this is often true for fiction. In these cases it is common practice to enclose a cover letter as an accompaniment to your manuscript. A cover letter is similar to a query in form, but even more concise, allowing the manuscript to speak for itself.

A cover letter should be a one-page business letter addressed to the appropriate editor. It can include the following:

1. Lead. Introduce the article or story enclosed. State its title, word length, and intended audience.

2. Description. Again, be brief. State the focus and slant of your piece and how it serves the magazine's readers. If not enclosed, state the availability of artwork and/or photos.

3. Experience. Mention any relevant experience and/or publishing credits. Refer to any additional enclosures such as a resume, author biography, published clips, or bibliography.

4. Closing. Indicate a simultaneous submission if applicable. Refer to the enclosed self-addressed, stamped envelope for response.

As with a query, a good cover letter is well written, neatly presented, and error free. It reflects your knowledge of the magazine and its interests.

HOW TO SUBMIT A MANUSCRIPT

Most editors will accept manuscripts that follow the standard format outlined below. Some, however, require a particular set-up or request additional information. Check the writer's guidelines and market listings for any special requirements before submitting your work.

Manuscript Format

Manuscripts should be neatly typed and double spaced. Allow generous top, bottom, and side margins—at least one inch—for editor's comments. On the first page, type your name, address, phone number, and social security number, single spaced, in the upper left corner. Type the approximate word length in the upper right corner. Center your title (and byline, if desired though not necessary) one-third of the way down the page. Begin your text two or three lines below the title. On subsequent pages, type your last name and the page number in the upper right corner. Space down three or four lines to continue your text.

A note about word lengths: There are several ways to divine the number of words in your manuscript. If you do your writing on a computer, most programs will provide word counts. If not, count the number of words in five lines and divide it by five. This will give you the average number of words per line. Then count the number of lines and multiply to find your total word count.

Presentation and Mailing

As with any business proposal, manuscript presentation counts, so be professional. Use heavy-weight 8.5x11 white bond paper that allows for minimal show-through. Erasable paper is flimsy and sloppy—avoid using it. Whether typewritten or computer printed, check that your manuscript type is dark, clean, and very legible. Many editors accept clear dot-matrix printouts and photocopies, but letter-quality originals are always preferred. Be sure your manuscript is neat and smudge free. Always keep a copy of the article or story for your files.

Short manuscripts, usually less than five pages, can be folded and mailed in a business-size envelope. Longer pieces should be mailed flat, unstapled, in a 9x12 or 10x13 envelope. Include a SASE marked First Class with sufficient return postage (see page 9 for rates) or International Reply Coupons (IRCs) if submitting to a foreign publication. Enclose a SAS postcard if you wish the editor to acknowledge receipt.

Wait the predetermined response time before following up on your submission, and then contact the editor by mail. Above all, be patient.

HOW TO SUBMIT YOUR WORK

FIRST CLASS POSTAGE RATES

The chart below will help you determine the amount of postage needed to mail manuscripts to prospective publishers in the U.S. and Canada, as well as return postage for self-addressed, stamped envelopes. When mailing to foreign countries, check with the Post Office for International Reply Coupon (IRC) rates and requirements.

The number of pages per ounce are based on using standard 20 lb. paper and standard-weight 9x12 envelopes. Costs may vary according to the quality and weight of the paper and envelopes used. A query or short manuscript can be mailed in a #10 business-size envelope with a $.29 stamp. A self-addressed postcard requires $.19 postage.

First-class pieces weighing over 11 ounces are considered Priority Mail and are priced according to geographical zone as well as weight. Check with the Post Office for rates and requirements.

Ounces	Number of pages plus 9x12 envelope and 9x12 SASE	First-class postage rates	Rates to Canada from U.S.
1	1–2 pages	$.39	$.63
2	3–7 pages	$.52	$.73
3	8–14 pages	$.75	$.86
4	15–20 pages	$.98	$1.09
5	21–27 pages	$1.21	$1.32
6	28–34 pages	$1.44	$1.55
7	35–40 pages	$1.67	$1.78
8	41–47 pages	$1.90	$2.01
9	48–54 pages	$2.13	$2.24
10	55–60 pages	$2.36	$2.47
11	61–66 pages	$2.59	$2.70

PROOFREADER'S SYMBOLS

Correction	Symbol	Correction	Symbol
Insert character	the wh̬te house	Spell out	at least ⑩ ⑤ₚ
Insert period	away⊙She saw it	Lowercase	choose Ẉisely /c
Insert comma	with them⸲but he	Uppercase	rev. Jonas (Cap)
Insert semicolon	this time⸔however	Set in italics	entitled Roots (ital)
Insert colon	as follows⁀	Set in boldface	in Chapter 1 (bf)
Insert hyphen	well⸗known dog	Set in small capitals	a limited time (sc)
Insert EM dash	this day⸺a day	New paragraph	brightly. ¶The new
Insert EN dash	12‖14 years	No new paragraph; run text in	in his way⸗ no¶ ⌐The next day
Insert space	today#they went		
Insert quotation	said, “Come back.”	Move left	⌐ nearly ten feet
Insert apostrophe	Elizabeth's room	Move right	nearly ⌐
Delete character	the churchⱦdoor	Move up	a dark ⌐sky⌐ above
Delete word	ask any questions	Move down	sharp ⌐rocks⌐ below
Delete and close space	tommorrow night	Move text	as he drove⸳Suddenly the wheel shifted.)He heard a crackling sound.
Close space	his text book		
Replace word	In the evening morning	Return to original	the only one (stet)
Transpose letters	at the wnidow	More than one correction per line	He left without a wrdd⊙ # /N/⊙
Transpose words	heard the ring bell		

USING THE MARKET LISTINGS

Our market listings are designed to help you make informed choices about the best opportunities for your work. The outline that follows introduces you to the listing format and the type of information presented under each subheading.

AT A GLANCE

This column allows you to assess quickly a magazine's interests, policies, and relevance to your writing. In this section you will find the following information:

- Religious/denominational and editorial focus (Ex.: Baptist, Family). For non-religious markets that accept inspirational writing, two primary editorial concerns are listed (Ex.: Fiction, Poetry).
- Opportunities for freelance writers. The percent of an average issue that is contributed by freelance writers.
- Opportunities for new writers. The percent of an average issue that is contributed by new/unpublished writers.
- Frequency. How often a magazine is issued per year.
- Circulation. The number of magazines sold per issue.
- Number of queries and/or unsolicited manuscripts received by the magazine each month. Allows you to assess the competition.
- Payment, if any.

From the Editor: First-hand advice for perspective writers on the publication's philosophy, interests, policies, and procedures.

Best Bet: The types of articles and stories most in demand by the publication, or areas, such as departments or columns, most open to freelance writing.

Avoid: Topics, writing styles, literary forms, language usages, or viewpoints an editor will not consider for publication.

Sample Copy: How to obtain an issue of the magazine, including sample and postage costs, SASE size, and guideline availability.

In the body of each listing, you will find:

Profile
A brief description of the publication, its editorial slant, publishing house, and any religious, denominational, or organizational affiliations. When available, we list the date established. In most cases, we provide a physical description: the size, cover stock, binding, presentation, and number of pages.

Focus and Audience
The flavor of the publication with an in-depth description of the publication's goals, editorial and publishing philosophy, primary interests, doctrinal concerns, political bent, and target audience.

Interests and Word Lengths
Information on specific editorial needs and interests. Categories include Fiction, Nonfiction, Departments, Poetry, Seasonal, Filler, Games, Reviews, and Artwork/Photos. Listed are the types of articles, stories, and illustrations accepted; subjects of interest; and minimum and maximum word-length requirements.

How to Submit
Details on how to approach a publication: whether to query first or send a complete manuscript; what to include with your submissions, i.e., cover letter, resume, writing samples, author biography or outline; and acceptable submissions forms, i.e., photocopies, computer printouts and disks, or fax submissions; and any special submissions restrictions or deadlines. We also indicate whether the publication accepts reprints and simultaneous submissions. Finally, we note the average time it will take an editor to respond to your query or manuscript.

Payment and Policies
An outline of general publication terms: the type of rights the publisher requests; whether payment is made on acceptance or publication; rates per word or per piece; the number of contributor's copies offered; and any special policies regarding contests or compensation.

Your research into the religious and inspirational markets can begin with a careful study of the listings. Refer to the Glossary on page 538 for information on specific terms.

SUBJECT INDEX

Apologetics
Christian Research Journal
Missiology
SCP Journal

Arts and Architecture
Anglican and Episcopal
    History
Christian Living
Church Recreation
Environment & Art Letter
Hadassah Magazine
Home Times
Jewish Press
Kaleidoscope
Lilith
Living Prayer
Mennonite Life
A Positive Approach
Touchstone

Bible Stories
Canada Lutheran
Focus on the Family
    Clubhouse
Focus on the Family
    Clubhouse Jr.
Gospel Advocate
Parish Teacher
Shining Star
Teachers Interaction

Bible Study
AABC Newsletter
The Anglican Digest
The Baptist Informer
Beyond Reality Newsletter
Bible Review
The Bible Today
Biblical Illustrator
The Canadian Catholic
    Review
Carolina Christian
The Catholic Exponent
The Christian Science
    Sentinel
Church of God Evangel
CoLaborer
Compass

The Congregationalist
Contempo
Cornerstone Connections
Daughters of Sarah
Discipleship Journal
Emmanuel
Faith at Work
Foursquare World Advance
FreeWay
Gospel Advocate
Gospel Herald
Group
Hallelujah!
Hamevaser
Home Altar
In Mission
Jewish Exponent
Light and Life
Living Today
The Lookout
The Lutheran Witness
Lutheran Woman Today
Marketplace Métier
The Mennonite
Message of the Cross
Ministry
New Covenant
The New Era
Northwestern Lutheran
The Other Side
The Plowman
Pockets
Praying
The Preacher's Magazine
The Presbyterian Outlook
Protestant Challenge
Quarterly Review
Royal Service
The Sabbath Sentinel
The Sacred Name
    Broadcaster
St. Anthony Messenger
Sojourners
StarLight
Student Leadership
TAL
Touch
Touchstone
U.S. Catholic

The Voice of the Gospel
Woman's Touch
Year One

Biography
Again
Anglican and Episcopal
    History
Brio
Compassion Magazine
Focus on the Family
    Clubhouse
Focus on the Family
    Clubhouse Jr.
Friends Journal
Gnosis
Harmony
High Adventure
Lifeglow
Lilith
Marketplace Métier
My Friend
Purpose
St. Willibrord Journal
The Shantyman
Young & Alive

Book Review
Again
Anglican and Episcopal
    History
Bible Review
Bridges
Broken Street
The Canadian Catholic
    Review
Carolina Christian
The Christian Courier
Christian Education Journal
Christian Info News
The Christian Librarian
Compass
Cornerstone
Creation Social Science &
    Humanities Quarterly
Cross Currents
Desert Call
Dimensions
Epiphany Journal

Church Worship
Clubhouse
Command
Compassion Magazine
Conqueror
Contact
Cornerstone
Counselor
The Covenant Companion
Creation Social Science & Humanities Quarterly
Creator Magazine
Current Thoughts & Trends
Daughters of Sarah
Desert Call
Discipleship Journal
Discoveries
The Door
Dreams & Visions
Educational Ministries Buyers
Emphasis on Faith and Living
Epiphany Journal
Evangel
Evangelizing Today's Child
Faith and Renewal
Faith 'n Stuff
Faith Today
Faith at Work
Focus on the Family Clubhouse
Focus on the Family Clubhouse Jr.
Free Press
FreeWay
God's Revivalist
God's World Today
Good Fortune
Good News Journal
Gospel Herald
Gospel Tidings
Group
Growing Churches
The Helping Hand
High Adventure
His Garden
Homelife
The Hymn

The Journal of Christian Camping
Journal of Christian Nursing
The Joyful Noiseletter
The Joyful Woman
Jr. High Ministry
Junior Trails
Just Between Us
Keys for Kids
The Kiln
Latin American Evangelist
Lifeglow
Listen (Kansas City)
Listen (Nampa)
Living
Living Prayer
Living Today
Logos
The Magazine for Christian Youth!
Manna
Marketplace Métier
Marriage Partnership
Message
Message of the Cross
Message of the Open Bible
Ministries Today
Missiology
Moravian
Na'amat Woman
National & International Religion Report
Nature Friend Magazine
A New Heart
Open Hands
Opening the Word
Oregon Association of Christian Writers
The Other Side
Parent Care
Parents of Teenagers
Parish Teacher
Pastor's Tax & Money
Pathway I.D.
Perspectives on Science and Christian Faith
The Plowman
Plus
Pockets

A Positive Approach
Power for Living
The Preacher's Magazine
Preaching
Primary Days
Probe
Progress Magazine
Pursuit
Quiet Revolution
RADAR
Radix
Renewal News
The Sabbath Sentinel
Salt
SCP Journal
Second Stone
The Secret Place
Seek
The Shantyman
Sharing
Shining Star
Silver Wings
Single Adult Ministries Journal
Sojourners
Sports Spectrum
StarLight
Straight
Student Leadership
Sunday Digest
Teen Power
Today's Better Life
Today's Christian Woman
Today's Family
Touchstone
21st Century Christian
Twin Cities Christian
Unity
The Upper Room
Venture
Virtue
Voice
The Voice of the Gospel
Vox Benedictina
The War Cry
Wherever
Women Alive!
Wonder Time
World Vision

Writers Information Network
Young & Alive
Young Salvationist
Your Church

Christian Living
Alive Now!
Associate Reformed
   Presbyterian
At Ease
The Baptist Standard
Bible Advocate
Bible Time 4s5s
Brigade Leader
Brio
Campus Life
Canada Lutheran
Catechumenate
The Catholic Answer
Catholic New York
Christian Leader
Christian Living
Christian Single
ChristianWeek
Command
Contact
Counselor
The Covenant Companion
Diaconalogue
Discipleship Journal
Family
Free Press
FreeWay
God's Revivalist
God's Special People
Guide Magazine
Herald of Holiness
High Adventure
Home Life
Homelife
Insight/Out
The Kiln
Light and Life
Liguorian
Live
Living Prayer
Living Today
Living with Children
Living with Preschoolers

Living with Teenagers
The Lutheran
Message of the Cross
Morning Glory
The New Era
Oblates
Parenting Treasures
Pathway I.D.
Plus
Praying
Presbyterian Record
Presbyterian Survey
Progress Magazine
Purpose
Quiet Revolution
Rejoice!
Renewal News
St. Anthony Messenger
Salt
Seek
Share
Signs of the Times
Sisters Today
Sojourners
Spirit
Standard
StarLight
Teens Today
Today's Better Life
21st Century Christian
The United Methodist
   Christian Advocate
Unity
Woman's Touch
Women Alive!
You!
Young Salvationist

Church Life
Advance
The Anglican Digest
Baptist Progress
Catholic Digest
The Christian Chronicle
The Christian Ministry
The Christian Reader
The Christian Science
   Journal
ChristianWeek

Church Administration
CoLaborer
Compass
The Cumberland
   Presbyterian
Evangel
The Evangelical Beacon
Faith at Work
Family Digest
Interchange
Joyful Noise
Leadership
Live
Lutheran Forum
The Lutheran
Mennonite Reporter
Message of the Open Bible
Ministries Today
Ministry
National Catholic Reporter
On the Line
Orthodox Observer
Our Family
Our Sunday Visitor
Pastor's Tax & Money
The Pentecostal Messenger
Plenty Good Room
The Preacher's Magazine
The Presbyterian Outlook
Presbyterian Record
Presbyterian Survey
U.S. Catholic
Your Church

Community
AIM
Areopagus
Banner High
Catholic Near East
Christian Living
Common Ground
Communities
Community Service
   Newsletter
Companion of St. Francis
   and St. Anthony
Evangel
Extension
Fellowship

Guide Magazine
Israel Horizons
Live
Morning Glory
People Who Care
Salt
Sojourners
Year One

Comparative Religion
The Anglican Journal
Anima
Areopagus
Christian*New Age
  Quarterly
Common Boundary
The Congregationalist
Crisis
Ecumenical Trends
Parabola
The Plowman
The Reader's Review
Sunstone
U.S. Catholic

Cultural and Ethnic Issues
AIM
AlFajr
The American Jewish
  World
Amit Woman
The Baptist Informer
The B'nai B'rith International
  Jewish Monthly
Bridges
Catholic Near East
Challenge (Washington)
The Christian Century
Christian Living
Christian Social Action
Common Boundary
Compass
The Congregationalist
Creation Spirituality
Crisis
Desert Call
Ecumenical Trends
Faith 'n Stuff
Focus on the Family

Clubhouse
Focus on the Family
Clubhouse Jr.
Friend
Friends Journal
Hadassah Magazine
Homevaser
Harmony International
  Screenwriting
Inside
Jewish Leader
Joyful Noise
Language Bridges
  Quarterly
Latin American Evangelist
The Lutheran Journal
The Magazine for Christian
  Youth!
Maryknoll
Mennonite Life
Message
Missiology
National Review
On the Line
Orthodox Observer
Plenty Good Room
The Plowman
RADAR
Radix
The Reporter
SCP Journal
Shofar
Skipping Stones
United Synagogue Review
The Wisconsin Jewish
  Chronicle
You!

Devotions
Alive Now!
The Annals of St. Anne de
  Beaupré
Broken Streets
Canadian Messenger of the
  Sacred Heart
Carolina Christian
Chastity and Holiness
The Christian Reader
Church of God Evangel

CoLaborer
Cornerstone Connections
The Covenant Companion
Evangel
Foursquare World Advance
Gospel Advocate
Home Altar
Keys for Kids
Leaves
Lifeglow
Light and Life
Lutheran Woman Today
Mennonite Brethren Herald
Ministry
Miraculous Medal
Opening the Word
Parent Care
Pockets
The Priest
Queen of All Hearts
Rejoice!
The Secret Place
Seek
Sliver Wings
Standard
StarLight
Take Five
Time of Singing
The Upper Room
The War Cry
The Word in Season
Young & Alive

Disabilities
Expressions
God's Special People
Kaleidoscope
Lifeglow
A Positive Approach
Quiet Revolution
Vintage Northwest
Young & Alive

Discipleship
Children's Ministry
Diaconalogue
Discipleship Journal
The Kiln
Leader

DISCIPLESHIP (CON.)–ENVIRONMENT AND NATURE

Youth!
My Friend
Nature Friend Magazine
On the Line
Our Family
Our Little Friend
Pax Christi USA
Primary Treasure
RADAR
Skipping Stones
Time of Singing
The War Cry
World Vision
The World

Essays
Alaska Quarterly Review
America
Bridges
Compass
Cornerstone
Diaconalogue
Living Prayer
National Catholic Reporter
The New Press Literary
  Quarterly
Now and Then
The Observer
Poetry Forum Short Stories
Renegade
Response (Jewish)
Skylark
Sunstone
Vox Benedictina
Year One

Ethics
AFA Journal
The Anglican Journal
Arlington Catholic Herald
The Catholic Exponent
Catholic Parent
The Catholic Worker
The Christian Century
The Christian Chronicle
Command
Contact
Epiphany Journal
Gospel Advocate

Harmony
Journal of Christian Nursing
The Kiln
Living
Pastoral Life
Reconstructionist
Salt
You!

Evangelism
The Advocate
Again
At Ease
The Baptist Informer
Bible Time 4s5s
Breakaway
Brigade Leader
Brown Gold
The Catholic Accent
Childlife
The Christian Chronicle
Christian Info News
Christian Research Journal
Church Recreation
Circuit Rider
Evangel
Evangelizing Today's Child
Extension
Faith and Renewal
Faith Today
Foursquare World Advance
Free Press
God's Special People
Good News Journal
Gospel Herald
Gospel Tidings
Growing Churches
Hallelujah!
Huron Church News
Insight/Out
The Journal of Christian
  Camping
The Joyful Woman
The Kiln
Librarian's World
Living Today
Marketplace Métier
The Mennonite
Mennonite Brethren Herald

Message of the Cross
Ministry
Missiology
Moravian
National & International
  Religion Report
New Covenant
Pentecostal Evangel
Perspectives on Science
  and Christian Faith
Power for Living
Preaching
The Priest
Progress Magazine
Protestant Challenge
Pursuit
Review for Religious
SCP Journal
The Shantyman
Signs of the Times
Sports Spectrum
The Star of Zion
Student Leadership
Sunday Digest
Teachers Interaction
Venture
Voice
The Voice of the Gospel
Whole Earth Newsletter
Wonder Time

Family
Act
AFA Journal
The Anglican Journal
Avotaynu
Baptist Progress
Catholic Digest
Catholic Forester
Catholic Parent
Catholic Sentinel
Changes
Christian Home & School
Christian Leader
Christian Living
Christian Parenting Today
Christian Woman
Command
Common Ground

The Christian Science
   Journal
The Christian Science
   Sentinel
Church of God Evangel
Common Boundary
Guideposts
Health Consciousness
Jewish Science Interpreter
The Lutheran Journal
Message of the Open Bible
New Covenant
Pentecostal Evangel
Sharing
Woman's Touch

Health
Alive!
A Better Tomorrow
Beyond Reality Newsletter
Catholic Digest
The Catholic Exponent
Changes
Christian Parenting Today
Christian Single
Christian Social Action
Clubhouse
Cornerstone Connections
Expressions
Health Consciousness
The Helping Hand
Hospice
Jewish Times
Jewish Vegetarians
   Newsletter
The Jewish Veteran
Journal of Christian Nursing
Lifeglow
The Lutheran Journal
Mature Living
Message
The Montana Catholic
A New Heart
Parent Care
A Positive Approach
The Star of Zion
Today's Better Life
Today's Family
Total Health

Unity
Vibrant Life
Women Alive!

History
Amit Woman
Anglican and Episcopal
   History
Avotaynu
Baptist History and Heritage
Bible Review
The B'nai B'rith International
   Jewish Monthly
Bridges
The Canadian Catholic
   Review
Catholic Forester
Catholic Near East
Christian History
The Congregationalist
Creation Social Science &
   Humanities Quarterly
Homevaser
Home Times
Ideals
Jewish Action
Jewish Education
Lifeglow
Lilith
Logos
The Lutheran
Martyrdom and Resistance
Mennonite Family History
Mennonite Life
Missiology
Now and Then
On the Line
Protestant Challenge
Purpose
Queen of All Hearts
Response (Jewish)
The Sabbath Sentinel
Touchstone
Unity
Whole Earth Newsletter
The World

How-to
The Acorn

Advance
Advent Christian Witness
Authorship
Baptist Leader
Baptist Record
Bookstore Journal
Brigade Leader
Brio
Byline
Challenge (Memphis)
The Christian Ministry
Christian Retailing
Church Administration
Church Teachers
The Congregationalist
Creator Magazine
Dimension
Discipleship Journal
Faith and Renewal
Family Digest
Group
Growing Churches
Housewife Writer's Forum
Insight
Insight/Out
Jr. High Ministry
Life Enrichment
Living with Children
Living with Preschoolers
Living with Teenagers
The Lutheran Journal
Ministries Today
Modern Liturgy
People Who Care
Plus
Preaching
Probe
Progress Magazine
Renewal News
Single Adult Ministries
   Journal
Sunday Digest
Teachers Interaction
Teen Power
Tickled by Thunder
Virtue
Vista
With
Writers Information Network

Your Church
Youth and Christian
   Education Leadership

Humor
The Acorn
Alive!
Baltimore Jewish Times
Byline
Catholic Digest
Catholic Forester
The Christian Reader
Clubhouse
The Door
Dreams & Visions
Faith Today
Family Digest
FreeWay
Greater Phoenix Jewish
   News
Guide Magazine
Housewife Writer's Forum
Jewish Action
The Joyful Noiseletter
The Kiln
Light and Life
The Lookout
The Magazine for Christian
   Youth!
Marriage Partnership
Maryknoll
Mature Living
The Mennonite
Parenting Treasures
Pursuit
Standard
The Star of Zion
Straight
Student Leadership
Teen Power
Today's Christian Woman
United Synagogue Review
Welcome Home
With

Inspirational
The Acorn
Advent Christian Witness
The Anglican Digest

The Annals of St. Anne de
   Beaupré
The Baptist Standard
A Better Tomorrow
Byline
Canada Lutheran
Canadian Messenger of the
   Sacred Heart
Caring People
The Catholic Accent
Catholic Digest
Catholic Twin Circle
Changes
Christian Info News
The Christian Reader
The Christian Science
   Journal
Christian Standard
Clubhouse
Emphasis on Faith and
   Living
Family
Family Digest
Free Press
Friends Journal
Glory Songs
Gospel Herald
Guideposts
Harmony International
   Screenwriting
The Helping Hand
His Garden
Housewife Writer's Forum
Ideals
Jewish Science Interpreter
Joyful Noise
Just Between Us
Lady's Circle
Language Bridges
   Quarterly
Life Enrichment
Lifeglow
Light and Life
Lotus
The Lutheran Journal
Manna
Mature Living
Message of the Open Bible
New Covenant

Northwestern Lutheran
Now and Then
The Oak
Oblates
Opening the Word
Oregon Association of
   Christian Writers
Plus
A Positive Approach
Purpose
Queen of All Hearts
Rejoice!
St. Anthony Messenger
Seek
The Senior Musician
Silver Wings
Standard
StarLight
Teachers Interaction
Time of Singing
21st Century Christian
Virtue
The War Cry
Welcome Home
Writer's Guidelines
Writers Information Network
Young & Alive

Interviews and Profiles
The Acorn
AIM
The American Jewish
   World
Areopagus
Arlington Catholic Herald
Authorship
Baptist Progress
A Better Tomorrow
Breakaway
The Canadian Catholic
   Review
Caring People
Catholic Forester
Catholic New York
Catholic Sentinel
The Christian Courier
Christian Educators Journal
Christian History
The Christian Librarian

Friend
God's World Today
Guide Magazine
High Adventure
Junior Trails
Keys for Kids
Listen (Kansas City)
My Friend
Nature Friend Magazine
On the Line
Our Little Friend
Pockets
Power and Light
Primary Days
Primary Treasure
RADAR
The Shantyman
Shofar
Story Friends
Story Mates
Touch
Venture
Wonder Time

Leadership
At Ease
Baptist Leader
The Bible Today
Brigade Leader
Children's Ministry
Christian Education Journal
Christian Standard
Church Administration
Church Recreation
Cornerstone Connections
Discipleship Journal
Educational Ministries
    Buyers
Episcopal Life
Evangelizing Today's Child
Faith and Renewal
Faith at Work
Glory Songs
Group
Growing Churches
The Hymn
Jewish Leader
The Journal of Christian
    Camping

Jr. High Ministry
Leader
Leader in the Church
    School Today
Leadership
Lutheran Partners
Ministries Today
Ministry
Reformed Worship
Single Adult Ministries
    Journal
Sports Spectrum
Student Leadership
Youth and Christian
    Education Leadership

Lifestyle
The Advocate
Alive!
The Anglican Journal
At Ease
Atlanta Jewish Times
Campus Life
Changes
Christian Single
Christian Woman
Common Boundary
Communities
Good Fortune
Greater Phoenix Jewish
    News
Guideposts
Hadassah Magazine
Home Times
Inside
Israel Horizons
The Jewish Review
Jewish Vegetarians
    Newsletter
Kashrus Magazine
Listen (Nampa)
The Lookout
The Lutheran Journal
Moment
The Montana Catholic
Now and Then
Purpose
Pursuit
Saints Herald

Shofar
Signs of the Times
Single Adult Ministries
    Journal
Standard
Total Health
United Synagogue Review
Vibrant Life
Vintage Northwest
Virtue
Wellsprings
Women Alive!
Young & Alive

Literary
Alaska Quarterly Review
Kaleidoscope
Lilith
The Pegasus Review
Renegade
Response (Jewish)
TAL
Vintage Northwest

Liturgy
The Canadian Catholic
    Review
Catechumenate
The Catholic Exponent
Celebration
Church Educator
Church Worship
Emmanuel
Environment & Art Letter
Liguorian
Liturgy 90
Lutheran Forum
Messenger
Modern Liturgy
Our Family
Pastoral Life
The Priest
Spirit
St. Willibrord Journal
U.S. Catholic

Marriage
Christian Woman
Dovetail

MARRIAGE (CON.)–NEWS AND CURRENT EVENTS

Focus on the Family
Herald of Holiness
Home Life
Lifeglow
Liguorian
Living
Marriage Partnership
The Montana Catholic
Our Family
Social Justice Review
Standard
Today's Christian Woman
Virtue
Welcome Home
Women Alive!

Media
AFA Journal
AlFajr
The Canadian Catholic
    Review
Christian Woman
Church Media Library
    Magazine
Church Teachers
Cornerstone
Current Thoughts & Trends
Home Times
Librarian's World
Lilith
Michigan Christian
    Advocate
The Presbyterian Outlook

Men's Issues
Brigade Leader
Contact
Joyful Noise
Marriage Partnership
Voice

Ministers
Advance
The Bible Today
Celebration
The Christian Century
The Christian Ministry
Circuit Rider
Company

The Cumberland
    Presbyterian
Emmanuel
Homiletic & Pastoral Review
Just Between Us
Leadership
Lutheran Forum
Lutheran Partners
Message
Ministry
Pastor's Tax & Money
Pastoral Life
The Preacher's Magazine
Preaching
The Presbyterian Outlook
The Priest
Quarterly Review
Reformed Worship
Renewal News
Review for Religious
Your Church
Youth and Christian
    Education Leadership

Missionary
Advent Christian Witness
The Advocate
Again
Alive!
The Baptist Informer
Baptist Record
Brown Gold
Catholic Near East
Challenge (Memphis)
Childlife
CoLaborer
Contempo
Dimension
Extension
Free Press
High Adventure
Homelife
In Mission
The Kiln
The Link & Visitor
The Lutheran Witness
The Magazine for Christian
    Youth!
Maryknoll

Message of the Cross
Missiology
Missionary Tidings
National & International
    Religion Report
New World Outlook
Response (Christian)
Royal Service
Saints Herald
The United Methodist
    Christian Advocate
The Voice of the Gospel
Wherever
Whole Earth Newsletter
World Vision

Music
Cornerstone
Creator Magazine
Glory Songs
Guide Magazine
The Hymn
Lilith
Moravian
The Music Leader
Plenty Good Room
The Preacher's Magazine
The Senior Musician
Young Salvationist

News and Current Events
The Advocate
Again
AlFajr
The American Jewish
    World
Atlanta Jewish Times
Baptist Record
The Baptist Standard
Carolina Christian
The Catholic Accent
Catholic Courier
Catholic New York
Catholic Sentinel
Catholic Telegraph
Christian Standard
Conqueror
Cornerstone
The Covenant

Current Thoughts & Trends
Epiphany Journal
Episcopal Life
Faith Today
God's World Today
Greater Phoenix Jewish
    News
Harmony
High Adventure
Home Times
Insight
Insight/Out
Interchange
Jewish Action
Jewish Exponent
The Jewish News
Jewish Press
Jewish Weekly News
The Jewish World
The Kansas City Jewish
    Chronicle
The Living Church
The Lutheran Layman
Mennonite Reporter
Mennonite Weekly Review
Messenger
Michigan Christian
    Advocate
Moment
National Catholic Reporter
National & International
    Religion Report
National Review
NCSE Reports
Northwestern Lutheran
The Observer
Orthodox Observer
Our Sunday Visitor
Pentecostal Evangel
The Presbyterian Outlook
Presbyterian Record
Saints Herald
Social Justice Review
The Star of Zion
Touchstone
U.S. Catholic
The United Methodist
    Review
United Synagogue Review

Washington Jewish Week
Youth Update

Opinion
America
Arlington Catholic Herald
The Baptist Standard
Bible Advocate
Catholic Courier
Catholic Sentinel
Catholic Twin Circle
Changes
The Christian Century
The Christian Chronicle
Christian Crusade
    Newspaper
ChristianWeek
Church & State
Common Boundary
The Covenant
Crisis
The Door
Dovetail
Episcopal Life
Friends Journal
Harmony
Heritage Florida Jewish
    News
The Hymn
Interchange
Jewish Action
Jewish Community
    Chronicle
Jewish Education
Jewish Exponent
The Jewish News
The Jewish Review
Jewish Times
Jewish Weekly News
Lilith
Living
The Living Church
The Lookout
The Lutheran Layman
Lutheran Partners
Mennonite Weekly Review
Messenger
Moment
The Montana Catholic

National Review
Orthodox Observer
The Other Side
Our Sunday Visitor
Peace Newsletter
The Presbyterian Outlook
Presbyterian Record
Presbyterian Survey
Reconstructionist
Salt
Second Stone
Sunstone
Twin Cities Christian
U.S. Catholic
United Synagogue
Vista
The World

Parables
Canada Lutheran
FreeWay
Insight
Insight/Out
Open Hands
With

Parenting
Catholic Parent
Christian Home & School
Christian Parenting Today
Christian Single
Fathers, Brothers, Sons
Focus on the Family
The Helping Hand
Home Education Magazine
Homelife
Jr. High Ministry
Liguorian
The Link & Visitor
Living with Children
Living with Preschoolers
Living with Teenagers
Parenting Treasures
Priority Parenting
St. Anthony Messenger
Today's Christian Woman
Today's Family
Welcome Home
Women Alive!

Personal Experience

The Annals of St. Anne de
  Beaupré
Areopagus
Associate Reformed
  Presbyterian
A Better Tomorrow
Bible Advocate
Brigade Leader
Byline
Campus Life
The Christian Courier
CoLaborer
Contempo
Counselor
Daughters of Sarah
Dimensions
Emphasis on Faith and
  Living
Expressions
Faith at Work
Friends Journal
Gospel Tidings
Guideposts
The Helping Hand
Home Altar
Hospice
The Jewish Veteran
Journal of Christian Nursing
Leadership
Life Enrichment
Living Prayer
Mennonite Family History
New Covenant
The New Era
A New Heart
New World Outlook
Oblates
Open Hands
The Other Side
Power for Living
Praying
Purpose
Pursuit
Religion Teacher's Journal
Salt
Standard
Student Leadership
Today's Better Life

Touchstone
The United Methodist
  Review
Unity
Vibrant Life
Virtue
The War Cry
Welcome Home
World Vision
Youth and Christian
  Education Leadership

Philosophy

Alaska Quarterly Review
Beyond Reality Newsletter
Changes
Creation Social Science &
  Humanities Quarterly
Cross Currents
Dimensions
Hamevaser
Living Prayer
The Lutheran
The New Press Literary
  Quarterly
Parabola
The Plowman
Response (Jewish)
Social Justice Review
Wellsprings

Poetry

The Acorn
Alaska Quarterly Review
Alive Now!
Areopagus
Beyond Reality Newsletter
Bible Advocate
Bridges
Broken Streets
Byline
Caring People
Chastity and Holiness
Christian Info News
The Christian Science
  Journal
The Christian Science
  Sentinel
The Church Herald and

Holiness Banner
Clubhouse
Command
Communities
Cornerstone
Daughters of Sarah
Diaconalogue
Emmanuel
Evangel
Expressions
God's Special People
Guideposts
Hallelujah!
Heritage Florida Jewish
  News
His Garden
Home Life
Home Times
Hospice
Housewife Writer's Forum
Ideals
Israel Horizons
Issues
Jewish Action
Jewish Science Interpreter
Kaleidoscope
Language Bridges
  Quarterly
Leader
Leaves
Life Enrichment
Light and Life
Liguorian
Lilith
Listen (Kansas City)
Listen (Nampa)
Liturgy 90
Live
Lutheran Partners
Manna
Maryknoll
Mennonite Family History
Mennonite Life
Message of the Open Bible
Miraculous Medal
The Montana Catholic
The Music Leader
Nature Friend Magazine
The New Press Literary

Quarterly
Now and Then
Oblates
On the Line
Open Hands
Parabola
Pentecostal Evangel
The Pegasus Review
The Plowman
Pockets
Poetry Forum Short Stories
Presbyterian Record
Priority Parenting
Probe
Queen of All Hearts
RADAR
Radix
Renegade
Response (Jewish)
Se La Vie Writer's Journal
Sharing
Silver Wings
Sisters Today
Skylark
The Shantyman
Sharing
StarLight
Student Leadership
Sunday Digest
TAL
Time of Singing
Touch
21st Century Christian
The United Methodist
  Christian Advocate
Unity
Whisper
With

Politics
AlFajr
Atlanta Jewish Times
The B'nai B'rith International
  Jewish Monthly
Bridges
Catholic Courier
The Catholic Worker
Challenge (Washington)
Christian Crusade

Newspaper
Christian Leader
Christian Woman
Church & State
Compass
Crisis
Dimensions
Friends Journal
Greater Phoenix Jewish
  News
Hadassah Magazine
Harmony
Israel Horizons
The Jewish Veteran
Jewish Weekly News
The Jewish World
Lilith
Maryknoll
National Review
The Other Side
Peace Newsletter
Reconstructionist
Report from the Capital
Social Justice Review
Twin Cities Christian
The Wisconsin Jewish
  Chronicle
Year One

Prayer
Aylesford Carmelite
  Newsletter
Broken Streets
Chastity and Holiness
The Christian Reader
Church Educator
Church Worship
Contempo
Counselor
Desert Call
Emmanuel
Family Digest
Fellowship Magazine
Foursquare World Advance
Free Press
God's Revivalist
Gospel Herald
Guideposts
The Helping Hand

Home Altar
Jewish Science Interpreter
Leaves
Liguorian
Living Prayer
The Mennonite
New Covenant
Our Family
Our Little Friend
Pastoral Life
The Plowman
Praying
The Priest
Primary Treasure
Rejoice!
Review for Religious
Royal Service
Share
Sisters Today
Spiritual Life
StarLight
Sunday Digest
Teen Power
U.S. Catholic
Virtue
Youth Update

Psychology
Anima
Beyond Reality Newsletter
Common Boundary
Communities
Creation Social Science &
  Humanities Quarterly
Creation Spirituality
Gnosis
Health Consciousness
Living Prayer
Lotus
St. Anthony Messenger
Singles Adult Ministries
  Journal
Sisters Today
Teachers Interaction

Recreation
Breakaway
Catholic Courier
Challenge (Memphis)

Breakaway
The Catholic Accent
Catholic New York
Catholic Twin Circle
Celebration
Challenge (Memphis)
Children's Ministry
The Christian Courier
Christian Home & School
Christian Info News
Christian Woman
Church Educator
Church of God Evangel
Church Teachers
Common Ground
Cornerstone Connections
FreeWay
Friend
Friends Journal
Gospel Herald
Greater Phoenix Jewish
    News
The Helping Hand
Herald of Holiness
Heritage Florida Jewish
    News
Ideals
Jewish Action
Jewish Community
    Chronicle
Jewish Exponent
Jewish Times
The Jewish World
Just Between Us
The Kansas City Jewish
    Chronicle
Kashrus Magazine
The Kiln
Leader in the Church
    School Today
Liturgy 90
The Lookout
Lutheran Woman Today
The Magazine for Christian
    Youth!
Martyrdom and Resistance
Mature Living
The Mennonite
Modern Liturgy

The Montana Catholic
Moravian
The Music Leader
Our Family
Our Little Friend
Plenty Good Room
Primary Treasure
Quarterly Review
Reconstructionist
Renewal News
The Reporter
St. Anthony Messenger
Shining Star
The Star of Zion
Teen Power
Time of Singing
Touchstone
The War Cry
Washington Jewish Week
Welcome Home
Woman's Touch

Self-Help
Authorship
Challenge (Memphis)
Changes
Listen (Nampa)
Lotus
My Friend
Tickled by Thunder
Vibrant Life
Vista
Welcome Home

Sermons
Advance
Bible Advocate
The Christian Ministry
Joyful Noise
Message of the Open Bible
Open Hands
Pastoral Life
The Preachers' Magazine
Preaching

Seniors
Alive!
A Better Tomorrow
The Catholic Exponent

Diaconalogue
The Jewish Veteran
The Lutheran Journal
Mature Living
The Montana Catholic
Oblates
Parent Care
The Senior Musician
The Star of Zion
Vintage Northwest
Women Alive!

Social Justice
Act
AIM
The Catholic Exponent
The Catholic Worker
Challenge (Washington)
The Christian Century
Christian Social Action
Cornerstone
Creation Spirituality
Episcopal Life
Fellowship
Harmony
Interchange
Israel Horizons
Latin American Evangelist
The Mennonite
The Other Side
Pax Christi USA
Peace Newsletter
Probe
Salt
Share
Social Justice Review
Sojourners
World Vision
Year One

Social and World Issues
Act
AFA Journal
America
The American Jewish
    World
Amit Woman
Arlington Catholic Herald
Baltimore Jewish Times

The Baptist Standard
Bible Advocate
The B'nai B'rith International
    Jewish Monthly
Catholic Courier
Challenge (Memphis)
Christian Crusade
    Newspaper
Christian Leader
Christian Parenting Today
Christian Social Action
Circuit Rider
Columbia
Communities
Compass
Compassion Magazine
The Congregationalist
Contempo
Creation Social Science &
    Humanities Quarterly
Crisis
Daughters of Sarah
The Door
Faith Today
God's World Today
Gospel Advocate
Hallelujah
Harmony
Herald of Holiness
Home Times
Huron Church News
Issues
Jewish Leader
The Jewish Veteran
Jewish Weekly News
The Jewish World
The Kiln
Light and Life
The Lutheran
The Lutheran Witness
The Magazine for Christian
    Youth!
The Mennonite
Message
Michigan Christian
    Advocate
Moment
National Catholic Reporter
National Review

People Who Care
Radix
Reconstructionist
Response (Jewish)
St. Anthony Messenger
Second Stone
Social Justice Review
Spes Nostra
Teachers in Focus
Touchstone
U.S. Catholic
Virtue
The War Cry
World Vision
You!

Spirituality/Spiritual Growth

The Anglican Journal
Anima
The Annals of St. Anne de
    Beaupré
Associate Reformed
    Presbyterian
Aylesford Carmelite
    Newsletter
A Better Tomorrow
Beyond Reality Newsletter
The Canadian Catholic
    Review
Canadian Messenger of the
    Sacred Heart
The Catholic Answer
Changes
Christian Living
The Christian Science
    Journal
The Christian Science
    Sentinel
Christian Woman
Circuit Rider
Common Boundary
Common Ground
Companion of St. Francis
    and St. Anthony
Compass
The Congregationalist
Conqueror
Cornerstone Connections

The Covenant Companion
Creation Spirituality
Crisis
Desert Call
The Door
Emmanuel
Emphasis on Faith and
    Living
Faith at Work
Family Digest
Fellowship Magazine
Friends Journal
Gnosis
God's Revivalist
Gospel Herald
Group
Growing Churches
Home Life
Homelife
Homiletic & Pastoral Review
Huron Church News
Issues
Jewish Science Interpreter
The Joyful Woman
Light and Life
Liguorian
Logos
Lotus
Lutheran Woman Today
Message of the Cross
New Covenant
The Other Side
Our Family
Our Sunday Visitor
Parish Teacher
Pastoral Life
Pax Christi USA
Pentecostal Evangel
The Pentecostal Messenger
Portland
Praying
The Priest
Reconstructionist
Review for Religious
St. Anthony Messenger
The Shantyman
Share
Signs of the Times
Sisters Today

Spiritual Life
Standard
Today's Better Life
Today's Christian Woman
U.S. Catholic
Unity
Virtue
Voice
Vox Benedictina
Wellsprings
Youth Update

Teen/Young Adult
AIM
Bread for God's Children
Breakaway
Brio
Caleb Issues and Answers
Campus Life
Challenge (Memphis)
Christian Home & School
Conqueror
Cornerstone
Crusader
FreeWay
Guide Magazine
Insight
Insight/Out
The Kiln
Listen (Nampa)
The Magazine for Christian
    Youth!
On the Line
Pathway I.D.
Purpose
Skipping Stones
Spirit
Straight
Student Leadership
Take Five
Teen Power
Teens Today
Venture
Wherever
With
You!
Young & Alive
Young Salvationist
Youth Update

Testimonies
Baptist Record
Bible Advocate
Challenge (Memphis)
Conqueror
Cornerstone
The Covenant Companion
Emphasis on Faith and
    Living
Good News Journal
Guideposts
Hallelujah!
High Adventure
Leaves
Message of the Open Bible
Parenting Treasures
Pathway I.D.
Power for Living
Progress Magazine
Pursuit
Renewal News
Seek
The Senior Musician
The Shantyman
Signs of the Times
Vista
Voice

Theology
Again
The American Jewish
    World
The Anglican Journal
Anglican and Episcopal
    History
Atlanta Jewish Times
The Baptist Informer
The Canadian Catholic
    Review
The Christian Century
The Christian Ministry
Christian Research Journal
Compass
Ecumenical Trends
Faith and Renewal
Fellowship Magazine
Homiletic & Pastoral Review
Living Prayer
Logos

The Lutheran
Lutheran Forum
Lutheran Partners
The Lutheran Witness
Mennonite Life
Ministry
Missiology
New Church Life
Open Hands
The Plowman
The Priest
Quarterly Review
The Reader's Review
The Sabbath Sentinel
St. Willibrord Journal
Sharing
Sisters Today
Social Justice Review
Sunstone
Teachers Interaction
U.S. Catholic
The World

Women's Issues
Amit Woman
Anima
Bridges
CoLaborer
Contempo
Daughters of Sarah
Faith at Work
Hadassah Magazine
Israel Horizons
The Joyful Woman
Just Between Us
Lady's Circle
Lilith
The Link & Visitor
Lutheran Woman Today
Marriage Partnership
Na'amat Woman
Probe
The Reporter
Response (Christian)
Share
Sisters Today
Today's Christian Woman
Virtue
Vox Benedictina

LISTINGS BY DENOMINATION

African Methodist Episcopal
The Star of Zion

Anglican/Episcopal
Anglican and Episcopal
    History
The Anglican Digest
The Anglican Journal
Cathedral Age
Episcopal Life
Huron Church News
Interchange
The Living Church

Assemblies of God
Advance
Live
Pentecostal Evangel
Take Five
Woman's Touch

Baptist
Baptist History and Heritage
Baptist Leader
Baptist Progress
God's Special People
In Mission
Report from the Capital
The Baptist Informer
The Link & Visitor

Calvinist
Crusader
Touch

Catholic
America
The Annals of St. Anne de
    Beaupré
Arlington Catholic Herald
Aylesford Carmelite
    Newsletter
The Canadian Catholic
    Review
Canadian Messenger of the

Sacred Heart
Catechumenate
The Catholic Accent
The Catholic Answer
Catholic Courier
Catholic Digest
The Catholic Exponent
Catholic Forester
Catholic Near East
Catholic New York
Catholic Parent
Catholic Sentinel
Catholic Telegraph
Catholic Twin Circle
The Catholic Worker
Columbia
Common Ground
Companion of St. Francis
    and St. Anthony
Company
Compass
Crisis
Emmanuel
Environment & Art Letter
Extension
Family
Family Digest
Homiletic & Pastoral Review
Leaves
Liguorian
Liturgy 90
Maryknoll
Messenger
Miraculous Medal
Modern Liturgy
The Montana Catholic
My Friend
National Catholic Reporter
New Covenant
Oblates
The Observer
Our Family
Our Sunday Visitor
Pastoral Life
Pax Christi USA

Plenty Good Room
Praying
The Priest
Queen of All Hearts
Religion Teacher's Journal
Review for Religious
St. Anthony Messenger
St. Willibrord Journal
Share
Sisters Today
Social Justice Review
Spes Nostra
Spirit
Spiritual Life
Today's Catholic Teacher
U.S. Catholic
You!
Youth Update

Christian Science
The Christian Science
    Journal
The Christian Science
    Sentinel

**Church of Christ/Churches
of Christ**
Carolina Christian
The Christian Chronicle
Christian Standard
Christian Woman
Gospel Advocate
Gospel Herald
The Lookout

Church of God
Bible Advocate
Church of God Evangel
Leader
Pentecostal Messenger
Youth and Christian
    Education Leadership

Congregationalist
The Congregationalist

Eastern Orthodox
Again

Evangelical Free Church of America
The Evangelical Beacon

Free Methodist
Light and Life
Missionary Tidings

Free Will Baptist
CoLaborer

Greek Orthodox
Orthodox Observer

Lutheran
Diaconalogue
Home Altar
The Lutheran
Lutheran Forum
The Lutheran Journal
Lutheran Partners
The Lutheran Witness
Lutheran Woman Today
Morning Glory
Northwestern Lutheran
Parenting Treasures
Parish Teacher
Teachers Interaction
The Word in Season

Mennonite
Christian Leader
Christian Living
The Mennonite
Mennonite Brethren Herald
Mennonite Family History

Mennonite Life
Mennonite Reporter
Mennonite Weekly Review
On the Line
Purpose
Rejoice!
Story Friends
Story Mates
With

Methodist
Hallelujah!

Mormon/LDS
Friend
The New Era
Saints Herald
Sunstone

Presbyterian
Associate Reformed
    Presbyterian
The Cumberland
    Presbyterian
The Presbyterian Outlook
Presbyterian Record
Presbyterian Survey

Quaker
Friends Journal

Seventh-day Adventist
Cornerstone Connections
Guide Magazine
Insight
Ministry
Our Little Friend
Primary Treasure
Signs of the Times

Southern Baptist
Baptist Record
The Baptist Standard
Biblical Illustrator
Challenge (Memphis)
Church Administration
Church Recreation
Contempo
Dimension
Glory Songs
Home Life
Living with Children
Living with Preschoolers
Living with Teenagers
Mature Living
The Music Leader
Royal Service
The Senior Musician

United Church of Canada
Fellowship Magazine

United Methodist
Christian Social Action
Leader in the Church
    School Today
Michigan Christian
    Advocate
New World Outlook
Quarterly Review
Response (Christian)
The United Methodist
    Christian Advocate
The United Methodist
    Review

Wesleyan Churches
Preacher's Magazine
Standard

AABC Newsletter

Dr. Randall E. Bell, Executive Director
P.O. Box 1523
Fayetteville, AR 72702
501-521-8164

AT A GLANCE:
AABC NEWSLETTER

- Christian, Education
- 25% freelance
- 25% new writers
- 3 issues per year
- Circ: 1,200
- Receives several queries and mss each month.
- No payment. Offers 1 contributor's copy.

From the Editor:
"We are distinctly Christian with a focus on undergraduate higher education. Relevant articles will be considered as space permits. Use a professional writing style."

Best Bet: Articles that inspire excellence in biblical higher education.

Sample copy: No information provided.

Profile
The American Association of Bible Colleges (AABC) newsletter focusing on undergraduate biblical higher education. 8.5x11; heavy bond paper; folded; 16 pages.

Focus and Audience
Aims to promote undergraduate Bible-centered higher education by promoting academic excellence, cooperation, and services that stimulate excellence. Serves as a news source for Bible college administrators and educators in the U.S. and Canada.

Interests and Word Lengths
- *Nonfiction:* Feature and sub-feature articles on Bible college education. Address a current issue or inspire readers to adopt a perspective or course of action that promotes academic excellence. Up to 2,500 words.

How to Submit
Send complete ms. Include SASE. Accepts photocopies, computer printouts, and Macintosh Microsoft Word disks. Reports 1 month before publication.

Payment and Policies
No payment. Authors receive 1 copy of the issue.

The Acorn

Betty Mowery, Editor
1530 Seventh Street
Rock Island, IL 61201
309-788-3980

AT A GLANCE:
THE ACORN

- Juvenile, Inspirational
- 100% freelance
- 90% new writers
- 6 times a year
- Circ: 100
- Receives 50 mss each month.
- No payment. Offers 1 contributor's copy.

From the Editor:
"Writers, young and adult, should slant material to K–12 students. Read a sample copy. Include your name, address, phone number, and age on your manuscript. Don't be afraid to keep submitting."

Best Bet: Articles and stories that are wholesome, entertaining, and informative.

Avoid: Violence, preachiness, or obvious religion.

Sample copy: $2. Send #10 SASE for guidelines.

Profile

A small-circulation compilation of inspirational prose and poetry for young readers. Most material is written by young adults. 8.5x11; photocopied; folded; 16 pages.

Focus and Audience

Publishes wholesome fiction, nonfiction, and poetry written by young authors and adults for young readers, kindergarten through high school.

Interests and Word Lengths

- *Fiction:* Adventure, folktales, mysteries, humor, and nature stories. Accepts seasonal material. Up to 500 words.
- *Nonfiction:* How-to articles, interviews, profiles, and personal experiences. Up to 500 words. Accepts filler.
- *Poetry:* Up to 32 lines.

How to Submit

Fiction, query with outline. Nonfiction, send complete ms with cover letter. Include SASE. Accepts legible handwritten submissions. Reports in 1 week.

Payment and Policies

First North American serial rights. No payment. Authors receive 1 copy of the issue.

Act

Laurie Przybysz, Editor
682 Twin Oak Drive
Pittsburgh, PA 14235
412-795-7156

AT A GLANCE:
ACT

- Christian, Family
- 5% freelance
- 5% new writers
- 8 issues a year
- Circ: 2,500
- Receives 1 mss each month.
- No payment. Offers 2 contributors copies.

From the Editor:
"We do not ordinarily solicit outside articles, however we do occasionally publish a free-lance article."

Best Bet: Articles on family-related or social action issues.

Sample copy: Free. Send #10 SASE for guidelines.

Profile
A newsletter for members of the Christian Family Movement, a family-life development organization of small discussion and action groups. 8.5x11; folded; 8 pages.

Focus and Audience
Family-related, social action, and news articles for members of the Christian Family Movement.

Interests and Word Lengths
- *Nonfiction:* Family and social action articles. Up to 500 words.
- *Filler:* Occasionally accepts filler, poetry and seasonal material.

How to Submit
Send complete ms with cover letter. Include SASE. Accepts photocopies, computer printouts, disks, and fax submissions. Simultaneous submissions okay. Reports in 2 weeks.

Payment and Policies
Authors retain rights. No payment. Authors receive 2 copies of the issue; more on request.

Advance

Harris Jansen, Editor
1445 Boonville Avenue
Springfield, MO 65802
417-862-2781

AT A GLANCE:

ADVANCE

- Assemblies of God, Ministers
- 5% freelance
- Monthly
- Circ: 32,000
- Receives 20–30 queries, 20–30 mss each month.
- Pays: Up to $.06 per word on acceptance.

From the Editor:
"We provide ministerial helps, administration aids, and program promotional material for Assemblies of God ministers and church leaders."

Best Bet: Articles on ministerial concerns and helps.

Sample copy: Free with SASE. Send #10 SASE for guidelines.

Profile

A monthly magazine for Assemblies of God ministers and church leaders. Published by the General Council of the Assemblies of God. 8.5x11; glossy cover; 2-color; 40–44 pages.

Focus and Audience

Serves as a vehicle of communication between local Assemblies of God ministers and the national headquarters ministries.

Interests and Word Lengths

- *Nonfiction:* Articles slanted to ministers on preaching, doctrine, and practice. 1,000–1,500 words. How-to features of interest to ministers and church leaders. Original sermon illustrations
- *Seasonal:* Accepts seasonal material that has social significance.

How to Submit

Send complete ms. Include SASE. Accepts photocopies, computer printouts, faxes, and submissions via modem. No simultaneous submissions. Reports in 2 months.

Payment and Policies

First North American serial rights. Pays on acceptance. Up to $.06 per word. Authors receive 2 copies of the issue.

Advent Christian Witness

Robert Mayer, Editor
P.O. Box 23152
Charlotte, NC 28227
704-545-6161

AT A GLANCE:

ADVENT CHRISTIAN WITNESS

• Advent Christian,
  Missions
• 20% freelance
• Monthly
• Circ: 4,000
• Receives 10–15 mss
  each month.
• Pays: $25 per piece
  on publication.

Best Bet: Holiday and
inspirational material
that promotes missions
work.

Avoid: Fiction; poetry;
politics; and doctrine.

Sample copy: Free.
Send #10 SASE for
guidelines.

Profile

A monthly missions magazine for Advent Christians. 20 pages.

Focus and Audience

Provides inspirational missions news and ideas for members and friends of the Advent Christian Church.

Interests and Word Lengths

• *Nonfiction:* Inspirational and how-to articles on missions work and activities for Advent Christians. Accepts holiday material. 1,000–1,500 words.
• *Photos:* Accepts prints with article.

How to Submit

Send complete ms with cover letter. Include SASE. Accepts photocopies, computer printouts, WordPerfect 5.1 and ASCII disks, and fax submissions (704-573-0712). Simultaneous submissions okay. Reports in 2–3 months.

Payment and Policies

One-time rights. Pays on publication. $25 per piece. Authors receive 2 copies of the issue.

The Advocate

Editor
1426 Lancaster Park, Box 30
Circleville, OH 43113
614-474-8856

AT A GLANCE:
THE ADVOCATE

- Christian, Evangelical
- 20% freelance
- 5% new writers
- Monthly
- Circ: 5,500
- Receives 5 mss each month.
- No payment. Offers 3 contributor's copies.

From the Editor:
"We speak to the needs of our constituency, and emphasize fundamental evangelical holiness."

Best Bet: Practical issues and current event articles.

Avoid: Anything contrary to evangelical Christian beliefs.

Sample copy: Free. No guidelines.

Profile
A monthly evangelical Christian news magazine. 8.5x11; 26 pages.

Focus and Audience
Emphasizes current events and world views that speak to the needs of fundamental evangelical Christians.

Interests and Word Lengths
- *Fiction:* Short stories with evangelical Christian themes.
- *Nonfiction:* News, informational articles, feature articles on news, current events, missionary work, and lifestyle.

How to Submit
Fiction, query with outline. Nonfiction, send complete ms with cover letter and resume. Include SASE. Accepts computer printouts, faxes, and Macintosh disks submissions. Simultaneous submissions okay.

Payment and Policies
One-time and reprint rights. No payment. Authors receive 3 copies of the issue.

AFA Journal

Randall Murphree, Articles Editor
107 Parkgate Drive
Tupelo, MS 38801
601-844-5036

AT A GLANCE:
AFA JOURNAL

- Christian, Family
- 11 issues a year
- Circ: 1,040,000
- Receives 20–25 mss each month.
- No payment. Offers contributor's copies.

From the Editor:
"We want to motivate readers with how-to information."

Best Bet: Articles on social and moral issues with impact on the family.

Avoid: Fiction.

Sample copy: Free. No guidelines.

Profile
Published by the American Family Association (AFA), a Christian organization promoting the biblical ethic of decency in American society. 8.5x11; self cover; glossy paper; 2-color; 24 pages.

Focus and Audience
Offers a Christian perspective on social and moral issues impacting the family, with a primary emphasis on TV and other media. Readers are AFA members.

Interests and Word Lengths
- *Nonfiction:* Articles on social or moral issues that impact the family: abortion, education, TV, media issues, pornography, victimization, fathering, etc. 1,000 words.
- *Photos:* B/W prints.

How to Submit
Query by phone or mail. Include outline and SASE if mailed. Accepts computer printouts. Simultaneous submissions okay. Reports in 2 months.

Payment and Policies
Reprint rights. No payment. Authors receive several copies of the issue.

Again

Deacon Raymond Zell, Managing Editor
P.O. Box 76
Ben Lomond, CA 95005
408-338-3644

AT A GLANCE:

AGAIN

- Eastern Orthodox, Theology
- 1% freelance
- 5% new writers
- Quarterly
- Circ: 4,000
- Payment is rare. Offers 3–5 contributor's copies.

From the Editor:
"We rarely accept freelance, and then it is for Eastern Orthodox thought only. All Scripture quotations should be from the *New King James Bible*."

Best Bet: Contemporary Eastern Orthodox thought.

Avoid: Dissertations and intellectualizing.

Sample copy: $2.50 with 8x11 SAE and $1.21 postage. No guidelines.

Profile

A quarterly magazine published by the Conciliar Press, a department of the Antiochian Orthodox Christian Archdiocese of North America. Each issue focuses on one theme. 8.5x11; glossy cover; full-color; 32 pages.

Focus and Audience

Provides a forum for contemporary Eastern Orthodox thought and tradition. Readers are Eastern Orthodox lay people and others interested in the Eastern Orthodox tradition.

Interests and Word Lengths

- *Nonfiction:* Lives of saints; personal-experience pieces within Eastern Orthodox tradition; current events and travel in traditional Orthodox countries; missions; evangelical and theological explanatory pieces. All material must relate to issue theme. 1,500–2,500 words.
- *Departments:* Book Reviews, Eastern Orthodox-related titles.
- *Photos:* B/W and color prints; line drawings.

How to Submit

Query with outline and resume. No unsolicited mss. Include SASE. Accepts photocopies, computer printouts, and Macintosh disk submissions. Simultaneous submissions okay. Reports in 4 months.

Payment and Policies

Rights are negotiable. Payment is rare. Authors receive 3–5 copies of the issue.

AIM
America's Intercultural Magazine

Ruth Apilado, Editor
7308 South Eberhart
Chicago, IL 60619
312-874-6184

AT A GLANCE:
AIM

- Multicultural, Young Adult
- 75% freelance
- 60% new writers
- Quarterly
- Circ: 7,000
- Receives 50 queries, 40 mss each month.
- Pays: $25 per piece on publication.

From the Editor:
"We do not solicit religious material. We are trying only to change bigoted points of view. Never write about the superiority of any race. Show that all can succeed."

Best Bet: Essays, articles, and short stories that address social issues as they help create a more equitable world and reduce racial tension.

Sample copy: $4 with $1.21 postage. Send #10 SASE for guidelines.

Profile

A quarterly journal that promotes racial harmony through the written word. 8.5x11; glossy cover; 48 pages.

Focus and Audience

Designed to show that people from various ethnic and racial backgrounds are more alike than they are different. Works to steer readers—high school and college-age youth—away from bigoted views.

Interests and Word Lengths

- *Fiction:* Submit to Dr. Myron Apilado, Managing Editor. Stories that illustrate the following: Good leadership is measured by open arms that include every race; hard work is rewarding; honesty is the best policy; and what is in the heart is more important than appearances. 2,000 words. Accepts poetry.
- *Nonfiction:* Personal experiences, interviews, and essays on subjects of social interest. 2,000 words.
- *Departments:* Point of View, opinion pieces. Profiles, individuals who are making positive contributions to their communities. 1,500 words.
- *Seasonal:* Accepts seasonal material that has social significance.
- *Artwork:* B/W photos; pen and ink illustrations.

How to Submit

Send complete ms with cover letter and resume, or send an outline of your material with resume. Include SASE. Accepts photocopies and computer printouts. Simultaneous submissions okay. Reports in 2 months.

Payment and Policies

First North American serial rights. Pays on publication. $25 per piece. Authors receive 1 copy of the issue.

Alaska Quarterly Review

Ronald Spatz, Editor
College of Arts and Sciences
3211 Providence Drive
Anchorage, AK 99508
907-786-1731

AT A GLANCE:
ALASKA QUARTERLY REVIEW

- Literary, Arts
- 100% freelance
- 2 issues per year
- Circ: 1,200
- Receives 150 queries and mss each month.
- Pays on publication. Rates vary.

From the Editor:
"*Alaska Quarterly Review* is very writer-oriented, yet demands work of the highest quality to meet its readers' expectations."

Best Bet: High-quality material that explores the relationship between philosophy and literature.

Avoid: Genre fiction.

Sample copy: $5. Send #10 SASE for guidelines.

Profile

A university journal devoted to contemporary literary art, criticism, and philosophy. 6x9; heavy bond cover; 176 pages.

Focus and Audience

Publishes high-quality literary works with special emphasis on the relationship between contemporary philosophy and literature. Its audience is discerning and academic.

Interests and Word Lengths

- *Fiction:* Fiction and drama of the highest quality and of all forms except genre fiction. Open to both traditional and experimental styles. No word-length restrictions.
- *Nonfiction:* Essays, literary criticism, and reviews with strong narratives that explore the relationship between philosophy and literature. No word-length restrictions.
- *Poetry:* High-quality traditional or experimental poems.
- *Photos:* B/W prints with Alaskan content.

How to Submit

Submit complete ms with author biography between August 25 and May 10. Include SASE. Accepts photocopies and computer printouts. Identify simultaneous submissions. Reports in 3 months.

Payment and Policies

First North American serial rights. Pays on publication. Payment is grant-based and varies. Authors receive 1 copy of the issue; additional copies available at reduced rates.

AlFajr

Jerusalem Palestinian Weekly

Editor
16 Crowell Street
Hempstead, NY 11550
516-485-5736

AT A GLANCE:

AlFajr

- Politics, Palestinian Affairs
- 25% freelance
- Weekly
- Circ: not available
- Receives 3 queries, 4 mss each month.
- No payment. Offers contributor's copies.

From the Editor:
"Our objective is to assert the rights and freedom of the press and religion within the Palestinian movement. If your work does not pass Israeli military censors, it may be published in the U.S."

Best Bet: Objective, factual articles that explore the plight of the Palestinians under occupation.

Sample copy: Free. No guidelines.

Profile

A weekly newspaper focusing on the conditions faced by Palestinians in Israeli-occupied territories. Tabloid-size; 16 pages.

Focus and Audience

Provides political and social commentary about Palestinians in Israel. Readers include universities, students of Mideast studies, libraries, research institutions, members of Congress and the State Department, and others concerned with the plight of the Palestinians.

Interests and Word Lengths

- *Nonfiction:* Personal accounts of those who have visited areas of occupation; Christian/Jewish dialog; and articles on the plight of Palestine, media bias, aid to Israel, the treatment of Palestinians, and related topics. No word-length restrictions.
- *Poetry:* Relevant poems.
- *Artwork:* Line drawings and cartoons.

How to Submit

Query with outline or send complete ms with cover letter. Include SASE. Accepts photocopies, computer printouts, and fax submissions. Simultaneous submissions okay. Reports in 1–2 months.

Payment and Policies

Non-exclusive reprint rights. All material is reviewed by Israeli censors. No payment. Authors receive copies of the issue as requested.

Alive!
A Magazine for Christian Senior Adults

June Lang, Office Editor
P.O. Box 46464
Cincinnati, OH 45246
513-825-3681

AT A GLANCE:
Alive!

- Christian, Seniors
- 33-50% freelance
- Bimonthly
- Circ: 6,000
- Receives over 100 mss each month.
- Pays: $.03–$.05 per word on publication.

From the Editor:
"Send clean manuscripts of not more than 1,200 words. Manuscripts will not be returned without a SASE."

Best Bet: Inspirational, informational, or humorous fiction of particular male interest.

Avoid: Sermons, lectures, and nostalgia. Publishes few poems.

Sample copy: Free with 5x7 or 8.5x11 SAE and $.52 postage. Send #10 SASE for guidelines.

Profile
A bimonthly magazine aimed at Christian senior adults age 55 and over. Primary interests include seniors, lifestyle, fiction, health, and missionary work. 8.5x11; 2-color, stapled. 12–16 pages.

Focus and Audience
Emphasis is on timely articles about Christian seniors in vital, productive lifestyles, travel, and ministries. Magazine is upbeat and activity oriented rather than nostalgic.

Interests and Word Lengths
- *Fiction:* Short stories or short-short stories. Needs stories of particular male interest. May be inspirational, informational, or humorous. 600–1,200 words.
- *Nonfiction:* Features, interviews, personal experiences of interest to Christian seniors, 600–1,200 words.
- *Departments:* Heart Medicine; "grandparent" stories, jokes, short humorous verse. 25–100 words.
- *Artwork:* Occasionally uses B/W photos and cartoons.

How to Submit
Send complete ms with cover letter. Include SASE. Accepts photocopies. No dot-matrix. Simultaneous submissions okay. Reports in 1–2 months.

Payment and Policies
First North American serial rights, or one-time and reprint rights. Pays $.03–$.05 per word upon publication. Authors receive 1 copy of the issue.

Alive Now!

George R. Graham, Editor
1908 Grand Avenue
P.O. Box 189
Nashville, TN 37202-0189

AT A GLANCE:
ALIVE NOW!

- Christian, Devotional
- Bimonthly
- Circ: not available
- Pays: $15–$20 per piece on acceptance.

From the Editor:
"Good writing from a Christian standpoint looks toward the hope presented by Christ rather than toward the despair that personal and social problems cause."

Best Bet: Short, practical, and inspiring devotions, meditations, poems, and prayers.

Avoid: Attributed stories and gimmicks; lengthy material.

Sample copy: Free. Send #10 SASE for guidelines/theme list.

Profile

A Christian magazine of devotional writing and spiritual nourishment. Published bimonthly by The Upper Room. Issues are thematic. 5.5x7.5; glossy cover; 4-color; 64 pages.

Focus and Audience

Connects Christian faith with daily living for those seeking a sacred way of living in today's world. Material should invite readers to reflection, prayer, and action. Readers are active Christians who want to grow spiritually and live their faith.

Interests and Word Lengths

- *Devotions:* Short devotions and Scripture-based meditations that are creative, grounded in reality, and celebrate the Christian faith. Invite readers to examine their beliefs, ask hard questions, and struggle to find the ways in which God is revealed to us in daily life. All must relate to issue theme. Past themes include Life-Changing Events, Reconciliation, and Remember Your Baptism.
- *Poetry:* Vivid, dynamic poems and prayers.
- *Seasonal:* Lenten/Easter and Advent/Christmas/New Year material. Avoid relating holidays with seasons of the year, i.e., Easter with Spring, as audience is international.
- *Photos:* B/W and color photos.

How to Submit

Request theme list before submitting. Then, send complete ms with cover letter. Include SASE. Accepts reprints. Reports in 2–3 weeks.

Payment and Policies

All or one-time rights. Pays on acceptance. $15–$20 per piece.

America

Father George Hunt, Editor
106 West 56th Street
New York, NY 10019
212-581-4640

AT A GLANCE:

AMERICA

- Catholic, Social and World Issues
- 100% freelance
- 5–10% new writers
- Weekly
- Circ: 36,000
- Receives 30 mss each month.
- Pays: $75–$250.

From the Editor:
"Carefully check the typing, the expression of thought, all dates, names, titles, and statistics."

Best Bet: Articles on current, controversial issues from a Catholic perspective.

Avoid: Fiction.

Sample copy: $1.50. Send #10 SASE for guidelines.

Profile

A national Catholic weekly magazine published by the Jesuits of the United States and Canada. 8.5x11; self cover; 24–32 pages.

Focus and Audience

Offers commentary on contemporary social issues and their affect on Catholic life in the U.S.

Interests and Word Lengths

- *Nonfiction:* Issue-related articles, essays, and opinion pieces on current controversial topics from a Catholic perspective. 1,500–2,000 words. Accepts poetry and seasonal material.

How to Submit

Query with outline and short author biography, or send complete ms with cover letter and short author biography. Include SASE. Accepts photocopies, computer printouts, and fax submissions (212-399-3596). Reports in 1 month.

Payment and Policies

Authors retain rights. Pays $75–$250 per piece. Authors receive 5 copies of the issue.

The American Jewish World

Marshall Hoffman, Managing Editor
4509 Minnetonka Boulevard
Minneapolis, MN 55416
612-920-7000

AT A GLANCE:

THE AMERICAN JEWISH WORLD

- Jewish, Regional
- 5% freelance
- 1% new writers
- Weekly
- Circ: 20,000
- Receives 50 queries,
  50 mss each month.
- Pays: $20–$75 on
  publication.

From the Editor:
"Keep your focus on items of Jewish interest. Save yourself postage by checking in advance to see if we are interested in your story."

Best Bet: Articles with a Minnesota slant.

Avoid: Folksy style; anything without a Jewish angle.

Sample copy: Free. Send #10 SASE for guidelines.

Profile
A weekly Jewish newspaper for Minnesota-area residents. Est.: 1912. Tabloid-size; newsprint; 12 pages.

Focus and Audience
Provides international, national, and local news of Jewish interest to readers in the upper Midwest.

Interests and Word Lengths
- *Nonfiction:* Feature articles on theological, cultural, and social issues. Interviews with Jewish personalities. Material with a Minnesota angle receives special consideration. 500–700 words.
- *Seasonal:* Jewish holiday material. 500–700 words.
- *Photos:* B/W or color prints of any size. Include SASE for return.

How to Submit
Query with outline. Include SASE. Accepts photocopies, computer printouts, Macintosh disks, and submissions via modem. Simultaneous submissions okay.

Payment and Policies
One-time rights. Pays on publication. $20–$75 per piece. Authors receive 2 copies of the issue.

Amit Woman

Micheline Ratzerdorfer, Editor-in-Chief
817 Broadway
New York, NY 10003
212-477-4720

AT A GLANCE:
AMIT WOMAN

- Jewish, Women
- 5% freelance
- 5% new writers
- 5 times a year
- Circ: 100,000
- Receives 10–20 queries and mss each month
- Pays: $50–$100 on publication.

From the Editor:
"Don't assume anything. Stand on your knowledge of Jewish/Yiddish history and culture."

Best Bet: Articles highlighting the history and/or culture of Israel.

Avoid: Politics; inspirational and personality pieces.

Sample copy: No information provided. Send #10 SASE for guidelines.

Profile

The national magazine of Amit Women, the major religious women's Zionist organization in the United States. 8.5x11; glossy cover; 2-color; 36 pages.

Focus and Audience

Concerned with Jews throughout the world, Israel, aspects of Judaism, and current world events as they affect all three. Readers are vital, enthusiastic Jewish women, committed to Israel, her tradition and her people.

Interests and Word Lengths

- *Nonfiction*: Articles and personal experiences on travel, history, Jewish/Yiddish culture, world events as they affect Israel, Judaism, and Jews. 1,000–2,000 words. Accepts some filler and seasonal material.
- *Artwork*: 5x7 B/W photos and line drawings. Accepts transparencies.

How to Submit

Prefers query with outline and clips. Accepts complete ms with cover letter. Accepts photocopies, computer printouts, and fax submissions. Simultaneous submissions okay. Reports in 3–8 months.

Payment and Policies

One-time rights. Pays on publication. $50–$100 per piece. Authors receive 10 copies of the issue.

The Anglican Digest

Rev. C.F. Barbee, Editor
P.O. Box 1107
St. Louis, MO 63105
314-721-1502

AT A GLANCE:
THE ANGLICAN DIGEST

- Anglican, Inspirational
- 25% freelance
- 90% new writers
- 6 issues a year
- Circ: 250,000
- Receives 45 queries and mss each month.
- No payment. Offers contributor's copies.

From the Editor:
"Write with brevity. Ours is a highly educated audience."

Best Bet: Inspirational and motivational articles that are a call to action and stimulate thought.

Avoid: Extremist and highly statistical writing.

Sample copy: Free. Send # 10 SASE for guidelines.

Profile

A non-profit, independent Anglican journal published by the Society for Promoting and Encouraging the Arts and Knowledge (SPEAK). 5x6; self cover; 2-color; 63 pages.

Focus and Audience

Aims to provide inspiration and motivation to an educated Episcopalian community. Readers are both laity and clergy.

Interests and Word Lengths

- *Nonfiction:* Features, interviews, essays, and personal experiences. Subjects include inspiration, opinion, Bible study, news, and church highlights. 1,000 words.
- *Departments:* And in All Places; News Snipits; We Recommend, book and film reviews.
- *Filler:* Humor.
- *Seasonal:* Church-related seasonal material.
- *Photos:* B/W or color prints, slides and line drawings.

How to Submit

Send complete ms with cover letter. Include SASE. Accepts photocopies, computer printouts, and fax submissions. Simultaneous submissions okay. Reports in 1 day.

Payment and Policies

Reprint rights. No payment. Authors receive 1–2 copies of the issue upon request.

Anglican and Episcopal History

Dr. John F. Woolverton, Editor
P.O. Box 261
Center Sandwich, NH 03227
603-284-6584

AT A GLANCE:

ANGLICAN AND EPISCOPAL HISTORY

- Anglican/Episcopal, History
- 90% freelance
- 25% new writers
- Quarterly
- Circ: 1,300
- Receives 4–5 queries, 4–5 mss each month.
- No payment. Offers 5 contributor's copies.

From the Editor:
"We seek lucidly written, solidly researched, clean copy. State thesis of essays clearly in relation to other writings on the same subject. Place material in its historical context and conclude essay critically."

Avoid: Self-serving denominational apologetics.

Sample copy: $4.25. Send #10 SASE for guidelines.

Profile

A quarterly journal covering the history of the Episcopal and Anglican Churches throughout the years. 125 pages.

Focus and Audience

Sole interest is in sound, critical, well-researched material on Anglican/Episcopal history, including the Church of England Episcopal Church in the U.S.A., the British Commonwealth Anglican Church, and the Latin American and Canadian Anglican churches.

Interests and Word Lengths

- *Nonfiction:* Biography; institutional and constitutional history; historical theology; sociological analysis; religious art and architectural history; history of church music; 16th-century English Reformation; 19th-century missions history; social gospel; and leading theologians. 20–40 typed, double-spaced pages. Submit missions and overseas material to Ian T. Douglas, Episcopal Divinity School, 99 Brattle Street, Cambridge, MA 02138.
- *Departments:* Book Reviews; biography, theology, and missions—send to J.B. Miller, P.O.Box L, Fuller Theological Seminary, Pasadena, CA 91162. Church Reviews, denominational services—send to David Homes, Dept. of Religion, College of William and Mary, Williamsburg, VA 23185. Film Reviews, religious/historical films—send to address above.
- *Artwork* 5x8 B/W glossy prints. Quality etchings.

How to Submit

Query with outline and resume, or send ms with cover letter. Include SASE. Accepts computer printouts. No simultaneous submissions. Reports in 3 months.

Payment and Policies

All rights. No payment. Authors receive 5 copies of the issue.

The Anglican Journal

Vianney (Sam) Carriere, News Editor
600 Jarvis Street
Toronto, ON M4Y 2J6
Canada
416-924-9192

AT A GLANCE:
THE ANGLICAN JOURNAL

- Anglican, Regional
- 10–15% freelance
- 5% new writers
- 10 issues a year
- Circ: 274,000
- Receives 5–10 queries, 5–10 mss each month.
- Pays: $35–$500 on publication.

From the Editor:
"Articles should be of interest to a national audience and written in a news style."

Best Bet: Articles that give voice to those within the church without a voice: Native peoples, women, the elderly, and the handicapped.

Avoid: Opinion pieces.

Sample copy: Free with SAE/IRC. Send #10 SAE/IRC for guidelines.

Profile
The national newspaper of the Anglican Church of Canada. Tabloid-size; 24 pages.

Focus and Audience
Covers news of the Anglican Church across Canada and around the world for its members. Readers are Canadian Anglicans and Anglican Bishops overseas.

Interests and Word Lengths
- *Nonfiction:* News features and articles of interest to Canadian Anglicans. Subjects include national events; local happenings that reflect the larger picture; unusual local events and issues; social and ethical issues; news and viewpoints of other faith groups; culture and ethnic pieces; religious education; world issues; family; and lifestyle. All must have an Anglican slant. Includes articles published in French. Up to 1,000 words.
- *Departments:* Reflections, theological or spiritual insights into issues of interest to church or society; Book Reviews. Up to 1,000 words.
- *Photos:* 8x10 B/W glossy or high-contrast color prints.

How to Submit
Query with outline and resume. Include SASE. U.S. authors send IRCs. Accepts computer printouts and 3.5-inch Macintosh disks. No simultaneous submissions. Reports in 1 month.

Payment and Policies
All rights. Pays on publication. Major features and Reflections, $200–$500. Lesser features and news stories, $75–$200. Book reviews, $35 plus the book. Authors receive copies of the issue.

Anima
The Journal of Human Experience

Barbara Rotz, Editor
1053 Wilson Avenue
Chambersburg, PA 17201-1247
717-267-0087

AT A GLANCE:
ANIMA

- Comparative Religion
- 90% freelance
- 50% new writers
- 2 issues a year
- Circ: 1,000
- Receives 30 queries, 20 mss each month.
- No payment. Offers 50 offprints with covers.

From the Editor:
"Our writers are renowned for their ability to reach into the stream of daily living and grasp new insights that awaken us, challenge us, and change us. It is very important to study a few issues of *Anima* before submitting. Your articles must be well studied."

Sample copy: No information provided.

Profile
Published in Spring and Fall issues, this magazine explores religion, spirituality, psychology, and the feminine. Primary interests include comparative religion, environment, personal experiences, and women's issues. 8.5x8.5; glossy cover; 72 pages.

Focus and Audience
Deals with human experience as informed by Western and Asian spiritualities, myth and ritual, Jungian thought, feminism, and the earth. Featured authors include Margaret Mead, Jean Houston, Joseph Campbell, and Madeleine L'Engle.

Interests and Word Lengths
- *Fiction:* Publishes very little fiction. Must fit the magazine's philosophy. No word-length restrictions.
- *Nonfiction:* Wholistic/holistic thought. Women's experience. No word-length restrictions.
- *Artwork:* Clear glossy prints.

How to Submit
Query with an outline or send complete ms with cover letter. Include SASE. Accepts computer printouts and IBM-compatible disks. Reports in 2 months.

Payment and Policies
First North American serial rights or all rights. No payment. Authors receive 50 offprints with covers.

The Annals of St. Anne de Beaupré

Roch Achard, C.Ss.R., Editor
9795 St. Anne Boulevard
St. Anne de Beaupré, Québec G0A 3C0
Canada
418-827-4530

AT A GLANCE:
THE ANNALS OF ST. ANNE DE BEAUPRÉ

- Catholic, Devotions
- 80% freelance
- 60–70% new writers
- 11 issues a year
- Circ: 45,000
- Receives 50+ queries, 50+ mss each month.
- Pays: $.03–$.04 per word on acceptance.

From the Editor:
"Write something educational, inspirational, objective, and uplifting."

Avoid: Current controversies that are of little interest to readers.

Sample copy: Free with International Reply Coupons. Send #10 SASE for guidelines.

Profile
A Catholic family magazine that promotes devotion to St. Anne, who is traditionally accepted to be the grandmother of Jesus. Published by the Redemptorist Fathers. Primary interests include devotions, family, and inspirational works. Est.: 1878. 8.5x11; glossy cover; 32 pages.

Focus and Audience
Promotes devotion to St. Anne and Catholic family values to a wide-ranging audience in Canada, Ireland, the Orient, Australia, and Scandanavia.

Interests and Word Lengths
- *Fiction:* Inspirational, religious fiction. 500–1,500 words. Buys approximately 100 stories per year.
- *Nonfiction:* Exposés, general interest, inspirational, and personal experience, all with a spiritual thrust. 500–1,500 words. Buys approximately 100 articles per year.

How to Submit
Send complete ms. Include SASE. U.S. authors send IRCs. Accepts computer printouts. Reports within 2 weeks.

Payment and Policies
First North American serial rights and one-time rights. Pays on acceptance. $.03–$.04 per word. Authors receive 3 copies of the issue.

Areopagus

John G. LeMond, Editor
33 Tao Fong Shan Christian Centre
Shatin, New Territories
Hong Kong
852-691-1904

AT A GLANCE:

AREOPAGUS

- Christian, Comparative Religion
- 75% freelance
- 75% new writers
- Quarterly
- Circ: 1,200
- Receives 10 queries, 5 mss each month.
- Pays: $25–$50 on publication.

From the Editor:
"We look for compassionate, direct, and unself-conscious prose that reflects a writer who is firmly rooted in his or her own tradition but unafraid to encounter other traditions."

Best Bet: Balanced, interreligious dialog. Virtually all departments are open to freelancers.

Avoid: Arcane religious conjecture; religious conspiracy; seeking to prove the superiority or inferiority of a particular religion.

Sample copy: $4. Send #10 SASE for guidelines.

Profile

A Christian magazine that provides a forum for dialog between the good news of Jesus Christ and people of faith in all major world religions and in new religious movements. Primary interests include comparative religion, missionary work, and interreligious dialog. 8.5x11; glossy cover; 4-color; 50 pages.

Focus and Audience

Seeks to engage its audience in a living encounter with today's religious world. Readers are interested in interreligious dialog, religious faith, and the points of contact that may be found among the living religions.

Interests and Word Lengths

- *Nonfiction:* Interviews with people in major religious movements or key figures in new religious movements, 3,500 words. Good News; vignettes of encounters with the Gospel, 250–300 words. Accepts religious news as fillers.
- *Departments:* Getting to Know, objective descriptions of major world religions, 4,000 words. Pilgrimage, stories of personal faith journeys, 3,000 words. People and Communities, descriptions and experiences of faith communities, 3,000 words.
- *Poetry:* Publishes 1–2 poems per year.
- *Photos:* Submit to Art Editor. Color transparencies preferred. Accepts B/W and color prints.

How to Submit

Send complete ms with cover letter. Include SASE. U.S. authors send IRCs. Accepts photocopies, computer printouts, faxes, and ASCII, Microsoft Word, WordPerfect, or Macintosh Microsoft Word disks. Simultaneous submissions okay. Reports in 2 months.

Payment and Policies

One-time rights. Pays $25–$50 on publication. Kill fee, 50%. Authors receive 2 copies of the issue.

Arkansas Catholic

Pete Hoelscher, Editor
P.O. Box 7417
Little Rock, AR 72217
501-664-0340

AT A GLANCE:
ARKANSAS CATHOLIC

- Catholic, Regional
- 5% freelance
- 80% new writers
- 40 issues a year
- Circ: 7,100
- Receives 5–10 queries and mss each month.
- Pays: $2.50 per column inch on publication.

From the Editor:
"Display a knowledge of Catholic issues, people, and the Diocese."

Best Bet: Diocesan news.

Avoid: Sensationalism.

Sample copy: Free with 9x12 SASE and 2 first-class stamps. Send #10 SASE for guidelines.

Profile

The official newspaper of the Diocese of Little Rock, AR. Tabloid-size; newsprint; 16 pages.

Focus and Audience

Reports on diocesan, national, and international news of interest to Arkansas-area Catholic clergy and lay people. Inspires readers to consider what it means to be Catholic today. All material must adhere to Catholic teachings.

Interests and Word Lengths

- *Nonfiction:* News on church-related issues. 2 typed, double-spaced pages. Articles in the following areas of interest: New Development in the Church, highlights of programs or parish models; Behind the Scenes Heroes, profiles of Catholic clergy or laity; Living the Faith, practical Christianity with everyday application. 5 typed, double-spaced pages.
- *Departments:* Viewpoint, issue-related opinion pieces. Scripture Speaks Today, Bible commentary. 500 words.
- *Filler:* Did You Know?, short fact pieces.
- *Illustrations:* B/W line drawings to accompany articles.

How to Submit

Query with outline, resume, writing samples, and clips. Include SASE. Accepts photocopies, letter-quality print-outs, 3.5-inch IBM-compatible disks, and fax submissions. Identify simultaneous submissions. Reports in 3 weeks.

Payment and Policies

First North American serial rights. Pays on publication. $2.50 per column inch. Authors receive 2 copies of the issue.

Arlington Catholic Herald

Michael Flach, Editor
200 North Glebe Road
Suite 614
Arlington, VA 22203
703-841-2590

AT A GLANCE:
ARLINGTON CATHOLIC HERALD

- Catholic, Regional
- 15–25% freelance
- Weekly
- Circ: 45,000
- Receives 20–50 queries, 10–20 mss each month.
- Pays: $50–$200 on publication.

From the Editor:
"We strictly adhere to the teachings of the Roman Catholic Church."

Best Bet: Accepts only Catholic-related material.

Avoid: Topics too controversial such as women's ordination, etc.

Sample copy: Free. Send #10 SASE for guidelines.

Profile

A weekly Catholic newspaper serving the Diocese of Arlington, Virginia. Member of the Catholic Press Association. Tabloid-size; newsprint; 24 pages.

Focus and Audience

Seeks material related to and within the teachings of the Roman Catholic Church. Readers are Arlington, Virginia-area Catholics.

Interests and Word Lengths

- *Nonfiction:* Features, profiles, and op/ed pieces about the Catholic Church or social and religious issues such as abortion, euthanasia, family life, and religious vocations. 500–2,000 words.
- *Departments:* Sports, Entertainment, School News. 500 words.
- *Photos:* 5x7 B/W prints; color slides.

How to Submit

Send complete ms with cover letter. Include SASE. Accepts photocopies, computer printouts, WordPerfect 5.1 disks, and fax submissions. No simultaneous submissions. Reports in 2 months.

Payment and Policies

One-time rights. Pays on publication. $50–$200 per piece. Authors receive 1 copy of the issue.

Associate Reformed Presbyterian

Ben Johnson, Editor
One Cleveland Street
Greenville, NC 29601
803-232-8297

AT A GLANCE:
ASSOCIATE REFORMED PRESBYTERIAN

- Presbyterian, Regional
- 10% freelance
- 5% new writers
- Monthly
- Circ: 63,000
- Receives 60 queries, 3 mss each month.
- Pays: $20–$50 on acceptance.

From the Editor:
"We are looking for Christ-centered material, not merely moral-value articles."

Best Bet: Morally uplifting writing with a biblical basis.

Avoid: Articles by or about female ordained ministers or liberals.

Sample copy: $1.50. Send #10 SASE for guidelines.

Profile
The official publication of the Associate Reformed Presbyterian Church. Member of the Evangelical Press Association. 8.5x11; full-color cover; 40 pages.

Focus and Audience
Aims to strengthen church members in their daily walk with Christ. Theological perspective is Reformed and evangelical. Readers are Associated Reformed Presbyterians of different ages, vocations, interests, and backgrounds. Most live in the Southeast.

Interests and Word Lengths
- *Fiction:* Children's stories that are of practical help to young readers. Use anecdotes and Scripture documentation. Up to 2,000 words.
- *Nonfiction:* Christ-centered articles that promote spiritual growth; personal experiences; new angles on familiar topics like pro-life, foster parenting, etc. 800–850 words.
- *Departments:* Higher Education; Witness and Outreach; World Missions. 200–500 words
- *Photos:* 5x7 B/W photos for contest. Occasionally accepts drawings.

How to Submit
Query with clips or send complete ms with cover letter and 50-word biographical sketch. Accepts photocopies and computer printouts. Simultaneous submissions okay. Reports in 1 month.

Payment and Policies
First North American or one-time rights. Pays on acceptance. $20–$50 per piece. Authors receive 3 copies of the issue.

At Ease

Chaplain Lemuel E. McElyea, Department Secretary
1445 Boonville Avenue
Springfield, MO 65802
417-862-2781

AT A GLANCE:

AT EASE

- Military, Outreach
- 90% freelance
- 25% new writers
- Bimonthly
- Circ: 28,000
- Receives 3 queries,
  20 mss each month.
- Pays: $.03 per word
  on publication.

From the Editor:
"We relate directly to military personnel and encourage them in the Word of God."

Best Bet: Articles that emphasize character development and/or Christian evangelism.

Sample copy: Free. Send #10 SASE for guidelines.

Profile

A bimonthly devotional newsletter distributed to military personnel. Published by Military Ministries, a division of The General Council of the Assemblies of God, Inc. 12x18; 2-color; 4 pages.

Focus and Audience

Serves as an outreach tool to minister to and encourage military personnel. Strong emphasis is placed on character building and the need to accept Jesus as personal savior.

Interests and Word Lengths

- *Nonfiction:* Military lifestyle; the problems and trials faced by members of the military; praise reports. 400–500 words.
- *Photos:* B/W or color prints and slides.

How to Submit

Send complete ms with cover letter. Include SASE. Accepts photocopies, computer printouts, and fax submissions. Simultaneous submissions okay. Reports in 6 weeks.

Payment and Policies

First or reprint rights. Pays on publication. $.03 per word. Authors receive 3 copies of the issue.

Atlanta Jewish Times

Neil Rubin, Assistant Editor
1575 Northside Drive
Suite 470
Atlanta, GA 30318
404-352-2400

AT A GLANCE:
ATLANTA JEWISH TIMES

- Jewish, Regional
- 30% freelance
- 5% new writers
- Weekly
- Circ: 10,000
- Receives 15 queries, 13 mss each month.
- Pays: $50–$125 on publication.

From the Editor:
"Our readers are interested in a broad array of issues, from local cooking contests to investigations of local neo-Nazis to analysis of Mid-east peace talks."

Avoid: Holocaust stories—has an abundance already.

Sample copy: Free. No guidelines.

Profile
A weekly publication serving metropolitan Atlanta's 70,000 Jews as well as Jewish communities in the region. Tabloid-size; newsprint; 64 pages.

Focus and Audience
Covers local, national, and international issues of interest to Atlanta-area Jewish residents. Readers are highly educated and interested in a wide range of topics.

Interests and Word Lengths
- *Nonfiction:* Travel articles, sports features, lifestyle pieces, and articles on politics and theology. Open to coverage of local news and events as well as worldwide issues of Jewish interest. No word length-restrictions.

How to Submit
Query with outline and clips. Include SASE. Accepts computer printouts, faxes, and submissions via modem. Identify simultaneous submissions. Reports in 2 months.

Payment and Policies
First North American serial rights. Pays on publication. $50–$125 per piece. Kill fee, 50%. Authors receive 2 copies of the issue.

Authorship

Sandra Whelchel, Editor
1450 South Havana
Suite 424
Aurora, CO 80012
303-751-7844

AT A GLANCE:
AUTHORSHIP

- Writing, Self-Help
- 65% freelance
- 50% new writers
- Bimonthly
- Circ: 3,000
- Receives 2–3 queries, 10 mss each month.
- No payment. Offers 2 contributor's copies.

From the Editor:
"Writers must be members of the National Writers Club to submit."

Best Bet: Articles on writing.

Avoid: Fiction; anything not related to writing.

Sample copy: $1 with 9x12 SAE and $.52 postage. No guidelines.

Profile
The official publication of the National Writers Club (NWC). Accepts submissions from NWC members only. 8.5x11; glossy cover; 20 pages.

Focus and Audience
Dedicated to self-help and informational articles for writers and about writing. Read and written by National Writer Club members.

Interests and Word Lengths
- *Nonfiction:* Interviews, how-tos, and self-help articles about writing. All material is geared toward or reports on NWC members and activities. 600–800 words.

How to Submit
Send complete ms with cover letter. Include SASE. Accepts photocopies, computer printouts, computer disks, faxes, and submissions via modem. Simultaneous submissions okay. Reports in 1 month.

Payment and Policies
First North American serial rights. No payment. Authors receive 2 copies of the issue.

Avotaynu

Sallyann Sack, Editor
P.O. Box 1134
1485 Teaneck Road
Teaneck, NJ 07666
201-837-8300

AT A GLANCE:
Avotaynu

- Jewish, Genealogy
- Quarterly
- Circ: 2,000
- Receives 1–5 queries, 1–5 mss each month.
- No payment. Offers 1–6 contributor's copies.

From the Editor:
"Our readers are Jewish persons who are tracing their family's history. We receive articles from persons who have information for people with this interest."

Best Bet: Articles on Jewish family history.

Sample copy: $7. Send #10 SASE for guidelines.

Profile
A quarterly publication of Jewish genealogy. 8.5x11; 68 pages.

Focus and Audience
Provides articles of interest to persons tracing their Jewish family history.

Interests and Word Lengths
- *Nonfiction:* Articles and first-person accounts of tracing Jewish family history. Up to 4,000 words.

How to Submit
Send complete ms with cover letter. Include SASE. Accepts photocopies, computer printouts, and IBM-compatible disk submissions. Reports in 2 months.

Payment and Policies
Authors retain rights. No payment. Authors receive 1–6 copies of the issue.

Aylesford Carmelite Newsletter

Rev. Aloysius Sieracki, O.Carm., Provincial Director
8501 Bailey Road
Darien, IL 60561
708-969-5050

AT A GLANCE:

AYLESFORD CARMELITE NEWSLETTER

- Catholic, Carmelite
- 20% freelance
- 5% new writers
- Quarterly
- Circ: 12,000
- Receives 2 queries, 1 ms each month.
- No payment.

From the Editor:
"Most writing is done by the editor and staff, with some reprints."

Best Bet: Articles of interest to the lay Carmelite community.

Sample copy: No information provided.

Profile

A quarterly newsletter for and about the Order of Carmelites. 8.5x11; folded; 4 pages.

Focus and Audience

Reports on matters of current interest to the Order of Carmelites and the Catholic Church. Strives to keep readers—lay Carmelites in the United States and Canada—knowledgeable about new movements.

Interests and Word Lengths

- *Nonfiction:* Articles, essays, and reflections on Carmelite spirituality, prayer, and happenings. Approximately 6 typed, double-spaced ms pages. Accepts poetry, filler, and seasonal material.

How to Submit

Send complete ms with cover letter. Include SASE. Accepts reprints.

Payment and Policies

No payment. Does not provide copies of the issue.

Baltimore Jewish Times

Barbara Pash, Editor
2104 North Charles Street
Baltimore, MD 21218
410-752-3504

AT A GLANCE: BALTIMORE JEWISH TIMES

- Jewish, Regional
- Weekly
- Circ: 20,000–22,000
- Receives 5–6 mss each month
- Pays on publication. Rates vary.

From the Editor:
"We are the largest Jewish weekly publication in the nation."

Best Bet: Topical articles of interest to the Jewish community.

Avoid: Holocaust-related pieces; poetry.

Sample copy: $2. Send #10 SASE for guidelines.

Profile

A weekly Jewish newspaper serving the Baltimore area. Tabloid-size; glossy cover; newsprint; 120 pages.

Focus and Audience

Serves to inform Jewish people in the Baltimore area about social and world issues.

Interests and Word Lengths

- *Nonfiction:* Articles and news of Jewish interest on social and world issues, travel, and Jewish holidays. Appreciates humor. 6–8 typed, double-spaced pages.
- *Photos:* B/W prints.

How to Submit

Query with outline or send complete ms with cover letter. Include SASE. Accepts photocopies and computer printouts. No simultaneous submissions. Report time varies.

Payment and Policies

One-time rights. Pays on publication. Rates vary. Authors receive copies of the issue.

Banner High

John Fullmer, Administrative Assistant
172 Lexington Avenue
New York, NY 10016
212-213-5454

AT A GLANCE:

BANNER HIGH

- Evangelical, Regional
- 30% freelance
- 10% new writers
- Bimonthly
- Circ: 4,000
- Receives 15 announcements each month.
- No payment.

From the Editor:
"Our vision is to unite the Body of Christ in one voice in New York City, and to lift up 'our banners' and declare Jesus is Lord."

Best Bet: News and reports on urban evangelism.

Avoid: Opinion pieces.

Sample copy: No information provided.

Profile
A bimonthly newsletter of New York City-area evangelistic activities. Published by the New York Bible Society. 8.5x11; glossy paper; folded; 6 pages.

Focus and Audience
Services the Christian community in the New York-area by providing news and articles concerning evangelistic events. Readers are churches, ministries, and individuals throughout New York City.

Interests and Word Lengths
- *Nonfiction:* News pieces and reporting articles on creative evangelistic outreach ideas for the urban community, including reaching the needy, youth ministries, and Christian counseling. 3–5 paragraphs. Announcements of upcoming events. 3–4 sentences.
- *Photos:* B/W prints.

How to Submit
Submit entire report or announcement. Accepts photocopies, computer printouts, Macintosh 3.5-inch disks, and fax submissions. Simultaneous submissions okay.

Payment and Policies
No payment. Material submitted on a voluntary basis.

Baptist History and Heritage

Lynn E, May, Jr., Editor
901 Commerce Street
Suite 400
Nashville, TN 37203-3630
615-244-0344

AT A GLANCE:

BAPTIST HISTORY AND HERITAGE

- Baptist, History
- 16% freelance
- 16% new writers
- Quarterly
- Circ: 2,000
- Receives 2 queries, varied number of mss each month.
- Pays for assigned articles only. $192 per piece.

From the Editor: "Send a query first. Articles must be based on primary sources. Write for scholars and non-academicians."

Best Bet: Articles on lesser-known aspects of Baptist history.

Avoid: Institutional histories or topics already covered in our previous issues.

Sample copy: Not provided. Send #10 SASE for guidelines.

Profile

A scholarly journal focusing on Baptist history, particularly Southern Baptist. Published by the Historical Commission of the Southern Baptist Convention and the auxiliary Southern Baptist Historical Society. 6x9; heavy bond cover; 64 pages.

Focus and Audience

Seeks to help readers understand the Baptist heritage as a foundation for a living faith in God in today's world. Readers include educators, pastors, and lay persons interested in Baptist history.

Interests and Word Lengths

- *Nonfiction:* Scholarly articles on Baptist history, especially lesser-known aspects. Up to 4,000 words.

How to Submit

Query with outline and resume. Include SASE. Accepts photocopies, computer printouts, and IBM and Macintosh disks. No simultaneous submissions. Reports in 2 months.

Payment and Policies

All rights. Pays for assigned articles. $192 per piece. Authors receive 3 copies of the issue.

The Baptist Informer

Archie D. Logan, Editor
603 South Wilmington Street
Raleigh, NC 27601
919-821-7466

AT A GLANCE:

THE BAPTIST INFORMER

- Baptist, Regional
- 10% freelance
- 1% new writers
- Monthly
- Circ: 10,000
- Receives 1–2 queries,
  3–4 mss each month.
- No payment. Offers 5
  contributor's copies.

From the Editor:
"By the word of truth,
by the power of God,
by the armour of right-
eousness. . . (II Corinthi-
ans 6:7)' is the publica-
tion's theme."

Best Bet: Family, community, church life,
and missionary work—
all with an African-
American focus.

Sample copy: Free. No
guidelines.

Profile

An African-American regional monthly organ of the General Baptist State Convention of North Carolina, Inc. Tabloid-size; newsprint; 16 pages.

Focus and Audience

Articles with an African-American focus for North Carolina-area members of the General Baptist State Convention.

Interests and Word Lengths

- *Fiction:* Stories on topics of interest to African-American Baptists.
- *Nonfiction:* African-American Baptist missionary work. African-American issues of family, community and church. Other interests include Bible study, devotions, doctrine, evangelism, prayer, religious education, self-help, social and world issues, theology, and worship.

How to Submit

Query with outline and resume, or send complete ms with cover letter and resume. Include SASE. Accepts computer printouts, Wordstar 2000 disks, and faxes (919-836-0061). Simultaneous submissions okay. Reports in 3 months.

Payment and Policies

Authors retain rights. No payment. Authors receive 5 copies of the issue.

Baptist Leader

Linda R. Isham, Editor
American Baptist Churches, USA
P.O. Box 851
Valley Forge, PA 19482-0851
215-768-2153

AT A GLANCE:

BAPTIST LEADER

- Baptist, Leadership
- 5% freelance
- Quarterly
- Circ: 6,000
- Receives 5 queries, 20 mss each month.
- Pays: $10–$50 on acceptance.

From the Editor:
"We emphasize Christian education administration and planning articles for church leaders."

Avoid: Politics, gay rights, abortion, and similar controversial topics.

Sample copy: $1.50 with 9x12 SAE and $.75 postage. Send #10 SASE for guidelines.

Profile

A leadership magazine supporting the teaching ministry and leader development in the American Baptist Church. 32 pages.

Focus and Audience

Provides practical, thought-provoking material for American Baptist lay leaders, pastors, and Christian education staff who support teaching ministries and leader development.

Interests and Word Lengths

- *Nonfiction:* Practical how-to articles on Christian education administration, planning, and leadership. 1,300–2,000 words.
- *Seasonal:* Seasonal and holiday programs or plays that have been tested in church. Submit 1 year in advance. Advent/Christmas programs due by September 1; Lent/Easter programs due by December 1. 1,300–2,000 words.
- *Filler:* Accepts poems and cartoons.

How to Submit

Send complete ms with cover letter. Include SASE. Accepts photocopies and computer printouts. Simultaneous submissions okay. Reports in 6 months.

Payment and Policies

First North American serial rights. Pays on acceptance. $10–$50 per piece. Authors receive 1 copy of the issue.

Baptist Progress

Danny Pope, Editor
632 Farley Street
Waxahachie, TX 75165
214-923-0756

AT A GLANCE:
BAPTIST PROGRESS

- Baptist, Regional
- 10% freelance
- Weekly
- Circ: 12,500
- No payment.

From the Editor:
"We are a conservative Baptist magazine but do carry articles of general, religious information."

Best Bet: Brief, concise articles on issues of interest to Baptist Missionary Association of Texas members.

Avoid: Politics.

Sample copy: Not provided. No guidelines.

Profile

A weekly denominational magazine published by the Baptist Missionary Association of Texas. 7.5x10; self cover; newsprint; 2-color; 16 pages.

Focus and Audience

Reports on the missions and church ministries of the Baptist Missionary Association of Texas for it members. Espouses a conservative Baptist perspective on family, social, and religious issues.

Interests and Word Lengths

- *Fiction:* Spiritual and religious fiction. Must be at least 4 typed, double-spaced pages. Accepts longer pieces for serialization.
- *Nonfiction:* Feature articles on issues pertaining to denominational church works, family life, church growth, and current religious and societal issues. Interviews with and profiles of religious leaders. Must be at least 4 typed, double-spaced pages.
- *Seasonal:* Submit 1 week in advance.
- *Artwork:* Accepts photos and illustrations of any size or style.

How to Submit

Query with writing samples. Include SASE. Accepts photocopies. No simultaneous submissions. Report time varies.

Payment and Policies

One-time rights. No payment. Does not provide contributor's copies.

Baptist Record

Guy Henderson, Editor
515 Mississippi Street
Jackson, MI 39205
601-968-3800

Profile

A weekly newspaper that serves as the official publication of the Mississippi Baptist Convention. Member of the Southern Baptist Press Association. Tabloid-size; newsprint; 12 pages.

Focus and Audience

Publishes news, events, and personalities of interest to Mississippi-area Southern Baptists.

Interests and Word Lengths

- *Nonfiction:* Interested in general news articles, mission stories, personal testimonies, and how-to articles. 200–400 words.
- *Seasonal:* Accepts only high-quality holiday stories. 200–400 words.

How to Submit

Send complete ms with resume and clips. Include SASE. Reports in 1–3 months.

Payment and Policies

One-time rights. No payment. Authors receive 6 copies of the issue.

The Baptist Standard

Dr. Presnall H. Wood, Editor
P.O. Box 660267
Dallas, TX 75266-0267
214-630-4571

AT A GLANCE:

THE BAPTIST STANDARD

- Southern Baptist, Regional
- 90% freelance
- Few new writers
- Weekly
- Circ: 230,000
- Receives many queries and mss each month.
- No payment. Offers contributor's copies.

From the Editor:
"*The Baptist Standard* is the largest Baptist paper in the Southern Baptist Convention."

Best Bet: Short, topical articles of interest to Baptists in Texas.

Sample copy: Free. No guidelines.

Profile

A weekly news magazine for Texas Southern Baptists. Published by Baptist Standard Publishing Company. Est.: 1888; 8.5x11; newsprint; 16–32 pages.

Focus and Audience

Aids and supports the Baptist General Convention of Texas and interprets events and movements that affect Texas Southern Baptists.

Interests and Word Lengths

- *Nonfiction:* Short topical and inspirational articles of interest to Texas Baptists. Interests include social and world issues and local news. Occasionally accepts poetry and seasonal material.
- *Photos:* B/W prints.

How to Submit

Submit complete ms with cover letter. Include SASE. Accepts photocopies, computer printouts, and fax submissions (214-638-8535). Simultaneous submissions okay if to a non-competitor. Reports in 1–2 months.

Payment and Policies

Authors retain rights. No payment. Authors receive copies of the issue upon request.

A Better Tomorrow

Cathy Constant, Assistant Editor
5301 Wisconsin Avenue NW
Suite 620
Washington, DC 20015
202-364-8000

AT A GLANCE:
A BETTER TOMORROW

- Christian, Seniors
- 5–10% freelance
- 5% new writers
- Quarterly
- Circ: 100,000
- Receives 5–10 queries, 10–15 mss each month.
- Pays: $.10 per word on publication.

From the Editor:
"We publish upbeat, positive, practical information for active Christian seniors. We recommend that writers read several issues of *A Better Tomorrow* before submitting queries. Articles should be consistent with traditional Christian values."

Best Bet: Personal experiences, opinion, profiles, and reflection stories.

Avoid: Talking down to seniors or offering vague information.

Sample copy: Not provided. Send #10 SASE for guidelines.

Profile
A quarterly magazine that inspires and informs Christian seniors. Published by Thomas Nelson, Inc. Est.: 1992; 8.5x11; glossy cover; 4-color; 110 pages.

Focus and Audience
Dedicated to helping readers make the most of their lives by featuring positive, uplifting articles on faith, fitness, and more. Readers are Christian seniors over 50 who take their faith, family, and fitness seriously and who recognize that the second half of life is the best.

Interests and Word Lengths
- *Departments:* Profiles, shows active Christian seniors who are doing extraordinary things, 1,000 words. My Story, personal experiences that teach a valuable lesson in spiritual and personal growth. Opinion and Reflections departments. 1,700–2,500 words.
- *Photos:* Color photos or slides to accompany Profiles.

How to Submit
Query with outline, resume, and writing samples. Include SASE. Accepts photocopies and computer printouts. No simultaneous submissions. Reports in 1 month.

Payment and Policies
All rights. Pays on publication. $.10 per word or $150–$200 per piece. Authors receive 1 copy of the issue.

Beyond Reality Newsletter

Grace Bubulka, Editor
2350 West Shaw
Fresno, CA 93711
209-431-0381

AT A GLANCE:

BEYOND REALITY NEWSLETTER

- Spirituality, Near-Death Experiences
- 25% freelance
- 25% new writers
- 6 issues a year
- Receives 3 queries, 2 mss each month.
- No payment. Offers 5 contributor's copies.

From the Editor:
"Handle this sensitive topic professionally and with an open mind. Appropriate submissions are clearly developed and respectful of our readers. Christian perspectives are most welcome."

Avoid: Belittling, antagonistic writing.

Sample copy: Not provided. No guidelines.

Profile

A spiritual newsletter addressing near-death experiences. 8.5x11; 4 pages.

Focus and Audience

Dedicated to those who have had or wish to understand more about the near death experience—from spiritual, medical, and psychological perspectives. Welcomes Christian experiences. Readers are bereaved families, medical staff, and those who wonder about what follows clinical death.

Interests and Word Lengths

- *Fiction:* Short-short stories on the process of death, the meaning of life, and spirituality. 200 words. Accepts poetry.
- *Nonfiction:* Personal experiences, essays, and opinion pieces. Topics include death, the afterlife, spiritual lifestyles, health, healing, philosophy, psychology, theology, and Bible study. 200 words.
- *Departments:* Network Corner; Calendar of Events; Research. 200 words.
- *Filler:* Quotes, thoughts, and ideas to ponder.
- *Artwork:* Line drawings and graphics.

How to Submit

Send complete ms with cover letter. Include SASE. Accepts photocopies and computer printouts. Simultaneous submissions okay. Reports in 1 month.

Payment and Policies

One-time rights. No payment. Authors receive 5 contributor's copies.

Bible Advocate

Roy A. Marrs, Editor
P.O. Box 33677
Denver, CO 80233
303-452-7973

AT A GLANCE:
BIBLE ADVOCATE

- Church of God (Seventh Day), Doctrine
- 5–10% freelance/year
- 5% new writers/year
- 11 issues a year
- Circ: 10,000
- Receives 1–3 queries, 10–20 mss each month.
- Pays: $10–$25 per page honorarium on publication.

From the Editor:
"We care about good writing, fresh ideas, and sound interpretation of the Bible. We are open to all writers who meet this criteria. Know the magazine and our style and doctrinal beliefs."

Avoid: Didactic, preachy styles. Traditional Christmas and Easter celebrations. Sing-songy rhyming poetry.

Sample copy: Free with 9x12 and 3 first-class stamps. Send #10 SASE for guidelines and doctrinal statement.

Profile

A Bible-teaching magazine published by the General Conference of the Church of God (Seventh Day). 8.5x11; glossy cover; 24 pages.

Focus and Audience

Reflects the teachings of the Church of God (Seventh Day)—send for doctrinal beliefs booklet. Features articles on Bible doctrine, social and religious issues, and Christian living. Most readers are 50- to 60-years old and are from a wide range of denominations.

Interests and Word Lengths

- *Nonfiction:* Features, testimonies, sermons, personal experiences, expositions on Bible passages. Interests include Church of God Bible doctrine, current social and religious issues, practical teaching on Bible topics, textual and biblical book studies, Christian lifestyle, and prophecy. 1,500–2,500 words. Filler, 100–500 words.
- *Departments:* Viewpoint, an opinion page on issues that affect Christians in today's society such as homosexuality, pornography, politics, education, and media. 700 words.
- *Poetry:* 5–25 lines.
- *Photos:* B/W prints. Color slides for cover.

How to Submit

Send complete ms with cover letter and clips. Accepts computer printouts, 3.5-inch Macintosh Microsoft Word 5.1 disks, and Timbuktu remote modem submissions. Simultaneous submissions okay. Reports in 1–2 months.

Payment and Policies

Authors retain rights. Pays on publication. $10–$25 honorarium for articles. No payment for Viewpoint pieces, poetry, or photos. Authors receive 1 copy of the issue.

Bible Review

Editorial Office
3000 Connecticut Avenue NW
Suite 300
Washington, DC 20008
202-387-8888

AT A GLANCE:

BIBLE REVIEW

- Bible Study, History
- 5% freelance
- Less than 5% new writers
- Bimonthly
- Circ: 40,000
- Receives 20–30 queries, 10–20 mss each month.
- Pays: Up to $300 on publication.

From the Editor:
"Query first. Make sure you read a sample of *Bible Review* before submitting a manuscript."

Best Bet: Interesting, historical, critical analysis of the Bible.

Avoid: Inspirational material; denominational focuses.

Sample copy: Not provided. No guidelines.

Profile

A popular magazine devoted to critical Bible scholarship. Published bimonthly by the non-profit Biblical Archaeology Society. 8.5x11; glossy cover; full-color; 80 pages.

Focus and Audience

Presents historical, critical Bible scholarship and interpretation to a lay audience.

Interests and Word Lengths

- *Nonfiction:* Critical essays and analysis of the Bible, both the Hebrew Scriptures and New Testament. Accepts interviews. No word-length restrictions.
- *Departments:* Bible Books, reviews of related titles. Bible Quiz, thematic quizzes.
- *Artwork:* Photos and illustrations of Bible art.

How to Submit

Query with outline preferred. Accepts complete ms with cover letter. Include SASE. Accepts photocopies and computer printouts. Simultaneous submissions okay. Reports in up to 1 year.

Payment and Policies

One-time rights. Pays on publication. Essays and interviews, up to $300. Authors receive 1–2 copies of the issue.

Bible Time 4s5s

Cathy Marie Walker, Editor
P.O. Box 632
Glen Ellyn, IL 60138
708-668-6000

AT A GLANCE:

BIBLE TIME 4S5S

- Christian, Children
- 50–70% freelance
- Weekly
- Circ: not available
- Receives 40–55 mss each month.
- Pays: $20–$30 on acceptance.

From the Editor:
"We seek to honor Jesus Christ in all our publishing efforts, and to help children come to know the Lord and be discipled in His ways. We are an evangelical publishing house."

Best Bet: Stories for preschool children that apply spiritual truths to everyday life.

Avoid: Bible stories.

Sample copy: Free with 6x9 SAE and $.29 postage. Send #10 SASE for guidelines.

Profile

A Sunday school take-home paper for preschool children. Correlated with the Scripture Press *Bible for Today* curriculum. 7x10; 4-color; folded; 4 pages.

Focus and Audience

Designed to help children, ages 4 and 5, apply Scripture lessons to everyday life situations and come to know Jesus Christ. Evangelical in nature.

Interests and Word Lengths

- *Fiction:* Concise stories that address the lives of 4- and 5-year-old children. Be realistic and illustrate spiritual truths applied in life. Keep in mind the characteristics and concrete thinking patterns of this age. 220–225 words.
- *Nonfiction:* True-life stories that address the lives of preschool children. 220–225 words.
- *Filler:* Activities to accompany stories.

How to Submit

Send complete ms with cover letter. Include SASE. Accepts photocopies and computer printouts. No simultaneous submissions. Reports in 4–6 weeks.

Payment and Policies

All rights. Pays on acceptance. $20–$30 per story. Authors receive 4 copies of the issue.

The Bible Today

Rev. Leslie J. Hoppe, O.F.M., Editor
The Liturgical Press
Collegeville, MN 56321-7500
612-363-2213

AT A GLANCE:
THE BIBLE TODAY

- Christian, Bible Study
- 20% freelance
- 5% new writers
- Bimonthly
- Circ: 9,000
- Receives 3 queries, 5–7 mss each month.
- No payment. Offers free subscription.

From the Editor:
"*The Bible Today* is a popular periodical. It attempts to bring the best in contemporary scholarship to biblically literate readers."

Best Bet: Non-technical articles that explore and explain Scripture and encourage prayerful Bible study.

Avoid: Fundamentalist views of the Bible or Bible scholarship.

Sample copy: Free. Send #10 SASE for guidelines.

Profile

A quarterly compilation of contemporary Bible scholarship. Published by a Roman Catholic publisher, but sensitive to ecumenical concerns. Est.: 1962. 6x9; glossy cover; 64 pages.

Focus and Audience

Promotes understanding and appreciation of Scripture. Written for both professional and paraprofessional readers, including parish ministers and leaders, Bible study groups, Scripture students, and all those attempting to relate Scripture to their own spiritual life.

Interests and Word Lengths

- *Nonfiction:* Considers biblical articles only. Articles that explain the meaning and context of biblical passages and books, explore topics or themes in light of the biblical tradition, and encourage a prayerful reading of the Bible. Bible study and biblical archaelology 2,000 words (7–8 typed, double-spaced pages).
- *Artwork:* Submit to Robin Pierzina, O.S.B., Managing Editor. Photos and illustrations that enhance articles.

How to Submit

Send complete ms with cover letter. Include SASE. Accepts computer printouts and IBM-compatible disks with hard copy. Reports in 2–3 months.

Payment and Policies

All rights. No payment. Offers authors a free 1-year subscription and 5 complimentary copies.

Biblical Illustrator

Design Editor
127 Ninth Avenue North
Nashville, TN 37234
615-251-3649

Profile

A quarterly Bible study publication. 8.5x11; 82 pages.

Focus and Audience

Provides biblical background articles for Southern Baptist Sunday school teachers, Bible students, and sermons.

Interests and Word Lengths

- *Nonfiction:* Biblical background articles that focus on specific Scripture passages. Writers must be Southern Baptist Church members. No word-length restrictions.
- *Photos:* Color slides of Biblical sites.

How to Submit

All material is assigned. Request writer qualifications. Then, send resume or curriculum vitae with writing samples. Include SASE.

Payment and Policies

All rights. Pays on acceptance. $.055 per word. Authors receive 2 copies of the issue.

The B'nai B'rith International Jewish Monthly

Jeff Rubin, Editor
1640 Rhode Island Avenue NW
Washington, DC 20036
202-857-6646

AT A GLANCE:
The B'nai B'rith International Jewish Monthly

- Jewish, Cultural
- 50% freelance
- 25% new writers
- 8 issues a year
- Circ: 200,000
- Receives 30 queries, 60 mss each month.
- Pays on publication. Rates vary.

From the Editor:
"We value clear, vibrant, engaging writing that tells a story completely but with a maximum of economy."

Best Bet: Non-religious topics related to the Jewish community.

Avoid: Fiction; political commentary; nostalgia; generalizations; clichés; and wordiness.

Sample copy: Not provided. Send #10 SASE for guidelines.

Profile

An international magazine of Jewish critical and political thought. Published by B'nai B'rith International. 8.5x11; glossy cover; full-color; 48–56 pages.

Focus and Audience

Explores the social, cultural, historical, and political issues that affect the Jewish community in the United States and abroad.

Interests and Word Lengths

- *Nonfiction:* Articles on any non-religious topic relevant to the Jewish community. Subjects include culture, politics, human interest, and service. Capture the spirit of the idea, person, or place. 750–3,000 words.
- *Photos:* B/W and color prints and illustrations. Include SASE.

How to Submit

Query with outline and clips. Include SASE. Accepts typewritten and Macintosh ASCII or WordPerfect disk submissions. No simultaneous submissions. Reports in 3 weeks.

Payment and Policies

First North American serial rights. Pays on publication. Rates vary. Authors receive 3 copies of the issue.

Bookstore Journal

Todd Hafer, Editor
P.O. Box 200
Colorado Springs, CO 80901
719-576-7880

AT A GLANCE:

BOOKSTORE JOURNAL

- Christian, Retail
- 30% freelance
- 10–20% new writers
- Monthly
- Circ: 7,000
- Receives 25–30 queries and mss each month.
- Pays: $.11–$.14 per word on publication.

From the Editor:
"Most of our articles are assigned to people who have expertise in retail management. We occasionally ask freelance writers to report on special industry events or interview selected authors, artists, suppliers, and retailers."

Best Bet: Articles that impact the professional lives of Christian retail owners, employees, and service people.

Sample copy: $5. Send #10 SASE for guidelines.

Profile

A monthly trade publication for Christian retailers. The official publication of the Christian Booksellers Association. 8.5x11; glossy cover; full-color; 175 pages.

Focus and Audience

Designed to help Christian retailers and suppliers have more effective ministries by providing them how-to articles, product information, and relevant industry news. Readers are owners, managers, and employees of Christian retail stores.

Interests and Word Lengths

- *Nonfiction:* How-to articles on financial management, retail business management and procedures, and marketing to consumers. Features on specific Christian retail stores, supplier companies, authors, and artists. 1,200–2,000 words.
- *Photos:* B/W and color prints.

How to Submit

Submit complete ms with cover letter and resume. Include SASE. Accepts photocopies, computer printouts, and DOS WordPerfect and DOS or Macintosh ASCII disks with hard copy. Simultaneous submissions okay if to a non-competitor. Reports in 1–2 months.

Payment and Policies

All or first rights. Pays on publication. Articles, $.11–$.14 per word. Photos, $20. Authors receive 1–2 copies of the issue.

Bread for God's Children

Anna Lee Carlton, Editor
P.O. Box 1017
Arcadia, FL 33821
813-494-6214

AT A GLANCE:
BREAD FOR GOD'S CHILDREN

- Christian, Youth
- 20% freelance
- Monthly
- Circ: 10,000
- Receives 40–50 mss each month.
- Pays $20–$40 on publication.

From the Editor:
"We want to help families live a consistent Christian life by lifting up Jesus and His teachings."

Best Bet: Non-preachy fiction that teaches Christian principles.

Avoid: Fantasy stories. Any strictly denominational slant.

Sample copy: Free with 9x12 SAE and 5 first-class stamps. Send #10 SASE for guidelines.

Profile

A non-denominational monthly magazine designed as a teaching tool for Christian families. Aimed at children, early teens, and their parents. 8.5x11; paper cover; 2-color; 28 pages.

Focus and Audience

Stories and articles that model Christian principles for children, 5–10 years, and teens, 11–15 years. Also publishes a section for parents.

Interests and Word Lengths

- *Fiction:* Uses 2 stories per issue. Teen stories, 800–1,600 words. Young children's stories, 500–900 words. True-to-life situations that weave biblical teaching into plots in a natural way. No preaching or moralizing. Show characters overcoming worldly problems through Christian living. No fantasy.
- *Departments:* Teen Page; Let's Chat. Subjects of concern to young people from a scriptural outlook. 500–800 words.

How to Submit

Send complete ms with cover letter. Include SASE. Accepts photocopies and computer printouts. Simultaneous submissions okay. May hold stories for several months.

Payment and Policies

First or second rights. Pays on publication. Teen stories, $40. Young children's stories, $30. Departments, $20. Authors receive 3 copies of the issue.

Breakaway

Greg Johnson, Editor
420 North Cascade
Colorado Springs, CO 80903
719-531-3400

AT A GLANCE:

BREAKAWAY

- Christian, Teens
- 60–70% freelance
- 10–20% new writers
- Monthly
- Circ: 90,000
- Receives 10 queries, 25 mss each month.
- Pays: $.12–$.15 per word on acceptance.

From the Editor:
"We have a conservative Christian bent, but don't use 'Christianese.' All material must appeal to a teen guy. Have a few people read your article and make suggestions before sending it in."

Best Bet: Humor, cartoons, and articles on friendship.

Avoid: First-person testimonies; hokey fiction that always turns out right; sermons; writing for adults.

Sample copy: Free with 8.5x11 SAE and 3 first-class stamps. Send #10 SASE for guidelines.

Profile

An inspirational, contemporary Christian magazine for 12 - to 17-year-old teenage boys. 8.5x11; glossy cover; 4-color; 24–32 pages.

Focus and Audience

Must appeal to and address topics of interest to the average teenage boy. The magazine has a conservative bent, but strives to be friendly enough for readers to pass on to non-church friends.

Interests and Word Lengths

- *Fiction:* Adventure, action, real-life high school situations and subjects such as sports, girls, etc. 1,200–2,200 words.
- *Nonfiction:* Features on professional athletes, students involved in positive activities, and general interest articles for teenage boys. 400–1,800 words. Accepts quizzes, sports facts, and cartoons.
- *Departments:* Plugged In, devotional page. 700–900 words.
- *Seasonal:* Submit 8 months in advance.

How to Submit

Query with clips. Include SASE. Accepts photocopies and computer printouts. Simultaneous submissions okay. Reports in 1 month.

Payment and Policies

First North American serial rights, one-time rights, or all rights. Pays on acceptance. $.12–$.15 per word. Kill fee, 33%–50% for assigned pieces. Authors receive 3 copies of the issue.

Bridges
A Journal for Jewish Feminists and Our Friends

Clare Kinberg, Managing Editor
P.O. Box 18437
Seattle, WA 98118

AT A GLANCE:
BRIDGES

- Jewish, Feminist
- 99% freelance
- 50% new writers
- Semi-annual
- Circ: 3,000
- Receives 2–3 queries, 15–20 mss each month.
- No payment. Offers 5 contributor's copies.

From the Editor:
"We want to provide a forum in which Jews, feminists, and activists can exchange ideas."

Best Bet: Material relevant to Jewish feminism.

Avoid: Anything that perpetuates anti-Jewish, anti-Arab, sexist, classist, racist, homophobic, or other biases.

Sample copy: Free. Send #10 SASE for guidelines.

Profile
A literary and political journal of Jewish feminism. Explores the relationship between Jewish feminism and activism. 7x10; heavy bond cover; 150 pages.

Focus and Audience
Combines Jewish identity and values with feminist and progressive activism. Showcases the creative work of Jewish feminists and welcomes work relevant to Jewish feminism by Sephardic and Mizrachi Jews, people of color, the old or the young, lesbians and gay writers, men, and non-Jewish women.

Interests and Word Lengths
- *Fiction:* Fiction with Jewish and feminist perspectives. Up to 35 typed, double-spaced pages.
- *Nonfiction:* Articles; commentary; discussions of politics and culture; scholarly essays written in an accessible style; archival material; interviews and oral histories; reviews. Up to 35 typed, double-spaced pages.
- *Departments:* Working Class Words.
- *Poetry:* Poetry in English or in its original language with an English translation. Submit no more than 10 poems at one time.
- *Artwork:* B/W photos, stats, or copies of artwork. No originals.

How to Submit
Send complete ms with cover letter and brief author biography. Include SASE. No reprints. Accepts photocopies, computer printouts, and disk submissions. No simultaneous submissions. Reports in 4–6 months.

Payment and Policies
One-time rights. No payment. Authors receive 5 copies of the issue.

Brigade Leader

Deborah Christensen, Managing Editor
765 Kimberly Drive
Carol Stream, IL 60188
708-665-0630

AT A GLANCE:

BRIGADE LEADER

- Christian, Men
- 50% freelance
- 10% new writers
- Quarterly
- Circ: 9,000
- Receives 0–5 queries, 0–5 mss each month.
- Pays: $.05–$.10 per word on publication.

From the Editor:
"We rarely accept unsolicited manuscripts. It's better to submit writing samples and be put on our list for possible future assignments."

Avoid: Academic treatises—keep it simple and practical.

Sample copy: $1.50 with 9x12 SAE with $.98 postage. Send #10 SASE for guidelines.

Profile

A membership magazine for men who are Christian Service Brigade (CSB) leaders. 8.5x11; glossy cover; 4-color; 24–32 pages.

Focus and Audience

Readers are leaders in Christian Service Brigade, a non-profit, nondenominational, evangelical Christian agency dedicated to winning and training boys to serve Jesus Christ.

Interests and Word Lengths

- *Nonfiction:* Features, how-tos, personal experiences on marriage, family, Christian living, and leadership in CSB. 1,500 words. Each issue includes Program-related articles, CSB program materials, and Leadership Aid articles, all practical tips of interest to men working with boys.
- *Photos:* Submit to Robert Fine. 8x10 B/W photos of family situations, camping, service opportunities, hobbies, sports, multi-racial/multi-ethnic, and outdoor adventure.

How to Submit

Query with writing samples. SASE. No unsolicited mss. Accepts photocopies, computer printouts, and faxes. Reports in 1 month.

Payment and Policies

First North American serial rights and reprint rights. Pays on publication. $.05–$.10 per word. Inside photos, $35. Cover photos, $75–$100. Kill fee, $35. Authors receive 2 copies of the issue.

Brio

Susie Shellenberger, Editor
420 North Cascade Avenue
Colorado Springs, CO 80903
719-531-3400

From the Editor:
"*Brio* is a fast-paced publication that uses articles and stories written in a bright, compelling, out-of-the-ordinary style. Study our magazine for our style and audience before submitting your work."

Best Bet: Articles for teen girls that deal with ordinary female problems: buying a bra, cramping, talking to guys. Solid fiction and short, fun quizzes are also needed.

Avoid: Christian lingo.

Sample copy: Free with 9x12 SASE. Send #10 SASE for guidelines.

Profile

A Christian magazine for teenage girls. Published monthly by Focus on the Family. 8x11; glossy cover; full-color; 32 pages.

Focus and Audience

Goal is to teach creatively, to entertain, to challenge, and to encourage teenage girls towards a strong relationship with Jesus Christ, a healthy relationship with the opposite sex, and a good self image.

Interests and Word Lengths

- *Fiction:* Short stories with realistic character development, fresh teen lingo, and plots that girls are immediately drawn to. Particularly interested in romance, sibling rivalry, and situations faced daily by teen girls. May contain a spiritual slant but should not preach. Up to 2,000 words.
- *Nonfiction:* Biographical articles and/or interviews with teens or adults who teens admire. Action-oriented articles of interest to teens. Past topics include Organizing Your Locker and Better Eyes. Accepts how-to articles on talking to boys, relating to parents; teachers and others in authority, spending money; etc. Interested in unique and creative youth group activities that show the fun and adventure Christian teens have together. No word-length restrictions.

How to Submit

Send complete ms with cover letter. Include SASE. Accepts photocopies, computer printouts, faxes, and submissions via modem. Identify simultaneous submissions. Reports in 1 month.

Payment and Policies

One-time rights. Pays on acceptance. $.08–$.15 per word depending on editing needed. Authors receive 3 copies of the issue.

Broken Streets

Ron Grossman, Editor
57 Morningside Drive East
Bristol, CT 06010

Profile

A forum for Christian poetry of all types. 5.5x8.5; glossy cover; 40–50 pages.

Focus and Audience

Open to Christian poetry, prayers, short prose, and filler.

Interests and Word Lengths

- *Poetry:* Christian poetry of 5–15 lines preferably, but accepts any length.
- *Nonfiction:* Devotionals, short prayers, filler. 500 words maximum.
- *Departments:* Book Reviews of Christian poetry books. Include book with submission. 500 words maximum.
- *Artwork:* B/W pen & ink drawings with Christian themes.

How to Submit

Query with writing samples or send complete ms with cover letter and clips. Include SASE. Accepts photocopies and computer printouts. Reports in 1 week.

Payment and Policies

One-time rights. No payment. Authors receive 1–2 copies of the issue.

Brown Gold

Macon Hare, Editor-in-Chief
1000 East First Street
Sanford, FL 32771
407-323-8430·

AT A GLANCE:
BROWN GOLD

- Missionary, Evangeli-
  cal
- Very little freelance
- Monthly
- Circ: 50,000
- Receives 20 queries,
  20 mss each month.
- No payment.

From the Editor:
"Since our ministry is so
specialized, our writers
are basically from our
own personnel out on
the fields of service."

Best Bet: Informative
and challenging
material on the world
evangelization efforts
of the New Tribes
Missions.

Sample copy: No information provided.

Profile

The monthly magazine of the New Tribes Missions, a
missionary organization dedicated to providing cross-
culture evangelism, church planting, and literacy development to peoples in remote areas. 8x10.5; 12
pages.

Focus and Audience

Reports on the New Tribes Missions work worldwide. Informs Christians as it challenges them to get involved in
world evangelization. Most material is provided by missionaries in field service.

Interests and Word Lengths

- *Nonfiction:* Positive reports on New Tribes Missions
  projects. Occasionally accepts outstanding freelance
  articles on evangelism and missionary work in line
  with the publication's goals.

How to Submit

Query with outline. Include SASE. Accepts photocopies
and computer printouts.

Payment and Policies

No payment. All material is donated.

Byline

Kathryn Fanning, Managing Editor
P.O. Box 130596
Edmond, OK 73013
405-348-5591

AT A GLANCE:

BYLINE

- Writing, Inspirational
- Monthly
- Circ: 3,000
- Pays: $15–$50 on acceptance.

From the Editor:
"It is our belief that tenacity is essential to success in writing. But while success as a writer is a great achievement, considerable merit attaches to the effort itself. Our message to writers is a simple one: Believe in yourself and keep trying."

Best Bet: Motivational articles for writers.

Avoid: Poems about writer's block, the muse, and inspiration in the middle of the night.

Sample copy: $3. Send #10 SASE for guidelines.

Profile

A national monthly magazine aimed toward helping writers succeed. Est.: 1981. 8.5x11; glossy cover; 28 pages.

Focus and Audience

Goal is to seek out and encourage unpublished writers and to provide a forum for the work of beginners and veterans alike.

Interests and Word Lengths

- *Fiction:* General short fiction. Good writing is the main criterion. 2,000–4,000 words.
- *Nonfiction:* Instructive feature articles of help or motivation to writers; how-to-write and how-to-sell to specific market pieces; interviews with editors or freelance friendly publications. 1,200–1,800 words. First-person stories and essays on writing that are humorous, inspirational, or philosophical for End Piece section, 800 words.
- *Departments:* First Sale, accounts of a writer's first sale, 300–600 words. Only When I Laugh, writing-related humor, 300–800 words.
- *Poetry:* Submit to Marcia Preston, Executive Editor. Poems on writers or writing. Seeks serious poetry about the writing experience.

How to Submit

Send complete ms with cover letter. Interviews, query with editor's name and sample of the publication. Include SASE. Report time varies.

Payment and Policies

First North American serial rights. Pays on acceptance. Features and fiction, $50. End Pieces, $35. Departments, $15–$35. Poetry, $5–$10.

Caleb Issues & Answers

Bill Jack, Managing Editor
Rt. 4, Box 274
West Frankfort, IL 62896
618-937-2348

AT A GLANCE:
CALEB ISSUES & ANSWERS

- Christian, Young Adult
- 30% freelance
- 5% new writers
- 9 issues a year
- Circ: 14,000
- No payment. Offers 10 contributor's copies.

From the Editor:
"Aim for high school students and address their interests, always presenting a Christian worldview."

Sample copy: Free with SAE and 2 first-class stamps. Send #10 SASE for guidelines.

Profile
A small, independent Christian paper for high school students. 8.5x11; newsprint; 16 pages.

Focus and Audience
Aims to present a Christian worldview of contemporary social and moral issues to high school students.

Interests and Word Lengths
- *Nonfiction:* Articles on academic and social issues. 2 typed, double-spaced pages.
- *Departments:* Interviews with professional athletes. 2 typed, double-spaced pages.

How to Submit
Query with outline. Include SASE. Accepts photocopies and computer printouts. Simultaneous submissions okay. Reports in 1–2 months.

Payment and Policies
All rights. No payment. Authors receive 10 copies of the issue.

Campus Life

Christopher Lutes, Manuscripts Editor
465 Gundersen Drive
Carol Stream, IL 60188
708-260-6200

AT A GLANCE:
CAMPUS LIFE

- Christian, Youth
- 10–25% freelance
- 5% new writers
- 10 issues a year
- Circ: 120,000
- Receives 25 queries each month.
- Pays: $.10–$.20 per word on acceptance.

From the Editor:
"We want to reach the typical American teenager where his or her needs are. We don't want to hit them over the head with religion; we want to show them, through their own experiences, why it makes good sense to turn to Christianity for answers."

Best Bet: True, as-told-to first-person stories.

Avoid: Preaching, sermonizing, clichés, Sunday school fiction.

Sample copy: $2 with 8.5x11 SAE and $.50 postage. Send #10 SASE for guidelines.

Profile
A Christian magazine with the purpose of helping teenagers navigate adolescence with their faith intact. Published by Christianity Today, Inc. 8.5x11; glossy cover; full-color; 64 pages.

Focus and Audience
Seeks to help young people understand how their Christian faith applies to all areas of life. Readers are both male and female and most are late high school or early college students.

Interests and Word Lengths
- *Fiction:* Prefers fiction from experienced writers. Contemporary fiction with situations that reflect experiences common to the average high school student. 1,200–3,500 words.
- *Nonfiction:* Highly descriptive personal-experience pieces, first-person stories, and real-life drama that reflect experiences common to the average high school student. 750–1,500 words.
- *Departments:* OnCampus, Going for It!, In My Mind's Eye, Making a Difference. Send for specific guidelines—very limited opportunities.
- *Filler:* Very short tips for today's high school students.

How to Submit
Query with outline and clips. Include SASE. Accepts computer printouts. Simultaneous submissions okay. Reports in 3–5 months.

Payment and Policies
First North American serial rights or one-time rights. Pays on acceptance. $.10–$.20 per word. Authors receive 2 copies of the issue.

Canada Lutheran

Kenn Ward, Editor
1512 St. James Street
Winnipeg, MB R3H 0L2
Canada
204-786-6707

AT A GLANCE:
CANADA LUTHERAN

- Lutheran, Inspirational
- 0–50% freelance
- 0–20% new writers
- 11 issues a year
- Circ: 26,000
- Receives 20 queries, 15 mss each month.
- Pays: $40–$110 on publication.

From the Editor:
"Material must reflect the confessional faith and positions of the ELCIC."

Best Bet: Articles with simple style, contemporary language, and fresh ideas, especially those portraying real experiences of faith.

Avoid: Religious clichés; proof-texting the Bible.

Sample copy: Not provided. Send #10 SAE/IRC for guidelines.

Profile

A publication of the Evangelical Lutheran Church in Canada (ELCIC). Member of the Canadian Church Press. 8.5x11; self cover; 2-color; 40 pages.

Focus and Audience

Seeks to provide information, inspiration, and interpretation for ELCIC members. All material must adhere to ELCIC teachings.

Interests and Word Lengths

- *Fiction:* Biblical stories and modern parables. 1,000–1,500 words.
- *Nonfiction:* Articles on any subject that would interest contemporary Christians, especially those that show real-life experiences of faith. Preference given to specific ELCIC personalities and institutions. Use a simple style and contemporary language. 1,000–1,500 words.

How to Submit

Query with outline, or send complete ms with cover letter. Include SASE. U.S. authors send IRCs. Accepts computer printouts and IBM or Macintosh WordPerfect 5.1 disks. Simultaneous submissions okay. Reports within 1 month.

Payment and Policies

One-time rights. Pays on publication. $40–$110 per piece. Authors receive 2 copies of the issue.

The Canadian Catholic Review

Donald Ward, Managing Editor
1437 College Drive
Saskatoon, SK S7N 0W6
Canada
306-966-8959

AT A GLANCE:
The Canadian Catholic Review

- Catholic, Theology
- 30% freelance
- 10% new writers
- 11 issues a year
- Circ: 1,200
- Receives 10–20 queries, 5–10 mss each month.
- Pays: $50–$300 (CAN) on publication.

From the Editor:
"We look primarily for good writing and what one subscriber has described as 'creative orthodoxy.' We are interested in all issues that touch on the Christian life, but they must be dealt with maturely and intelligently."

Avoid: Devotional or pietistic treatments. Extremes of either conservatism or liberalism; fiction and poetry.

Sample copy: $3 with 9x12 SAE/IRC. Send #10 SASE/IRC for guidelines.

Profile

A magazine of Catholic theology and tradition founded and largely sponsored by the Congregation of St. Basil, a teaching order that evangelizes by example and through education. 8x10.5; 2-color; 40 pages.

Focus and Audience

Seeks to carry on the Catholic intellectual tradition, which is moderate, objective, sophisticated, and ultimately Christian. Readers are mature, educated Catholic and other Christian lay people and clergy.

Interests and Word Lengths

- *Nonfiction:* Serious articles and interviews on historical, theological, or contemporary issues of interest to the mature believer and his or her spirituality; whimsical essays that make a point; profiles of heroic sanctity (i.e., Maximilian Kolbe). 500–6,000 words.
- *Columns:* American Notes, Liturgy, Scripture, Television, Movies, and Spirituality. 500–1,200 words. Book Reviews, 300–700 words.
- *Artwork:* Line drawings; B/W photos.

How to Submit

Query with outline. Include SASE. U.S. authors include IRCs. Accepts photocopies, computer printouts, MS-DOS Microsoft Word or WordPerfect disks, and fax submissions. Reports in 2 months.

Payment and Policies

First North American serial rights. Pays on publication. Articles, $50–$300 (CAN) depending on length. Book Reviews, $25. Columns, $50. Authors receive 2 copies of the issue.

Canadian Messenger of the Sacred Heart

F.J. Power, S.J. and Alfred De Manche, Editors
661 Greenwood Avenue
Toronto, ON M4J 4B3
Canada
416-466-1195

AT A GLANCE:

CANADIAN MESSENGER OF THE SACRED HEART

- Catholic, Spirituality
- 40% freelance
- 10% new writers
- 11 issues a year
- Circ: 18,000
- Receives 1 query, 30 mss each month.
- Pays: $.04 per word on publication.

From the Editor:
"Develop a story that sustains interest to the end. Aim to move the heart as well as the mind. If you can, add a light touch or sense of humor to the story."

Best Bet: Inspirational stories and articles.

Avoid: Scripture dramas with imagined thoughts or dialog; poetry.

Sample copy: $1. Send #10 SASE/IRC for guidelines.

Profile

An inspirational Catholic magazine published by the Apostleship of Prayer. 7x10; glossy cover; 3-color; 32 pages.

Focus and Audience

Stresses the great value of ordinary actions and lives. Readers are Canadian and U.S. Catholics interested in developing a life of prayer and spirituality.

Interests and Word Lengths

- *Fiction:* Religious and inspirational short stories, humor, and drama about people, adventure, and heroism. End stories with impact, leaving a moral or faith message, but do not preach. Use the plot and characters to convey the message or theme. Up to 1,500 words.
- *Nonfiction:* Inspirational and informative articles of a non-controversial nature on spirituality, doctrine, and devotions. Use a conversational style. Up to 1,500 words.

How to Submit

Send complete ms with cover letter. Include SASE. U.S. authors include IRCs. Accepts photocopies and computer printouts. No simultaneous submissions. Reports in 1 month.

Payment and Policies

First North American serial rights. Pays on publication. $.04 per word. Authors receive 3 copies of the issue.

Caring People

Suzanne Kieffer
513 C Street NE
Washington, DC 20002
202-547-0655

AT A GLANCE:
CARING PEOPLE

- Inspirational, Volunteerism
- 0% freelance
- Quarterly
- Circ: 5,000
- Open to article ideas and suggestions.
- No payment. Offers contributor's copies.

From the Editor:
"We do not accept material from outside sources. We do, however, welcome your interview suggestions. We distribute approximately 5,000 free copies of *Caring People* each quarter."

Sample copy: No information available.

Profile

A non-profit quarterly magazine that profiles individuals dedicated to volunteerism and public service. 8.5x11; glossy cover; 4-color; 80 pages.

Focus and Audience

Profiles individuals who portray the spirit of caring, compassion, and integrity through volunteer and public service. Readership varies according to content.

Interests and Word Lengths

- *Nonfiction:* All articles are written in-house. Accepts ideas, suggestions, and recommendations for interviews with committed people who have excellent records of volunteering or supporting human rights. Considers short pieces as fillers.
- *Poetry:* Open to poetry that reflects the spirit of the magazine.
- *Photos:* Submit to Suzanne Kieffer. B/W or color prints or slides. No Polaroids or 110-film prints.

How to Submit

Send suggestions for possible interviews with writing samples or clips. Include photos if available. SASE. Accepts computer printouts, Macintosh 3.5-inch disks, and fax submissions. Simultaneous submissions okay. Report time varies.

Payment and Policies

All rights. No payment. Authors receive 1 or more copies of the issue.

Carolina Christian

Johnny R. Melton, Editor
R.R. 2, Box 137
Conover, NC 28613-9609
704-465-6739

AT A GLANCE:

CAROLINA CHRISTIAN

- Churches of Christ, Regional
- 35–50% freelance
- 10% new writers
- Monthly
- Circ: 2,200
- No payment. Offers 1–10 contributor's copies.

From the Editor:
"Write what you believe. Base your convictions on solid biblical basis. Write from the heart to a popular, rather than technical, audience."

Best Bet: Materials that are Christ-centered, God-honoring, and biblically based.

Sample copy: Free with 6x9 SAE and $.52 postage. No guidelines.

Profile

A monthly regional magazine that promotes the Churches of Christ in the Carolinas. 5.5x8.5; 20 pages.

Focus and Audience

Primary focus is on the regional activities of Carolina-based Churches of Christ. Readers include Carolinians as well as Christians across the country interested in the progress of this regional denomination.

Interests and Word Lengths

- *Nonfiction:* Features involving Churches of Christ and its members. Essays on biblical subjects. Articles of a solid devotional nature. Bible studies. 800–1,500 words.
- *Departments:* News, 50–150 words. Submit to Mike Mobley, News Editor, P.O. Box 312, Mooresville, NC 28115. Book reviews, 50–150 words. Submit to Tim Sensing, Book Review Editor, 2409 Blanche Drive, Burlington, NC 27215.

How to Submit

Submit complete ms with cover letter and resume. Include SASE. Accepts photocopies, letter-quality computer printouts, and IBM-compatible disk submissions. No simultaneous submissions. Reports in 2–3 months.

Payment and Policies

One-time rights. No payment. Authors receive 1–10 copies of the issue upon request.

Catechumenate

A Journal Christian Initiation

Victoria Tufano, Editor
1800 North Hermitage Avenue
Chicago, IL 60622-1101
312-486-8970

AT A GLANCE:

CATECHUMENATE

- Catholic, Conversion
- 95% freelance
- 20% new writers
- 6 issues a year
- Circ: 6,000
- Receives 1–2 queries, 1–2 mss each month.
- Pays: $250 per piece on publication.

From the Editor:
"All material should be in accordance with Vatican II teaching."

Best Bet: Articles on Catholic rites of initiation and reconciliation.

Avoid: Pious meditations and catechetical content.

Sample copy: Free. Send #10 SASE for guidelines.

Profile

A bimonthly journal for individuals converting to Catholicism through the Rite of Christian Initiation for Adults (RCIA). Published by Liturgy Training Publications. 6x9; glossy cover; 2-color; 48 pages.

Focus and Audience

Scholarly or experiential articles focusing solely on the Catholic rites of initiation or reconciliation. Adheres to Vatican II teaching. Written for individuals studying for or ministering in the field of Christian initiation: catechumens, clergy, religious educators, and seminarians.

Interests and Word Lengths

- *Nonfiction:* Articles and personal experiences on the RCIA process, liturgy, conversion, and reconciliation. 10 typed, double-spaced pages.
- *Poetry:* Poems themed or imaged around reconciliation or initiation.

How to Submit

Query with outline, resume, and writing samples; or send complete ms with cover letter. Include SASE. Accepts photocopies, computer printouts, 3.5- or 5.25-inch IBM-compatible WordPerfect disks, and faxes (1-800-933-7094). Identify simultaneous submissions. Reports in 2–3 months.

Payment and Policies

All rights. Pays on publication. Articles, $250. Authors receive 2 copies of issue.

Cathedral Age

Kelly Ferguson, Editor
Office of Public Affairs
Massachusetts and Wisconsin Avenues NW
Washington, DC 20016-5098
202-537-6247

AT A GLANCE:
CATHEDRAL AGE

- Episcopal, Cathedral Events
- Quarterly
- Circ: 35,000
- Pays: $125 on publication.

Best Bet: Articles covering Washington National Cathedral events and concerts.

Avoid: Editorials.

Sample copy: Free. Send #10 SASE for guidelines.

Profile

A quarterly magazine covering events at the Washington National Cathedral. 8.5x11; 32 pages.

Focus and Audience

Focuses solely on the religious, social, and recreational activities offered by the Washington National Cathedral.

Interests and Word Lengths

- *Nonfiction:* Straight-forward, journalistic articles reporting on Cathedral events and concerts. Events include religious services, forums on current issues and how they relate to persons of faith, choir concerts, and a Summer Festival free concert series. 1,000–2,000 words.

How to Submit

Query with outline and related writing samples. Include SASE. Accepts photocopies, computer printouts, and fax submissions (202-364-6600). No simultaneous submissions. Report time varies.

Payment and Policies

All rights. Pays on publication. $125 per piece. Authors receive 1–2 copies of the issue.

The Catholic Accent

Alice Laurich, Editor
P.O. Box 850
Greensburg, PA 15601
412-834-4010

AT A GLANCE:
THE CATHOLIC ACCENT

- Catholic, Regional
- Weekly
- Circ: 48,000
- Receives 2 mss each month.
- Payment varies.

From the Editor:
"We seek to inform, inspire, and evangelize."

Best Bet: Inspirational articles.

Avoid: Sensationalism.

Sample copy: $.35. No guidelines.

Profile

The official newspaper of the Diocese of Greensburg, PA. Published by Greensburg Catholic Accent and Communications Inc. Tabloid-size; newsprint; 20 pages.

Focus and Audience

Serves to inform and inspire Catholics in Western and Southwestern Pennsylvania.

Interests and Word Lengths

- *Nonfiction:* Articles of interest to Greensburg, PA Catholics. Interests include evangelism, inspiration and religious education. Accepts seasonal material. 1.5–2 typed, double-spaced pages.

How to Submit

Send complete ms with cover letter. Include SASE. Accepts original copies and fax submissions (412-836-5650). No simultaneous submissions. Reports in 1–2 months.

Payment and Policies

Authors retain rights. Payment schedule and rates vary. Authors receive 2 copies of the issue.

The Catholic Answer

Fr. Peter M. J. Stravinskas, Editor
207 Adams Street
Newark, NJ 07105
219-356-8400

AT A GLANCE:
The Catholic Answer

- Catholic, Spirituality
- Bimonthly
- Circ: 60,000
- Pays: $100 per piece on publication.

From the Editor:
"Scripture quotations, if from other than the *New American Bible*, should be noted accordingly."

Best Bet: Explanations of the tenets of Catholic faith and how it applies to daily living.

Avoid: Purple prose and polemics.

Sample copy: Free. Send #10 SASE to 200 Noll Plaza, Huntington, IN 46750 for guidelines.

Profile
A bimonthly publication of traditional Catholic faith. Published by Our Sunday Visitor. 5.5x8.5; 64 pages.

Focus and Audience
Concerned with answering questions about the Catholic faith. Readers are Catholic lay people, primarily over 40 years old.

Interests and Word Lengths
- *Nonfiction:* Articles on the application and explanation of the tenets of traditional Catholic faith; Catholic heritage; and how to apply faith to daily living. 5–7 typed, double-spaced pages.

How to Submit
Query with outline. Include SASE. Accepts photocopies, computer printouts, and 5.25-inch IBM-compatible disks. No simultaneous submissions. Report time varies.

Payment and Policies
First North American serial rights. Pays on publication. $100 per piece. Authors receive 2 copies of the issue.

Catholic Courier

Karen M. Franz, Editor
1150 Buffalo Road
Rochester, NY 14624
716-328-4340

Profile

A weekly Roman Catholic newspaper of the 12-county Diocese of Rochester, NY. It is a diocese-sponsored but independent publication. Tabloid-size; newsprint; 20 pages.

Focus and Audience

Primary emphasis is on Rochester, NY-area news. Also reports on national and international church issues of interest to Catholic readers.

Interests and Word Lengths

- *Nonfiction:* Hard news, features, and commentary on local, national, and international news of the Catholic Church, as well as related political and social issues. 1,200 words.
- *Departments:* Columns, Opinion, Et Cetera, Sports, Youth, and Leisure. 750 words.
- *Artwork:* 5x7 or larger clear B/W prints. Also accepts line art.

How to Submit

Query with outline, resume, and writing samples or clips, or send complete ms with cover letter, resume and clips. Include SASE. Accepts photocopies, computer printouts, and ASCII disks. Simultaneous submissions okay. Reports in 1–2 months.

Payment and Policies

One-time rights. Pays on publication. Articles and Departments, $30–$100 depending on length. Authors receive up to 5 copies of the issue.

Catholic Digest

Henry Lexau, Editor
P.O. Box 64090
St. Paul, MN 55164-0090

Profile

A national Catholic general-interest publication of inspirational writing. Published by the University of St. Thomas. 5x7.5; glossy cover; full-color; 128 pages.

Focus and Audience

Articles and fillers on a wide variety of topics of interest to a general Catholic audience. Most articles used are reprinted from other publications.

Interests and Word Lengths

- *Nonfiction:* Submit to Articles Editor. Articles on a variety of topics including religion, family, science, health, human relationships, nostalgia, good works, and the like. 1,000–3,000 words.
- *Filler:* Submit to Filler Editor. Open Door, true incidents that brought people back to the Catholic Church. People Are Like That, true stories that illustrate the instinctive goodness of human nature. The Perfect Assist, original accounts of gracious or tactful remarks or actions. Hearts Are Trumps, true cases of unseeking kindness. 200–500 words. Signs of the Times, amusing or significant signs. In Our Parish, stories of parish life, 50–300 words. Also accepts jokes, anecdotes, quizzes, and informational paragraphs, 10–500 words.

How to Submit

Original material, submit complete ms. Reprints, send copy or tear sheet, including name, address, editor, copyright line, and issue date of original source. Include SASE. Accepts photocopies and computer printouts. No simultaneous submissions.

Payment and Policies

Original articles, $200. Reprints, $100. Filler, $50 except Signs of the Times, $4, and In Our Parish, $20.

The Catholic Exponent

Denny Finneran, Editor
144 West Wood Street
P.O. Box 6787
Youngstown, OH 44501-6787
216-744-5251

AT A GLANCE:
THE CATHOLIC EXPONENT

- Catholic, Regional
- 20% freelance
- 5% new writers
- Biweekly
- Circ: 37,000
- Receives many queries and mss each month.
- Pays on publication. Rates vary.

From the Editor:
"Writers should be familiar with our newspaper and the Catholic faith."

Best Bet: Pieces on Catholic spiritual, moral, and ethical issues.

Avoid: Poetry and editorials.

Sample copy: Free. No guidelines.

Profile

The official newspaper of the Diocese of Youngstown, Ohio covering local, national, and international events. Member of the Catholic Press Association. Tabloid-size; newsprint; 24 pages.

Focus and Audience

A family-oriented paper covering Catholic spiritual, moral, and ethical issues for Catholic adults living in northeast Ohio.

Interests and Word Lengths

- *Nonfiction:* Submit to Elaine Polomsky Soos, Managing Editor. Articles on careers, retirement and aging, youth, vocations, respect for life, environment, health, family life, spirituality, and moral and ethical issues such as social justice, women's rights, and pro-life. Up to 500 words.
- *Departments:* Submit to Elaine Polomsky Soos, Managing Editor. Scripture, Liturgy, Family Life, Entertainment, and Recipes as well as general commentary. Up to 250 words.
- *Artwork:* Submit to Edmund Sullivan, Associate Editor. B/W photos and illustrations with good contrast.

How to Submit

Query with outline. Include SASE. Accepts computer printouts, Display Write 4 3.5-inch disks, and faxes. Simultaneous submissions okay.

Payment and Policies

One-time rights. Pays on publication. Rates vary according to length and subject. Authors receive copies of the issue.

Catholic Forester

Barbara Cunningham, Editor
355 Shuman Boulevard
P.O. Box 3012
Naperville, IL 60566
708-983-4920

AT A GLANCE:
CATHOLIC FORESTER

- Catholic, Membership News
- 25% freelance
- 10% new writers
- Bimonthly
- Circ: 140,000
- Receives 200 mss each month.
- Pays: $.05–$.20 per word on acceptance.

From the Editor:
"We look for work in which the basics of good, clear writing have been observed: a good lead, style, rhythm, and a lack of clutter."

Avoid: Unnecessary and long words or sentences; jargon.

Sample copy: Free with 8.5x11 SAE with $1.50 postage. Send #10 SASE for guidelines.

Profile

The membership magazine of the Catholic Order of Forester, a fraternal organization. 8.5x11; glossy cover; full-color; 36 pages.

Focus and Audience

Informs members of organizational news and events and serves as an outreach tool for non-members. Offers readers a variety of general- and Catholic-interest articles and stories.

Interests and Word Lengths

- *Fiction:* Contemporary fiction, adventure, humor, mainstream, mysteries, and suspense. Considers children's stories. 2,000–2,500 words.
- *Nonfiction:* General-interest, informative articles suitable for family reading on a wide variety of topics including travel, nostalgia, and timely material on current issues. Accepts historical and contemporary pieces, interviews and profiles, opinion and viewpoint pieces, personal experiences, and articles of special interest to Catholics. Welcomes seasonal material. Up to 2,500 words.
- *Filler:* Humorous anecdotes and jokes.
- *Artwork:* Welcomes photos and illustrations to accompany articles. Prefers color, but accepts B/W.

How to Submit

Send complete ms with cover letter. Include SASE. Accepts photocopies, computer printouts, and disk submissions. Simultaneous submissions okay. Reports in 2 months.

Payment and Policies

One-time or all rights. Pays on acceptance. $.05–$.20 per word. Authors receive 1 copy of the issue.

Catholic Near East

Michael La Civita, Editor
1011 First Avenue
New York, NY 10022-4195
212-826-1480

AT A GLANCE:
CATHOLIC NEAR EAST

- Catholic, Missions
- 60% freelance
- 40% new writers
- Bimonthly
- Circ: 100,000
- Receives 10 queries, few mss each month.
- Pays $.20 per word on acceptance.

From the Editor:
"Articles should not be academic, rather they should weave current life and lifestyles with issues and needs. Know your topic, stay away from piety, interview people when applicable, and write clearly and succinctly."

Avoid: Articles with political leanings.

Sample copy: Free. Send #10 SASE for guidelines.

Profile

A publication of the Catholic Near East Welfare Association, a papal agency for humanitarian and pastoral support that serves Eastern Christian communities. Member of the Catholic Press Association of the United States and Canada. 6x9; glossy cover; full-color; 32 pages.

Focus and Audience

Strives to inform American Catholics about the traditions, faith, history, culture, and churches of Ethiopia, India, the Middle East, and the former Soviet Union. Also serves as an ecumenical and interfaith tool.

Interests and Word Lengths

- *Nonfiction:* Non-academic features and profiles of communities in the Middle East, India, and the former Soviet Union. Communities can be Catholic, Orthodox, Jewish, or Muslim. Up to 1,500 words.
- *Photos:* Professional quality 35-mm color slides or prints.

How to Submit

Query with outline, resume, and writing samples. Include SASE. Accepts photocopies, computer printouts, Macintosh 3.5-inch disks, and fax submissions. No simultaneous submissions. Reports in 3 months.

Payment and Policies

First North American serial rights. Pays on acceptance and approval. $.20 per edited word. Authors receive 6 copies of the issue.

Catholic New York

Anne Buckley, Editor-in-Chief
1011 First Avenue, 17th Floor
New York, NY 10022
212-688-2399

AT A GLANCE:
CATHOLIC NEW YORK

- Catholic, Regional
- 10% freelance
- 5% new writers
- Weekly
- Circ: 130,000
- Receives 8–10 queries, 4 mss each month.
- Pays: $15–$100 on publication.

From the Editor:
"Read our publication before submitting. We look for timeless material."

Best Bet: Articles that combine work, hobbies, or special interests with the Catholic faith.

Avoid: Controversial, newsy, trite, or over-done pieces.

Sample copy: $1. No guidelines.

Profile

A weekly newspaper serving New York-area Catholics. Covers New York City and seven counties. Tabloid-size; 44 pages.

Focus and Audience

Informs readers of local, regional, national, and international affairs of the Catholic Church. Aims to incorporate real people into the church's activities and goals. Readers are New York Catholics.

Interests and Word Lengths

- *Nonfiction:* Issue-oriented features, interviews, and personal experiences that incorporate the Catholic faith into everyday living. 500–800 words.
- *Departments:* Catholic New Yorkers, profiles of unique individuals; Comment. 325 words.
- *Seasonal:* Accepts holiday material for Op/Ed page.
- *Photos:* B/W prints to accompany article only.

How to Submit

Prefers query with outline; accepts complete ms with cover letter. Include SASE. Accepts photocopies, computer printouts, and fax submissions. No simultaneous submissions. Reports in 1 month.

Payment and Policies

One-time rights. Pays on publication. $15–$100 per piece. Authors receive copies of the issue upon request.

Catholic Parent

Woodeene Koenig-Bricker, Editor
200 Noll Plaza
Huntington, IN 46750
219-356-8400

AT A GLANCE:
CATHOLIC PARENT

- Catholic, Parenting
- 90% freelance
- Bimonthly
- Circ: not available
- Pays on acceptance. Rates vary.

From the Editor:
"Write a tight story or feature on an issue of concern to parents. Keep it anecdotal and practical. Don't preach, but share your wisdom."

Best Bet: Parenting articles with a Catholic focus.

Avoid: Preaching, pontificating, and boring the reader.

Sample copy: Not available. Send #10 SASE for guidelines.

Profile
A parenting magazine directed to Catholic parents. Published by Our Sunday Visitor, Inc. Est.: 1993. 8.5x11; glossy cover; full-color; 48 pages.

Focus and Audience
Offers a specifically Catholic focus and approach to child-rearing and family issues.

Interests and Word Lengths
- *Nonfiction:* Anecdotal, practical feature articles, personal experiences, and some essays on child-rearing, relationships, education, moral values, and other issues confronting today's parents, all with a Catholic slant. Up to 1,500 words.
- *Departments:* This Works!, parenting tips.

How to Submit
Query with outline and writing samples, if available, or send complete ms with cover letter. Include SASE. Accepts photocopies and computer printouts. Disk and fax submissions need prior approval. Reports in 1 month.

Payment and Policies
First North American serial rights. Pays on acceptance. Rates vary. Authors receive copies of the issue.

Catholic Sentinel

Robert Pfohman, Editor
P.O. Box 18030
Portland, OR 97218
503-281-1191

AT A GLANCE:

CATHOLIC SENTINEL

- Catholic, Regional
- 10% freelance
- 2% new writers
- Weekly
- Circ: 16,500
- Receives 1–2 queries,
  3–4 mss each month.
- Pays on publication.
  Rates vary.

From the Editor:
"Please read the publication."

Best Bet: Material directly relevant to Oregon Catholics.

Sample copy: Free with 9x12 SASE. No guidelines.

Profile

The official newspaper for the Archdiocese of Portland, Oregon, and the Baker Diocese of Eastern Oregon. Published by Oregon Catholic Press. Est.: 1870. Tabloid-size; newsprint; 20 pages.

Focus and Audience

Publishes material that is directly relevant to Oregon-area Catholics.

Interests and Word Lengths

- *Nonfiction:* News from the world, nation, state, and parish that affects Catholics. Personality profiles of Catholics living out their faith. 600–1,200 words.
- *Columns:* Lively, thought-provoking personal observations and opinion pieces on how the Catholic faith relates to today's events, family life, etc. 500–700 words.
- *Artwork:* B/W or color prints. Considers illustrations, especially calligraphy.

How to Submit

Query with outline and clips. Include SASE. Accepts photocopies, computer printouts, disks (call first), faxes, and ASCII submissions via modem. No simultaneous submissions. Reports in 1–2 months.

Payment and Policies

One-time rights. Pays on publication. Rates vary. Kill fee offered if piece is assigned. Authors receive 2 copies of the issue.

Catholic Telegraph

Jennifer Roedersheimer, Managing Editor
100 East Eighth Street
Cincinnati, OH 45202
513-421-3131

AT A GLANCE:
CATHOLIC TELEGRAPH

- Catholic, Regional
- 10% freelance
- 2% new writers
- Weekly
- Circ: 40,000
- Receives 1 query each month.
- Pays on publication. Rates vary.

From the Editor:
"Be knowledgeable about the Catholic faith. New writers should speak with experienced writers—they will tell you what to write about."

Best Bet: News of interest to Cincinnati-area Catholics.

Avoid: Queries and unsolicited manuscripts.

Sample copy: Free. Guidelines sent after acceptance.

Profile

The official newspaper of the Archdiocese of Cincinnati, Ohio. Tabloid-size; newsprint; 16 pages.

Focus and Audience

Seeks to further the goals of the Catholic Church by informing Cincinnati-area Catholics about their faith. All material is assigned.

Interests and Word Lengths

- *Nonfiction:* Feature articles on Cincinnati-related news of interest to Catholics. Assignment only.
- *Filler:* Press releases and community news.
- *Photos:* B/W prints.

How to Submit

Send resume and writing samples. Accepts photocopies, computer printouts, faxes, and submission via modem if contacted in advance. No simultaneous submissions. Reports in 2–3 weeks.

Payment and Policies

All rights. Pays on publication. Rates vary depending on the amount of work necessary. Kill fee varies. Authors receive 1 copy of the issue.

Catholic Twin Circle

Loretta G. Seyer, Editor
12700 Ventura Boulevard
Suite 200
Studio City, CA 91604
818-766-2270

AT A GLANCE:
CATHOLIC TWIN CIRCLE

- Catholic, Family
- 45% freelance
- 5% new writers
- Weekly
- Circ: 30,000
- Receives dozens of queries and mss each month.
- Pays: At least $.10 per word on publication.

From the Editor:
"Good writing with solid sources is essential. First person is fine, but there should be a strong point underlying it. Strong analysis is a plus."

Avoid: Fiction. Syrupy writing. Speaking down to the readers.

Sample copy: $2. Send #10 SASE for guidelines.

Profile

A national weekly Catholic newspaper that focuses on family and social issues. Tabloid-size; newsprints; 20 pages.

Focus and Audience

Publishes articles on any topic from an orthodox Catholic perspective. Geared toward adult readers who want news of the Church and the world presented in a lively style.

Interests and Word Lengths

- *Nonfiction:* Factual, inspirational, and informational articles. Open to any topic that relates in some way to family or religion, Catholic or others. Accepts seasonal material. 750–2,200 words. Prefers 1,200–2,000 words.
- *Departments:* Opinion/Editorial on any topic of interest to Catholics or Catholic families. 600–800 words.
- *Artwork:* Color slides, B/W photos, and cartoons.

How to Submit

Send complete ms with cover letter. Include SASE. Accepts photocopies, computer printouts, IBM-compatible disks, faxes, and submissions via modem. No simultaneous submissions. Reports in 2 months.

Payment and Policies

First North American serial rights. Pays on publication. Rates start at $.10 per word and vary according to author's experience. Authors receive 1 copy of the issue.

The Catholic Worker

Editor
36 East First Street
New York, NY 10003
212-777-9617

AT A GLANCE:
THE CATHOLIC WORKER

- Catholic, Social Justice
- 25% new writers
- 8 issues a year
- Circ: 89,000
- Receives 6–12 queries, 6–12 mss each month.
- No payment. Offers 1 contributor's copy.

From the Editor:
"We espouse St. Thomas Aquinas' doctrine of the Common Good, a vision of a society where the good of each member is bound to the good of the whole in the service of God."

Best Bet: Articles that speak out against poverty and war.

Sample copy: Free. No guidelines.

Profile
The official organ of The Catholic Worker Movement, founded in 1933 by Dorothy Day and Peter Maurin. Tabloid-size; newsprint; 8 pages.

Focus and Audience
Reflects the aims of the Catholic Worker Movement: to live in accordance with the justice and charity of Jesus Christ. To this end, it advocates personalism, a decentralized society, a green revolution, nonviolence, works of mercy, manual labor, and voluntary poverty. Uses as sources the Hebrew and Greek Scriptures as handed down in the teachings of the Roman Catholic Church, and as inspiration, the lives of the saints.

Interests and Word Lengths
- *Nonfiction:* Features, interviews, essays, and personal experiences that explore issues of justice and peace in politics, economics, labor, morals, and the arms race. Up to 7 typed, double-spaced pages.
- *Illustrations:* B/W line drawings.

How to Submit
Query with outline, or send complete ms with cover letter. Include SASE. Accepts photocopies and computer printouts. No simultaneous submissions. Reports in 2 months.

Payment and Policies
Authors retain rights. No payment. Authors receive 1 copy of the issue; more upon request.

Celebration

Bill Freburger, Editor
207 Hillsboro
Silver Spring, MD 20902
301-681-4927

AT A GLANCE:
CELEBRATION

- Christian, Clergy
- Some freelance
- 15% new writers
- Monthly
- Circ: 9,000
- Receives few queries and mss each month.
- Pays: $.10 per word on acceptance.

Best Bet: Articles that assist Christian clergy—Catholic, Episcopalian, Lutheran, Presbyterian, etc.—in putting together Sunday celebrations.

Avoid: Devotionals; pious pieces; and pieces that focus only on faith in times of crisis.

Sample copy: Free. No guidelines.

Profile

An interdenominational magazine published monthly for Christian clergy. 8.5x11; 48 pages.

Focus and Audience

Articles assist Christian clergy in preparing for Sunday celebrations. Readers are priests, ministers, and liturgy teams.

Interests and Word Lengths

- *Nonfiction:* Practical, programmatic articles that assist Christian clergy in preparing for Sunday celebrations, including, liturgy, baptism, marriage, funerals, and issues in the field of worship. No word-length restrictions.
- *Seasonal:* Material for Advent and Lenten Sunday celebrations.
- *Artwork:* Prefers B/W prints; accepts color. Line drawings and cartoons.

How to Submit

Query with outline. Include SASE. Accepts photocopies, computer printouts, and 5.25-inch computer disks from major word processing programs. No simultaneous submissions. Reports within 2 weeks.

Payment and Policies

First North American serial rights. Pays on acceptance. $.10 per word. Authors receive 3 copies of the issue.

Challenge

Jeno Smith, Editor
1548 Poplar Avenue
Memphis, TN 38128
901-272-2461

AT A GLANCE:
CHALLENGE

- Southern Baptist, Youth
- 40%–50% freelance
- 10% new writers
- Monthly
- Circ: 32,000
- Receives 40 queries, 50 mss each month.
- Pays: $.05 per word on publication.

From the Editor:
"We focus on the interests of young men while supporting a missions education program."

Best Bet: Articles and photo essays that focus on current interests of and issues affecting teenagers, especially those with a biblical emphasis.

Avoid: Fiction; preachy and dated articles.

Sample copy: Free with 9x12 SAE and $.75 postage. Send #10 SASE for guidelines.

Profile

A monthly missions magazine for Southern Baptist young men. Published by the Baptist Brotherhood Commission. 8.5x11; glossy cover; 4-color; 24 pages.

Focus and Audience

Committed to encouraging the spiritual growth, missions awareness, and missions involvement among Southern Baptist young men, ages 12–18.

Interests and Word Lengths

- *Nonfiction:* Articles on teen interests and issues such as sex, AIDS, relationships, and improving grades; profiles of professional athletes and personalities with strong Christian testimonies; how-to sports articles; self-improvement features; seasonal and holiday articles. 700–900 words.
- *Departments:* Fun and Games, games that encourage teamwork and character building. What's Your Interest?, puzzles pertaining to biblical topics, crafts, hobbies, and outdoor recreation.
- *Photos:* 5x7 or 8x10 prints. Color transparencies.

How to Submit

Query with writing samples, or send complete ms. Include SASE. Accepts photocopies and computer printouts. Simultaneous submissions okay. Reports in 1 month.

Payment and Policies

One-time rights and reprint rights. Pays on publication. $.05 per word. Authors receive 1 copy of the issue.

Challenge
Faith and Action in the Americas

c/o EPICA
1470 Irving Street NW
Washington, DC 20010
202-332-0292

AT A GLANCE:
CHALLENGE

- Ecumenical, Social Justice
- 98% freelance
- 20% new writers
- 3 issues a year
- Circ: 1,000
- Receives 1 query, 1 ms each month.
- No payment. Offers 10–20 contributor's copies.

From the Editor:
"We strive to educate and build solidarity for Central America and the Caribbean from the perspective of those living and working in these areas."

Best Bet: Reports of Central American or Caribbean popular movements and progressive churches.

Avoid: Anything not relevant to Central America and the Caribbean.

Sample copy: Free. No guidelines.

Profile

A publication of the Ecumenical Program in Central America and the Caribbean (EPICA) that centers around issues pertinent to those regions. Issues are thematic. 8.5x11; self cover; 16 pages.

Focus and Audience

Reflects on contemporary struggles of life and faith as expressed by Central American and Caribbean people. Informs and mobilizes North Americans on hemispheric issues of social justice and self-determination.

Interests and Word Lengths

- *Nonfiction:* Features, interviews, essays, and personal experiences related to the human, political, and social issues of Central America and the Caribbean. Analysis of religious/progressive faith. 800–2,000 words. Accepts filler and poetry.
- *Artwork:* Accepts photos and illustrations.

How to Submit

Query with outline, or send complete ms with cover letter. Include SASE. Accepts photocopies, computer printouts, disks, and fax submissions. Simultaneous submissions okay. Reports immediately.

Payment and Policies

All rights. No payment. Authors receive 10–20 copies of the issue upon request.

Changes

Jeffrey Laign, Managing Editor
3201 SW 15th Street
Deerfield, FL 33442
800-851-9100

AT A GLANCE: CHANGES

- Recovery, Inspirational
- 25% freelance
- 6 issues a year
- Circ: 100,000
- Receives 400 mss each month.
- Pays: $.15 per word on publication.

From the Editor:
"Read a few issues of *Changes* before submitting. We appreciate a new slant on old issues."

Best Bet: Recovery-related self-help articles, social-conscience pieces, and in-depth features.

Avoid: Personal-experience pieces; blasphemy.

Sample copy: Free. Send #10 SASE for guidelines.

Profile
A self-help recovery magazine for adults. Published by U.S. Journal, Inc. Est.: 1986. 8.5x11; 100 pages.

Focus and Audience
Established as a recovery magazine for adult children of alcoholics, the magazine has expanded to include a full spectrum of recovery issues. Readers are primarily women age 30–50.

Interests and Word Lengths
- *Fiction:* Unique short stories appropriate to the magazine's concerns. Themes include family, healing, inspiration, and women's, social, and world issues. Up to 2,000 words. Accepts poetry.
- *Nonfiction:* In-depth features, how-to and self-help pieces, and articles on contemporary issues. Interests include women in the workplace, recovery, family, healing, health, inspiration, lifestyle, philosophy, opinion, 12-step, and social and world issues. Accepts seasonal material. Up to 2,000 words.
- *Departments:* Living Better; articles on recreation, feelings, self-esteem, bodywork, spirituality. Advice; Family Secrets; Sexuality & You; News Form the Front; Reflections.
- *Photos:* B/W prints and illustrations.

How to Submit
Query with outline or send complete ms with cover letter. Include SASE. Accepts photocopies, computer printouts, 5.25-inch ASCII disks, faxes, and submissions via modem. Simultaneous submissions okay. Reports in 2–4 months.

Payment and Policies
One-time rights. Pays on publication. Features and short stories, $.15 per word. Kill fee, $15. Authors receive 2 copies of the issue.

Chastity and Holiness

Cecil Justin Lam, Editor
22006 Thorncliffe P.O.
Toronto, ON M4H 1N9
Canada
416-696-2350

AT A GLANCE:

CHASTITY AND HOLINESS

- Christian, Poetry
- 55% freelance
- 15% new writers
- Biannually
- Circ: 500
- Receives 25–50 queries, 27 mss each month.
- Little to no payment. Offers 1 contributor's copy.

From the Editor:
"Our publication is relatively revelatory and deep in scope and content."

Best Bet: Genuine witnesses and testimony. Prefers prose or poetry.

Avoid: Fiction; obscene material; racial biases; lies and slander; Satanic verse.

Sample copy: $5 with 8.5x14 SAE/IRC. Send #10 SASE/IRC for guidelines.

Profile

A small Christian paper of revelatory and devotional poetry and prose. Primary interests include poetry, evangelism, and theology. 7x8.5; self cover; photocopied; 32 pages.

Focus and Audience

Publishes writings that reveal a personal encounter and witness of God, Jesus Christ, and the Holy Spirit.

Interests and Word Lengths

- *Nonfiction:* Features, interviews, essays, personal experiences, heroic stories, witnesses, and testimony. Devotions and prayers should accompany each submission. Up to 10,000 words.
- *Poetry:* Poetry that reveals the writer's relationship with God.

How to Submit

Send complete ms with cover letter. Include SASE. U.S. authors send IRCs. Accepts photocopies, computer printouts, disks, faxes and submissions via modem. Simultaneous submissions okay. Reports in 1 month.

Payment and Policies

All rights. Little to no payment. Authors receive 1 copy of the issue.

Childlife

Senior Editor
919 West Huntington Drive
Monrovia, CA 91016
818-357-7979

AT A GLANCE:

CHILDLIFE

- Christian, Child Sponsorship
- 5% new writers
- Quarterly
- Circ: 249,114
- Receives 2 mss each month.
- No payment. Offers contributor's copies.

From the Editor:
"We do not accept freelance articles for *Childlife* magazine, but use our in-house staff."

Best Bet: Short pieces for Samaritan Sampler department.

Sample copy: Free with 9x12 SAE and $1 postage. No guidelines.

Profile

A quarterly publication of World Vision Inc., a non-profit Christian humanitarian agency. 8.5x11; glossy cover; full-color; 16 pages.

Focus and Audience

Reports on World Vision projects in the Third World and shares success stories of children and their World Vision sponsors. Virtually all material is written in-house by those who have contact with World Vision sponsored projects and children.

Interests and Word Lengths

- *Departments:* Submit to Tamera Marko, Associate Editor. Samaritan Sampler, short reports on the environment, missions opportunities, children's issues, evangelism, poverty, or spiritual issues. 50–180 words.
- *Artwork:* Query Don Aylard, Art Director before submitting art, prints, or slides. Most artwork is commissioned.

How to Submit

Query first. Include SASE. Accepts computer printouts, 3.5-inch Macintosh disks, and fax submissions. Simultaneous submissions okay. Reports in 2–6 weeks.

Payment and Policies

First North American serial rights. No payment. Authors receive copies of the issue.

Children's Ministry

Barbara Beach, Departments Editor
2890 North Monroe Avenue
Loveland, CO 80538
303-669-3836

AT A GLANCE:
CHILDREN'S MINISTRY

- Christian, Youth
  Ministry
- 90% freelance
- 40% new writers
- Bimonthly
- Circ: 36,000
- Receives 30 queries,
  30 mss each month.
- Pays: $25–$100 on
  acceptance.

From the Editor:
"We need practical articles on working with volunteers, disciplining, and connecting with children about faith, morals, money, friends, grades, and choices."

Best Bet: Articles that are practical and easy for children's workers to apply.

Avoid: Fiction, poetry, or anything preachy.

Sample copy: No information provided.

Profile

An interdenominational magazine for Christian adults who work with children from birth through the 6th grade. 8.5x11; glossy cover; full-color; 48–52 pages.

Focus and Audience

Supplies practical ideas to help adults encourage children to grow spiritually. Readers include teachers, child-care workers, and youth ministers.

Interests and Word Lengths

- *Nonfiction:* Feature articles about working with volunteers, disciplining, and communicating with children about faith, morals, money, friends, and choices. Programming articles include Sunday school programs, skits, songs, and puppet shows. 500–1,200 words.
- *Departments:* Emergency Lessons include three lessons on one topic: one for pre-kindergarten, one for grades 1–3, and one for grades 4–6. 1,200 words. Crafts, Group Games, 5-Minute Messages, Preschool Program, and Teacher Tips, 150 words. Seasonal activities, 50 words.
- *Photos:* State availability of photos with submission; model releases and identification of subjects required.

How to Submit

Query with writing samples, or send ms with cover letter. Include SASE. Accepts photocopies, computer printouts, Macintosh Microsoft Word disks, and fax submissions. Simultaneous submissions okay. Reports in 1 month.

Payment and Policies

All rights. Pays on acceptance. $25–$100 based on article length and type. Kill fee, $25. Authors receive 2 copies of the issue.

The Christian Century

James M. Wall, Editor
407 South Dearborn Street
Chicago, IL 60605
312-427-5380

AT A GLANCE:
THE CHRISTIAN CENTURY

- Protestant, Theology
- 90% freelance
- 10% new writers
- Weekly
- Circ: 35,000
- Receives 200 mss each month.
- Pays: Up to $125 on publication.

From the Editor:
"We are interested in the continuing task of appropriating and embodying Christian faith amid the cultural realities of our time."

Best Bet: Articles that explore the public meaning of Christian faith.

Sample copy: $1.75. Send #10 SASE for guidelines.

Profile
An ecumenical weekly of contemporary Christian thought that relates faith to social and political issues. 8.5x11; self cover; 2-color; 46 pages.

Focus and Audience
Examines developments in the contemporary church and probes the religious and moral issues of modern culture. Many readers are ministers or college-level teachers of religion; all are familiar with the main themes in Christian history and theology.

Interests and Word Lengths
- *Nonfiction:* Articles on the public meaning of faith that brings the resources of religious tradition to bear on such topics as poverty, human rights, economic justice, international relations, national priorities, and popular culture. Articles that examine or critique the theology and ethos of individual religious communities. Articles that find fresh meaning in old traditions and that adapt or apply religious traditions to new circumstances. 3,000 words. Editorials, reports, and personal reflections. Up to 1,500 words.

How to Submit
Send complete ms with cover letter. Include SASE. Accepts photocopies and computer printouts. No simultaneous submissions or reprints. Reports in 1 month.

Payment and Policies
All rights. Pays on publication. Feature articles, up to $125. Authors receive 1 copy of the issue and additional copies at reduced rates.

The Christian Chronicle

Glover Shipp, Managing Editor
P.O. Box 11000
Oklahoma City, OK 73136
405-425-5070

AT A GLANCE:

THE CHRISTIAN CHRONICLE

- Church of Christ, Evangelical
- 5% freelance
- 3–5% new writers
- 10 times a year
- Circ:112,000
- Receives varied number of queries, 15–20 mss each month.
- Pays on acceptance. Rates vary.

From the Editor:
"We accept few items from non-members of the Church of Christ. Keep it short."

Best Bet: Short, timely news items, editorial, and inspirational pieces.

Avoid: Political issues.

Sample copy: Free. No guidelines.

Profile

An international newspaper for members of the Churches of Christ. Published monthly by Oklahoma Christian University of Science and Arts. Est.: 1943; tabloid-size; newsprint; 32 pages.

Focus and Audience

Purpose is to tell good news of the Churches of Christ, to support the evangelization of the world, and, when necessary, to present bad news in a constructive manner. Readers are members of Churches of Christ in 100 countries.

Interests and Word Lengths

- *Nonfiction:* Articles on matters of moral and spiritual character; religious values; and human interest. All must pertain to Churches of Christ and members. Up to 1,000 words.
- *Departments:* Opinion.
- *Photos:* B/W action or human interest prints of exciting people and places.

How to Submit

Send complete ms with cover letter. Include SASE. Accepts computer printouts, Macintosh disks, and fax submissions. No simultaneous submissions. Reports in 2–3 weeks.

Payment and Policies

One-time rights. Pays on acceptance. Rates vary. Authors receive up to 10 copies of the issue.

Christian Courier

Bert Witvoet, Editor
4-261 Martindale Road
St. Catharines, ON L2W 1A1
Canada
416-682-8311

AT A GLANCE:
CHRISTIAN COURIER

- Christian, Opinion
- 15% freelance
- 5% new writers
- Weekly
- Circ: 6,000
- Receives 5 queries, 15 mss each month.
- Pays: $.05–$.10 per word on publication.

From the Editor:
"We are willing to make an effort to help nurture beginning writers, but only when we have time."

Avoid: Sentimental stories, stories that spiritualize problems, fundamentalist and liberal interpretation of Scripture.

Sample copy: Free with 8.5x11 SASE/IRC. Send #10 SAE/IRC for guidelines.

Profile
An independent weekly newspaper that seeks the truth, care, and rule of Jesus Christ as it reports on news in the Christian community and the world. Provides opportunities for contact and discussion for the Christian community. Est: 1945. Tabloid-size; newsprint; 20 pages.

Focus and Audience
Seeks material that shows how faith is relevant to all areas of life and tackles important issues and current events. Opinions are based on Scripture and Spirit and rooted in a Reformed perspective.

Interests and Word Lengths
- *Fiction:* Short stories. Occasionally accepts serial fiction. Up to 2,000 words. Accepts poetry.
- *Nonfiction:* Features, essays, personal experiences, and occasional interviews. Up to 1,000 words.
- *Departments:* Submit to Bob Vander Vennen, Book Review Editor. Book Reviews, reviews fiction, children's literature, poetry, and books on education, theology, and society. 100–500 words.
- *Seasonal:* Interests include Christmas, Easter, Mother's Day, Ascension Day, Pentecost, Father's Day, Canada Day, Back-to-School, Labour, Thanksgiving, Reformation Day, Remembrance Day. Up to 1,000 words.
- *Artwork:* B/W or color photos. Line drawings and illustrations.

How to Submit
Send complete ms with cover letter. Include SASE. U.S. authors send IRCs. Accepts photocopies, computer printouts, and IBM-compatible WordPerfect disks. Simultaneous submissions okay. Reports in 1 month.

Payment and Policies
One-time rights. Pays on publication. $.05–$.10 per word. Authors receive 1 copy of the issue upon request.

Christian Crusade Newspaper

Billy James Hargis, Publisher
P.O. Box 279
Neosho, MO 64850
918-438-4234

AT A GLANCE:
CHRISTIAN CRUSADE NEWSPAPER

- Christian, Politics
- 50% freelance
- Few new writers
- Monthly
- Circ: 25,000
- Receives few queries and mss each month.
- Pays on publication. Rates vary.

From the Editor:
"Articles must be accurate beyond litigation, pro-Christian, and pro-American."

Best Bet: Religious and political articles.

Sample copy: Free. No guidelines.

Profile

A monthly Christian and pro-American newspaper. Tabloid-size; 24 pages.

Focus and Audience

Offers a pro-Christian, pro-American perspective on current political and social affairs. Most material is staff-written.

Interests and Word Lengths

- *Nonfiction:* Religious and political commentary and opinion on social and world issues.
- *Photos:* 8x10 B/W glossy prints.

How to Submit

Query with outline. Include SASE. Accepts computer printouts and fax submissions (417-451-4319). No simultaneous submissions. Reports in 2 months.

Payment and Policies

All rights. Pays on publication. Rates are negotiable. Authors receive copies of the issue upon request.

Christian Drama Magazine

Judy Tash, Editor
1824 Celestia Drive
Walla Walla, WA 99362-3612
509-529-0089

AT A GLANCE:

CHRISTIAN DRAMA MAGAZINE

- Christian, Drama
- 75–90% freelance
- 25% new writers
- Quarterly
- Circ: 300
- Receives 2 queries, 10 mss each month.
- Pays: $25 per piece on publication.

From the Editor:
"In plays, close attention is paid to the amount of conflict, the quality of dialog, the completeness of development, and the message."

Avoid: Anything patently not Christian.

Sample copy: Free with 9x12 SAE and $.75 postage. Send #10 SASE for guidelines.

Profile

A quarterly publication that promotes the use of Christian drama in worship and spreads the Gospel of Jesus Christ. 7x8.5; self cover; stapled; 28 pages.

Focus and Audience

Open to a variety of styles and accepts a wide range of Christian thought, but rejects material that is patently not Christian. Readers are creative people, primarily in churches, who are looking for help in finding and producing sketches and plays.

Interests and Word Lengths

- *Drama:* Plays and dramatic readings on any subject within the scope of Christianity. No word-length restrictions.
- *Nonfiction:* How-to, inspirational, and personal-experience articles on any subject within the scope of Christianity. How-to articles should be concise and have diagrams and pictures. 500–1,000 words.
- *Departments:* Letters to the Editor; Questions & Answers; Network. Drama-related material. Up to 400 words.
- *Artwork:* Prefers 5x7 B/W photos, but accepts wallet-size to 8x10. Accepts line drawings and color prints. No slides.

How to Submit

Send complete ms with cover letter and an author photo. Include SASE. Accepts photocopies, computer printouts, and 5.25-inch double-sided, double-density disks in Wordstar 5 or ASCII. Simultaneous submissions okay. Reports in 3 months or longer.

Payment and Policies

One-time rights. Pays on publication. Articles and drama, $25 per piece. Photos and drawings, $10. Authors receive 3 copies of the issue upon request.

Christian Education Journal

Ronald R. Ramsey, Executive Editor
P.O. Box 650
Glen Ellyn, IL 60138
708-260-6440

AT A GLANCE: CHRISTIAN EDUCATION JOURNAL

- Christian, Education
- 3 issues a year
- Circ: 2,500
- Receives 4 queries, 8 mss each month.
- Pays: $100 honorarium on publication.

From the Editor:
"We provide a forum for the expression of facts, ideas, and opinions on Christian education."

Best Bet: Christian education and related topics.

Sample copy: Free. Send #10 SASE for guidelines.

Profile

A tri-annual peer-reviewed journal promoting Christian education and Bible scholarship. Published by Scripture Press Ministries. 6.5x10; glossy cover; 130 pages.

Focus and Audience

Designed to promote growth and advancement in the field of Christian education by stimulating scholarly study of the Bible and related fields. Aimed at Christian education professionals, teachers, students, and lay people.

Interests and Word Lengths

- *Nonfiction:* Articles on topics directly related to Christian education, including church ministry and church leadership as well as commentary on current or past *Journal* articles. 5–15 typed, double-spaced pages.
- *Book Reviews:* Submit to Book Review Editor, One Pennsylvania Avenue, Glen Ellyn, IL 60137. Considers reviews on publications in the categories of Christian education, church ministry, leadership development, and related Christian education topics.

How to Submit

Send complete ms with a 50-word summary. Include SASE. Accepts photocopies, computer printouts, disks, and fax submissions. Simultaneous submissions okay. Reports in 2 months.

Payment and Policies

All rights. Pays on publication. $100 honorarium per article. Authors receive 1 copy of the issue.

Christian Educators Journal

Lorna Van Gilst, Managing Editor
Dordt College English Department
Sioux Center, IA 51250-1697
712-722-6252

AT A GLANCE:
CHRISTIAN EDUCATORS JOURNAL

- Christian, Education
- 50% freelance
- 15% new writers
- Quarterly
- Circ: 4,200
- Receives 5–10 queries, 5–10 mss each month.
- Pays: $30 per piece on publication.

From the Editor:
"Our objectives and principles are consistently biblical, integrating Christian theory and practice."

Avoid: Sunday school articles; quoting Scripture out of context to prove a point; and exclusive language.

Sample copy: $1 or SAE with $.98 postage. Send #10 SASE for guidelines.

Profile
A quarterly journal that serves as a channel of communication for educators committed to evangelical Christian day schools. 8.5x11; glossy cover; 36 pages.

Focus and Audience
Sole concern is evangelical Christian day education. Readers are elementary, secondary, and college-level educators.

Interests and Word Lengths
- *Fiction:* Short stories and drama about Christian school classrooms, faculty rooms, and student concerns and dilemmas. 600–1,200 words.
- *Nonfiction:* Articles, interviews, features, essays, or personal experiences on any topic related to Christian day school students, teachers, or administrators. 600–1,200 words.
- *Departments:* Christian School News, Profile, Media Eye, Thinking Thirteen, Idea Bank, Query, and Book Reviews. Most are staff-written.
- *Photos:* B/W prints accompanying articles.

How to Submit
Send complete ms with cover letter. Include author biography and SASE. No footnoting; use internal documentation or list references. Accepts computer printouts, and faxes. Simultaneous submissions okay. Reports in 1 month.

Payment and Policies
One-time rights. Pays on publication. $30 per article. Authors receive 1–2 copies of the issue.

Christian History

Kevin A. Miller, Editor
465 Gundersen Drive
Carol Stream, IL 60188
708-260-6200

AT A GLANCE:
CHRISTIAN HISTORY

- Christian, History
- 75% freelance
- Quarterly
- Circ: 60,000
- Receives 5 queries, 1 ms each month.
- Pays $.10 per word on publication.

From the Editor:
"Use anecdotes and quotations to enliven your historical research."

Best Bet: The history of Christianity.

Sample copy: $4.40. Send #10 SASE for guidelines.

Profile

A quarterly magazine that focuses on the history of the Christian church. Published by Christianity Today, Inc. 8x10.5; glossy cover; full-color; 50 pages.

Focus and Audience

Attempts to present the history of the Christian church in an engaging and accurate way to a lay audience of history buffs.

Interests and Word Lengths

- *Nonfiction:* Articles that explore the history and personalities of Christianity throughout the centuries. 1,000–2,500 words.
- *Photos:* Historical photos relating to articles.

How to Submit

Query with outline. Include SASE. Accepts photocopies, computer printouts, and disk submissions. No simultaneous submissions. Reports in 1 month.

Payment and Policies

First North American serial rights. Pays on publication. $.10 per word. Authors receive 1 copy of the issue.

Christian Home & School

Gordon Bordewyk, Executive Editor
3350 East Paris Avenue SE
Grand Rapids, MI 49508
616-957-1070

AT A GLANCE:
CHRISTIAN HOME & SCHOOL

- Christian, Education
- 50% freelance
- 15% new writers
- 6 issues a year
- Circ: 51,000
- Receives 8 queries, 40 mss each month.
- Pays: $75–$150 on publication.

From the Editor:
"Present ideas from a Christian viewpoint; don't simply tack on a Bible verse. Use an informal, easy-to-read style."

Best Bet: Practical, concrete articles about 12- to 17-year-old children.

Avoid: A preachy writing style.

Sample copy: Free with 9x12 SAE and 4 first-class stamps. Send #10 SASE for guidelines.

Profile

A Christian Schools International publication that promotes and explains the concept of Christian education. 8.5x11; glossy cover; 2-color; 32 pages.

Focus and Audience

Aims to promote Christian education while encouraging parents in their walk with Christ and helping in their parenting skills. Articles should be written from a Christian viewpoint. Readers are parents who support Christian day schools.

Interests and Word Lengths

- *Fiction:* Short-short stories about school experiences, family, and parenting situations. 1,200–2,000 words.
- *Nonfiction:* First-person accounts of and practical features about school experiences, family issues, and parenting skills. Of current interest are articles about 12- to 17-year-old children. 1,200–2,000 words.
- *Seasonal:* Interests include back-to-school, Christmas, Easter, end of school year, graduation, summer activities, and vacations. 1,200–2,000 words.
- *Artwork:* Submit to Roger Schmurr. Full bleed, vertical color transparencies or slides. 8x10 B/W prints.

How to Submit

Send complete ms with cover letter. Include SASE. Accepts photocopies, computer printouts, and Macintosh or DOS 3.5-inch disks. Simultaneous submissions okay. Reports in 1 month.

Payment and Policies

First North American serial rights. Pays on publication. 1–25 column inches, $75. 26–42 column inches, $100. 43–55 column inches, $125. 56–up column inches, $150. Authors receive 5 copies of the issue.

Christian Info News

Alan Stanchi, Publisher
19414 96th Avenue, #4
Surrey, BC V4N 4C2
Canada
604-888-4447

Profile

An interdenominational Christian newspaper for the Greater Vancouver area. Tabloid-size; 24 pages.

Focus and Audience

Evangelical in nature, it provides inspirational reading to a multi-denominational audience of all ages. Distributed in 650 churches in the Greater Vancouver area as well as drop-in centers, municipal libraries, and Christian bookstores.

Interests and Word Lengths

- *Nonfiction:* Interviews, essays, and personal-experience pieces that are inspirational in nature. Open to all topics with Christian relevance. No word-length restrictions. Considers longer pieces for serialization.
- *Departments:* Book and music reviews.
- *Poetry:* Inspirational poems.
- *Seasonal:* Christmas and Easter material.
- *Photos:* 5x7 B/W and color prints.

How to Submit

Query with resume, writing samples, and clips. Include SASE. U.S. authors include IRCs. Accepts photocopies, computer printouts, disks, and fax submissions. Simultaneous submissions okay. Reports in 2 months.

Payment and Policies

One-time rights. Pays 1 month after publication. $25–$50 per piece. Provides byline. Kill fee, $25. Authors receive 25 copies of the issue.

Christian Leader

Don Ratzlaffe, Editor
P.O. Box L
Hillsboro, KS 67063
316-947-5543

Profile
A denominational magazine published monthly by the U.S. Conference of Mennonite Brethren. 8.5x11; 36 pages.

Focus and Audience
Provides issue-oriented, anecdotal articles for Mennonite Brethren in the U.S. Adheres to traditional Anabaptist theology. Preference given to Mennonite writers.

Interests and Word Lengths
• *Nonfiction:* Features and personal-experience pieces that integrate faith in everyday life. Interests include family, politics, and social and world issues. 1,200–1,500 words.
• *Seasonal:* Christmas and Easter material.
• *Photos:* B/W prints.

How to Submit
Query with outline. Include SASE. Accepts reprints. Accepts photocopies and computer printouts. Simultaneous submissions okay. Reports in 1 month.

Payment and Policies
First North American serial rights. Pays on publication. First rights, $.06 per word. Second rights, $.03 per word. Authors receive 2 copies of the issue.

The Christian Librarian

Ron Jordahl, Editor
Prairie Bible College, Box 4020
Three Hills, AB T0M 2A0
Canada
403-443-5511

AT A GLANCE:
THE CHRISTIAN LIBRARIAN

- Christian, Librarians
- 25% freelance
- 10% new writers
- Quarterly
- Circ: 450
- No payment. Offers 2 contibutor's copies.

From the Editor:
"*The Christian Librarian* is directed primarily to Christian librarians in institutions of higher learning."

Best Bet: Scholarly articles geared toward Christian librarians.

Sample copy: $5. Send #10 SASE/IRC for guidelines.

Profile
The quarterly journal of the Association of Christian Librarians. 8.5x11; heavy bond cover; 32 pages.

Focus and Audience
A practical, scholarly journal directed primarily to Christian librarians in institutions of higher learning.

Interests and Word Lengths
- *Nonfiction:* Articles on Christian interpretation of librarianship, and the theory and practice of library science; bibliographic essays; interviews; reviews; and human interest articles relating to books in libraries. Subjects include information technology, censorship, and intellectual freedom. 1,000–5,000 words.
- *Reviews:* Review copies may be obtained from the Review Editor. Book reviews should include the subject and scope of the author's thesis. Reveal the nature of treatment—reference, scholarly, textbook— with synopsis of contents. General reviews, 150–300 words. Critical reviews, 500 words or more.

How to Submit
Articles, query with outline, or send complete ms with cover letter. Reviews, request assignment from Review Editor. Include SASE. U.S. authors include IRCs. Accepts photocopies, computer printouts, disks, and fax submissions. Identify simultaneous submissions. Reports in 1 month.

Payment and Policies
One-time rights. No payment. Authors receive 2 copies of the issue.

Christian Living

David Graybill, Editor
616 Walnut Avenue
Scottdale, PA 15683
412-887-8500

AT A GLANCE:

CHRISTIAN LIVING

- Mennonite, Lifestyle
- 60% freelance
- 15% new writers
- 10 issues a year
- Circ: 6,300
- Receives 4–5 queries, 50 mss each month.
- Pays: Up to $.05 per word on acceptance.

From the Editor:
"We believe in the power of stories and the importance of expressing faith in ethical living. Write clearly and concisely and use lots of anecdotes and examples."

Best Bet: Pieces with a cross-cultural dimension or that connect the arts to community, family, or spiritual growth.

Avoid: Religious jargon; material that identifies God closely with the U.S. or a specific political agenda.

Sample copy: Free with 9x12 SAE and $.75 postage. Send #10 SASE for guidelines.

Profile

A magazine about people and faith today. Published by Mennonite Publishing House. 8x10; glossy cover; spot color; 28 pages.

Focus and Audience

Contents stress the spiritual growth of individuals, families, and communities. Seeks to help readers learn about people from different cultures and put their faith into practice in everyday life. Audience includes Mennonites and others who identify with Anabaptist beliefs about community, peacemaking, and service.

Interests and Word Lengths

- *Fiction:* Short stories about spirituality, community, family, the arts, and cross-cultural issues. 700–1,200.
- *Nonfiction:* Personal experiences, features, and essays on spirituality, community, family, the arts, and cross-cultural issues. Illustrate articles with anecdotes and examples. 700–1,200 words.
- *Photos:* Prefers B/W prints but accepts color prints with good contrast.

How to Submit

Send complete ms with cover letter. Include SASE. Accepts computer printouts and 3.5- or 5.25-inch disk files in a major word processing format such as WordPerfect. Reports within 1–2 months.

Payment and Policies

One-time rights. Pays on acceptance. Up to $.05 per word. Authors receive 2 copies of issue.

The Christian Ministry

James M. Wall, Editor
407 South Dearborn Street
Chicago, IL 60605
312-427-5380

AT A GLANCE:
THE CHRISTIAN
MINISTRY

- Protestant, Ministers
- 90% freelance
- 10% new writers
- Bimonthly
- Circ: 12,000
- Receives 30 mss each month.
- Pays: $10–$75 on publication.

From the Editor:
"We seek to be inclusive or non-sexist in language and presentation. Therefore, use inclusive language when referring to people, including clergy. We respect an author's view in references to God."

Best Bet: Practical articles for Protestant ministers.

Sample copy: $2.25. Send #10 SASE for guidelines.

Profile

A bimonthly magazine aimed at mainline Protestant ministers. Published by the Christian Century Foundation. Member of the Associated Church Press. Est.: 1929. 8.5x11; self cover; 2-color; 40–50 pages.

Focus and Audience

Addresses the issues confronting local parish ministers in their day-to-day work. Most readers are ministers in mainline Protestant denominations and include chaplains, denominational workers, and church counselors.

Interests and Word Lengths

- *Nonfiction:* Essays and practical articles on all aspects of ministry, from theological treatments of a particular issue to how to put together a church budget. Areas include: Ministry Focus, articles focused around one theme; Ministers' Workshop, useful and provocative articles about issues related to parish ministry; and From the Pulpit, sermons—2 or 3 published in each issue. Up to 2,500 words.
- *Departments:* Brief Encounters, short, often amusing items about events and happenings related to religion and the parish.

How to Submit

Send complete ms with cover letter. Include SASE. Accepts photocopies and computer printouts. No simultaneous submissions or reprints. Reports in 1 month.

Payment and Policies

First North American serial or all rights. Pays on publication. Ministry Focus, $75. Ministers' Workshop, $60. From the Pulpit, $50. Brief Encounters, $10. Authors receive 1 copy of the issue and additional copies at reduced rates.

Christian*New Age Quarterly

Catherine Groves, Editor
P.O. Box 276
Clifton, NJ 07011-0276

AT A GLANCE:
CHRISTIAN•NEW AGE QUARTERLY

- Christian, New Age
- 80% freelance
- 20% new writers
- Quarterly
- No payment. Offers free subscpription or contributor's copy.

From the Editor:
"Avoid confusing subjective beliefs with objective reality. Use 'I believe,' not 'truth is.' Be mindful that both Christians and New Agers are valuable contributors to our forum."

Avoid: Condescending or deprecating tones.

Sample copy: $3.50. Send #10 SASE for guidelines.

Profile
A forum for dialog between Christians and New Agers. Espouses no specific philosophy, but respects the diversity of beliefs. 7x8.5; self cover; stapled; 20 pages.

Focus and Audience
Publishes articles and contemplative essays that seek to clarify the differences, while improving communication between Christianity and the New Age movement.

Interests and Word Lengths
- *Nonfiction:* Scholarly or contemplative essays and personal pieces on topics relevant to the relationship of Christianity and the New Age movement. Also accepts purely Christian or New Age pieces, but they must hold general interest. Topical articles, 400–1,500 words. Contemplative essays, 600 words.
- *Departments:* A Pensive Pause, contemplative, personal essays, 600 words. The Letters Library, reader responses.
- *Artwork:* Small B/W line drawings and cartoons.

How to Submit
Prefers complete ms with cover letter. Accepts queries with outline. Include SASE. In cover letter, state whether you are open to revision and/or editing. Accepts photocopies and computer printouts. Reports in 1–2 months.

Payment and Policies
One-time rights. No payment. Offers a free, 1-year subscription for essays. Authors receive 1 copy of the issue.

Christian Parenting Today

Brad Lewis, Managing Editor
P.O. Box 850
Sisters, OR 97759
503-549-8261

AT A GLANCE:

CHRISTIAN PARENTING TODAY

- Christian, Parenting
- 50% freelance
- 5% new writers
- Bimonthly
- Circ: 250,000
- Receives 50 queries, 30 mss each month
- Pays: $.15–$.25 on publication.

From the Editor:
"Voice and tone are extremely important! Write as if you are visiting with your neighbor about her kids—not talking to a congregation or a seminar."

Best Bet: Articles with a biblical perspective that take a positive, practical, problem-solving approach.

Avoid: Verbiage that might offend or distance any part of the Christian community.

Sample copy: $2.95 with 9x12 SAE and 5 oz. postage. Send #10 SASE for guidelines.

Profile

A practical parenting magazine for Christians. Published by Good Family Magazines. 8.5x11; glossy cover; full-color; 80 pages.

Focus and Audience

Offers positive, practical, problem-solving advice and authoritative guidance on raising successful families. Readers represent a broad spectrum of Christians—parents in traditional family units, single parents, and parents in blended families.

Interests and Word Lengths

- *Nonfiction:* Articles targeting the real needs of today's parents: social issues, education, values and morals, practical parenting, discipline, spiritual development, nutritional health, extended family, fathering, marriage and love, money management, children with disabilities, and grandparents. Also accepts profiles of families in action, humor, reflections, heartwarming, inspirational stories, and page-turners. 850–2,000 words.
- *Departments:* Parent Exchange, problem-solving ideas from other parents, 25–100 words. My Story, first-person human-interest story of how a family or parent overcame a parenting challenge, 800–1,500 words. Life in Our House, humorous, insightful anecdotes, 25–100 words. Address Parent Exchange and Life in Our House to that particular department editor.

How to Submit

Query with outline and writing samples. Include SASE. Accepts photocopies, computer printouts, and faxes. No simultaneous submissions. Reports in 2–3 months.

Payment and Policies

First North American serial rights. Pays on publication. $.15–$.25 per word. Authors receive 2 copies of the issue.

The Christian Reader

Bonnie Steffen, Editor
465 Gundersen Drive
Carol Stream, IL 60188
708-260-6200

AT A GLANCE:
THE CHRISTIAN READER

- Christian, Inspirational
- 90% freelance
- Bimonthly
- Circ: 220,000
- Receives 10 queries, 100 mss each month.
- Pays: $.10 per word on acceptance.

From the Editor:
"Start with a compelling story and tell it clearly."

Best Bet: Encouraging Christian writing.

Avoid: Confrontational styles; heavily opinionated pieces.

Sample copy: Free with 5x8 SAE and $.50 postage. Send #10 SASE for guidelines.

Profile

A bimonthly digest of quality Christian reading. Published by Christianity Today, Inc. 5x8; glossy cover; full-color; 110 pages.

Focus and Audience

Aims to inspire and encourage Christians. Reaches a church audience, primarily women over 35.

Interests and Word Lengths

- *Nonfiction:* Personal-experience, devotional, and humorous articles on church life, family, social concerns, evangelism, missions, prayer, and conversion. 250–1,500 words.
- *Departments:* Ordinary Heroes; Kids of the Kingdom, child humor; Lite Fare, adult church humor; Rolling Down the Aisle, wedding humor. Up to 250 words.

How to Submit

Send complete ms with cover letter. Include SASE. Accepts photocopies and computer printouts. No simultaneous submissions. Reports in 1 month.

Payment and Policies

First North American serial rights. Pays on acceptance. Up to $.10 per word; $25 per piece minimum. Authors receive 1 copy of the issue.

Christian Research Journal

Elliot Miller, Editor
P.O. Box 500
San Juan Capistrano, CA 92693-0500
714-55-4428

AT A GLANCE:
CHRISTIAN RESEARCH JOURNAL

- Christian, Apologetics
- 80% freelance
- Few new writers
- Quarterly
- Circ: 28,000
- Pays on publication. Rates vary.

From the Editor:
"Western culture is deeply embroiled in a spiritual crisis. In the face of many conflicting, confusing claims to human allegiance, may believers be prepared to give logically and historically sound reasons for faith in Jesus Christ."

Best Bet: In-depth articles on religious movements and trends in the context of traditional Christianity.

Avoid: Fiction; poetry; conspiracy theories; personal testimonies; interviews; features.

Sample copy: $4. Send #10 SASE for guidelines.

Profile

A quarterly publication of education, evangelism, and theological apologetics. Published by the Christian Research Institute. 8.5x11; glossy cover; full-color; 48 pages.

Focus and Audience

Dedicated to furthering the proclamation and defense of the historic gospel of Jesus Christ, and to facilitating people's growth in sound doctrine and spiritual discernment. Serves both evangelical and educational purposes.

Interests and Word Lengths

- *Nonfiction:* Analysis of religious movements and trends in the context of traditional Christianity. Themes include non-Christian sects and cults; occult practices, phenomena, and movements; issues of contemporary theological and apologetic concern (e.g., aberrant Christian teachings and practices, philosophical and historical speculations that challenge biblical reliability, and sensational conspiracy theories). Articles should be scholarly, yet popular and readable, offering rational and biblical analysis. 5,000 words.
- *Departments:* Book Reviews; Witnessing Tips; News Watch.
- *Photos:* Prefers color prints and illustrations; accepts B/W prints.

How to Submit

Query with outline. Include SASE. Accepts photocopies, computer printouts, and fax submissions (714-855-4428). Simultaneous submissions okay. Report time varies.

Payment and Policies

First and reprint rights. Pays on publication. Rates vary. Authors receive 2 copies of the issue.

Christian Retailing

Brian Peterson, Editor
600 Rinehart Road
Lake Mary, FL 32746
407-333-0600

AT A GLANCE:
CHRISTIAN RETAILING

- Christian, Business
- 60% freelance
- 60% new writers
- 18 issues a year
- Circ: 10,000
- Receives 50 queries each month.
- Pays: $.10–$.20 per word on publication.

From the Editor:
"Be familiar with Christian retailing."

Best Bet: Articles related to setting up and running a Christian business.

Avoid: Anything non-trade.

Sample copy: $3. Send #10 SASE for guidelines.

Profile

A trade magazine for Christian retailers. Published by Strang Communications Company. 11.5x14.5; glossy cover; full-color; 72 pages.

Focus and Audience

All editorial relates to establishing and operating a successful Christian business. Distributed free to bookstores, readers include the owners, managers, and staff of both Christian and general bookstores.

Interests and Word Lengths

- *Nonfiction:* Reports on bookstore operations that detail unique methods of merchandising, advertising, display. Include photos of store interior and exterior. 1,500–2,000 words. Personality profiles of bookstore managers, authors, musicians, publishers, etc. Lengths vary. Informative, inspirational how-to articles of managerial expertise, marketing techniques, and successful financial programs used in store operation. 500–1,500 words. Personal motivation anecdotes based on actual store personnel management. 500–1,500 words. Success stories about bookstores with unusual ministries, effective distribution, or unusual growth. 1,000–2,000 words.
- *Photos:* B/W photos of store interior and exterior to accompany Bookstore Reports. Welcomes B/W photos with all articles.

How to Submit

Query with outline. No unsolicited mss. Include SASE. Accepts photocopies, computer printouts, and disk submissions. No simultaneous submissions. Reports in 6 weeks.

Payment and Policies

Rights negotiable; all rights preferred. Pays on publication. $.10–$.20 per word. Authors receive 1 copy of the issue.

The Christian Science Journal

William Moody, Editor
One Norway Street
Boston, MA 02115
617-450-2051

AT A GLANCE:
THE CHRISTIAN
SCIENCE JOURNAL

- Christian Science,
  Inspirational
- Monthly
- Circ: not available

From the Editor:
"Experience in writing,
though desirable, is not
essential. Love for God
and man, a spiritual
discernment of the
challenges of these
times, and a demon-
strated understanding
of Christian Science are
even more important.
Spiritual insights gained
through healing mark
the very presence of
Christ and are the real
substance of Christian
Science Literature."

Best Bet: Christian Science articles with a
strong healing content.

Avoid: Generalizations;
unkind statements
about other religions.

Sample copy: $3.50.
Send #10 SASE for
guidelines.

Profile
The official organ of The First Church of Christ, Scientist, in Boston. Contributors are students of Christian Science or Church members. Est.: 1883. 8.5x11; glossy cover; 4-color; 82 pages.

Focus and Audience
Offers an ongoing record of Christian healing since 1883, church news, and a directory of churches and practitioners. Readers are members of the Christian Science Church.

Interests and Word Lengths
- *Nonfiction:* Articles that focus on a specific metaphysical point. Themes include healing, error, prayer, spirituality, and truth. Healing testimonies must meet requirements outlined in guidelines. All should have a strong healing content and a Christian Science perspective.
- *Poetry:* Accepted on the basis of healing content and distinctness and clarity of the Christian Science message.

How to Submit
Query with outline. Include SASE. Accepts photocopies, computer printouts, and disk submissions. No simultaneous submissions. Acknowledges upon receipt.

Payment and Policies
Rights and payment information unavailable. Offers contributor's copies.

The Christian Science Sentinel

William Moody, Editor
One Norway Street
Boston, MA 02115
617-450-2051

AT A GLANCE:
THE CHRISTIAN SCIENCE SENTINEL

- Christian Science, Inspirational
- Weekly
- Circ: not available

From the Editor:
"Experience in writing, though desirable, is not essential. Love for God and man, a spiritual discernment of the challenges of these times, and a demonstrated understanding of Christian Science are even more important. Spiritual insights gained through healing mark the very presence of Christ and are the real substance of Christian Science Literature."

Best Bet: Christian Science articles with a strong healing content.

Avoid: Generalizations; unkind statements about other religions.

Sample copy: $3.50. Send #10 SASE for guidelines.

Profile
A weekly inspirational magazine for Christian Scientists. Contributors are students of Christian Science or Church members. Est.: 1889. 5.5x7.5; glossy cover; 4-color; 48 pages.

Focus and Audience
Offers first-hand experiences that confirm that spirituality is a powerful influence for good in any situation. Aims to awaken a solid reassurance of God's nearness. Readers are Christian Scientists and those interested in Christian Science.

Interests and Word Lengths
- *Nonfiction:* Articles on Christian Science healing and practice and Bible study; first-person experiences of healing; articles for children.
- *Poetry:* Accepted on the basis of healing content and distinctness and clarity of the Christian Science message.

How to Submit
Query with outline. Include SASE. Accepts photocopies, computer printouts, and disk submissions. No simultaneous submissions. Acknowledgment upon receipt.

Payment and Policies
Rights and payment information not available. Offers contributor's copies.

Christian Single

Stephen Felts, Editor
127 Ninth Avenue North
Nashville, TN 37234
615-251-2228

AT A GLANCE:
CHRISTIAN SINGLE

- Christian, Lifestyle
- 45% freelance
- 10% new writers
- Monthly
- Circ: 70,000
- Receives 50 queries,
  100 mss each month.
- Pays on acceptance.
  Rates vary.

From the Editor:
"Deal with real-life issues. Write to evoke emotion. Be concrete, and don't be 'churchy'."

Best Bet: In-depth, well-researched, biblically based articles that will touch single Christian adults.

Avoid: Christian sub-culture language.

Sample copy: Free with 9x12 SAE and $.98 postage. Send #10 SASE for guidelines.

Profile

A non-denominational evangelical magazine for single Christian adults. Published monthly by the Sunday School Board of the Southern Baptist Convention. 8.5x11; glossy cover; 2-color; 52 pages.

Focus and Audience

Purpose is to help Christian single adults, ages 25–45, incorporate their faith into daily life and reveal to non-Christian singles the reality of a living faith.

Interests and Word Lengths

- *Fiction:* Short stories of interest to single adults. 1,200–2,000 words.
- *Nonfiction:* Features, interviews, essays, personal experiences, and how-to articles on current events, health, single parenting, and relationships. 1,200–1,800 words. Accepts seasonal material and filler.
- *Departments:* Submit to David Hargrove, Department Editor. Micro-Info, short tips or humor related to single life. Single Parenting; He Said . . . She Said; Relationship Talk; The Body Shop; Reviews and Entertainment; Q&A. Up to 500 words.

How to Submit

Query with outline. Include SASE. Accepts photocopies, computer printouts, Macintosh and IBM 3.5-inch high-density disks with hard copy, and fax submissions. No simultaneous submissions. Reports in 2 months.

Payment and Policies

First North American serial, one-time, or all rights. Pays on acceptance. Rates negotiable. Authors receive 3 copies of the issue.

Christian Social Action

Lee Ranck, Editor
100 Maryland Avenue NE
Washington, DC 20002
202-488-5621

AT A GLANCE:

CHRISTIAN SOCIAL ACTION

- United Methodist, Social Issues
- 5% freelance
- 10% new writers
- Monthly
- Circ: 3,500
- Receives 20 queries, 25 mss each month.
- Pays: $125 per piece on publication.

From the Editor:
"We emphasize knowledge of the issues and often seek issue-experts who can write rather than writers who will have to research the topic."

Best Bets: Social analysis from a Christian viewpoint.

Avoid: Shallow presentation of issues; pious pronouncements.

Sample copy: Free with 6x9 SAE and $1.25 postage. Send #10 SASE for guidelines.

Profile

A monthly journal offering a Christian view on national public policy and critical issues facing the nation. Published by the General Board of Church and Society of The United Methodist Church. 8.5x11; self cover; 48 pages.

Focus and Audience

Information and analysis of social issues from the perspective of the Christian faith and, more specifically, based on the social policy positions of the United Methodist Church.

Interests and Word Lengths

- *Nonfiction:* Articles from a Christian perspective on a wide range of social issues, e.g., drugs and alcohol, peace, criminal justice, racial strife, terrorism, abortion, human welfare, health care, and immigration. 1,800–2,000 words.
- *Photos:* 5x7 or 8x10 B/W glossy prints.

How to Submit

Query with outline. Include SASE. Accepts computer printouts, WordPerfect 5.1 disks, and fax submissions. No simultaneous submissions. Reports in 1–3 months.

Payment and Policies

All rights. Pays on publication. $125 per article. Authors receive 3 copies of the issue.

Christian Standard

Sam Stone, Editor
8121 Hamilton Avenue
Cincinnati, OH 45231
513-931-4050

AT A GLANCE:

CHRISTIAN STANDARD

- Churches of Christ, Leadership
- 60% freelance
- 10% new writers
- Weekly
- Circ: 62,000
- Receives 65 mss each month.
- Pays on publication. Rates vary.

From the Editor:
"Writers for *Christian Standard* are, for the most part, its readers. While there is no deliberate attempt to limit writership, these are the people who share our convictions."

Best Bet: Doctrinal, practical, and inspirational articles on New Testament Christianity.

Sample copy: $1. Send #10 SASE for guidelines.

Profile

A weekly journal of New Testament Christianity for Churches of Christ leaders. Published by the Standard Publishing Company. 8.5x11; self cover; 2-color; 16–24 pages.

Focus and Audience

Devoted to "the restoration of New Testament Christianity, its doctrine, its ordinances, and its fruits." Designed to develop a thoughtful, well-indoctrinated, and consecrated membership among undenominational Christian churches. Readers include preachers, educators, church leaders, and lay people.

Interests and Word Lengths

- *Nonfiction:* Essays on doctrinal, practical, and inspirational themes that profile people or congregations that have made unusual accomplishments in ordinary circumstances. Express timeless truths in new ways. Essay features, 1,000–1,600 words. Shorter essays, 400–1,000 words.
- *Departments:* News reports from churches and individuals who are committed to undenominational Christianity. Interests include church renovations, special programs, evangelistic meetings, conventions, and new churches.
- *Photos:* B/W and color prints to accompany articles.

How to Submit

Send complete ms with cover letter. Include SASE. Accepts photocopies and computer printouts. No simultaneous submissions. Reports in 2 months.

Payment and Policies

One-time rights. Pays on publication. Rates vary. Authors receive 10 copies of issue.

ChristianWeek

Harold Jantz, Editor
507-228 Notre Dame Avenue
Winnipeg, MB R3B 1N7
Canada
204-943-1147

AT A GLANCE:

CHRISTIANWEEK

- Christian, News
- 10–15% freelance
- 5% new writers
- Biweekly
- Circ: 11,000–12,000
- Receives 5 queries,
  5–10 mss each
  month.
- Pays: $20–$100 fol-
  lowing publication.

From the Editor:
"Be news oriented and
specifically Canadian.
Stories should be tight-
ly written, reflect an
understanding of
evangelical Christiani-
ty, and have a gen-
uine news hook."

Best Bet: News and
features that illuminate
Christian faith and
practice in Canada.

Avoid: Features and
articles about the U.S.

Sample copy: No information provided.

Profile

An evangelical tabloid of news and comment about
Christian faith and life in Canada. Published by the Fellowship for Print Witness. Tabloid-size; newsprint; 16–20
pages.

Focus and Audience

Aims to help readers gain a sense of important developments and issues in the life and witness of followers
of Christ in Canada. Readers are Christian leaders, students, and laity.

Interests and Word Lengths

- *Nonfiction:* Submit to Doug Koop, Managing Editor, or
  Debra Fieguth, Associate Editor. Articles and features
  on activities of the church world-wide, events about
  the faith and life of Christians in Canada, news on
  how God is at work in the world, opinion, and other
  related issues and topics. 200–800 words.
- *Departments:* Query first. 500–600 words.

How to Submit

Query with resume. Include SASE. Accepts photocopies, computer printouts, disks, and fax submissions
(204-947-5632). No simultaneous submissions. Reports in
1 month.

Payment and Policies

One-time rights. Pays following publication. $20–$100
per piece depending on quality and length. Authors receive 5 copies of the issue.

Christian Woman

Sandra Humphrey, Editor
4113 East Encinas Avenue
Higley, AZ 85236-9265
615-254-8781

AT A GLANCE:

CHRISTIAN WOMAN

- Church of Christ,
  Women
- 85% freelance
- 75% new writers
- Bimonthly
- Circ: 20,000
- Pays: $25 per piece
  on publication.

From the Editor:
"Stress the practical—
what the reader can
do differently to be a
better person after
reading your article."

Best Bet: Uplifting, encouraging articles and
stories with broad out-
reach.

Avoid: Political advocacy.

Sample copy: Free.
Send #10 SASE for
guidelines.

Profile

A women's magazine for Church of Christ members.
Published bimonthly by Gospel Advocate Company.
8.5x11; glossy cover; full-color; 64 pages.

Focus and Audience

Seeks to enhances spiritual growth and moral stability
of readers, primarily Church of Christ women, ages
35–45. Appeals to a broad category of women—single,
married, older, younger, working in or out of the home.

Interests and Word Lengths

- *Fiction:* Short stories with wholesome Christian content. 1,200–1,400 words.
- *Nonfiction:* Practical, positive articles and essays with
  strong Christian emphasis on family life, children,
  married and single lifestyles, media, home remodel-
  ing, and political and moral issues such as abortion,
  AIDS, and homosexuality. Accepts interviews with
  Church of Christ members. Accepts seasonal material
  and filler. 1,200–1,400 words.
- *Departments:* A Matter of Taste, recipes. Creative Corner, crafts. Your Image, beauty and fashion. Dollars
  and Sense, finances. 1,200–1,400 words.
- *Poetry:* Short poems. Publishes 2–3 per issue.
- *Artwork:* Submit to Joel Butts, Graphic Designer. Accepts color photos and illustrations.

How to Submit

Query with outline or send complete ms with cover letter. Include SASE. Accepts photocopies, computer printouts, Macintosh Quark Xpress or DOS-ASCII disks, and
fax submissions. Simultaneous submissions okay. Reports in up to 2 years.

Payment and Policies

First rights. Rights revert to author after 1 year. Pays on
publication. Articles and stories, $25. Poems, $5. Authors receive 3 copies of the issue.

Church Administration

George Clark, Editor
MSN 157
127 Ninth Avenue North
Nashville, TN 37234
615-251-2060

AT A GLANCE:
CHURCH ADMINIS-TRATION

- Southern Baptist, Leadership
- 65% freelance
- Monthly
- Circ: not available
- Pays: $.055–$.065 per word on acceptance.

From the Editor:
"Be conversant with how Southern Baptists do things. We are a practical, nuts-and-bolts kind of magazine."

Best Bet: Practical, how-to articles for church administrators.

Avoid: Poetry; sermons; Bible study; theology; scholarly works.

Sample copy: Free. Send #10 SASE for guidelines.

Profile

A monthly magazine for church administrators. Published by The Sunday School Board of the Southern Baptist Convention. Uses as doctrinal guidelines the 1963 statement of The Baptist Faith and Message. 8.5x11; 50 pages.

Focus and Audience

Seeks to help Southern Baptist pastors, church staff, church officers, church council, and church committee members understand and preform their administrative and pastoral ministries tasks.

Interests and Word Lengths

- *Nonfiction:* Practical articles in the areas of leadership; pastoral care; ministers of education; proclamation and worship; weekday education; deacon work; public relations; and religious vocational guidance. Church planning and evaluation, coordination, staffing, property and space, building, government and polity, business administration, finances, housekeeping, secretarial work, committees, and staff relations. Accepts seasonal material. 1,600–2,000 words.
- *Photos:* Occasionally accepts B/W prints.

How to Submit

Prefers query with outline. Accepts complete ms with cover letter. Include SASE. Accepts photocopies, computer printouts, and disk submissions. No simultaneous submissions. Report time varies.

Payment and Policies

All rights. Pays on acceptance. $.055–$.065 per word. Authors receive 3 copies of issue.

Church Educator

Robert Davidson, Editor
165 Plaza Drive
Prescott, AZ 86303
800-221-0910

AT A GLANCE:
CHURCH EDUCATOR

- Christian, Education
- 75% freelance
- Publishes 1 new
  writer per month
- Monthly
- Circ: 3,000
- Receives several
  hundred mss each
  month.
- Pays: $.03 per word
  on publication.

From the Editor:
"We strive to be a valuable resource for Christian educators."

Best Bet: Examples of successful Christian education programs for children, youth, adults, or families.

Avoid: Testimonials.

Sample copy: Free with 9x12 SAE and $.75 postage. Send #10 SASE for guidelines.

Profile

A monthly publication serving an ecumenical readership of Christian educators. 8.5x11; glossy cover; 2-color; 28 pages.

Focus and Audience

Comprehensive in scope, it presents practical education resources for ministers, teachers, and administrators involved in Christian education programs in large and small churches of all denominations.

Interests and Word Lengths

- *Nonfiction:* Accepts four categories of articles: Children's Ministry: general educational features; lesson plans on seasonal and special themes; prayers and liturgies that help children celebrate God's love; learning center activities and projects; and craft projects and games. Youth Ministry: youth programs and program outlines including discussion starters and activities; guidelines for small group activities; guidelines for small group encounters; celebration service ideas, and youth ministry leadership education. Adult Ministry: outlines for study groups and study programs; features on pastoral care and counseling; educator's meditations. Intergenerational: how-to articles for all church programs; events and celebrations; family programs. Up to 1,500 words.
- *Photos:* Occasionally accepts B/W prints.

How to Submit

Send complete ms. Include SASE. Accepts photocopies, computer printouts, and fax submissions. No simultaneous submissions. Reports in 2–3 months.

Payment and Policies

First North American serial rights. Pays on publication. $.03 per word. Authors receive 2 copies of the issue.

The Church Herald and Holiness Banner

Ray Crooks, Editor
7405 Metcalf
P.O. Box 4060
Overland Park, KS 66204
913-432-0331

AT A GLANCE:
THE CHURCH HERALD AND HOLINESS BANNER

- Evangelical, Bible Study
- Biweekly
- Circ: 2,500
- No payment. Offers 1 contributor's copy.

From the Editor:
"This is a conservative evangelical paper. Request writer's guidelines before submitting."

Best Bet: Evangelical church-related features and news.

Sample copy: Not provided. Send #10 SASE for guidelines.

Profile

An evangelical biweekly publication published by Herald and Banner Press. 8x10; self cover; stapled; 20 pages.

Focus and Audience

General features and church-related news aimed at a conservative evangelical audience.

Interests and Word Lengths

- *Nonfiction:* Doctrinal and inspirational pieces, Bible studies, biographies and autobiographies, and devotional writing. 200–800 words. Accepts poetry, filler, and seasonal material.

How to Submit

Query with writing samples, or send complete ms with cover letter. Include SASE. Accepts computer printouts and 3.5- and 5.25-inch disks. Simultaneous submissions okay. Reports in 2 months.

Payment and Policies

Authors retain rights. No payment. Authors receive 1 copy of the issue.

Church of God Evangel

Homer G. Rhea, Editor-in-Chief
1080 Montgomery Avenue
Cleveland, TN 37311
615-476-4512

AT A GLANCE: CHURCH OF GOD EVANGEL

- Church of God, Denominational
- 40% freelance
- 10% new writers
- Monthly
- Circ: 50,000
- Receives 10 queries, 50 mss each month.
- Pays: $.02–$.05 per word on publication

From the Editor:
"Know the denomination. Write when you feel the importance of the words you have to proclaim. Every line should be saturated with prayer."

Best Bet: Writing with strong evangelistic appeal.

Avoid: Fiction and poetry.

Sample copy: Free with 9x12 SAE and 3 oz. postage cost. Send #10 SASE for guidelines.

Profile

A monthly denominational magazine that serves as the official journal of the Church of God Evangel. Member of the Evangelical Press Association and the International Pentecostal Press Association. 8.5x11; glossy cover; 2-color; 36 pages.

Focus and Audience

Seeks evangelistic, doctrinal, and devotional material from a fundamental Christian perspective and in keeping with the Church of God statements of faith. Read primarily by Church of God members, but aims to appeal to other Christians and non-Christians.

Interests and Word Lengths

- *Nonfiction:* Evangelistic pieces aimed at the non-Christian, 400–500 words. Doctrinal articles pertaining to salvation, holiness, divine healing, heaven, hell, Bible prophecy, etc., 600–800 words. Devotionals on prayer, fasting, stewardship, Bible reading, and Church attendance, 400–800 words. Personal experiences of soul-winning, outstanding conversions, unusual answers to prayer, Christian service, and personality features on outstanding Christians, 400–1,200. Articles dealing with social problems from a Christian perspective, and pieces on how to make a strong Christian home, 400–1,200 words.
- *Seasonal:* New Year's, Christmas, Mother's Day, Pentecost Sunday, Thanksgiving, and Memorial Day pieces. Submit 3 months in advance.

How to Submit

Send complete ms. Include SASE. Accepts photocopies and computer printouts. Simultaneous submissions okay, but not encouraged. Reports in 1 month.

Payment and Policies

One-time rights. Pays on publication. $.02–$.05 per word. Authors receive 2 copies of issue.

Church Media Library Magazine

Floyd B. Simpson, Editor
127 Ninth Avenue North
Nashville, TN 37234
615-251-2752

AT A GLANCE:
Church Media Library Magazine

- Christian, Media Libraries
- 10% freelance
- 2% new writers
- Quarterly
- Circ: 36,000
- Receives 1 query, 2 mss each month.
- Pays: $.055 per word on acceptance.

From the Editor:
"Our goal is to develop stronger Christian churches through effective, fully functioning church media libraries."

Best Bet: Material that inspires and guides church media library operation.

Sample copy: Free with 8.5x11 SASE. Send #10 SASE for guidelines.

Profile

A quarterly resource designed to aid in developing a church media library. Published by The Sunday School Board of the Southern Baptist Convention. 8x11; glossy cover; 2-color; 52 pages.

Focus and Audience

Provides general and specialty articles to assist churches in establishing and operating a church media library. Directed primarily to church media librarians, pastors, program leaders, and church staff.

Interests and Word Lengths

- *Nonfiction:* Articles on establishing, operating, improving, enlarging, and utilizing church media libraries. Material that will help libraries support personal Christian growth and their church's educational programs, counseling, and outreach ministries. Skits or other promotional ideas that highlight the services of a church library. Human interest stories of individuals whose lives were impacted by the ministry of a church media library. 825–1,750 words.

How to Submit

Send complete ms with cover letter. Include SASE. Accepts computer printouts. Simultaneous submissions okay. Reports within 2 months.

Payment and Policies

All rights. Will opt for first North American serial or one-time rights at reduced rates. Pays on acceptance. $.055 per word. Authors receive 3 copies of the issue.

Church Recreation

Laura Stallins, Assistant Editor
127 Ninth Avenue North
Nashville, TN 37234
615-251-3841

AT A GLANCE:
CHURCH RECREATION

- Southern Baptist, Recreation
- 70% freelance
- 20% new writers
- Quarterly
- Circ: 17,000
- Receives 10–15 queries, 25–30 mss each month.
- Pays: $.055 per word on publication.

From the Editor:
"We want to surprise, encourage, and entertain our readers to the point that they can't wait to try the next issue full of ideas. We care very little for the philosophy of *why*; tell us *how!*"

Best Bet: Short, direct, exciting, innovative, crazy ideas for all ages.

Avoid: Wordy, philosophical, footnoted material. Instead, make it interesting.

Sample copy: Free with SASE. Send #10 SASE for guidelines.

Profile

A quarterly magazine focusing on the effective use of recreation in all church programs. Follows as doctrinal guidelines the 1963 statement of The Baptist Faith and Message. 8x11; glossy cover; 2-color; 60 pages.

Focus and Audience

Provides ideas and plans for a variety of church, family, and social recreation. Readers are ministers and volunteers who organize and plan activites for children, youth, and seniors.

Interests and Word Lengths

- *Fiction:* Drama, puppetry, clowning. Interested in scripts for all occasions, stunts, skits, and monologues. 800–1,200 words.
- *Nonfiction:* Sports evangelism, articles on how sports have affected an individual's life in Christ. 800 words.
- *Departments:* Games, twist on familiar games. Family Recreation, family activities and outings. Crafts, craft ideas. Fitness, recipes for fitness or camping. Retreats, retreat plans—games, food, locations. Social Recreation; Sports. 800–1,200 words.

How to Submit

Query with outline, or send comple ms with cover letter and resume. Include SASE. Accepts photocopies, computer printouts, MS-DOS and Macintosh disks, and faxes with cover sheet. Simultaneous submissions okay if noted in cover letter. Reports in 1 month or less.

Payment and Policies

One-time or all rights. Pays on publication. Fiction and nonfiction, $.055 per word. Game or activity ideas, $25 each. Authors receive 3 copies of the issue.

Church & State

Joseph L. Conn, Managing Editor
8120 Fenton Street
Silver Spring, MD 20910
301-589-3707

AT A GLANCE:
CHURCH & STATE

- Religion, Politics
- 5% freelance
- 5% new writers
- 11 issues a year
- Circ: 30,000
- Receives 10–20 queries, 10–20 mss each month.
- Pays: $150–$250 on publication.

From the Editor:
"*Church & State* is not a religious magazine. Articles must promote separation of church and state and be non-sectarian in approach."

Best Bet: Issues of church–state separation only.

Avoid: Sectarianism.

Sample copy: Free with 9x12 SAE and $.75 postage. Send #10 SASE for guidelines.

Profile

An association publication of Americans United for Separation of Church and State, a non-profit corporation dedicated to preserving church-state separation. 8x11; self cover; 32 pages.

Focus and Audience

Promotes religious liberty and separation of church and state. Articles are political, not religious, in nature. Readers come from across the entire religious spectrum.

Interests and Word Lengths

- *Nonfiction:* News stories and features on local church-state issues. 2,000–3,000 words.
- *Departments:* Viewpoint, opinion pieces on church-state issues. 500–1,000 words.
- *Photos:* B/W prints to accompany articles.

How to Submit

Query with outline. Include SASE. Accepts photocopies and computer printouts. Simultaneous submissions okay. Reports in 1–2 months.

Payment and Policies

All rights. Pays on publication. $150–$250 per piece. Authors receive copies of the issue upon request.

Church Teachers

Shirley Strobel, Editor
1119 Woodburn Road
Durham, NC 27705
919-490-5552

AT A GLANCE:
CHURCH TEACHERS

- Christian, Religious Education
- 33% freelance
- 5 times a year
- Circ: 6,000
- Receives many queries and mss each month.
- Pays: $25–$40 per page on publication.

From the Editor:
"An effort is made to include Roman Catholic, Orthodox, and Protestant writers."

Best Bet: Articles based on actual teaching experiences; success stories, especially from volunteer teachers.

Avoid: Short stories; poetry; testimonials.

Sample copy: $1. Send #10 SASE for guidelines.

Profile

A practical professional journal by and for Christian education teachers. Est.: 1973; 8.5x11; 40 pages.

Focus and Audience

Provides successful classroom-tested teaching strategies and creative ideas. Prefers writers with teaching experience. Readership is ecumenical, comprised of volunteer teachers in Sunday church schools and religious education programs.

Interests and Word Lengths

- *Nonfiction:* Teaching methods, how-to and curriculum-related articles, and workshops that have proven success in religious education classes. Themes such as creativity, drama, adult education, and creative media are announced regularly. 500–1,500 words.
- *Seasonal:* Articles on Advent, Christmas, Epiphany, Lent, and Easter. 500–1,500 words.
- *Photos:* Clear, sharp B/W glossy prints of any size.

How to Submit

Send complete ms with cover letter. Include SASE. Accepts photocopies, computer printouts, and Macintosh disk submissions. No simultaneous submissions. Reports in 1–2 months.

Payment and Policies

All rights. Pays on publication. Articles, $25–$45 per page. Photos, $10–$20. Authors receive 2 copies of the issue.

Church Worship

Henry Rust, Editor
165 Plaza Drive
Prescott, AZ 86303
602-771-8601

AT A GLANCE:
CHURCH WORSHIP

- Christian, Worship
- 75% freelance
- 10% new writers
- Monthly
- Circ: 1,200
- Receives 100 queries, 50 mss each month.
- Pays: $.03 per word on publication.

From the Editor:
"We serve mostly mainline Protestant churches."

Best Bet: Worship resources.

Avoid: Testimonials and fundamentalist theology.

Sample copy: Free with 9x12 SAE and $.75 postage. Send #10 SASE for guidelines.

Profile
A monthly magazine that serves as resource for innovative worship in mainline Protestant churches. 8.5x11; 2-color; 24 pages.

Focus and Audience
Worship resources such as prayers, dedications, and youth services presented for use by mainline Protestant ministers, worship leaders, and deacons.

Interests and Word Lengths
- *Resources:* Prayers, litanies, dedications, responsive readings, complete worship services—indoor, outdoor, formal, informal—for children, young adults, and adults.

How to Submit
Send complete ms with cover letter. Include SASE. Accepts photocopies and computer printouts. Simultaneous submissions okay. Reports in 2–3 months.

Payment and Policies
First North American serial rights. Pays on publication. $.03 per word. Authors receive 2 copies of the issue.

Circuit Rider

Rich Peck, Editor
201 Eighth Avenue South
Nashvillle, TN 37202
615-749-6137

AT A GLANCE:

CIRCUIT RIDER

- United Methodist, Clergy
- 3% freelance
- 1% new writers
- Monthly
- Circ: 40,000
- Receives 50 queries, 30 mss each month.
- Pays $100–$300 on publication.

From the Editor:
"Don't write what you wouldn't read if you weren't the author. Write about what excites you. A new twist to an old idea makes good reading. Test your ideas on some clergy friends to see how they react."

Best Bets: Scholarly articles that are practical and viable for ministry of the church.

Avoid: Academic writing style.

Sample copy: Not available. Send #10 SASE for guidelines.

Profile

A monthly professional journal for the applied practice of Christian ministry for United Methodist clergy. Published by The United Methodist Publishing House. 8.5x11; glossy cover; 28 pages.

Focus and Audience

Attempts to cover all of the functional areas of a pastor's ministry and offer uncommon insights into common experiences. It is sent to all United Methodist clergy and to retired clergy upon request.

Interests and Word Lengths

- *Nonfiction:* Practical articles that discuss the problems and challenges of ministry and offer creative solutions. Topics include doctrine, evangelism, spirituality, social and world issues, and the environment. Up to 1,800 words. Prefers shorter articles.
- *Departments:* The Pastor/Administrator, The Pastor/Priest, The Pastor/Teacher, The Pastor/Preacher, The Pastor/Counselor, The Pastor/Student, The Pastor/Evangelist, The Pastor/Prophet. Departments are usually assigned. 350–1,800 words.

How to Submit

Query with outline, or send comple ms with cover letter. Include SASE. Accepts photocopies, computer printouts, and ASCII disks. Simultaneous submissions okay. Reports in 1 month.

Payment and Policies

All rights. Pays on publication. $100–$300 per piece. Authors receive 5 copies of the issue.

Clubhouse

Elaine Trumbo, Editor
464 West Ferry, Box 15
Berrien Springs, MI 49103
616-471-9009

AT A GLANCE:
CLUBHOUSE

- Christian, Juvenile
- 80% freelance
- 10% new writers
- 6 issues a year
- Circ: 8,000
- Receives 200+ mss each month.
- Pays: $25–$35 after acceptance.

From the Editor:
"Remember to make kids the 'good guys' in *Clubhouse* stories—not kids who need to be reformed or do silly, unwise, selfish deeds."

Best Bet: First-person stories that demonstrate the good qualities and capabilities of young people.

Avoid: Santa; elves; Halloween items; the Easter Bunny; fairy tale and occult themes.

Sample copy: Free with 6x9 SAE and 3 oz. postage. Send #10 SASE for guidelines.

Profile
A bimonthly Christian children's magazine of inspiring stories and puzzles. 6x9; self cover; folded; 32 pages.

Focus and Audience
Designed to help young people feel good about themselves. Material is not overtly religious, but represents Christian principles of behavior in action. Readers are Christian children, ages 9–14.

Interests and Word Lengths
- *Fiction:* Stories that demonstrate the good qualities and capabilities of young people by relating clever, selfless, brave, or heroic adventures. Accepts humor, suspense, drama, and inspirational stories. 1,000–1,200 words.
- *Nonfiction:* Articles demonstrating the good qualities of young people. Can be health-related, historical, or human interest. 1,000–1,200 words.
- *Poetry:* Humor or mood pieces on themes of interest to children. 4–24 lines.
- *Filler:* Word searches, mind-benders, deduction puzzles, secret codes, crafts, and recipes for nutritious snacks, easy entrées, and seasonal beverages.

How to Submit
Send complete ms with cover letter. Include SASE. Accepts photocopies and computer printouts. Simultaneous submissions okay. Reports in 2 months.

Payment and Policies
One-time, first, second, or reprint rights. Pays 6 months after acceptance. Articles and stories, $25–$35. Filler and poems, $5–$12. Authors receive 2 copies of the issue.

CoLaborer

Melissa L. Riddle, Editor
5233 Mt. View Road
Antioch, TN 37013-2306
615-731-6812

AT A GLANCE:
CoLaborer

- Free Will Baptist, Women
- 50% freelance
- 10% new writers
- Bimonthly
- Circ: 14,000
- Receives 10–15 queries, 2–5 mss each month.
- No payment. Offers 3 contributors copies.

From the Editor:
"We look for material that is original, creative, expressive, and concise. Our audience appreciates fresh new materials."

Best Bet: Inspirational, instructional, and personal experience pieces aimed at edifying and strengthening Christian women.

Avoid: Over-analytical, jargon-filled, exegesis-type articles.

Sample copy: $1.25 with 9x12.5 SASE. Send #10 SASE for guidelines.

Profile
A bimonthly women's magazine published by the Women's National Auxiliary Convention of the National Association of Free Will Baptists. 8.5x11; 2-color; stapled; 32 pages.

Focus and Audience
Reflects Christian women's issues especially as they relate to personal evangelism and world missions. Readers are Free Will Baptist women of different ages and from different geographical locations.

Interests and Word Lengths
- *Fiction*: Christian fiction, drama, and comedy reflecting women's issues. 750–1,000 words.
- *Nonfiction:* Personal experiences of crisis and faith and devotionals on a variety of topics such as Christian and family issues, missions, evangelism, and church life. 250–750 words.
- *Departments:* Life!, action column for youth. The Minister's Wife; Crosswinds; Bible Studies. 250–1,000 words. Accepts filler, poetry, and facts of interest.
- *Photos:* B/W prints.

How to Submit
Query with outline, writing samples, and clips. Include SASE. Accepts computer printouts and IBM-compatible disks, preferably WordPerfect. Simultaneous submissions okay. Reports in 2 months.

Payment and Policies
One-time rights. No payment. Authors receive 3 copies of the issue.

Columbia

Richard McMunn, Editor
Columbus Plaza
New Haven, CT 06510
203-772-2130

AT A GLANCE:

COLUMBIA

- Catholic, Membership
- 30% freelance
- 10% new writers
- Monthly
- Circ: 1.5 million
- Receives 5–10 queries, 5–10 mss each month.
- Pays: $250–$500 on acceptance.

From the Editor:
"We suggest that you become familiar with the magazine and its readers before submitting."

Best Bet: Features about Knights of Columbus programs or personalities. Articles of general Catholic interest.

Avoid: Controversial or sensational Catholic Church-related topics; first-person opinion pieces.

Sample copy: Free. Send #10 SASE for guidelines.

Profile

The membership magazine for the Knights of Columbus (KC), a Catholic volunteer service organization. 8.5x11; glossy cover; full-color; 92 pages.

Focus and Audience

Publishes topics of general Catholic interest, but readership consists mainly of members of the Knights of Columbus and their families.

Interests and Word Lengths

- *Nonfiction:* Features, interviews, and occasional essays on KC personalities and unique KC volunteer programs. Topics of interest to Catholics, i.e., current events; societal trends; social problems; family life; Catholic practice and teaching as it relates to the world; and Catholic Church programs, institutions, and personalities. Up to 1,500 words.

How to Submit

Query with outline. Include SASE. Accepts photocopies and computer printouts. No simultaneous submissions. Reports in up to 2 months.

Payment and Policies

First North American serial rights. Pays on acceptance. $250–$500 per piece. Kill fee, $125. Authors receive 2 copies of the issue.

Command

Col. Don Martin, Jr., USAR, Editor
3784 South Inca
Englewood, CO 80110-3408
303-761-1984

Profile

A Christian magazine for military personnel. Published by the Officers' Christian Fellowship (OCF) of the United States of America for its members. Member of the Evangelical Press Association. 8.5x11; glossy cover; 4-color; 32 pages.

Focus and Audience

Provides biblically based perspectives on professional and family life and on Christian outreach and service in the military. Written and edited by and for OCF members—Christian officers and their spouses in the U.S. Armed Forces.

Interests and Word Lengths

- *Nonfiction:* Features, essays, and personal experiences on the integration of biblical teaching with the military profession; professional ethics; American foreign and military policy; family life in the military; and Christian ministry in the military. 750–1,500 words.
- *Departments:* Commentary, how Scripture applies to controversial issues concerning the military profession, its values, traditions, and actions. 500 words.
- *Poetry:* Occasionally publishes devotional or topical poetry.

How to Submit

Query with outline. Include SASE. Accepts photocopies, computer printouts, Macintosh or DOS disks, and fax submissions. Simultaneous submissions okay. Reports in 6 months.

Payment and Policies

One-time rights. Rarely offers payment. Payment is negotiated on occasion. Authors receive 5 copies of the issue.

Common Boundary

Mark Judge, Editorial Assistant
4304 East-West Highway
Bethesda, MD 20874
301-652-9495

AT A GLANCE:
COMMON BOUNDARY

- Spirituality, Psychology
- 50% freelance
- 10% new writers
- Bimonthly
- Circ: 26,000
- Receives 20 queries, 20 mss each month.
- Pays on publication. Rates depend on author's experience.

From the Editor:
"We are ecumenical, discerning, and look for well-crafted and well-argued articles. Send for several back issues and look at our magazine."

Avoid: The new age.

Sample copy: $5. Send #10 SASE for guidelines.

Profile
A bimonthly ecumenical magazine that explores the relationship between psychotherapy and spirituality. 8.5x11; glossy cover; 2-color; 64 pages.

Focus and Audience
Focus is on the relationship between psychotherapy and spirituality. Aimed at readers from a variety of backgrounds who are interested in the inner experience.

Interests and Word Lengths
- *Nonfiction:* Feature articles examining spirituality, psychology, healing, comparative religion, cultural and ethnic issues, the environment, lifestyle, and metaphysics. 3,000–4,000 words.
- *Departments:* Innovations; Trends; Viewpoint; Playback, audio and video reviews; In Your Own Words. 1,500–1,800 words.
- *Filler:* News Briefs, 200–600 words.

How to Submit
Query with outline. Include SASE. Accepts photocopies. Simultaneous submissions okay. Reports in 3–6 months.

Payment and Policies
First North American serial rights. Pays on publication. Rates depend on author's experience. Kill fee, usually 33%. Authors receive 2 copies of the issue.

Common Ground

Sandra A. LaBlanc, Communications Director
11625 Beaver Avenue
Des Moines, IA 50310-2199
515-270-2634

AT A GLANCE:
COMMON GROUND

- Catholic, Community Living
- 25% freelance
- 25% new writers
- 10 issues a year
- Circ: 2,500
- Receives 5 queries, 1 ms each month.
- Pays: $.20 per word on publication.

From the Editor:
"A query letter is a must for possible article ideas. Writers should be conversant with the Catholic Church as well as the mission of NCRLC."

Best Bet: National Catholic Rural Life Conference-related articles.

Sample copy: $1 with 9x12 SAE and $.52 postage. Send #10 SASE for guidelines.

Profile

A newsletter of community living. Published by the National Catholic Rural Life Conference (NCRLC). 8.5x11; folded; 2-color; 4 pages.

Focus and Audience

Works to promote a family farm system of agriculture, a healthy environment, and strong rural communities from a Catholic faith perspective. Inclusive in nature and serves an active, informed constituency.

Interests and Word Lengths

- *Nonfiction:* Features, interviews, essays, and personal experiences on food, agriculture, rural communities, environment, and faith. 500–1,000 words. Accepts seasonal material.
- *Departments:* Spiritual Food, faith perspective in agriculture, rural communities, and the environment. 250–500 words.
- *Photos:* B/W prints and line drawings.

How to Submit

Query with outline, writing samples, and clips. Include SASE. Accepts computer printouts, Macintosh disks, and fax submissions. No simultaneous submissions. Reports in 6–12 months.

Payment and Policies

First North American serial rights. Pays on publication. $.20 per word. Authors receive 5 copies of the issue.

Communities
Journal of Cooperative Living

Editor
Route 1, Box 155
Rutledge, MO 63563
816-883-5543

AT A GLANCE:
COMMUNITIES

- Community Living, Lifestyle
- 90% freelance
- 50% new writers
- Quarterly
- Circ: 4,000
- Receives 3 queries, 2 mss each month.
- No payment. Offers contributor's copies.

From the Editor:
"Writing works much better for us if it is grounded in concrete and personal examples, not just theory."

Best Bet: Prose and poetry that address cooperative living and explore the ways in which people are learning to get along with others. Stress positive choices.

Sample copy: $4. Send #10 SASE for guidelines.

Profile
An ecumenical publication promoting cooperation but no particular style of community living. Published by Fellowship for Intentional Community. 8.5x11; glossy cover; 56–64 pages.

Focus and Audience
Aims to be the source of up-to-date and comprehensive information about community living, and a forum for exploring issues and ideas in community lifestyles.

Interests and Word Lengths
- *Fiction:* Considers any fiction that is suitable for the content of its message and the theme of the publication. No word-length restrictions.
- *Nonfiction:* Features, interviews, essays, and personal experiences on community living and cooperation, lifestyle, social and world issues, and psychology, as they relate to cooperative living. No word-length restrictions.
- *Poetry:* Suitable poems that illustrate cooperative living.
- *Photos:* B/W prints and line drawings.

How to Submit
Send complete ms with cover letter. Include SASE. Accepts photocopies and computer printouts. Simultaneous submissions okay. Reports in 1 month.

Payment and Policies
One-time rights. No payment. Authors receive 3 copies of the issue.

Community Service Newsletter

Jane Morgan, Editor
114 East Whiteman Street
P.O. Box 243
Yellow Springs, OH 45387
513-767-2161

AT A GLANCE:
COMMUNITY SERVICE NEWSLETTER

- Community, Family
- 90% freelance
- Bimonthly
- Circ: 350
- Receives 2 queries, 2–3 mss each month.
- No payment. Offers a free subscription and 2–5 contributor's copies.

From the Editor:
"We do not want articles about how great a community might be, but articles about how a community is actually working in a school, workplace, church, or hometown."

Best Bet: Articles about how people actually improved their communities.

Avoid: Wordy, hypothetical articles not based on fact.

Sample copy: $.50 with 4x9 SAE and $.29 postage. Send #10 SASE for guidelines.

Profile

A bimonthly newsletter with practical information on small community building. 7x8.5; self cover; stapled; 12 pages.

Focus and Audience

Promotes the small community as a basic social institution involving organic units of economic, social, and spiritual development. Readers are concerned about improving their own communities.

Interests and Word Lengths

- *Nonfiction:* Practical, factual features and essays on community development. Interests include family, the environment, economics, education, and land trusts. 2,000 words maximum.
- *Departments:* Readers Write, announcements about communities and community service, up to 300 words.
- *Artwork:* Silhouettes and line drawings.

How to Submit

Query, or send complete ms. Accepts clear computer printouts. Reports in 1 month.

Payment and Policies

One-time rights. No payment. Authors receive a free one-year subscription and 2–5 copies of the issue.

Companion of St. Francis and St. Anthony

B. McCrimmon, Managing Editor
P.O. Box 535, Station F
Toronto, ON M4Y 2L8
Canada
416-463-5442

AT A GLANCE:
COMPANION OF ST. FRANCIS AND ST. ANTHONY

- Catholic, Family
- 50% freelance
- 11 issues a year
- Circ: 5,000
- Receives 10 queries, 10 mss each month.
- Pays: $.06 (CAN) per word on publication.

From the Editor:
"We stress Franciscan values of simplicity, peace, and joy."

Best Bet: Anything fostering personal and spiritual growth from a Franciscan perspective.

Avoid: Sexist viewpoints.

Sample copy: Free with SAE and postage/IRCs. Send #10 SASE/IRCs for guidelines.

Profile

A Catholic family magazine of spiritual growth and renewal. 5.5x8.5; 31 pages.

Focus and Audience

Values personal and spiritual growth, church renewal, and a sense of community as seen through a Franciscan perspective.

Interests and Word Lengths

- *Fiction:* Short stories, 1,200–1,500 words.
- *Nonfiction:* Articles and personal experiences on Franciscan spirituality, family life, and social and world issues. 1,200–1,500 words.

How to Submit

Fiction, query with outline or send complete ms with cover letter. Nonfiction, send complete ms with cover letter. Include SASE. U.S. authors send IRCs. Accepts photocopies and computer printouts. No simultaneous submissions.

Payment and Policies

First North American serial rights. Pays on publication. $.06 (CAN) per word. Authors receive 3 copies of the issue.

Company
A Magazine of the American Jesuits

E.J. Mattimoe, S.J., Editor
3441 North Ashland Avenue
Chicago, IL 60657
312-281-1534

AT A GLANCE:

COMPANY

- Catholic, Jesuit
- 90% freelance
- Quarterly
- Circ: 125,000
- Receives 15–20 queries, 10–15 mss each month
- Pays: $50–$100 on publication.

From the Editor:
"Articles must have some relationship to Jesuits. Actual quotes and detail are prized."

Best Bet: Concrete stories of Jesuit-sponsored ministries and narratives that describe ongoing projects.

Avoid: Sermons; drawing very large conclusions from insufficient data.

Sample copy: Free with 9x12 SAE and $1 postage. Send #10 SASE for guidelines.

Profile

A national public-relations magazine of the Jesuits, a Catholic religious order formally known as the Society of Jesus. Est.: 1983. 8.5x11; glossy cover; 32 pages.

Focus and Audience

Aims to make known the ideas and ideals of the American Jesuits and those who work with them.

Interests and Word Lengths

- *Nonfiction:* Articles about Third World experience, teaching, retreat or city ministries, and narrative pieces on people who are doing good work. All articles must relate in some way to Jesuits. Appreciates articles that use concrete details, quotes, and some humor. 1,000–2,000 words.
- *Departments:* Minims & Maxims, items of interest from Jesuit ministries around the country. 100–200 words.
- *Photos:* All articles must be accompanied by B/W photos.

How to Submit

Send complete ms with cover letter. Include SASE. Accepts photocopies, computer printouts, and WordPerfect 5.1 disks. No simultaneous submissions. Reports in 1 month.

Payment and Policies

One-time and reprint rights. Pays on publication. $50–$100 per piece. Rates for photos vary. Authors receive 6 copies of the issue.

Compass: A Jesuit Journal

Robert Chodos, Editor
Ten St. Mary Street, Suite 300
Toronto, ON M4Y 1P9
Canada
416-921-0653

AT A GLANCE:

COMPASS

- Catholic, Canadian
- 25% freelance
- 2% new writers
- 6 issues a year
- Circ: 3,000
- Receives 5 queries, 2 mss each month.
- Pays: $50–$500 (CAN) on publication.

From the Editor: "Avoid pious and religious language and try to engage the secular world."

Best Bet: Creative approaches to religious and social issues.

Avoid: Shallow theologizing; excessive emotionalism; uncritical dogmatism; unthinking criticism of church.

Sample copy: Free with 8.5x11 SASE/IRC. No guidelines.

Profile

A magazine of social and religious thought published by the Jesuits of the Upper Canada Province. Member of the Canadian Magazine Publishers Association and the Catholic Press Association. 8.5x11; self cover; 2-color; 48 pages.

Focus and Audience

Ecumenical in spirit, the magazine provides a forum for lively debate and an ethical perspective on social and religious experience. Emphasizes Canadian content. Readers are educated, but not specialized.

Interests and Word Lengths

- *Nonfiction:* Essays and opinion pieces on topics of current interest, church issues, spirituality, social and political topics, and culture. 750–2,000 words.
- *Departments:* Testament, Colloguay, Disputatio, Saints, and Book Reviews. Biblical, theological, and spiritual reflection. 750–2,000 words.

How to Submit

Query with outline and writing samples, or send complete ms with cover letter and resume. Include SASE. U.S. authors send IRCs. Accepts computer printouts and WordPerfect disks. No simultaneous submissions. Reports in 2 months.

Payment and Policies

All rights. Pays on publication. $50–$500 (CAN) per piece. Authors receive 3 copies of the issue.

Compassion Magazine

Steve Wamberg, Editor
3955 Cragwood Drive
Colorado Springs, CO 80918
719-594-9900

AT A GLANCE:

COMPASSION

- Christian, Child Development
- 5% freelance
- Bimonthly
- Circ: 160,000
- Receives 2 queries, 1 ms each month.
- Pays: $.09–$.15 per word on publication.

From the Editor:
"Our conservative theology has lead to the cutting-edge social interaction in *Compassion*'s history and its present."

Best Bet: Factual, case study-type articles with pictorial support and sidebars.

Avoid: Fiction and poetry.

Sample copy: $.25 with 9x12 SAE and $.52 postage. Send #10 SASE for guidelines.

Profile

A Christian magazine focusing on child-development issues. 8.5x11; 16 pages.

Focus and Audience

Explores the social dimension of child development issues by presenting factual case studies on a particular child or area. Embraces a conservative theology.

Interests and Word Lengths

- *Nonfiction:* Interviews and specific case studies that focus on the sociology of the poor in U.S. inner cities, Native Americans, and rural areas. Offer opinions of the poor and those who work with them. Appreciates photos and sidebars to accompany articles. 150–900 words.
- *Departments:* In Brief, short biographical sketches of child-development workers, projects, and children. Up to 200 words.
- *Photos:* Prefers slides, B/W or color. Accepts clear prints of any size.

How to Submit

Query with outline. Include SASE. Accepts photocopies, computer printouts, and fax submissions. No simultaneous submissions. Reports in 2–3 months.

Payment and Policies

All rights; grants authors reprint rights. Pays on publication. $.09–$.15 per word. Authors receive 12 copies of the issue.

The Congregationalist

Joseph B. Polhemus, Editor
1105 Briarwood Road
Mansfield, OH 44907
419-756-5526

AT A GLANCE:
THE CONGREGATION-
ALIST

- Congregationalist, Social Issues
- 20% freelance
- 10% new writers
- Bimonthly
- Circ: 4,000
- Receives 4–5 queries, 2–3 mss each month.
- No payment. Offers 2–3 contributor's copies.

From the Editor:
"Limit theorizing and be objective. Submit action photographs with your manuscript."

Best Bet: Articles dealing with Congregationalism and written by Congregationalists.

Avoid: Editorializing.

Sample copy: Free. No guidelines.

Profile

A bimonthly denominational magazine serving Congregational churches and their members. 8.5x11; 28 pages.

Focus and Audience

Reports on Congregational churches, personalities, and history and offers social commentary relevant to Congregational lay people and ministers.

Interests and Word Lengths

- *Nonfiction:* Articles on Congregational history, churches, and individuals—past and present, as well as objective social commentary on issues such as abortion and homosexuality. How-to articles offering Congregationalist success stories and how success was achieved. Interests include spirituality, prayer, Bible study, comparative religion, cultural and ethnic issues, missionary work, and women's issues. 1,200–1,500 words.
- *Departments:* Book reviews on religious subjects.
- *Artwork:* 5x7 B/W or color prints; line drawings.

How to Submit

Send complete ms with cover letter. Include SASE. Accepts photocopies, computer printouts, IBM-compatible ASCII disks, faxes, and submissions via modem. No simultaneous submissions. Reports in 1 month.

Payment and Policies

All rights. No payment. Authors receive 2–3 copies of the issue.

The Conqueror

Editor
8855 Dunn Road
Hazelwood, MO 63042-2299

AT A GLANCE:

THE CONQUEROR

- Pentecostal, Teens
- 60% freelance
- 40% new writers
- 7 issues a year
- Circ: 6,000
- Receives 50 mss each month.
- Pays $20–$30 on publication.

From the Editor:
"A good story or article must have conflict— deal with it in a realistic manner. Before writing, make sure you have a good story item. Know where you are taking your reader. Be sensitive, creative, and specific."

Best Bet: Articles and stories relevant to Pentecostal teens.

Sample copy: Free with 9x12 SASE. Send #10 SASE for guidelines.

Profile

A denominational magazine for teenagers. Published by the General Youth Division of the United Pentecostal Church International. 8.5x11; glossy cover; 4-color; 16 pages.

Focus and Audience

Primary objective is to inspire young people by portraying happy, victorious living through faith in God. Readers are Pentecostal teenagers.

Interests and Word Lengths

- *Fiction:* Short Christian fiction on subjects relevant to single youth. 600–900 words for a single-page article; 1,200–1,800 words for a double-page article. Accepts poetry.
- *Nonfiction:* Articles pertaining to spiritual growth and development; missionary-related stories; character stories; personal testimonies and experiences; and current events, all of interest to teenagers. Use anecdotes and illustrations. In quoting Scripture, use the Cambridge Bible, King James Version. 600–900 words for a single-page article; 1,200–1,800 words for a double-page article.
- *Seasonal:* Publishes one Christmas piece a year. Submit 1 year in advance.

How to Submit

Send complete ms with cover letter. Include SASE. Accepts photocopies and computer printouts. Simultaneous submissions okay. Reports in up to 1 year.

Payment and Policies

All rights. Pays on publication. $20–$30 per piece. Authors receive 1 copy of the issue.

Contact

Robert J. Tamasy, Editor
1800 McCallie Avenue
Chattanooga, TN 37404
615-698-4444

AT A GLANCE:
CONTACT

- Christian, Business
- 5% freelance
- 5% new writers
- Bimonthly
- Circ: 18,000
- Receives 10 queries,
  5 mss each month.
- Pays: $25–$50 on
  publication.

From the Editor:
"Our desire is to enable
our readers to see
practical and relevant
ways to apply their
faith in Jesus Christ to
everyday work de-
mands."

Best Bet: Articles with
specific relevance to
the needs and chal-
lenges of Christians in
the secular business
environment.

Avoid: Esoteric theology and generic plati-
tude pieces.

Sample copy: $2.50
with 9x12 SASE. No
guidelines.

Profile

The membership magazine of the Christian Business
Men's Committee of the U.S.A (CBMC), a non-denominational international evangelical organization of business and professional men. Member of the Evangelical
Press Association. 8.5x11; glossy cover; full-color; 24
pages.

Focus and Audience

Seeks to enable Christians in business to effectively integrate their faith in the workplace by offering practical
and relevant applications. Readers are primarily members of local CBMC groups. Prefers to work with writers
who are personally familiar with the ministry of CBMC
and its mission and with the 1990s business world.

Interests and Word Lengths

- *Nonfiction:* Personality profiles of committed Christians
  in business; features on everyday issues in business
  viewed from a biblical perspective; personal financial
  management; stress; ethics; change; and Christian
  perspective on work, integrity, sexual temptation,
  and work relationships. 700–1,000 words.
- *Artwork:* Color and B/W photos and slides and original line drawings related to article topics.

How to Submit

Query with outline, resume, writing samples, and clips.
Include SASE. No reprints. Accepts computer printouts
and Macintosh Microsoft Word disk submissions. No simultaneous submissions. Reports in 3 months.

Payment and Policies

One-time rights. Pays on publication. $25–$50 per
piece. Authors receive 5–10 copies of the issue.

Contempo

Cindy Lewis Dake, Editor
P.O. Box 830010
Birmingham, AL 35242
205-991-8100

AT A GLANCE:
CONTEMPO

- Southern Baptist,
  Women
- 95% freelance
- 20% new writers
- Monthly
- Circ: 65,000
- Receives 5–10
  queries, several mss
  each month.
- Pays: $.055 per word
  on publication.

From the Editor:
"Evidence of good writing can result in assignments. Verification of all facts must accompany manuscripts. Ninety-nine percent of our writers are Southern Baptist women."

Best Bet: Reports on Southern Baptist missions enterprises.

Avoid: Feministic writing; poetry; fiction; humor; and mushy devotions.

Sample copy: No information provided.

Profile

A monthly missions education magazine for Southern Baptist women. Published by the Women's Missionary Union, Auxiliary to Southern Baptist Convention. 8.5x11; glossy cover; 2-color; 48 pages.

Focus and Audience

Reports on missions enterprises involving Southern Baptist missionaries. Readers are conservative Christian women, 18–34 years of age.

Interests and Word Lengths

- *Nonfiction:* Mission action ideas, features, interviews, and personal experiences on women and family issues, Bible study, prayer, and current world and societal issues. Up to 600 words.
- *Departments:* Potpourri, includes mission action ideas, family ministry ideas, short pieces about women making a difference in families, churches, communities, and world. Up to 100 words.

How to Submit

Send complete ms with cover letter and resource list varifying factual statements. Include SASE. Many articles are assigned to freelance writers. Accepts photocopies, computer printouts, and IBM-compatible 3.5-inch disks. Reports in 12–18 months.

Payment and Policies

All rights. Pays on publication. $.055 per word. Does not offer contributor's copies.

Cornerstone

Jennifer Ingerson, Submissions Editor
939 West Wilson Avenue
Chicago, IL 60640
312-989-2080

AT A GLANCE:

CORNERSTONE

- Christian, Young Adult
- 20–60% freelance
- Bimonthly
- Circ: 50,000
- Receives 4–8 queries, 130 mss each month.
- Pays: $.08–$.10 per word on publication.

From the Editor:
"We are known as very avant garde, but we attempt to express orthodox belief in the language of the nineties. We read and consider all material received, but only respond if interested."

Best Bet: Fiction and nonfiction with a biblical worldview.

Avoid: Pornography; Christian clichés; cheap shots at non-Christians; unrealistic or syrupy fiction; undocumented research articles.

Sample copy: Free with 9x12 SAE and 5 first-class stamps. Send #10 SASE for guidelines.

Profile

A bimonthly magazine of progressive Christian thought and attitudes for young adults. 8.5x11; glossy cover; full-color; 64 pages.

Focus and Audience

Attempts to communicate doctrinal truth based on Scripture. Promotes the cultural freedom to participate in the complex world of today, while taking up the responsibility of impacting that world. Challenges readers—young adults, ages 18–35—to look through the window of biblical reality.

Interests and Word Lengths

- *Fiction:* Creative short stories and short-short stories on almost any topic. No pornography or unrealistic or syrupy fiction. 250–2,500 words.
- *Nonfiction:* Articles, essays, personal experiences, testimonies, and interviews on contemporary issues in the church, homelessness, current world events, the poor, and social justice. Document research and investigative articles. Up to 2,700 words.
- *Departments:* Music, book, and film reviews. Music interviews should show the artists' values and worldview as reflected in their music. 500–1,000 words.
- *Poetry:* Avant garde, free verse, haiku, and light verse. Submit up to 5 poems, no longer than 2 pages.
- *Photos:* B/W or color, 8x10 prints or 35 mm slides. Identify subject. Submit with manuscript.

How to Submit

Send complete ms with cover letter. MS not returned. Accepts photocopies, computer printouts, and faxes. Simultaneous submissions okay. Reports if interested.

Payment and Policies

First serial rights. Pays on publication. Fiction and nonfiction, $.08–$.10 per word. Poetry, 1–15 lines, $10; 16+ lines, $25. Authors receive 6 copies of the issue.

Cornerstone Connections

Mark Ford, Editor
55 West Oak Ridge Drive
Hagerstown, MD 21740
301-791-7000

Profile

A quarterly magazine for Seventh-day Adventist youth leaders. 8x10.5; 48 pages.

Focus and Audience

Serves as a resource and outreach tool for Seventh-day Adventist youth leaders. While published for leaders, much of its material is used by young people and reflects their vocabulary and interests. All material adheres to Seventh-day Adventist doctrinal standards and ideals for youth.

Interests and Word Lengths

- *Fiction:* Plays, activities, and skits, 800 words. Outreach and social activities, 200 words. All on themes relevant to today's youth such as interpersonal relationships, spiritual growth, holidays, environmental issues, family life, health, Bible study, and devotions.
- *Artwork:* B/W or color prints; cartoons.

How to Submit

Send complete ms with cover letter. Include SASE. Accepts computer printouts with IBM-compatible WordPerfect disks. Identify simultaneous submissions.

Payment and Policies

One-time rights. Pays $35–$100 per piece. Authors receive 1 copy of the issue.

Counselor

Janice K. Burton, Editor
P.O. Box 632
Glen Ellyn, IL 60187
708-668-6000

AT A GLANCE:
COUNSELOR

- Christian, Juvenile
- 50–70% freelance
- Uses new writers
- Weekly
- Circ: not available
- Receives 40–55 mss each month.
- Pays $.05–$.10 per word on acceptance.

From the Editor:
"We seek to honor Jesus Christ in all our publishing efforts, and to help children come to know the Lord and be discipled in His ways. We are an evangelical publishing house."

Avoid: Subjects that are more appropriate for older readers such as abuse, AIDS, abortion, eating disorders, dating, sex, suicide, etc.

Sample copy: Free with 6x9 SAE and $.29 postage. Send #10 SASE for guidelines.

Profile

A Sunday school take-home paper for children. Correlated with the Scripture Press *Bible for Today* curriculum. 8x11; 4-color; folded; 4 pages.

Focus and Audience

Designed to help children, ages 8–12, apply Scripture lessons to everyday life situations and come to know Jesus Christ. Evangelical in nature.

Interests and Word Lengths

- *Fiction:* Short stories on topics such as response to authority, accepting responsibility, cheating, divorce, interpersonal relationships, family, friends, justice, lying, peer pressure, prayer, prejudice, salvation, trusting God, and witnessing. 950–1,100 words. Avoid stories on subjects more appropriate for older readers.
- *Nonfiction:* Personal experiences, interviews, and true stories with photos if possible. See *Fiction* for subjects of interest. 950–1,100 words.
- *Departments:* World Series, stories from around the world reflecting God at work in children's lives. Kids in Action and Nature Stories. Photos required. 400–700 words.
- *Filler:* Puzzles and creative activities that reflect a spiritual truth. Must be solvable with both the *King James* and *New International* Bible versions.
- *Photos:* B/W or color slides to accompany material.

How to Submit

Send complete ms with cover letter. Query for World Series features. Include SASE. Accepts photocopies and computer printouts. No simultaneous submissions. Reports in 4–6 weeks.

Payment and Policies

First North American, one-time, or all rights. Pays on acceptance. $.05–$.10 per word depending on rights offered and editing required. Authors receive 4 copies.

The Covenant

Debbie Cohen, Assistant Editor
15 Hove Street
Downsview, ON M3H 4Y8
Canada
416-633-6224

AT A GLANCE:

THE COVENANT

- Jewish, Canadian
- 10–20% freelance
- 50% new writers
- Monthly
- Circ: 55,000
- Receives 4 queries each month.
- Pays: $25–$50 on publication.

From the Editor:
"We are open to working with writers. Be familiar with the Mideast, Israel, and Jewish issues."

Best Bet: Journalistic articles related to Jewish issues and culture.

Avoid: Fiction; poetry; lengthy articles.

Sample copy: Free with 9x11 SAE/IRCs. No guidelines.

Profile

Canada's largest Anglo-Jewish monthly newspaper. Published by B'nai Brith Canada, a Jewish fellowship that serves to combat anti-Semitism, bigotry, and racism in Canada and abroad; and support activities that insure the security and survival of the State of Israel and Jewish communities worldwide. Tabloid-size; newsprint; 20 pages.

Focus and Audience

Offers regional, national, and international news of interest to the Jewish community in Canada.

Interests and Word Lengths

- *Nonfiction:* Personality profiles, opinion pieces, and sports articles of interest to the Jewish community in Canada. Interests include regional, national, and international news, particularly the Mideast, Israel, and Jewish issues. 500–700 words.
- *Photos:* B/W prints and line drawings.

How to Submit

Query with writing samples and clips. Include SASE. Accepts photocopies, computer printouts, faxes, and Macintosh disk submissions. Simultaneous submissions okay. Reports in 1 week.

Payment and Policies

One-time rights. Pays on publication. Articles, $50. Student submissions, $25. Does not provide copies of the issue.

The Covenant Companion

Rev. James R. Hawkinson, Editor
5101 North Francisco Avenue
Chicago, IL 60625
312-784-3000

AT A GLANCE:
THE COVENANT COMPANION

- Evangelical, Christian Living
- 10% freelance
- 10% new writers
- Monthly
- Circ: 22,500
- Receives 5 queries, 20 mss each month.
- Pays: $15–$35 per piece on publication.

From the Editor:
"Our magazine is addressed to people who care about commitment but are open to ideas and experiences. Articles should explore what it means to claim Jesus Christ as Savior and follow Him as Lord."

Best Bet: Articles from a Christian perspective that deal with life and faith issues together.

Avoid: Know-it-all attitudes.

Sample copy: $2.25 with 9x12 SAE and $1.25 postage. Send #10 SASE for guidelines.

Profile

The official organ of The Evangelical Covenant Church. Member of the Associated Church Press and Evangelical Press Association. 8x11; glossy cover; full-color; 44 pages.

Focus and Audience

Seeks to inform, stimulate, and gather The Evangelical Covenant Church by putting its members in touch with each other and assisting them in interpreting contemporary issues.

Interests and Word Lengths

- *Nonfiction:* Features, essays, and personal-experience pieces that witness to and deal with life and faith issues from an evangelical perspective. Topics include denominational issues, devotions, doctrine, the environment, evangelism, family concerns, health and healing, inspiring others, children and teenagers, lifestyle, missionary work, prayer, religious education, seniors, social and world issues, spirituality, theology, women's issues, and worship. 500–1,000 words.
- *Seasonal:* Material for the church year. Submit 8–10 weeks in advance.
- *Poetry:* Accepts poetry.
- *Photos:* B/W prints, any size.

How to Submit

Send complete ms with cover letter stating author's faith persuasion and church affiliation. Include SASE. Accepts computer printouts and DOS ASCII, WordPerfect, or Microsoft Word disks with hard copy. Simultaneous submissions okay. Reports in 2–3 months.

Payment and Policies

First North American serial, one-time, or all rights. Pays on publication. $15–$35 per piece. Authors receive 3 copies of the issue.

Creation Social Science & Humanities Quarterly

Dr. Paul D. Ackerman, Editor
1429 North Holyoke
Wichita, KS 67208
316-683-3610

AT A GLANCE:
CREATION SOCIAL SCIENCE & HUMANITIES QUARTERLY

- Christian, Social Science
- 50% freelance
- 20% new writers
- Quarterly
- Circ: several hundred
- Receives 2 queries, 2 mss each month.
- No payment. Offers 6 contributor's copies.

From the Editor:
"We are strict biblical creation-believing Christians. We want articles written with a calm, professional, courteous attitude and a clear style."

Best Bet: Studies of the social sciences or humanities from a biblical creation view.

Avoid: Theological polemics.

Sample copy: Free. Send #10 SASE for guidelines.

Profile

A quarterly journal that presents a biblical creation model of origins for the social sciences and humanities. Est: 1977. 5.5x8.5; 32 pages.

Focus and Audience

Studies and comments on the social sciences—psychology, sociology, history, philosophy—and humanities—literature, fine arts, music—from the biblical creation perspective. Readers are college-educated and share views on the origins of creation.

Interests and Word Lengths

- *Nonfiction:* Well-researched and documented articles and essays that address the social sciences and humanities in light of a biblical view of creation. Writers should have a professional/academic background in either the humanities or social sciences. 3,000 words.
- *Departments:* Submit to Mrs. Ellen Myers, Book Review Editor. Book Reviews. 1,000–2,000 words.
- *Poetry:* Poems under 1 page. Brief devotions.
- *Artwork:* B/W illustrations that are reproducible by a printer. Must accompany article.

How to Submit

Query with outline, or send complete ms with cover letter. Include SASE. Accepts photocopies, computer printouts, and IBM-compatible disks. Reports in 3 months.

Payment and Policies

All rights. No payment. Authors receive 6 copies of the issue.

Creation Spirituality

Dan Turner, Editor
P.O. Box 19216
Oakland, CA 94619
510-482-4984

AT A GLANCE:

CREATION SPIRITUALITY

- Spirituality, Social Justice
- 75% freelance
- Bimonthly
- Circ: 15,000
- Pays: $.02 per word upon request.

From the Editor:
"We come from a very specific perspective. Please be familiar with our magazine and the writing of Matthew Fox before submitting, or it will most probably be rejected. We embrace panentheism, the belief that divinity permeates all things."

Avoid: Fiction; sentimental poetry; theological proofs; fundamentalist positions; and new age lingo.

Sample copy: Free. Send #10 SASE for guidelines.

Profile

A bimonthly magazine that seeks to rediscover the earliest tradition of the Hebrew Bible and medieval European mystics. Prospective writers should be familiar with the writings of Matthew Fox. 8.5x11; glossy cover; full-color; 56 pages.

Focus and Audience

Strives to awaken authentic mysticism, revitalize Western religion and culture, and promote social and ecological justice by bringing together the wisdom of ancient spiritual traditions, the insights of contemporary science, and the expression of the arts.

Interests and Word Lengths

- *Nonfiction:* Submit to John R. Mabry, Managing Editor. Spirituality, psychology, feminism, ecology, racial issues, cosmology, and ecumenism. 1,200–2,000 words.
- *Departments:* Submit to John R. Mabry, Managing Editor. Creating Ritual, Art-as-Meditation, Voices of the Mystics, and Deep Ecumenism. All concern practical daily spirituality, rituals, and awakening the artist or mystic within. 500–1,500 words.
- *Artwork:* Submit to Andrea DuFlon, Art Director. Accepts B/W and color prints and slides, line drawings, and illustrations.

How to Submit

Send complete ms with cover letter, resume, and a brief author biography. Include SASE. Accepts original manuscripts or disks.

Payment and Policies

Authors retain rights. Pays $.02 per word upon request only to those who make their living writing. Authors receive 5 copies of the issue.

Creator Magazine

Marshall Sanders, Publisher
4631 Cutwater Lane
Hilliard, OH 43026
614-777-7774

AT A GLANCE:

CREATOR MAGAZINE

- Christian, Church Music
- 20% freelance
- 60% new writers
- 6 issues a year
- Circ: 5,500
- Receives 20 queries, 10 mss each month.
- Pays: $10–$60 on publication.

From the Editor:
"Creator Magazine is for church music leaders of all Christian denominations."

Best Bet: Instructional, detailed, how-to articles on church music programs.

Avoid: First- and second-person writing; cute or personal articles.

Sample copy: Free with 9x12 SAE and $1.44 postage. Send #10 SASE for guidelines.

Profile

A non-denominational Christian magazine that promotes excellence and integrity in church music programs. 8x10.5; 52 pages.

Focus and Audience

Believes in and fosters a balanced music program with any church, regardless of heritage and tradition. Readers are music leaders—church choir directors, organists, and support staff members.

Interests and Word Lengths

- *Nonfiction:* How-to articles, interviews, and program experiences on choir management, choral skills development, music program ideas and descriptions, and children's and youth choir management and program ideas. Write in the third person. 1,000–4,000 words.
- *Departments:* Hints & Humor, short helpful ideas or anecdotes of unique or humorous church or choir happenings, 50–250 words. Composer Spotlight, short profiles of past or present composers, 750–1,500 words. Belltips, focusing on hand bells, 1,000–4,000 words. Small Church; Children; Youth; Repertoire; 1,000–4,000 words.
- *Artwork:* Prefers 5x7 or larger B/W or color prints. Accepts slides and B/W drawings.

How to Submit

Query with outline, resume, and writing samples; or send complete ms with cover letter and resume. Include SASE. Accepts photocopies, computer printouts, DOS or Macintosh disks, and fax submissions. Simultaneous submissions okay. Reports in 3–5 months.

Payment and Policies

Rights negotiable. Pays on publication. Articles, $35–$60. Composer Spotlight, $20. Hints & Humor, $10. Authors receive 2 copies of the issue.

Crisis

A Journal of Lay Catholic Opinion

David A Bovenizer, Executive Editor
1511 K Street NW, Suite 525
Washington, DC 20005
202-347-7411

AT A GLANCE:
CRISIS

- Catholic, Opinion
- 90% freelance
- 20% new writers
- Monthly
- Circ: 9,500
- Receives 50 queries,
  20 mss each month.
- Pays: $100–$500 on
  publication.

From the Editor:
"Though a journal of
Catholic lay opinion,
we welcome submis-
sions from contributors
of all faiths."

Best Bet: Thematic or
reportorial contribu-
tions from lay people
that indicate the inter-
relationship of faith
and public life.

Avoid: Superficiality,
subjectivism, and di-
dacticism.

Sample copy: $4. Send
#10 SASE for guidelines.

Profile

A monthly journal of lay Catholic opinion that explores
the interrelationship of faith and public life. 8.5x11; 60
pages.

Focus and Audience

Attentive to the deepening dialog on questions of cultural life in the U.S. with an emphasis on reports of pre-
scriptive efforts.

Interests and Word Lengths

- *Nonfiction:* Issue-related reportorial articles. Interests
  include spirituality, social and world issues, and culture. No word-length restrictions.
- *Departments:* Issue-related opinion pieces. Public Ar-
  guments; In View, news and editorials; Miscellany;
  Major Essays; Book Reviews; Judaism; Evangelical
  Protestantism; National Conference of Catholic Bishops; Constitutional Cases; Common Wisdom.
  850–2,500 words.

How to Submit

Query with outline, resume, writing samples, and clips;
or send complete ms with cover letter and resume. Include SASE. Accepts photocopies, computer printouts,
disks, faxes, and submissions via modem. Simultaneous
submissions okay. Reports within 3 months.

Payment and Policies

All rights. Pays on publication. $100–$500 per piece.
Authors receive copies of the issue.

Cross Currents

William Birmingham, Editor
College of New Rochelle
New Rochelle, NY 10805-2308
914-654-5425

AT A GLANCE:
CROSS CURRENTS

- Interfaith, Interdisciplinary
- 90% freelance
- 50% new writers
- Quarterly
- Circ: 4,000
- Receives 100 mss each month.
- No payment. Offers 3–4 contributor's copies.

From the Editor:
"We are for the general reader, so do not get too technical or specialized."

Best Bet: Interdisciplinary religious writings.

Avoid: Technical, specialized writing.

Sample copy: Free. Send #10 SASE for guidelines.

Profile

An international, interfaith, and interdisciplinary journal published quarterly by the Association for Religion and Intellectual Life. 6x9; heavy bond cover; 144 pages.

Focus and Audience

Serves as a forum for critical dialog between persons searching to integrate their religious and intellectual commitments. Reaches a general audience.

Interests and Word Lengths

- *Nonfiction:* Features, interviews, essays, and personal experiences on a wide-range of subjects appropriate to the publication's goals. Up to 5,000 words.
- *Departments:* Correspondence Department, comments on past articles; Book Reviews.
- *Seasonal:* Accepts seasonal material and poetry.
- *Photos:* Illustrations to accompany articles only.

How to Submit

Query with outline, or send complete ms with cover letter. Include SASE. Accepts photocopies, computer printouts and Macintosh or IBM disks. Simultaneous submissions okay. Reports in 4–6 weeks.

Payment and Policies

Authors retain rights. No payment. Authors receive 3–4 copies of the issue.

Crusader

G. Richard Broene, Editor
1333 Alger SE
Grand Rapids, MI 49507
616-241-5616

AT A GLANCE:

CRUSADER

- Calvinist, Youth
- 40% freelance
- 5–10% new writers
- 7 issues a year
- Circ: 13,000
- Receives 0–5 queries, 65–70 mss each month.
- Pays: $.02–$.05 per word on acceptance.

From the Editor:
"*Crusader* is written for boys, 9- to 14-years old, who are members of the Calvinist Cadet Corps."

Best Bet: Fiction in keeping with issue themes.

Avoid: Fantasy stories.

Sample copy: Free with 9x12 SAE and 3 first-class stamps. Send #10 SASE for theme list.

Profile

A membership magazine of The Calvinist Cadet Corps, a Christian organization for boys. Issues are thematic. 8.5x11; 2-color; 24 pages.

Focus and Audience

Aims to show boys how God is at work in their lives and in the world around them. Readers are 9- to 14-year-old Calvinist Cadet Corps members.

Interests and Word Lengths

- *Fiction:* Adventures and mysteries of a devotional nature focusing on issue themes. Past themes have included Feed My Lambs, Choices—Consequences, and ComLink with God. 1,000–1,500 words.
- *Nonfiction:* Articles on nature and the environment. 400–1,000 words.

How to Submit

Obtain theme list before submitting. Accepts complete ms with cover letter. Include SASE. Accepts photocopies, computer printouts, and fax submissions. Simultaneous submissions okay. Reports in 1–2 months.

Payment and Policies

First North American serial or one-time rights. Pays on acceptance. First publication, $.04–$.05 per word. Reprints, $.02–$.03 per word. Authors receive 1 copy of the issue.

The Cumberland Presbyterian

Rev. M. Jacqueline Warren, Editor
1978 Union Avenue
Memphis, TN 38104
901-276-4572

AT A GLANCE:
THE CUMBERLAND PRESBYTERIAN

- Presbyterian, Regional
- Monthly
- Circ: 7,600
- No payment.

From the Editor:
"Articles that glorify God and minister to people will be considered for publication."

Best Bet: Material of interest to members of the Cumberland Presbyterian Church.

Sample copy: Not provided. No guidelines.

Profile
The denominational magazine of the Cumberland Presbyterian Church of Memphis, Tennessee. Member of the Associated Church Press. 8.5x11; glossy cover; 2-color; 32 pages.

Focus and Audience
Serves as a medium for the communication of the Gospel. Contains general feature articles and church news. Readers are primarily, but not limited to, Cumberland Presbyterians.

Interests and Word Lengths
- *Fiction:* Children's stories and sermons.
- *Nonfiction:* Features, personal experiences, interviews, and essays on biblical themes, life experiences, and church stories. 4 typed, double-spaced ms pages.
- *Department:* A Little Child Shall Lead Them; Viewpoints; For the Record; Bethel College; Church in the World; Church Life; Gray Matters; On Ministry.
- *Poetry:* Christian poetry.
- *Seasonal:* Features related to the church calendar year.
- *Photos:* Color prints.

How to Submit
Submit complete ms with cover letter and author photo. Include SASE. Accepts photocopies and computer printouts. Simultaneous submissions okay. Reports in 3 months.

Payment and Policies
All rights. No payment. Does not provide copies of the issue.

Current Thoughts & Trends

Dennis Cone, Editor
7899 Lexington Drive
Colorado Springs, CO 80920
719-531-3585

AT A GLANCE:
CURRENT THOUGHTS & TRENDS

- Christian, Article Summaries
- 30% freelance
- 2% new writers
- Monthly
- Circ: 8,000
- Receives 1 query each month.
- Pays: $15 per piece on publication.

From the Editor:
"A limited number of summaries are assigned to freelance writers."

Best Bet: Objective summarizations, paraphrased from original articles.

Avoid: Reviewing, commenting on, or simply condensing articles.

Sample copy: $2 with 9x12 SAE and $.98 postage. Send #10 SASE for guidelines.

Profile
A monthly journal of article summaries for use by those in Christian ministries. Published by The Navigators. 8.5x11; self cover; 2-color; 32 pages.

Focus and Audience
Its mission is to enhance the ministry of Christian leaders by providing concise timely summaries of contemporary trends in Christian and secular thought as reported in a wide variety of periodicals. Over 80 percent of readers are pastors.

Interests and Word Lengths
- *Summaries:* Objective, unbiased summaries of articles from the religious and secular media that are of particular interest to pastors and Christian leaders. Up to 450 words.
- *Artwork:* Considers cartoons, line drawings, and B/W prints.

How to Submit
Send summaries with cover letter, resume, and a photocopy of the original article. Include SASE. Accepts computer printouts, DOS PCWrite disks, and fax submissions. No simultaneous submissions. Reports in 1 month.

Payment and Policies
One-time rights. Pays on publication. $15 per summary. Authors receive 1 copy of the issue.

Daughters of Sarah

Cathi Falsani, Assistant Editor
3801 North Keeler
Chicago, IL 60641
312-736-3399

AT A GLANCE:

DAUGHTERS OF SARAH

- Christian, Women
- 85% freelance
- 65% new writers
- Quarterly
- Circ: 5,000+
- Receives 10 queries, 35 mss each month.
- Pays: $15 per printed page on publication.

From the Editor:
"We are a forum for a wide range of viewpoints that are both Christian and feminist. We invite you to enter into our open exchange of ideas."

Best Bet: Explorations of social issues and their effects on women.

Avoid: Subjects not directly related to women or women's issues; gender exclusive language when referring to God.

Sample copy: $3. Send #10 SASE for guidelines and theme list.

Profile

A quarterly magazine by Christian women calling for justice, mutuality, and reconciliation in the church and the world. Issues are thematic. 5.5x8.5; glossy cover; 64 pages.

Focus and Audience

Committed to biblical and feminist concepts of wholeness and liberation. Addresses contemporary social concerns and their effects on women. Tone is provocative and personal. Readers are Christian feminists.

Interests and Word Lengths

- *Fiction:* Publishes little fiction. Send for guidelines and current theme list. 1,200 words
- *Nonfiction:* Interviews, first-person accounts, investigative reporting, expository articles, and short prose. Send for theme list. 900–2,000 words.
- *Departments:* Submit to Reta Finger, Editor. Segue, feminist women in mainline churches. Dear Daughters, letters to the editor. Bible as Feminist Pilgrim, theological/biblical interpretation. 800–1,500 words. Also accepts book reviews.
- *Poetry:* Send for guidelines.
- *Artwork:* Submit to Kari Sandhaas, Art Director. B/W artwork, drawings, and photos.

How to Submit

Query with outline, or send complete ms with cover letter. Include brief author biography. Include SASE. Accepts computer printouts. Simultaneous submissions okay. Reports in 2 months.

Payment and Policies

First North American serial or one-time rights. Pays on publication. $15 per printed page. Offers kill fee, rates vary. Authors receive 2 copies of the issue.

Desert Call

Editor
Box 219
One Carmelite Way
Crestone, CO 81131
719-256-4778

AT A GLANCE:
DESERT CALL

- Christian, Contemplative Prayer
- 33% freelance
- 33% new writers
- 4 issues a year
- Circ: 3,000
- Receives 4 mss each month.
- No payment. Offers 2 contributor's copies.

From the Editor:
"We do not want sentimental pietism, nor do we seek scholarly papers. Rather, we seek intelligent, witty, reverent reflections that are creatively subversive of *all* parochialisms."

Best Bet: Articles and poetry that reflect and evoke contemplation.

Avoid: Preciosity, sanctimony, parochialism, political correctness.

Sample copy: $2 with 8.5x11 SAE and $.98 postage. Guidelines not available.

Profile

An ecumenical magazine focusing on contemplative prayer, especially as influenced by the Carmelite tradition. Sponsored by The Spiritual Life Institute, a small Roman Catholic ecumenical monastic community of men and women. 8.5x11; 2-color; 28 pages.

Focus and Audience

Portrays contemplation as the highest and most distinctively human act. Focuses primarily on the earthy mysticism of the Judeo-Christian tradition, but open to other religions and to keen cultural criticism.

Interests and Word Lengths

- *Nonfiction:* Features, interviews, essays, and personal experiences that represent spiritual practice as a humanizing activity and explore the role of passion in the quest for humanization. Also accepts cultural criticism from a contemplative view, and profiles of saints and heroes. 500–3,500 words.
- *Poetry:* Submit to Poetry Editor. Reflect a sense of sacramentality and passionate commitment to life, love, beauty, truth, and freedom. Up to 2 pages.
- *Departments:* Submit to Department Editor. Forethought/Frontiers. Includes book reviews, cultural and spiritual trends, and reflections on classic works.
- *Artwork:* B/W photos. B/W illustrations, preferably pen and ink, scratchboard, or cut paper.

How to Submit

Query with outline, resume, and writing samples, or send complete ms with cover letter and resume. Include SASE. Accepts photocopies, computer printouts, and WordPerfect 5.1 files on 5.25-inch double-density disks. Simultaneous submissions okay. Reports in 2 months.

Payment and Policies

No payment. Authors receive 2 copies of the issue.

Diaconalogue

Dot Nuechterlein, Editor
1304 LaPorte Avenue
Valparaiso, IN 46383
219-464-0909

Profile

A service-oriented publication of the Lutheran Deaconess Association. 8.5x11; 4–6 pages.

Focus and Audience

Designed to affirm, encourage, educate, and support lay people who perform "diakonia" or service. Readers are Christians who minister to one another.

Interests and Word Lengths

- *Nonfiction:* Features, interviews, essays and personal experiences that offer examples of how individuals care for others—their family, the elderly, hungry or homeless people, etc. Also considers profiles of caregivers. 1,000 words.
- *Poetry:* Free-verse poems that illustrate some aspect of caring for those in need of love and assistance.

How to Submit

Send complete ms with cover letter. Include SASE. Accepts photocopies and computer printouts. No simultaneous submissions. Reports within 1 month.

Payment and Policies

All rights; permits reprints with attribution. Pays on publication. Articles, $25. Authors receive 5–10 copies of the issue upon request.

Dimension

Judith Edwards, Editor
P.O. Box 830010
Birmingham, AL 35283
205-991-4063

AT A GLANCE:

DIMENSION

- Southern Baptist, Missions
- 75% freelance
- 25% new writers
- Quarterly
- Circ: 45,000
- Receives 15 mss each month.
- Pays: $.05 per word on publication.

From the Editor:
"Give suggestions on how to involve church members of all ages in missions activities."

Best Bet: Fresh, practical how-to's on missions activities.

Avoid: Trite, over-used subject matter.

Sample copy: $3. No guidelines.

Profile

A quarterly missions magazine for the Southern Baptist Church and missions leadership. 8.5x11; 52 pages.

Focus and Audience

Offers practical suggestions and ideas on Southern Baptist missions activities.

Interests and Word Lengths

- *Nonfiction:* Practical how-to articles on ways to involve congregations in missions activities; personal experiences of Southern Baptist missionary work. Accepts seasonal material. Up to 1,000 words.

How to Submit

Send complete ms with cover letter. Include SASE. Accepts photocopies, computer printouts, IBM-compatible disks, and fax submissions (205-991-4990). Simultaneous submissions okay. Reports in 6–8 weeks.

Payment and Policies

All rights. Pays on publication. $.05 per word. Authors receive 3 copies of the issue.

Dimensions

A Journal of Holocaust Studies

Dennis B. Klein, Editor
Braun Center for Holocaust Studies, ADL, 823 United Nations Plaza
New York, NY 10017
212-490-2525

AT A GLANCE:

DIMENSIONS

- Jewish, Holocaust
- 100% freelance
- 90% new writers
- 2–3 issues a year
- Circ: 10,000
- Receives 10 queries, 8–9 mss each month.
- Pays: $250–$500 on acceptance.

From the Editor:
"*Dimensions* explores the breadth and implications of the Holocaust and is an excellent resource for the classroom."

Best Bet: Clear, lucid prose, and an ability to reach non-specialist readers.

Sample copy: Available upon request. No guidelines.

Profile

A general resource that provides indepth coverage of the Holocaust. Published by the Anti-Defamation League's Braun Center for Holocaust Studies. 8.5x11; glossy cover; 48–50 pages.

Focus and Audience

Explores the causes and consequences of the Holocaust. Doubles as a classroom resource. Readers include teachers, students, religious organizations, libraries, individuals, Yeshivas, Hillels, and the media.

Interests and Word Lengths

- *Nonfiction:* Interviews and essays on and personal experiences about the Holocaust. Interests include philosophical and political treatments related to the Holocaust. 4,000–5,000 words.
- *Departments:* In Brief: Books New and Noteworthy. In Other Journals: A Review of Periodical Literature. The Last Word: International Calendar of Events.
- *Artwork:* Submit to Carol Perkins. 8x10 glossy B/W photos. Illustrations.

How to Submit

Query with outline. Include SASE. Accepts photocopies, computer printouts, WordPerfect disks, and faxes. No simultaneous submissions. Reports in 2 months.

Payment and Policies

All rights. Pays on acceptance. $250–$500 depending on assignment and length. Kill fee, usually 50%. Authors receive 2 copies of the issue.

Discipleship Journal

Deena Davis, Associate Editor
7899 Lexington Drive
Colorado Springs, CO 80920
719-531-3530

AT A GLANCE:
DISCIPLESHIP JOURNAL

- Christian Living
- 95% freelance
- Bimonthly
- Circ: 95,000
- Receives 60–70 queries each month.
- Pays: $.20 per word on acceptance.

From the Editor:
"Our articles are meaty, not fluffy. Study writer's guidelines and back issues and try to use similar approaches. Don't preach. Polish your articles before submitting."

Best Bet: Practical articles on Christian discipleship.

Avoid: Personal testimonies; devotionals, humor, politically partisan articles; and anything not distinctly Christian.

Sample copy: Free with 9x12 SAE and $1.67 postage. Send #10 SASE for guidelines.

Profile

A practical bimonthly magazine on Christian discipleship and daily ministry. Published by The Navigators. 8.5x11; glossy cover; full-color; 80 pages.

Focus and Audience

Designed to help Christians develop a deeper faith through a greater understanding of Scripture and how it can be applied to daily life and ministry.

Interests and Word Lengths

- *Fiction:* Occasionally accepts short stories or short-short stories with Christian emphasis. 2,000–3,000 words.
- *Nonfiction:* Practical how-to articles on growing in Christian faith and discipling, ministering to others, serving people in need, and understanding and applying the Bible. No personal testimonies. 1,500–3,000 words.

How to Submit

Query first with outline, resume, writing samples, and clips. No unsolicited mss. Include SASE. Accepts photocopies and computer printouts. Identify simultaneous submissions. Reports in 2 months.

Payment and Policies

First North American serial, one-time, and second serial rights. Pays on acceptance. Original articles and stories, $.20 per word. Reprints, $.05 word. Authors receive 2 copies of the issue.

Discoveries

Latta Jo Knapp, Editor
6401 The Paseo
Kansas City, MO 64131
816-333-7000

AT A GLANCE:
DISCOVERIES

- Evangelical, Sunday School
- 100% freelance
- Weekly
- Circ: 5,500
- Receives 100 queries, 150 mss each month.
- Pays: $.05 per word on publication.

From the Editor:
"Write on a 3rd- to 4th-grade reading level. Send for guidelines and theme list."

Best Bet: Realistic, true-to-life portrayals of 8- to 10-year-old children.

Avoid: Extensive cultural or holiday references, especially those distinctly American; fantasy or science fiction stories; abnormally mature or precocious characters; personification of animals.

Sample copy: With guidelines and theme list, free with #10 SASE.

Profile

A weekly story paper for 3rd- and 4th-grade children that correlates directly with the WordAction Sunday school curriculum. Published by WordAction Publishing Company. 8.5x11; full-color; folded; 4 pages.

Focus and Audience

Designed to connect Sunday school learning with the daily growth of 8- to 10-year-old children. Themes and outcomes should conform to the theology and practices of denominations having a Wesleyan-Aminian theological heritage. Readership is international.

Interests and Word Lengths

- *Fiction:* Contemporary, true-to-life short stories, particularly adventures, showing character building or scriptural application. Use an active voice and write in the third person. 500–700 words.
- *Departments:* Bible Trivia, 100–500 words.
- *Puzzles:* Simple puzzles correlating with the middler Sunday school lessons. Send for middler curriculum theme list. Include instructions on a separate sheet.
- *Artwork:* Accepts humorous cartoons involving children. Other B/W or color illustrations are assigned; submit portfolio for consideration.

How to Submit

Query with writing samples, or send complete ms with cover letter. SASE. Accepts photocopies, computer printouts, and fax submissions. Reports in 1–2 months.

Payment and Policies

Multiple-use rights. Pays on publication. Stories, $.05 per word. Puzzles, $15. Authors receive 4 copies of issue.

The Door

Bob Darden, Editor
P.O. Box 530
Yreka, CA 96097
916-842-2701

AT A GLANCE:
The Door

- Evangelical, Humor
- 40% freelance
- 15% new writers
- Bimonthly
- Circ: 10,000
- Receives 20 queries, 15 mss each month.
- Pays: $60–$200 on publication.

From the Editor:
"Thoroughly familiarize yourself with the magazine. We go after 'sacred cows' and endeavor to get readers to THINK. We don't agree with everything we print."

Best Bet: Humor and satire that promotes reform and renewal in the evangelical church.

Avoid: "Cute" pieces.

Sample copy: Free with 9x12 SASE. Send #10 SASE for guidelines.

Profile

A quarterly publication of satire and humor aimed at the evangelical church, of which its editors and readers are a part. 8.5x11; glossy cover; 2-color; 36 pages.

Focus and Audience

Seeks reform and renewal of the evanagelical church through satire, humor, and honest evaluation of issues concerning the church. Readers are evangelical Christians with a sense of humor.

Interests and Word Lengths

- *Nonfiction:* National Lampoon-type humorous and satirical essays and opinion pieces that look honestly at the issues concerning the evangelical church. Written in a spirit that promotes reform and renewal. Topics of interest include spirituality and social and world issues. 750–1,500 words.

How to Submit

Query with a short excerpts. Include SASE. No unsolicited manuscripts. Accepts computer printouts. Simultaneous submissions okay. Reports in 3 months.

Payment and Policies

First North American serial rights or one-time rights. Pays on publication. $60–$200 per piece. Authors receive 6 copies of the issue.

Dovetail

A Newsletter By and For Jewish-Christian Families

Joan C. Hawxhurst, Editor
3014A Folsom Street
Boulder, CO 80304
303-444-8713

AT A GLANCE:

DOVETAIL

- Interfaith, Family
- 60% freelance
- 50% new writers
- Bimonthly
- Circ: 800
- Receives 3–4 queries, 0–1 ms each month.
- Pays: $20 per piece on publication.

From the Editor:
"Believing that there are no definitive answers to the questions facing interfaith couples, *Dovetail* strives to be open to all ideas and opinions."

Best Bet: Anything relating to Jewish-Christian relationships or families.

Avoid: Negative, judgmental, dogmatic pieces.

Sample copy: $3.50 with 6x9 SAE and $.52 postage. No guidelines.

Profile

A bimonthly newsletter devoted exclusively to the challenges and opportunities facing Jewish-Christian interfaith families. Written primarily by members of interfaith families or family therapy professionals. 8.5x11; self cover; 12 pages.

Focus and Audience

Provides a channel of communication for interfaith couples, their parents, and children. Seeks to balance and respect the perspectives of both Jewish and Christian partners and offers information and resources. Read by interfaith partners, their families, clergy, therapists, and counselors.

Interests and Word Lengths

- *Nonfiction:* Personality profiles of interfaith couples. Profiles of interfaith and family programs and resources. Opinion pieces, statistics, and book reviews. Material must relate to life in a Jewish-Christian family. 600–1,000 words.
- *Photos:* B/W and color prints.

How to Submit

Query with outline and writing samples, or send complete ms with cover letter. Include SASE. Accepts photocopies, computer printouts, Macintosh 3.5-inch disks, faxes, and submissions via modem. Simultaneous submissions okay. Reports in 1–2 months.

Payment and Policies

One-time rights. Pays on publication. $20 per piece. Authors receive up to 5 copies of the issue.

Dreams & Visions

Steve Stanton, Editor
RR 1
Washago, ON L0K 2B0
Canada

AT A GLANCE:
DREAMS & VISIONS

- Christian, Fiction
- 100% freelance
- 80% new writers
- 3 issues a year
- Circ: 300
- Receives 20 queries, 20 mss each month.
- No payment. Offers $100 honorarium for best work of year.

From the Editor:
"Know that certain topics have already been exhausted by our authors in the first few years. Please study several back issues before submitting."

Best Bet: New, innovative, or unique Christian fiction.

Avoid: Poetry; stories that glorify violence or perversity; rehashed Bible stories; and "scientific" explanations for miracles.

Sample copy: $3.95. Send #10 SASE/IRC for guidelines.

Profile

A serialized literary anthology of short Christian fiction. Est.: 1989. 5.5x8.5; heavy bond cover; 52 pages.

Focus and Audience

Showcases Christian authors of short literary fiction that might not otherwise be published in commercial markets because of Christian content. Ultimate purpose is to glorify Jesus Christ and lead readers to a deeper relationship with Him.

Interests and Word Lengths

- *Fiction:* Short stories based on orthodox biblical norms or traditions that portray spiritual truths in a new, innovative, or unique way. Accepts all literary forms and genres: metafiction, science fiction, humor, fantasy, magic realism as well as contemporary and inspirational fiction. No rehashed Bible stories in modern or ancient garb or "scientific" explanations of historical miracles. 2,000–6,000 words.

How to Submit

Send complete ms with cover letter. Include SASE. U.S. authors send IRCs. Accepts photocopies, computer printouts, 3.5- and 5.25-inch disks, and submissions via modem by appointment. Simultaneous submissions okay. Reports in 2 months.

Payment and Policies

First North American serial rights and non-exclusive reprint rights. No payment. Stories are eligible for a $100 honorarium that accompanies the annual Dreams & Visions Award for the Best of the Year. Authors receive 1–2 copies of the issue.

Ecumenical Trends

William Carpe, Editor
P.O. Box 16136
Ludlow, KY 41016
606-581-6216

AT A GLANCE: ECUMENICAL TRENDS

- Interfaith, Theology
- 95% freelance
- Monthly
- Circ: 1,700
- Pays on publication. Rates vary.

From the Editor:
"We solicit all of the material we publish."

Best Bet: Comparative analysis of all world religions.

Sample copy: Not provided. Send #10 SASE for guidelines.

Profile
A monthly magazine of interreligious dialog and analysis. Published by the Graymoor Ecumenical and Interreligious Institute. 8.5x11; 16 pages.

Focus and Audience
Emphasizes ecumenical and comparative views on all world religions. Read by the ecumenical officers of churches and dioceses, pastors, religious educators, and interested lay people.

Interests and Word Lengths
- *Nonfiction:* All material is assigned. Articles, essays, and comparative analyses of the doctrines, theologies, and cultures of all world religions. 3,000–4,000 words.
- *Photos:* B/W prints.

How to Submit
Query with outline and writing samples. Include SASE. Accepts photocopies, computer printouts, and IBM-compatible disks. Report time varies.

Payment and Policies
Rights vary. Pays on publication. Rates vary. Authors receive 2 copies of the issue.

Educational Ministries Buyers

Editor
165 Plaza Drive
Prescott, AZ 86303
800-221-0910

Profile

A monthly publication for Christian educators. 8.5x11; 28–32 pages.

Focus and Audience

Offers practical suggestions and ideas for use in church groups and programs. Readers are ministers, principals and others associated with Christian education.

Interests and Word Lengths

- *Nonfiction:* Practical how-to articles on program ideas that have proven success in church groups. Categories are children's programs, youth programs, and adult programs. 500–1,500 words. Accepts seasonal material.

How to Submit

Send complete ms with cover letter. Include SASE. Accepts photocopies, computer printouts, and fax submissions (602-771-8621). No simultaneous submissions. Reports in 1–2 months.

Payment and Policies

One-time rights. Pays on publication. $.03 per word. Authors receive 2 copies of the issue.

Emmanuel

Rev. Anthony Schueller, S.S.S., Editor
5384 Wilson Mills Road
Cleveland, OH 44143-3092
216-449-2103

AT A GLANCE:

EMMANUEL

- Catholic, Clergy
- 33% freelance
- 20% new writers
- 10 issues a year
- Circ: 5,100
- Receives 6 mss each month.
- Pays: $100 per piece on publication.

From the Editor:
"Be practical and inspirational."

Best Bet: Articles that stress eucharistic spirituality.

Avoid: Exclusive (i.e., gender specific) language.

Sample copy: $3. Send #10 SASE for guidelines.

Profile

A magazine of eucharistic spirituality for those in the Catholic ministry. 5.5x8.5; 64 pages.

Focus and Audience

Aimed at Catholic priests, religious, and others in church ministry with the belief that spirituality and liturgy cut across ideological lines, are motivating and uplifting.

Interests and Word Lengths

- *Nonfiction:* Articles on prayer, eucharistic spirituality, liturgy, and biblical exegesis and application. 2,000–2,500 words.
- *Poetry:* Publishes 1 poem per issue.

How to Submit

Send complete ms with cover letter and resume. Include SASE. Accepts photocopies, computer printouts, and WordPerfect 5.1 disk submissions. No simultaneous submissions. Reports in 1 month.

Payment and Policies

First North American serial rights. Pays on publication. $100 per article. Authors receive 5 copies of the issue.

Emphasis on Faith and Living

Robert Ransom, Editor
P.O. Box 9127
Fort Wayne, IN 46899
219-747-2027

AT A GLANCE:
EMPHASIS ON FAITH AND LIVING

- Christian, Denominational
- 0–10% freelance
- 0–2% new writers
- Bimonthly
- Circ: 13,000
- Receives 1 query, 10 mss each month.
- Pays: $.03–$.04 per word on publication.

From the Editor:
"We select only a few unsolicited articles due to space parameters."

Best Bet: Short articles that offer spiritual inspiration and foster Christian growth.

Avoid: Purely anecdotal material; handwritten submissions.

Sample copy: Free with 9x12 SAE and $.52 postage. Send #10 SASE for guidelines.

Profile
A national denominational magazine of the Missionary Church, Inc. 8.5x11; 16 pages.

Focus and Audience
Contains inspirational personal testimonies of faith and spiritual growth for members of the Missionary Church.

Interests and Word Lengths
- *Fiction:* Inspirational short stories, 300–500 words.
- *Nonfiction:* Short, inspirational feature articles, essays, and personal experiences of Christian spiritual growth. 300–500 words.

How to Submit
Fiction, send complete ms with cover letter. Nonfiction, query with outline or send complete ms with cover letter. Include SASE. Accepts photocopies, computer printouts, 3.5-inch IBM-compatible disks, and fax submissions. Simultaneous submissions okay. Reports in 2–6 months.

Payment and Policies
One-time rights. Pays on publication. $.03–$.04 per word. Authors receive 1 copy of the issue.

Environment & Art Letter

David Philippart, Editor
1800 North Hermitage Avenue
Chicago, IL 60622-1101
312-486-8970

AT A GLANCE:
ENVIRONMENT & ART LETTER

- Catholic, Art and Architecture
- 90% freelance
- 15% new writers
- Monthly
- Circ: 3,000
- Receives 2–3 queries, 1 ms each month.
- Pays: $25 per manuscript page on publication.

From the Editor:
"We place heavy emphasis on visuals. Submit photos, drawings, and illustrations with articles."

Best Bet: Articles on religious art and architecture.

Sample copy: Free. Send #10 SASE for guidelines.

Profile

A forum on religious art and architecture. Published monthly by Liturgy Training Publications under the auspices of the Archdiocese of Chicago. 8.5x11; glossy cover; 12 pages.

Focus and Audience

Explores religious and secular architecture, art, and how physical surroundings can influence and enhance liturgy and worship. Aimed at Roman Catholic and other High Liturgy churches: Methodist, Lutheran, Episcopalian, and Presbyterian. Promotes Vatican II reforms.

Interests and Word Lengths

- *Departments:* User's Guides, addresses building maintenance. Viewpoint, opinion pieces. Exchange, short news items. A Place to Visit, short profiles with accompanying color photo of beautiful secular architectural structures that use space creatively.
- *Artwork:* B/W and color prints or slides to accompany manuscripts. Accepts line drawings and floor plans.

How to Submit

Query with outline. Include SASE. Prefers WordPerfect disk submissions. Accepts photocopies, computer printouts, and faxed queries. Simultaneous submissions okay. Reports in 4 months.

Payment and Policies

All rights. Pays on publication. $25 per ms page. Authors receive 5 copies of the issue.

Epiphany Journal

Fr. Michael Crowley, Editor
P.O. Box 2250
South Portland, ME 04116-2250
207-767-1889

AT A GLANCE:

EPIPHANY JOURNAL

- Christian, Contemporary Issues
- 90% freelance
- 40–50% new writers
- Quarterly
- Circ: not available
- Receives few queries, 1–2 mss each month.
- No payment. Offers 2 contributor's copies.

From the Editor:
"Write with a Christian slant on issues such as invitro fertilization."

Best Bet: Articles on education and ecology viewed from a traditional Christian spirituality.

Avoid: Fiction; fundamentalist or evangelical viewpoints.

Sample copy: Free. Send #10 SASE for guidelines.

Profile

A quarterly journal of commentary on contemporary issues for Christians. 8x10; 48–96 pages.

Focus and Audience

Offers a look at contemporary religious and social issues from a traditional Christian viewpoint. Readers are those interested in how a traditional Christian would deal with controversial modern issues.

Interests and Word Lengths

- *Nonfiction:* Essays, articles, and interviews that offer Christian perspectives on issues such as spirituality, education, ethics, social and world issues, and ecology and the environment. Essays, 1,000–3,000 words. Articles, 2,000–5,000 words.
- *Departments:* Book Reviews, 800–1,000 words.

How to Submit

Query with outline and writing samples. Include SASE. Accepts photocopies, computer printouts, and IBM-compatible disks. Simultaneous submissions okay. Reports in 2 months.

Payment and Policies

Rights vary No payment. Authors receive 2 copies of the issue.

Episcopal Life

Edward Stannard, News Editor
Nan Cobbey, Features Editor
815 Second Avenue
New York, NY 10017
800-334-7626

AT A GLANCE:

EPISCOPAL LIFE

- Episcopal, News
- 40–50% freelance
- 10% new writers
- Monthly
- Circ: 170,000
- Receives 15 queries; 60 mss each month.
- Pays: $50–$200 on publication.

From the Editor:
"Inform, challenge, and educate Episcopalians. Write in a newspaper style."

Best Bet: Articles on ministries among Hispanics, Blacks, and migrant workers relevant to the Episcopal Church.

Avoid: Long articles.

Sample copy: Free. No guidelines.

Profile

The national publication of the United States Episcopal Church, published monthly by The Domestic and Foreign Missionary Society under the auspices of the General Convention of the Episcopal Church. Tabloid-size; newsprint; 32 pages.

Focus and Audience

News and features of regional, national, and international interest to Episcopalians.

Interests and Word Lengths

- *Nonfiction:* News interviews, and features of regional, national, or international interest to Episcopalians. Ministries among Hispanics, Blacks, and migrant workers are of particular interest. 900–1,000 words.
- *Departments:* As I See It, personal opinions on current topics relevant to the church and society. 900–1,000 words.
- *Filler:* Short poetry and seasonal material.
- *Artwork:* Query first; B/W prints and illustrations.

How to Submit

Query with outline, or send complete ms with cover letter. Include SASE. Accepts photocopies, computer printouts, Macintosh and WordPerfect disks, and fax submissions. Simultaneous submissions okay. Reports in 2 months.

Payment and Policies

Authors retain rights. Pays on publication. $50–$200 per piece. Kill fee, 50%. Authors receive 1 copy of the issue.

Evangel

Vera Bethel, Editor
P.O. Box 535002
Indianapolis, IN 46253-5002
317-244-3660

AT A GLANCE:

EVANGEL

- Evangelical, Fiction
- 100% freelance
- 50% new writers
- Weekly
- Circ: 25,000
- Receives 300 mss each month.
- Pays: $25–$45 on acceptance.

From the Editor:
"Material needs to have a definitely Christian frame of reference in dealing with current affairs. Because we have a long-range publication schedule, however, don't focus on news that is too timely."

Best Bet: Male viewpoint stories and Christmas stories.

Avoid: Sermonic, encyclopedic writing. Stories you wouldn't read yourself.

Sample copy: Free with 6x9 SAE and $.52 postage. Send #10 SASE for guidelines.

Profile

An evangelical Christian Sunday school take-home paper for adults. 5.5x8; paper cover; spot color; 8 pages.

Focus and Audience

Compelling fiction and personal experiences with an evangelical Christian frame of reference. Most readers are married women who live in small towns or rural areas.

Interests and Word Lengths

- *Fiction:* Heart-stopping contemporary stories involving a young adult who faces a crisis. Must have a Christian viewpoint but not necessarily a happy ending. Begin stories with action, not setting. Interested in stories written from a male perspective and Christmas stories. 1,200 words.
- *Nonfiction:* Personal experiences—heart warming or chilling—of people who have made significant contributions to church or community projects. Use facts, quotes, and anecdotes. 1,000 words.
- *Filler:* Devotionals that are not preachy and explore a single concept. 300–500 words.
- *Poetry:* Short, evocative poetry, rhyming or free verse. 8–16 lines.
- *Photos:* B/W photos, especially to illustrate articles.

How to Submit

Send complete ms. Include SASE. Accepts computer printouts. Simultaneous submissions okay. Reports in 1 month.

Payment and Policies

One-time rights. Pays on acceptance. Fiction, $45. Personal experiences, $25. Authors receive 2 copies of the issue.

The Evangelical Beacon

Susan Brill, Assistant Editor
901 East 78th Street
Minneapolis, MN 55420
612-853-8491

AT A GLANCE:

THE EVANGELICAL BEACON

- Evangelical, Denominational
- 15% freelance
- 5% new writers
- 8 times a year
- Circ: 37,000
- Receives 25 queries, 75 mss each month.
- Pays: $.03–$.07 on publication.

From the Editor:
"Articles should fit themes on the editorial calendar and be compatible with the twelve articles of the EFCA Statement of Faith."

Best Bet: Articles relating to the EFCA, individual Free Churches, or individuals associated with the Evangelical Free Church.

Avoid: Controversy; dividing forces.

Sample copy: Free. Send #10 SASE for guidelines.

Profile

The official magazine of the Evangelical Free Church of America (EFCA). 8.5x11; glossy cover; 4-color; 40 pages.

Focus and Audience

Role is to support and encourage, unite and edify, members and friends of the EFCA. Readers are members and friends of the Evangelical Free Church and include a spectrum of age groups, economic levels, professions, and heritage.

Interests and Word Lengths

- *Nonfiction:* Articles relating to the EFCA and/or of interest its members. Subjects include lay counseling, prophecy, and issues confronting the church. All should fit themes on editorial calendar. 500–2,000 words.
- *Filler:* News blurbs.
- *Photos:* B/W prints and illustrations.

How to Submit

Send complete ms with cover letter. Accepts photocopies, computer printouts, ASCII and Macintosh disks, and fax submissions. Simultaneous submissions okay. Reports in 4–6 weeks.

Payment and Policies

First rights, $.07 per word. Reprints, $.03 per word. Pays on publication. Authors receive 3 copies of the issue.

Evangelizing Today's Child

Elsie Lippy, Editor
Box 348
Warrenton, MO 63383
314-456-4321

AT A GLANCE:

Evangelizing Today's Child

- Christian, Religious Education
- 10–25% freelance
- 10–25% new writers
- Bimonthly
- Circ: 22,000
- Receives 25 queries, 40 mss each month.
- Pays: $.06–$.10 per word on publication.

From the Editor:
"We look for practical, innovative, and educationally sound material, plus a skillful writing style. We prefer writers who are actively involved with children."

Best Bet: Fiction and educational material that can be used by teachers to bring children to Christ.

Avoid: Denomination issues.

Sample copy: Free with 9x12 SAE and 5 first-class stamps. Send #10 SASE for guidelines.

Profile

A bimonthly magazine for Christian education leaders. Published by the Child Evangelism Fellowship, an organization of born-again Christians who work to evangelize children with the Gospel. 8.5x11; glossy cover; full-color; 64 pages.

Focus and Audience

Equips Christians to win the world's children to Christ and disciple them. Readers are Sunday school teachers, Christian education leaders, and children's workers that minister to children up to 12 years old.

Interests and Word Lengths

- *Fiction:* Short stories for children dealing with real-life problems. Must be contemporary and have a scriptural solution worked into the story practically and believably. 800–1,000 words.
- *Nonfiction:* Feature articles that include teaching principles, reader instruction, and classroom illustrations, 1,200–1,500 words. Impact Features are human interest accounts of a conversion experienced by a person when he or she was under 12 years of age, 700–900 words. Resource Center includes short, creative teaching tips such as seasonal ideas and Bible drills. Must fit on a 3- x 5-inch card. See guidelines.
- *Photos:* Prefers color transparencies. Accepts B/W or color prints for inside illustrations.

How to Submit

Query with outline. Include writing samples for fiction. SASE. Accepts photocopies and letter-quality printouts. Simultaneous submissions okay. Reports in 1–2 months.

Payment and Policies

First North American serial or all rights and reprint rights. Pays on publication. Features, $.08–$.10 per word. Fiction, $.06 per word. Resource Center, $10–$25. Kill fee, 25% if assigned. Authors receive 1 copy of issue.

Expressions

Sefra Kobrin Pitzele, Editor
P.O. Box 16294
St. Paul, MN 55116-0294
612-451-1208

AT A GLANCE:

EXPRESSIONS

- Disabilities, Health
- 100% freelance
- 40% new writers
- 2 issues a year
- Circ: 500
- Receives 25–50 queries, 10–15 mss each month.
- No payment. Offers 2 contributor's copies.

From the Editor:
"*Expressions* is open to anyone who has a disability or health problem, regardless of publishing history. Please follow our guidelines."

Avoid: Limericks, pornography, and poor-me stories.

Sample copy: $5 with 6x9 SAE and $1.04 postage. Send #10 SASE for guidelines.

Profile

A semi-annual magazine featuring the writings and art of people with disabilities or chronic illnesses. 5.5x8.5; glossy cover; B/W; 72 pages.

Focus and Audience

Open to writing on any topic from writers with disabilities or chronic health problems. Readers are those who have, are interested in, or care for others with ongoing health issues.

Interests and Word Lengths

- *Fiction:* All topics are welcome. Must be written by a person with a disability or illness. Up to 1,500 words.
- *Nonfiction:* All topics are welcome. Must be written by a person with a disability or illness. 1,500 words maximum. Book reviews, 2–4 per issue on health-related books.
- *Poetry:* Up to 75 lines. No rhyming poetry or limericks.

How to Submit

Send $2 reading fee for each item submitted. Request guidelines before submitting. Prefers complete ms with SASE. Include a 4–5 sentence author biography noting author's disability or illness. Accepts photocopies, computer printouts, legible handwritten submissions, and faxes (612-552-1209). Audio tapes accepted for submissions under 25 lines. Simultaneous submissions okay. Reports in 3 months.

Payment and Policies

One-time rights. No payment. Authors receive 2 copies of the issue.

Extension

Marianna Bartholomew, Managing Editor
35 East Wacker Drive, Room 400M
Chicago, IL 60601-2105
312-236-7240

AT A GLANCE:

EXTENSION

- Catholic, Missions
- 20% freelance
- 9 times a year
- Circ: 95,000
- Receives 4–5 queries, 2 mss each month
- Pays: $350–$450 on acceptance.

From the Editor:
"We are not academic. *Extension* is nearly all human interest stories about mission work. We try to cover topics of current interest before they hit the other magazines."

Best Bet: Regional articles about local church customs in the South, Southwest, and Alaska. Also ethnic church customs.

Avoid: Poetry and fiction.

Sample copy: Free. Send #10 SASE for guidelines.

Profile

A Catholic mission magazine. Published by the Catholic Church Extension Society of the United States for its members. Est.: 1906. 8.5x11; glossy cover; full-color; 32 pages.

Focus and Audience

Reports on the Catholic mission work done in rural and remote parts of the U.S. and American territories. Aims to describe and explain current Catholic teachings and practices as it serves as a fund raising vehicle for the Extension Society. Distributed free to donors.

Interests and Word Lengths

- *Nonfiction:* Features, personality profiles, and personal experiences concerning current issues involving missionary work, religious education, evangelization, vocations, campus ministry, and development of mission areas served by Extension. Articles should describe how issues impact the home missions, what historical trends have shaped the missionary church, and what new innovations home missionaries are using to evangelize their local communities. Up to 1,500 words.
- *Photos:* B/W or color prints or slides. Needs full-color photos of church scenes in rural America.

How to Submit

Query with outline, resume, and clips. Include SASE. Accepts photocopies, computer printouts, and Macintosh or IBM-ASCII disk submissions. Simultaneous submissions okay.

Payment and Policies

One-time rights. Pays on acceptance. $350–$450 per piece. Authors receive copies of the issue.

Faith and Renewal

Joan Blattner, Editor
P.O. Box 7354
Ann Arbor, MI 48107
313-761-8505

AT A GLANCE:
FAITH AND RENEWAL

- Christian, Leadership
- 10% freelance
- 1% new writers
- Bimonthly
- Circ: 8,000
- Receives 5–6 queries each month.
- Pays: Up to $100 on publication.

From the Editor:
"Consult back issues to ascertain what we are about before writing us."

Best Bet: How-to articles.

Avoid: First-person and personality pieces.

Sample copy: Not provided. No guidelines.

Profile
An ecumenical, interdenominational journal for Christian leaders. Published bimonthly. 8.5x11; 16 pages.

Focus and Audience
Provides practical information and advice to pastors and lay leaders—especially those involved in church renewal.

Interests and Word Lengths
- *Nonfiction:* How-to articles for Christian leaders. Interests include theology, evangelism, and family life. 4,000 words.

How to Submit
Send complete ms with cover letter. Include SASE. Accepts photocopies and computer printouts. No simultaneous submissions. Reports within 1 month.

Payment and Policies
First North American serial rights. Pays on publication. Up to $100 per piece. Authors receive copies of the issue.

Faith 'n Stuff

Editor
16 East 34th Street
New York, NY 10016
212-251-8100

AT A GLANCE:
FAITH 'N STUFF

- Christian, Juvenile
- 15% freelance
- 5% new writers
- Bimonthly
- Circ: 100,000+
- Receives 200+ mss each month.
- Pays on acceptance. Rates vary.

From the Editor:
"We are not a Sunday school take-home paper—no preachy stories about Bible-toting kids. Be original and make it fun, kid-friendly, and good. We are not afraid to tackle tough or controversial subjects."

Best Bet: Relevant, playful, fun stories and articles with international flavor.

Avoid: Preachy stories; wisdom-giving adults.

Sample copy: $3.25 with 10x13 SAE and $1.21 postage. Send #10 SASE for guidelines.

Profile
A nondenominational Bible-based recreational magazine for children. 8.5x11; full-color; 132 pages.

Focus and Audience
Aims to provide fun, kid-friendly, Bible-based, value-centered writing that respects children and their intelligence and sensibilities. Seeks creative, thought-provoking, issue-oriented, controversial material of interest to 7- to 12-year-old readers.

Interests and Word Lengths
- *Fiction:* Submit to Lurlene McDaniel. Mysteries, fantasy and historical stories, and science fiction, especially those with international themes. No adult problem-solving. Write to an 11- to 12-year-old level. 1,200–1,500 words.
- *Nonfiction:* Submit to Wally "Sailor" Metts. Issue-oriented features on topics of interest to children, especially the issues about which kids need to know. Interviews with kids who are doing fun or unusual things. Features, 1,500 words. Secondary features, 700 words.
- *Departments:* Submit to Wally "Sailor" Metts. Featuring Kids, profiles of winners, achievers, overcomers, and creators as well as stories of kids from other cultures, foreign or domestic. 300–600 words. Tips from the Top, interviews with Christian celebrities. 600 words.
- *Filler:* Trivia, up to 300 words. Original puzzles and mazes; no Bible word searches or the like.

How to Submit
Fiction, send complete ms with cover letter. Nonfiction, query with outline, or send ms with cover letter. Include SASE. Accepts photocopies and computer printouts. Simultaneous submissions okay. Reports in 6–8 weeks.

Payment and Policies
All rights. Pays on acceptance. Rates vary but are competitive. Authors receive copies of the issue.

Faith Today

Audrey Dorsch, Managing Editor
175 Rivera Drive, #1
Markham, ON L3R 5J6
Canada
416-479-5885

Profile

A news and feature magazine for the evangelical Christian community in Canada. Published by the Evangelical Fellowship of Canada. Member of the Canadian Church Press. 8.5x11; glossy cover; full-color; 4 pages.

Focus and Audience

Aims to track "the footprints of God across the land," giving insights on current issues and informing about people and resources active in Canada. Readers are professionals, business people, pastors, and Christian leaders between the ages of 25–45.

Interests and Word Lengths

- *Nonfiction:* Features of current topics and issues of concern to Canadian church and society; brief news accounts of Canadian interest; profiles of Canadian evangelicals outstanding for some aspect of their faith in practice. Up to 2,000 words.
- *Comics:* Humorous depictions of foibles observable in Christians and the Church.
- *Photos:* To accompany profiles.

How to Submit

Query with outline and clips. Include SASE. U.S. Authors include IRCs. Accepts photocopies, computer printouts, WordPerfect disks, faxes, and modem submissions. No simultaneous submissions. Reports in 2 months.

Payment and Policies

First North American serial rights. Pays on acceptance. $65–$600 (CAN). Authors receive 2 copies of the issue.

Faith at Work

Marjory Zoet Bankson, Editor
150 South Washington Street, Suite 204
Falls Church, VA 22046
703-237-3426

AT A GLANCE:
FAITH AT WORK

- Christian, Spiritual Growth
- 50% freelance
- 6 issues a year
- Circ: 20,000
- Receives 10 queries, 5 mss each month.
- No payment.

From the Editor:
"Tell your own experience of how and where God is working in your life, particularly in relationships at home, at work, and in your community."

Best Bet: Stories of personal or public spiritual growth.

Avoid: Advice-giving—tell your own story. Be spare and brief.

Sample copy: Free with 9x12 SASE. Send #10 SASE for guidelines.

Profile

A bimonthly interdenominational Christian magazine that witnesses personal spiritual growth and public ministry. Published by Faith at Work, Inc, a national network of Christian leaders and learners. 8.5x11; glossy cover; full-color; 16 pages.

Focus and Audience

Focuses on personal stories of putting faith to work in the world and ministry in daily life. Promotes small healing groups modeled after 12-step programs. Readers are college-educated, middle-class church-goers from across many denominations.

Interests and Word Lengths

- *Nonfiction:* First-person accounts of spiritual growth, both personal and public, especially ministry in daily life. No word-length requirements, but be concise and brief.
- *Departments:* Small Group Life; Relational Bible Study; Book Reviews; Church Renewal Events/Structures; Women's Ministry. 1,000 words.
- *Poetry:* Accepts poetry.
- *Artwork:* Line drawings.

How to Submit

Query with outline and writing samples, or send complete ms with cover letter. Include SASE. Accepts photocopies, computer printouts, faxes, and submissions via modem. Simultaneous submissions okay. Reports in 1 month.

Payment and Policies

One-time rights. No payment.

The Family
A Catholic Perspective

Submissions Editor
50 St. Paul's Avenue
Boston, MA 02130

Profile

A Catholic family magazine. Published by the Daughters of St. Paul. 8.5x11; glossy cover; 2-color; 40 pages.

Focus and Audience

Committed to helping Catholic families grow in the awareness of their heritage, in reverence for the dignity of persons, in understanding of Catholic teaching, and in holiness of purpose. Articles must be in accord with Catholic Church teachings, though many authors are of other faith traditions.

Interests and Word Lengths

- *Fiction:* Short stories, preferably drama. 1,000–1,200 words.
- *Nonfiction:* Features on family life: especially interested in interviews and true-life stories exemplifying faith at work in family life. 1,200–2,000 words. Uplifting and spiritually encouraging articles on family living. Instructional articles on living the Catholic faith today. 1,500 words.
- *Photos:* 5x7 or larger clear B/W or color prints to accompany manuscripts.

How to Submit

Fiction, submit complete ms. Features, query first. Articles under 1,500 words, authors may submit complete ms. Include SASE. Accepts letter-quality computer printouts. No simultaneous submissions. Reports in 6–8 weeks.

Payment and Policies

First North American serial rights. Pays on publication. Rates are negotiated per piece. Kill fee, 33%. Authors receive 3 copies of the issue.

The Family Digest

Corine B. Erlandson, Editor
P.O. Box 40137
Fort Wayne, IN 46804

AT A GLANCE:
THE FAMILY DIGEST

- Catholic, Family
- 85% freelance
- Bimonthly
- Circ: 150,000
- Receives several 100 mss each month.
- Pays: $.05 per word on acceptance.

From the Editor:
"Send for a sample copy and guidelines and then submit appropriate articles. Please don't send a query."

Best Bet: Articles on Catholic family and parish life.

Avoid: Fiction and poetry.

Sample copy: Free with 6x9 SAE and $.52 postage. Send #10 SASE for guidelines.

Profile
A bimonthly publication for Catholic families. Formerly *Parish Family Digest*. 5.5x7.5; 48 pages.

Focus and Audience
Edited with the concerns of Catholic families in mind—family life, parish life, and living their faith in today's world.

Interests and Word Lengths
- *Nonfiction:* Humorous, inspirational, seasonal, personal experiences, profiles, and how-to pieces on prayer, family life, parish life, religious education, and spiritual growth. 600–1,200 words.
- *Filler:* Short, real-life anecdotes.

How to Submit
Send complete ms; no queries. Include SASE. Accepts computer printouts. No simultaneous submissions. Reports in 1 month.

Payment and Policies
First North American serial rights. Pays on acceptance. $.05 per word. Authors receive 2 copies of the issue.

Fathers, Brothers, Sons

Flo McLaughlin, Publisher
1346 Joan Drive
Southampton, PA 18966-4341
215-322-1346

AT A GLANCE:

FATHERS, BROTHERS, SONS

- Men's Issues, Family
- 95% freelance
- 50% new writers
- Quarterly
- Circ: 1,000
- Receives 3 queries, 20 mss each month.
- No payment. Offers a free subscription.

From the Editor:
"Beginning writers are most welcome. Send us your reflections on the positive value of the men in your life. Share the word that most men are good men."

Best Bet: Experiences and memories of grandparents and co-workers.

Avoid: Violence; sexual overtones; negative stereotypes; dull stories or depressing biographies.

Sample copy: $3. Send #10 SASE for guidelines.

Profile

A quarterly newsletter of stories for and about men, their family relationships, and their perspective on today's values. Welcomes the work of beginning writers. 8.5x11; photocopied; stapled; 8 pages.

Focus and Audience

Offers men an opportunity to exchange ideas, experiences, and information about life's adventures. Fosters an awareness of the positive influence that good men have on their families and in other relationships. Readers are men and women who understand the importance of this positive influence in today's society.

Interests and Word Lengths

- *Fiction:* Short stories and short-short stories about men in general and their relationships with children, family, and friends. 100–1,000 words.
- *Nonfiction:* Features, essays, interviews and profiles, and true experiences about men and their relationships with the important people in their lives. Suggested topics include memories of grandparents and co-workers, father/son outings, close male friendships, a male view of childbirth and parenting, and career choices and changes. 100–1,000 words.
- *Poetry:* Encouraging, informative poems about men or from a male perspective.

How to Submit

Obtain and read guidelines before submitting. Then, send complete ms with cover letter. Include SASE. Accepts computer printouts and IBM-compatible ASCII files on 3.5- or 5.25-inch disks. Simultaneous submissions okay. Reports in 1 month.

Payment and Policies

One-time rights. No payment. Authors receive a free one-year subscription and 4 copies of the issue.

Fellowship

Richard Deates, Editor
521 North Broadway
Nyack, NY 10960
914-358-4601

AT A GLANCE:

FELLOWSHIP

- Interfaith, Non-violence
- 80% freelance
- 20% new writers
- Bimonthly
- Circ: 6,000
- No payment. Offers free subscription and copies.

From the Editor:
"Inspire, inform, and challenge contemporary thinking and non-violent action."

Best Bet: Articles on non-violent solutions to conflict and oppression.

Sample copy: $2. Send #10 SASE for guidelines.

Profile

The magazine of the Fellowship of Reconciliation, an interfaith association of women and men who have joined together to explore the power of love and truth for resolving human conflict. 8.5x11; self cover; 32 pages.

Focus and Audience

Geared toward clergy, social workers, teachers, community leaders, and others interested in non-violent solutions to conflict and oppression.

Interests and Word Lengths

- *Nonfiction:* Features, interviews, essays, personal experiences, true-stories, and group movements on non-violent solutions to resolve conflicts. 200–2,000 words.
- *Departments:* In My Opinion, op-ed; Non-Violent Problem Solving Column. Up to 750 words.
- *Filler:* Short poetry and seasonal material.
- *Photos:* B/W prints and illustrations; sharp color prints.

How to Submit

Send complete ms with cover letter. Include SASE. Accepts photocopies, computer printouts, Macintosh Microsoft Word disks, faxes, and modem submissions. Identify simultaneous submissions. Reports in 2 weeks.

Payment and Policies

One-time rights. No payment. Authors receive 10 copies of the issue and a free subscription.

Fellowship Magazine

Lori Gwynne, Managing Editor
Box 237
Barrie, ON L4M 4T3
Canada
519-323-3804

AT A GLANCE:

FELLOWSHIP MAGAZINE

- United Church of Canada, Renewal
- 20% freelance
- 5% new writers
- 5 issues a year
- Circ: 5,000
- Receives 10 queries, 10 mss each month.
- Pays on publication. Rates vary.

From the Editor:
"We generally consider only renewal-minded Canadian writers who are present or past members of a mainline denomination."

Best Bet: Practical, personal articles on church renewal.

Sample copy: Free with $.43 (CAN) postage. No guidelines.

Profile

A renewal-minded magazine for members of the United Church of Canada. Published by the United Church Renewal Fellowship. 8.5x11; glossy cover; 32 pages.

Focus and Audience

Committed to upholding the historic Christian faith within the United Church of Canada. Read and written primarily by renewal-minded Canadians in the United Church or other mainline denominations.

Interests and Word Lengths

- *Nonfiction:* Practical, first-person articles on church renewal and theological topics. Interests include denominational concerns, family issues, prayer, social and world issues, and spirituality. No word-length restrictions.
- *Seasonal:* Accepts Christmas and Easter articles.
- *Artwork:* Open to all styles and types of photos and illustrations.

How to Submit

Query with outline and resume. Include SASE. U.S. authors include IRCs. Accepts computer printouts. Simultaneous submissions okay. Reports in 2–3 months.

Payment and Policies

Rights negotiable. Pays on publication. Rates vary. Authors receive 2–3 copies of the issue.

Focus on the Family

Mike Yorkey, Editor
8655 Explorer Drive
Colorado Springs, CO 80920
719-531-3400

AT A GLANCE:
FOCUS ON THE FAMILY

- Christian, Family
- 20% freelance
- 5% new writers
- Monthly
- Circ: 1,800,000
- Receives 10–20
  queries, 40–60 mss
  each month.
- Pays: $100–$500 on
  acceptance.

From the Editor:
"The Focus on the Family ministry produces several radio programs and magazines as well as family-oriented books, films, videos, and audio cassettes."

Best Bet: First-person experience articles dealing with marriage and parenting.

Avoid: Articles on the death or illness of a child or spouse.

Sample copy: Free with 9x12 SAE with $.52 postage. Send #10 SASE for guidelines.

Profile
An organizational publication of the Focus on the Family ministry, which produces a variety of family-oriented media. Member of the Evangelical Christian Publishers Association. 8x11; glossy cover; full-color; 16 pages.

Focus and Audience
Dedicated to strengthening the home and family.

Interests and Word Lengths
- *Nonfiction:* Articles and first-person pieces on family, marriage, and parenting issues, all from a Christian perspective. No word lengths specified.

How to Submit
Send complete ms with cover letter and resume. Include SASE. Accepts computer printouts and WordPerfect disks. Simultaneous submissions okay. Reports in 1 month.

Payment and Policies
One-time rights. Pays on acceptance. $100–$500 per piece. Kill fee, 33%. Authors receive up to 100 copies of the issue.

Focus on the Family Clubhouse

Linda Piepenbrink, Editor
25 North Cascade Avenue
Colorado Springs, CO 80903
719-531-3400

AT A GLANCE:
FOCUS ON THE FAMILY CLUBHOUSE

- Christian, Juvenile
- 2% freelance
- 1% new writers
- Monthly
- Circ: 100,000
- Receives 3–5 queries, 30–40 mss each month
- Pays: $75–$425 on acceptance.

From the Editor:
"The best stories are the products of writers who share in the adventure, exploring the characters they have created."

Best Bet: Fresh exciting literature with descriptive prose, interesting, well-developed characters, and good plot.

Avoid: Stereotypes; Christian clichés; moralizing and preaching.

Sample copy: Free with 9x12 SAE and $.52 postage. Send #10 SASE for guidelines.

Profile
A monthly Christian magazine for children ages 8–12. Published by Focus on the Family. 9x12; glossy cover; 16 pages.

Focus and Audience
Aims to promote biblical thinking, values, and behavior in every area of life, not just in the religious arena, for 8- to 12-year-old children.

Interests and Word Lengths
- *Fiction:* Stories built upon a Christian foundation. Fantasy and science fiction that reflects Christian views. Bible stories. Read-to-me stories for parents to read aloud 500–1,400 words.
- *Nonfiction:* Biographies of famous people from other ages and cultures whose Christian experience holds lessons today; science and nature; human interest about remarkable contemporary children and adults. Read-to-me articles, 200–1,000 words.
- *Seasonal:* Submit 6–9 months in advance.
- *Poetry:* Should capture intense experiences or thoughts by means of creative, evocative language. Up to half a page.
- *Filler:* Creative and some biblically based puzzles and games. Humorous cartoons.

How to Submit
Send complete ms with cover letter and resume. Include SASE. Accepts photocopies and computer printouts. No simultaneous submissions. Reports in 4–6 weeks.

Payment and Policies
First North American serial rights. Pays on acceptance. Fiction and nonfiction, $75–$425 depending on length, subject, and editing required. Poetry, $5–$25. Authors receive 2 copies of the issue.

Focus on the Family Clubhouse Jr.

Linda Piepenbrink, Editor
25 North Cascade Avenue
Colorado Springs, CO 80903
719-531-3400

AT A GLANCE:

FOCUS ON THE FAMILY CLUBHOUSE JR.

- Christian, Juvenile
- 2% freelance
- 1% new writers
- Monthly
- Circ: 100,000
- Receives 3–5 queries, 30–40 mss each month
- Pays: $75–$425 on acceptance.

From the Editor:
"The best stories are the products of writers who share in the adventure, exploring the characters they have created."

Best Bet: Fresh exciting literature with descriptive prose, interesting, well-developed characters, and good plot.

Avoid: Stereotypes; Christian clichés; moralizing and preaching.

Sample copy: Free with 9x12 SAE and $.52 postage. Send #10 SASE for guidelines.

Profile

A monthly Christian magazine for children ages 4–8. Published by Focus on the Family. 9x12; glossy cover; 16 pages.

Focus and Audience

Aims to promote biblical thinking, values, and behavior in every area of life, not just in the religious arena, for 4- to 8-year-old children.

Interests and Word Lengths

- *Fiction:* Stories built upon a Christian foundation. Fantasy and science fiction that reflects Christian views. Bible stories. Read-to-me stories for parents to read aloud. 500–1,100 words. Beginning reader stories. 250–650 words.
- *Nonfiction:* Biographies of famous people from other ages and cultures whose Christian experience holds lessons today; science and nature; human interest about remarkable contemporary children and adults. Read-to-me articles, 200–1,000 words.
- *Seasonal:* Submit 6–9 months in advance.
- *Poetry:* Should capture intense experiences or thoughts by means of creative, evocative language. Up to half a page.
- *Filler:* Creative and some biblically based puzzles and games. Humorous cartoons.

How to Submit

Send complete ms with cover letter and resume. Include SASE. Accepts photocopies and computer printouts. No simultaneous submissions. Reports in 4–6 weeks.

Payment and Policies

First North American serial rights. Pays on acceptance. Fiction and nonfiction, $75–$425 depending on length, subject, and editing required. Poetry, $5–$25. Authors receive 2 copies of the issue.

Foursquare World Advance

Ronald D. Williams, Editor
1910 West Sunset Boulevard
Suite 200
Los Angeles, CA 90026
213-484-2400

Profile

The official publication of the International Church of the Foursquare Gospel. 8.5x11; glossy cover; full-color; 24 pages.

Focus and Audience

Provides devotional material and church-related information to members of the International Church of the Foursquare Gospel.

Interests and Word Lengths

- *Fiction:* Topics of interest to church members, 1,200 words.
- *Nonfiction:* Bible study, doctrine, evangelism, family life, personal experiences, prayer, social and world issues, women's issues, and worship. 1,200 words.

How to Submit

Send complete ms. Include SASE. Accepts computer printouts. Simultaneous submissions okay. Reports in 1 month.

Payment and Policies

First North American serial or one-time rights. Pays on publication. $75 per piece. Authors receive 3–5 copies of the issue.

Free Press

Rebecca A. Shank, Editor
P.O. Box 685
Hagerstown, MD 21741
301-739-1166

AT A GLANCE:

FREE PRESS

- Christian, Evangelical
- Monthly
- Circ: 35,000–40,000
- Receives varied number of mss each month.
- No payment. Offers contributor's copies.

From the Editor:
"Review several copies of *Free Press* before submitting your work."

Best Bet: Gospel-based articles.

Avoid: Controversial political issues.

Sample copy: Free. No guidelines.

Profile
An inspirational newspaper for evangelical Christians. Published monthly by the Union Rescue Mission. Tabloid-size; newsprint; 24 pages.

Focus and Audience
Gospel-based articles that teach, inspire and inform a diverse group of Christian readers.

Interests and Word Lengths
- *Fiction:* Does not presently publish fiction but is willing to review well-written short stories appropriate to the magazine's interests.
- *Nonfiction:* Features, interviews, essays, and personal experiences that present biblical values to Christians. Interests include evangelism, inspiration, prayer, and missionary work. 350–1,000 words.
- *Photos:* B/W glossy prints.

How to Submit
Query with outline. Include SASE. Accepts photocopies, computer printouts, and fax submissions (301-739-1169). No simultaneous submissions. Report time varies.

Payment and Policies
Authors retain rights. No payment. Authors receive copies of the issue.

FreeWay

Amy J. Cox, Editor
1825 College Avenue
Wheaton, IL 60187
708-668-6000

AT A GLANCE:
FreeWay

- Christian, Young Adults
- Weekly
- 95% freelance
- 25% new writers
- Circ: not available
- Receives 60–120 mss each month.
- Pays: $.06–$.10 per word on acceptance.

From the Editor:
"We accept only material with a conservative, evangelical slant. Get to know *FreeWay* before you submit. *Show,* don't tell, through your writing."

Best Bet: Contemporary, realistic articles and stories that show God's character.

Avoid: Preaching, moralizing, sermonizing, or talking down to young people.

Sample copy: And guidelines free with #10 SASE.

Profile

A conservative, evangelical Sunday school take-home paper for young adults. Published quarterly in weekly sections. 8.5x11; folded; 4 pages.

Focus and Audience

Seeks to show high school- and college-age young people how biblical principles for Christian living can be applied to everyday life.

Interests and Word Lengths

- *Fiction:* True-to-life and humorous stories, allegories, and parables. Write about everyday issues such as friendship, peer pressure, witnessing to friends, taking a stand for what you believe, family life, honesty, and prayer. 600–1,200 words.
- *Nonfiction:* Especially interested in true personal experiences of those living the Christian life. Also accepts interviews and profiles, self-help/how-to pieces, anecdotes, Bible studies, and articles on friendship, dating, and other topics relevant to young adults. Up to 1,200 words.
- *Poetry:* Occasionally accepts poetry.
- *Seasonal:* Submit 6 months in advance. Material on Christian holidays. Avoid strictly American holidays such as the Fourth of July or Thanksgiving.
- *Photos:* Submit to Sue Jensen.

How to Submit

Send complete ms with cover letter. Include SASE. Submit seasonal material 6 months in advance. Accepts photocopies and computer printouts. Reports in 2–3 months.

Payment and Policies

One-time rights. Pays on acceptance. $.06–$.10 per word. Authors receive 4 copies of the issue.

Friend

Rex D. Pinegar, Editor
50 East North Temple, 23rd Floor
Salt Lake City, UT 84037
801-240-2210

AT A GLANCE:
FRIEND

- Mormon, Juvenile
- Monthly
- Circ: 235,000
- Receives 300+ mss each month
- Pays: $.10 per word on acceptance.

From the Editor:
"All submissions are carefully read by our staff and those not accepted are returned within two months when a SASE is enclosed."

Best Bet: Stories of boys and girls resolving a conflict; stories of substance for younger children; humorous pieces.

Avoid: Biographies of living people.

Sample copy: $.75 with 9x12 SAE and $1 postage. Send #10 SASE for guidelines.

Profile

Published monthly by The Church of Jesus Christ of Latter-day Saints (LDS) for boys and girls up to 12 years of age. 8.5x11; glossy cover; full-color; 48 pages.

Focus and Audience

Publishes stories and articles with universal settings, conflicts, and characters. Geared towards LDS children ages 3–12.

Interests and Word Lengths

- *Fiction:* Short stories that focus on character-building qualities and are wholesome without moralizing. Stories showing children resolving conflicts are of particular interest. Up to 1,000 words.
- *Nonfiction:* Wholesome, character-building articles on topics including sports, science, holidays, and other cultures. Up to 250 words for younger readers; up to 1,000 words for older readers.
- *Poetry:* Uplifting and of substance, evoking positive emotions and worthy aspirations without over attention to rhyme. Picturable poems with catchy cadence for pre-schoolers.
- *Activities:* Handicrafts, science, homemaking projects, games, cartoons, simple recipes, and puzzles about pets, nature, history, and religion.

How to Submit

Send complete ms with cover letter. Include SASE. Accepts computer printouts. No simultaneous submissions. Reports in 6–8 weeks.

Payment and Policies

All rights. Pays on acceptance. $.10 per word. Authors receive 2 copies of the issue.

Friends Journal

Vinton Deming, Editor
1501 Cherry Street
Philadelphia, PA 19102-1497
215-241-7277

Profile

A monthly inspirational magazine published in association with the Religious Society of Friends, commonly known as Quakers. 8.5x11; self cover; 32–48 pages.

Focus and Audience

Values a positive, experiential approach to life and religious thought in keeping with Quaker ways and concerns. Readers are unprogrammed Friends—Quakers with no minister.

Interests and Word Lengths

- *Nonfiction:* Inspirational, experience-oriented biographies and articles on current events, racial issues, spoken ministry, politics, personal meaning, and travel. Accepts spiritual articles that are grounded in fact and Quaker-related humor. Prefers a positive approach to problems and inclusive language. 2,000–2,500 words. Accepts poetry.
- *Departments:* Viewpoint; Book reviews. 500 words.
- *Seasonal:* Publishes a Christmas issue, an Educational issue (Fall), and a Travel/Vacation issue (Spring).
- *Artwork:* Submit to Barbara Benton, Art Editor. Accepts B/W photos or illustrations.

How to Submit

Query with outline, or send complete ms with cover letter. Include SASE. Accepts photocopies, computer printouts, DOS ASCII disks, and fax submissions. Simultaneous submissions okay. Reports within 6 months.

Payment and Policies

Authors retain rights. No payment. Authors receive 4 copies of the issue.

Glory Songs

Editor
Church Music Department, MSN 170
127 Ninth Avenue North
Nashville, TN 37234

AT A GLANCE:
GLORY SONGS

- Southern Baptist, Music
- Quarterly
- 100% freelance
- Circ: 85,000
- Pays: $.055 per word on acceptance.

From the Editor:
"Never be satisfied with your first draft. Write, then rewrite. Then rewrite again. Remember the saying, 'The best writing is rewriting.' That saying is true."

Best Bet: Articles and church music for non-professional choir directors and members.

Avoid: Slang, jargon, and overly technical terms.

Sample copy: Free. Send #10 SASE for guidelines.

Profile

A quarterly magazine containing both church music and music-related articles. Published by the Sunday School Board of the Southern Baptist Convention. Uses as doctrinal guidelines the 1963 statement of The Baptist Faith and Message. 7x10.5; glossy cover; 2-color; 26 pages.

Focus and Audience

Designed for the small church volunteer or part-time music director and choir members.

Interests and Word Lengths

- *Nonfiction:* Articles on choir membership, music training, hymn knowledge, ministry opportunities, inspirational testimonies, and thoughts about personal growth and development through music. Also seeks choir music and anthems that are easily learned and very singable. Length requirements vary. Write with an active, conversational voice and use simple, clear language.
- *Photos:* Prefers B/W glossy prints. Accepts color prints with negatives. Photos must be captioned.

How to Submit

Send complete ms. Include SASE. Accepts typed, double spaced mss on white bond paper. No more than 25 lines per page. See guidelines for additional submissions requirements. Simultaneous submissions okay.

Payment and Policies

First North American serial rights. Pays on acceptance. $.055 per word. Authors receive 2 copies of the issue.

Gnosis

Richard Smoley, Editor
P.O. Box 14217
San Francisco, CA 94114
415-255-0400

AT A GLANCE:

GNOSIS

- Western Spirituality
- 75% freelance
- 40–50% new writers
- Quarterly
- Circ: 16,000
- Receives 10 queries, 20 mss each month.
- Pays: $75–$250 on publication.

From the Editor:
"We publish issues on selected themes and give strong preference to articles that fit in with those themes."

Best Bet: Balanced, intelligent, fresh, and literate perspectives on the Western esoteric traditions.

Avoid: Fiction and poetry; doctrinal sell-jobs; puff pieces on New Age personalities.

Sample copy: $6 with a 9x12 SASE. Send #10 SASE for guidelines.

Profile
A quarterly journal on Western inner traditions. Published by the Lumen Foundation. Issues are thematic. 8.5x11; glossy cover; 88 pages.

Focus and Audience
Covers the esoteric and mystical traditions of Western civilization, including but not limited to Christianity, Judaism, and Islam.

Interests and Word Lengths
- *Nonfiction:* Features and essays on Western spirituality, metaphysics, psychology, and topics relating to issue's themes. Send for guidelines on upcoming topics. 3,000–5,000 words.
- *Departments:* Book reviews on recently published books on topics relating to the Western inner traditions. 250–1,000 words.
- *Artwork:* B/W photos or art for inside. Color art for cover.

How to Submit
Query with outline, resume, and writing samples or clips. Include SASE. Accepts photocopies, computer printouts, and Macintosh disks. No simultaneous submissions. Reports in 1 month.

Payment and Policies
One-time rights. Pays on publication. $75–$250 per piece. Authors receive 4 copies of the issue.

God's Revivalist

Ron Shew, Editor
1810 Young Street
Cincinnati, OH 45210
513-721-7944

AT A GLANCE:
GOD'S REVIVALIST

- Christian, Renewal
- 80% freelance
- 5% new writers
- Monthly
- Circ: 21,000
- Receives 12 mss each month.
- No payment. Offers contributor's copy.

Best Bet: Articles on holy living, spirited growth and depth, and family.

Avoid: Politics; current world issues; feminism; Friends ideas.

Sample copy: $.50. Send #10 SASE for guidelines.

Profile

A monthly magazine of Christian living. Interdenominational in scope. 8.5x11; 24 pages.

Focus and Audience

Concerned with revival and holy living. Serves a conservative, interdenominational Christian audience. Most readers are conservative and follow the Wesleyan-Arminian tradition.

Interests and Word Lengths

- *Nonfiction:* Articles and personal-experience pieces on prayer, holy living, revival, spirituality, family life, and spiritual activities. 600–1,400 words.
- *Departments:* Revival Page.
- *Seasonal:* Holiday material.
- *Photos:* To accompany articles only.

How to Submit

Send complete ms with cover letter. Include SASE. Accepts photocopies, computer printouts, and fax submissions. Simultaneous submissions okay. Reports in 2 months.

Payment and Policies

Authors retain rights. No payment. Authors receive 1 copy the issue.

God's Special People

Dan Lindsey, Editor
P.O. Box 729
Ocean Shores, WA 98569
206-289-2540

AT A GLANCE:
GOD'S SPECIAL PEOPLE

- Baptist, Disabilities
- 100% freelance
- 10% new writers
- Quarterly
- Circ: 400
- Receives 1–2 queries, 1–2 mss each month.
- No payment. Offers a free subscription.

From the Editor:
"Articles must be Christian and discuss disabilities. We are Fundamental Christians and the magazine is the ministry of a Baptist Church."

Best Bet: Personal-experience articles showing how Christian faith helped one cope with a disability.

Avoid: New age thought such as visualization, power of positive thinking, visions, and after-death experiences.

Sample copy: $2. Send #10 SASE for guidelines.

Profile

A Christian magazine for and about people with disabilities. Conservative and fundamental; doctrinal statement is available upon request. Published by Ocean Shores Baptist Church. 7.5x10; 3-color; 36 pages.

Focus and Audience

Committed to the biblical fundamentals of Christian faith, moral absolutes, scriptural separation, the vital necessity of the local church, and world evangelization. Proclaims the Gospel and the importance of every person, including those who are disabled.

Interests and Word Lengths

- *Nonfiction:* Personal experiences concerning disabilities that share how faith in Jesus Christ has helped in coping. Includes children and adults with disabilities, comfort and encouragement, and articles that define particular disabilities. Interviews are rare but accepted. Up to 1,000 words. Prefers shorter pieces.
- *Poetry:* Accepts few poems. Must concern disabilities.
- *Photos:* Photo submissions encouraged. Returned upon request only. Considers line drawings.

How to Submit

Send complete ms. Include SASE. Accepts photocopies, computer printouts, and WordPerfect disks. Simultaneous submissions okay. Reports in 1–2 months.

Payment and Policies

Authors retain rights. No payment. Offers a free one-year subscription. Authors receive up to 10 copies of the issue.

God's World Today

Norman W. Bomer, Editor
P.O. Box 2330
Asheville, NC 28803
704-253-8063

AT A GLANCE:
GOD'S WORLD
TODAY

- Christian, Juvenile
- 16% freelance
- Weekly during school year
- Circ: 260,000
- Receives 10 mss each month.
- Pays: $75 per piece on acceptance.

From the Editor:
"Use simple vocabulary and simple sentence structure."

Best Bet: Social commentary on any topic suitable for upper elementary or junior-high school students.

Avoid: Poetry and fiction.

Sample copy: Free. Send #10 SASE for guidelines.

Profile

A current-events newsweekly for Christian students. Published in five editions for kindergarten through junior high. Member of the Evangelical Press Association. 8.5x11; self cover; full-color; 8 pages.

Focus and Audience

Offers commentary and analysis of current world events and social issues from an evangelical Christian perspective. Readers are kindergarten through junior-high school students primarily in Christian schools and home schools.

Interests and Word Lengths

- *Nonfiction:* Feature articles, commentary, and activities related to social and world events or any topic suitable for young readers. Present a Christian worldview without being moralistic. Use simple vocabulary and sentence structure. 600–900 words.
- *Photos:* Color prints or slides related to feature articles.

How to Submit

Send complete ms with cover letter. Include SASE. Accepts computer printouts and Macintosh disk submissions. No simultaneous submissions. Reports in 2 months.

Payment and Policies

One-time rights. Pays on acceptance. $75 per piece. Authors receive copies of the issue upon request.

Good Fortune

David Leventhal, Publisher
1435 51st Street
Brooklyn, NY 11219
718-438-0939

AT A GLANCE:
GOOD FORTUNE

- Jewish, Regional
- 50% freelance
- 25% new writers
- 9 issues a year
- Circ: 100,000
- Payment varies.

From the Editor:
"We are kind of like a
People Magazine for
Jewish interests."

Best Bet: Articles about
Jewish personalities
and experiences.

Avoid: Anything that
causes tension be-
tween sects of Ju-
daism.

Sample copy: Free.
Send #10 SASE for
guidelines.

Profile
A lifestyle magazine for Jewish people in the New York
area. 8.5x11; 200 pages.

Focus and Audience
Offers personality and lifestyle articles of interest to New
York-area Jewish people.

Interests and Word Lengths
- *Fiction:* Short stories, short-short stories, novellas,
  drama, and genre fiction of any topic with a Jewish
  theme. 1,000–2,000 words.
- *Nonfiction:* Features, interviews, essays, personal experiences, personality profiles, and lifestyle pieces. All
  of interest to New York-area Jewish people. 1,000–
  2,000 words. Accepts filler and seasonal material.
- *Departments:* Home Beautiful; Baby; Fashion;
  Beauty & Health; Party.
- *Photos:* B/W prints and illustrations.

How to Submit
Query with outline or send complete ms with cover letter. Include SASE. Accepts photocopies, computer printouts, and fax submissions. Simultaneous submissions
okay. Report time varies.

Payment and Policies
First North American serial rights. Payment schedule
and amount varies. Authors receive 1 copy of the issue
upon request.

Good News Journal

Teresa Parker, Editor
P.O. Box 1882
Columbia, MO 65205
314-875-8755

AT A GLANCE:
GOOD NEWS JOURNAL

- Christian, Evangelism
- 50% freelance
- 5% new writers
- Monthly
- Circ: 50,000
- Receives 2–5 mss each month.
- No payment. Offers 2 contributor's copies.

From the Editor:
"We are interested in personal testimonies of how God turns the negative into positive, especially when related to the heartland of Missouri."

Best Bet: Real-life stories about God's workings in the world.

Avoid: Preachy articles, poems, and devotionals.

Sample copy: Free with 9x12 SAE and $.75 postage. No guidelines.

Profile
A regional Christian newspaper that is distributed free throughout churches and businesses in several Missouri cities. Tabloid-size; newsprint; 16 pages.

Focus and Audience
Looks for personal testimonies of God's workings in today's world. Readers are Missouri residents and church-goers.

Interests and Word Lengths
- *Nonfiction:* Features, interviews, and first-person experiences and testimonies about what God is doing in the world today, deliverance from drugs, alcohol, and other substance abuse. Personal testimonies require documentation from a pastor. 900–1,000 words.
- *Departments:* Family Finance, Family Gatherings, Book Reviews. Most are staff-written.
- *Photos:* B/W or color prints.

How to Submit
Send complete ms with cover letter and resume. Include SASE. Accepts computer printouts and Macintosh disks. Simultaneous submissions okay. Reports in 2 months.

Payment and Policies
Authors retain rights. No payment. Authors receive 2 copies of the issue.

Gospel Advocate

F. Furman Kearley, Editor
P.O. Box 167
Monahans, TX 79756
615-254-8781

AT A GLANCE:
GOSPEL ADVOCATE

- Church of Christ, Social Issues
- 90% freelance
- 75% new writers
- Monthly
- Circ: 16,000
- Receives 100 mss each month.
- No payment. Offers 3 contributor's copies.

From the Editor:
"You need to stress the practical—what the reader can do differently to be a better person after reading your article."

Best Bet: Essays on social issues from a Christian perspective.

Avoid: Satire; sarcasm; instrumental music.

Sample copy: Free. Send #10 SASE for guidelines.

Profile

A denominational magazine for members of the Church of Christ. Est.: 1885; 8.5x11; glossy cover; 68 pages.

Focus and Audience

Stresses positive articles with practical applications that explore contemporary social and world issues from a Christian perspective. All material should be consistent with the teaching of the Church of Christ.

Interests and Word Lengths

- *Nonfiction:* Essays, feature articles, and personal-experience pieces offering a Christian perspective of social and moral issues such as abortion and AIDS, as well as devotional writing and Bible stories. Be practical and positive. Use Scripture generously and include statistics, quotations, and examples. Document all facts and quotes. 800–1,700 words.
- *Photos:* B/W and color prints to accompany articles.

How to Submit

Query with outline, or send complete ms with cover letter. Include SASE. Accepts photocopies and computer printouts. Simultaneous submissions okay. Reports in 6–8 months.

Payment and Policies

First rights. Rights revert to authors after 1 year. No payment. Authors receive 3 copies of the issue.

Gospel Herald

Eugene C. Perry, Co-Editor
4904 King Street
Beamsville, ON L0R 1B6
Canada
416-563-7503

AT A GLANCE:
GOSPEL HERALD

- Churches of Christ, Doctrinal
- 40% freelance
- 5% new writers
- Monthly
- Circ: 1,500
- Receives 1 query, 1–2 mss each month.
- No payment. Offers 1 contributor's copy.

From the Editor:
"We do not pay for our material. All work is submitted on a voluntary basis by those wishing to serve the cause. Most writers are members of the Churches of Christ."

Sample copy: $1 with 9x12 SAE and $1 postage. Send #10 SASE/IRC for guidelines.

Profile

A doctrinal magazine published monthly by the non-profit Gospel Herald Foundation for members of Churches of Christ. 8.5x11; self cover; 20 pages.

Focus and Audience

Promotes New Testament Christianity. All material must be compatible with Churches of Christ doctrine.

Interests and Word Lengths

- *Nonfiction:* Submit to R.D. Merrit, 46 Elsbury Bay, Winnipeg, MB, R2N 2H8. Doctrinal, exegetical, and inspirational pieces. Bible studies, prayer, spirituality, evangelism, worship, and family, women's, and children's issues. Accepts seasonal material. 900–1,000 words.
- *Departments:* Women's Page; Family Ties; Christian Youth; Book Reviews; News East; News Prairies; News For West.
- *Filler:* Quotations.
- *Artwork:* B/W or color prints. Line drawings.

How to Submit

Send complete ms with cover letter and resume. Include SASE. U.S. authors send IRCs. Accepts photocopies, computer printouts, and faxes. Simultaneous submissions okay. Reports in 1–2 months.

Payment and Policies

Authors retain rights. No payment. Authors receive 1 copy of the issue.

Gospel Tidings

Robert L. Frey, Editor
5800 South 14th Street
Omaha, NE 68107-3584
402-731-4780

AT A GLANCE:

GOSPEL TIDINGS

- Evangelical, Family
- 80% freelance
- 10% new writers
- Bimonthly
- Circ: 2,200
- Receives 2–5 queries, 2–5 mss each month.
- Pays: $35 on publication.

From the Editor:
"Our purpose is to encourage, educate, and edify members of the Fellowship of Evangelical Bible Churches."

Sample copy: Free. No guidelines.

Profile

A denominational bimonthly magazine published by the Fellowship of Evangelical Bible Churches. Member publication of the Evangelical Press Association. 8.5x11; self cover; 2-color; 16–20 pages.

Focus and Audience

Encourages and educates church members.

Interests and Word Lengths

- *Fiction:* Fiction for adults, children, youth, and the entire family. Short stories, 1,000–2,500 words. Short-short stories, 500–1,000 words.
- *Nonfiction:* Topical and inspirational features and personal experiences. 1,000–2,500 words.
- *Photos:* B/W prints.

How to Submit

Send complete ms with cover letter. Include SASE. Accepts photocopies, computer printouts, and IBM-compatible disks, preferably WordPerfect. Simultaneous submissions okay.

Payment and Policies

One-time rights. Pays on publication. $35 per piece. Authors receive copies of the issue.

Greater Phoenix Jewish News

Leni Reiss, Editor
7220 North 16th Street, Suite G
Phoenix, AZ 85020
602-870-9470

Profile
A weekly community newspaper for Jewish people in the Phoenix metropolitan-area. Tabloid-size; 24–52 pages.

Focus and Audience
Covers Jewish-related news and events for readers in the Phoenix metropolitan-area.

Interests and Word Lengths
- *Nonfiction:* Features, interviews, and personal experiences. Interests include current political viewpoints, humor, and news and events of interest to a diverse Jewish population. Accepts seasonal material. Up to 1,000 words.
- *Departments:* Editorial Column; Holidays; Lifestyle.

How to Submit
Prefers query with outline. Accepts complete ms with cover letter. Include SASE. Accepts photocopies and computer printouts. Identify simultaneous submissions. Reports in 2–3 weeks.

Payment and Policies
Reprint rights. Pays on publication. Rates vary. Authors receive copies of the issue upon request.

Group

Barbara Beach, Departments Editor
2890 North Monroe Avenue
Loveland, CO 80538
303-669-3269

AT A GLANCE:
GROUP

- Christian, Youth Ministry
- 50% freelance
- 5% new writers
- 8 issues a year
- Circ: 50,000
- Receives 5 queries, 20–30 mss each month.
- Pays: $25–$100 on acceptance.

From the Editor:
"We need articles on successful youth groups or youth group projects involving music, drama, art, and helping others."

Best Bet: Practical how-to articles that are fun and experiential—active learning based. How-to articles on personal spiritual growth and time management.

Avoid: Fiction, prose, poetry or anything preachy.

Sample copy: $1.25 with 9x12 SASE.

Profile
An interdenominational magazine for youth group leaders that encourages Christian growth in children and youth. 8.5x11; glossy cover; full-color; 56 pages.

Focus and Audience
Supplies ideas, practical help, inspiration and training for Christian youth leaders.

Interests and Word Lengths
- *Nonfiction:* How-to articles on issues vital to working with young people such as programming ideas, active learning meetings and retreats, spiritual growth, time management, leadership skills, membership building, worship planning, and handling specific problems. 500–2,000 words and up.
- *Departments:* Try This One, short ideas for group use like games, fund-raisers, crowd-breakers, Bible studies, helpful hints, and discussion starters. Hands-On Help, tips for youth leaders for managing personal life, their youth group, volunteers, parents, and outreach ideas. Strange But True, strange, funny, or remarkable youth ministry experiences.
- *Photos:* State availability of photos with submission; model releases and identification of subjects required.

How to Submit
Query with outline and writing samples, or send ms with cover letter. Include SASE. Accepts computer printouts, Macintosh Microsoft Word disks, and fax submissions. Simultaneous submissions okay. Reports in 1 month.

Payment and Policies
All rights. Pays on acceptance. $25–$100 based on length and type of article. Kill fee, $25. Authors receive 2 copies of the issue.

Growing Churches

David T. Seay, Design Editor
127 Ninth Avenue North
Nashville, TN 37234
615-251-2485

AT A GLANCE:
GROWING CHURCHES

• Christian, Evangelism
• Quarterly
• Circ: 13,00
• Pays: $.055–$.06 per
  word on acceptance.

From the Editor:
"We are designed to
help church leaders
apply strategies for
church growth."

Best Bet: Practical,
how-to pieces on
church growth and
evangelism.

Avoid: Poetry and
fiction.

Sample copy: Free with
8.5x11 SASE. Send #10
SASE for guidelines.

Profile

A practical magazine promoting church growth and evangelism. 8x11; 4 pages.

Focus and Audience

Designed to help pastors, church staff, and other church leaders understand and apply church-growth strategies.

Interests and Word Lengths

• *Nonfiction:* How-to articles on the principles of church growth, evangelism, missions, outreach, leadership, and personal and spiritual growth, as well as church-growth success stories. Word-lengths not indicated.

How to Submit

Query with outline. Include SASE. Accepts photocopies, computer printouts, disks, and fax submissions. No simultaneous submissions. Reports in 1 month.

Payment and Policies

All or one-time rights. Pays on acceptance. $.055 per word. $.06 per word if submitted on diskette. Authors receive 3 copies of the issue.

Guide Magazine

Jeannette Johnson, Editor
55 West Oak Ridge Drive
Hagerstown, MD 21740
301-791-7000

AT A GLANCE:
GUIDE MAGAZINE

- Seventh-day Adventist, Youth
- 25% freelance
- 25% new writers
- Weekly
- Circ: 40,000
- Receives 3 queries, 80–100 mss each month.
- Pays: $.03–$.05 per word on acceptance.

From the Editor:
"Our most successful writers present stories from a young person's viewpoint. They find fresh angles and fill their stories with mystery, action, suspense, surprise, humor, and adventure."

Best Bet: Positive, upbeat, exciting, fresh stories that address kid's issues honestly.

Avoid: Preaching, moralizing, adult sentiments.

Sample copy: Free with #10 SAE and 2 first-class stamps. Send #10 SASE for guidelines.

Profile
A weekly Christian journal geared toward young people, ages 10–14. Sponsored by the Seventh-day Adventist Church. 6x9; glossy cover; 2-color; 32 pages.

Focus and Audience
Committed to helping young readers develop their own value system based on sound principles. Material presented is relevant to the needs of today's young people and emphasizes positive aspects of Christian living.

Interests and Word Lengths
- *Fiction:* Believable, fact-based stories. Interests include adventure, humor, choices and decision making, self-esteem, friendship, changes, nature, peer pressure, and family relationships. Write with an active voice and use plenty of dialog. Up to 1,200 words.
- *Nonfiction:* Feature articles about sports, music, achievements, and community service. Interview with people of strong moral worth. Personal experiences. All presented with reader's interests and viewpoint in mind. Up to 1,200 words.
- *Filler:* Activities and puzzles, preferably something more innovative than crossword and word search.

How to Submit
Query with outline, or send complete ms with cover letter. Include SASE. Accepts photocopies and letter-quality computer printouts. Simultaneous submissions okay. Reports in 1 month.

Payment and Policies
First North American serial or one-time and reprint rights. Pays on acceptance. $.03–$.05 per word, up to $75 per piece. Authors receive 3 copies of the issue.

Guideposts

Fulton Oursler, Jr., Editor-in-Chief
16 East 34th Street
New York, NY 10016
212-251-8100

AT A GLANCE:
GUIDEPOSTS

- Judeo-Christian, Inspirational
- 40% freelance
- 10% new writers
- Monthly
- Circ: 3.9 million
- Receives 4,000 mss each month.
- Pays: $50–$400 on acceptance.

From the Editor:
"Stories should make a single, practical spiritual point that the reader can use."

Best Bet: Shorter pieces of 250–750 words, such as third-person stories for the Quiet People department.

Avoid: Essays and opinion pieces. Stories not within the Judeo-Christian tradition.

Sample copy: Free. Send #10 SASE for guidelines.

Profile

An inspirational, interfaith magazine for the general reader that fosters courage, strength, and positive attitudes through faith in God. 5x7.5; glossy cover; full-color; 48 pages.

Focus and Audience

True stories of lay people who demonstrate faith in action through dealing with personal crises in a way that can help and inspire others.

Interests and Word Lengths

- *Nonfiction:* True first-person stories within the Judeo-Christian tradition that demonstrate faith overcoming trials. Stories can involve action or drama, business, celebrities, sports, healing and overcoming. May be ghost-written. 750–1,500 words.
- *Departments:* Submit to Rick Hamlin, Features Editor. Quiet people, accounts of helpful individuals, 750 words. His Mysterious Ways, experiences of divine intervention. This Thing Called Prayer, practical suggestions for praying. Up to 250 words. Accepts filler.
- *Poetry:* Submit to Rick Hamlin, Features Editor. Accepts few poems.
- *Photos:* Submit to Courtney Reid-Eaton. Prefers color slides.

How to Submit

Send complete ms with cover letter. Include SASE. Accepts photocopies and computer printouts. Simultaneous submissions okay. Reports in 1 month.

Payment and Policies

All rights. Pays on acceptance. Articles, $200–$400. Departments, $50–$200. Filler/shorts, $10–$25.

Hadassah Magazine

Joan Michel, Editor
50 West 58th Street
New York, NY 10019
212-333-5946

AT A GLANCE:

HADASSAH MAGAZINE

- Jewish, Women
- 80% freelance
- 10% new writers
- Monthly
- Circ: 300,000
- Receives 100 queries, 100 mss each month.
- Pays: $300–$400 on publication.

From the Editor:
"Stories and articles should focus on shared Jewish experiences but be told in fresh new ways, whether dealing with past traditions or grappling with new problems."

Best Bet: Articles on family, art, and travel that conform to the guidelines of each department.

Avoid: Speeches and research reports.

Sample copy: Free with 9x12 SAE and $2 postage. Send #10 SASE for guidelines.

Profile

A monthly Jewish women's magazine published by Hadassah, the Women's Zionist Organization. 8.5x11; glossy cover; 4-color; 60 pages.

Focus and Audience

Provides timely articles and stories on local, national, and international issues and events of interest to Jewish women. Readers are members of Hadassah.

Interests and Word Lengths

- *Fiction:* Short stories on Jewish life in the U.S., Israel, and around the world. Focus on shared Jewish experiences. Immigrant sagas and Holocaust tales need to be of outstanding quality to be considered. 1,500–2,500 words.
- *Nonfiction:* Articles on Jewish life in the U. S., Israel, and the world. Focus on shared Jewish experience. Interests include women's issues, lifestyle, culture, politics, and social and world issues. Feature articles for the Jewish Traveler must conform to guidelines; query before submitting. 1,500 words.
- *Departments:* Book Reviews; Family and Arts columns must conform to guidelines; query before submitting.
- *Photos:* Relating to story or article.

How to Submit

Prefers query with outline and writing samples; accepts complete ms with cover letter. Include SASE. Accepts photocopies and computer printouts. Identify simultaneous submissions. Reports in 3 months.

Payment and Policies

First North American serial or all rights. Pays on publication. Features, $300 minimum. Travel and Family articles, $400. Authors receive 1–2 copies of the issue.

Hallelujah!

Wesley H. Wakefield, Editor-in-Chief
Box 223, Postal Station A
Vancouver, BC V6C 2M3
Canada
604-498-3895

AT A GLANCE:

HALLELUJAH!

- Wesleyan/Methodist, Evangelistic
- 60% freelance
- 2% new writers
- Bimonthly
- Circ: 10,000
- Receives 1–5 queries, 3–8 mss each month.
- Pays: $15 and up on acceptance.

From the Editor:
"Writing must be tight with no frills."

Best Bet: Biblically based, non-academic articles on doctrine and social issues in keeping with Wesleyan standards.

Avoid: Slang; colloquialism; politics; attacks on other denominations (though they can be challenged); any form of Calvinism or dispensational premillenialism; ecumenism.

Sample copy: Free. Send #10 SASE/IRCs for guidelines.

Profile

An international magazine of aggresive evangelistic Christianity. Published by The Bible Holiness Movement, an international, inter-racial, Wesleyan Christian association that serves members in 88 countries. Est.: 1949; 5.5x8.5; 40 pages.

Focus and Audience

Aims to be an evangel for repentance, faith, and scriptural holiness with a commitment to social activism. Advocates red-hot revivals of scriptural Christianity with a Methodist/Salvationist Christian evangelical emphasis. Readership is culturally diverse, primarily people of color.

Interests and Word Lengths

- *Nonfiction:* Doctrinal articles and Bible studies; personal testimonies; articles on social issues such as slavery, child labor, hunger, etc. Avoid illustrations that conflict with Movement standards. Stresses tight writing, universal application, and biblical basis. Up to 3,000 words.
- *Poetry:* Poems with a hymn or song quality.
- *Artwork:* B/W photos; keep screens between 80–120%. Subjects depicted should adhere to Movement dress standards. Accepts line drawings but not religious humor. No illustrations glorifying war or anything contrary to Christian peace teachings.

How to Submit

Prefers query with outline. Accepts complete ms with cover letter. Include SASE. U.S. authors send IRCs. Accepts photocopies and computer printouts. Simultaneous submissions okay. Reports within 1 month.

Payment and Policies

One-time rights. Pays on acceptance. Rates vary. $15 and up depending on length and type of article. Authors receive 1 copy of the issue.

Hamevaser

Reuben Spolter, Executive Editor
500 West 185th Street
New York, NY 10033
212-928-3244

AT A GLANCE:

HAMEVASER

- Jewish, Bible Study
- 10–15% freelance
- 5–10% new writers
- 6 issues a year
- Circ: 4,000
- Receives 3–5 queries, 2–3 mss each month.
- No payment.

From the Editor:
"We will give serious consideration to well-written, thought-provoking submissions."

Best Bet: Well-researched articles on Jewish thought, history, philosophy, and Bible scholarship.

Avoid: Inflammatory, non-traditional Jewish topics.

Sample copy: Not provided. No guidelines.

Profile

A journal of Jewish thought, published by students at Yeshiva University. 16–20 pages.

Focus and Audience

Publishes articles relating to Jewish history, philosophy, and Bible scholarship for students and rabbinical alumni of Yeshiva University.

Interests and Word Lengths

- *Fiction:* Publishes one Purim issue each year dedicated to all types of fiction.
- *Nonfiction:* Submit to Dov Chelst. Interviews with important Jewish figures; articles on Jewry outside the U.S.; profiles of incidents and individuals affecting the Jewish world; thought-provoking pieces on Jewish thought, philosophy, and history. All material must be thoroughly researched and documented with traditional Jewish sources. 1,000–2,000 words.
- *Artwork:* Submit to A. Greengart. Line drawings no larger than 11x17. B/W prints.

How to Submit

Query with resume and writing samples. Include SASE. Accepts computer printouts and WordPerfect 5.0 or 5.1 disks. Simultaneous submissions okay. Reports in 2–3 months.

Payment and Policies

Authors retain rights. No payment. Does not offer copies of the issue.

Harmony
Voices for a Just Future
Rose Evans, Managing Editor
P.O. Box 210056
San Francisco, CA 94121
415-221-8527

AT A GLANCE:

HARMONY

- Social Justice, Pro-Life
- 75% freelance
- 25% new writers
- Bimonthly
- Circ: 1,200
- Receives 10 queries, 8 mss each month.
- No payment. Offers 6 contributor's copies.

From the Editor:
"We support human rights and social justice. We oppose violence—war, abortion, the death penalty, and euthanasia."

Best Bet: Articles and poetry that promote a reverence for all life.

Avoid: Judgmentalism and condemnations.

Sample copy: $2 with 9x12 SAE and $.98 postage. Send #10 SASE for guidelines.

Profile
A bimonthly independent journal dedicated to promoting a consistent reverence for life. Primary interests include pro-life issues, philosophy, politics, social issues, and women's issues. 8.5x11; self cover; stapled; 28 pages.

Focus and Audience
Espouses a philosophy of courtesy and goodwill. Articles must have a pro-life theme, which means anti-war, anti-death penalty, anti-abortion, and pro-peace and justice. Readers include professors, writers, and activists.

Interests and Word Lengths
- *Nonfiction:* Biographies and articles on current events. Interests include conflict resolution, peace and justice, and pro-life issues. 1,000–4,000 words.
- *Departments:* Off Key, reports of outrageous happenings and ethical inconsistencies. 300–600 words.
- *Poetry:* Poems that illustrate a reverence for all life.

How to Submit
Query with outline, or send complete ms with cover letter. Include SASE. Accepts photocopies and computer printouts. Simultaneous submissions okay. Reports in 2 months.

Payment and Policies
First North American serial rights. No payment. Authors receive 6 copies of the issue.

Harmony International Screenwriting

Fred C. Wilson, III, President
901 South Ashland Avenue
No. 218A
Chicago, IL 60607
312-666-7650

Profile

Launched in 1993 as the bimonthly newsletter of the Harmony International Screenwriting Group. 4 pages.

Focus and Audience

Publishes inspirational material of interest to aspiring screenwriters.

Interests and Word Lengths

- *Fiction and Nonfiction:* Accepts all categories of writing provided that they pertain to screenwriting and inspire those interested in writing. Interests include theology, social and world issues, politics, lifestyle, cultural and ethnic themes, women's issues, and the environment. No word-length restrictions. Also accepts seasonal material, filler, and poetry.
- *Photos:* B/W prints and illustrations.

How to Submit

Query with outline or send complete ms with cover letter. Include SASE. Accepts computer printouts. Simultaneous submissions okay. Reports in 2 weeks.

Payment and Policies

One-time rights. No payment. Authors receive 5 copies of the issue.

Health Consciousness

Assistant Editor
P.O. Box 550
Oviedo, FL 32765
407-365-6681

AT A GLANCE:

HEALTH CONSCIOUSNESS

- Health, Healing
- 50% new writers
- Bimonthly
- Circ: 10,000
- Receives 30–40 queries each month.
- No payment.

From the Editor:
"We're holistic, non-confrontational, and success-driven. We let the reader be informed by the contents themselves."

Best Bet: Health and healing success stories.

Sample copy: Free. No guidelines.

Profile

A bimonthly publication of holistic health practices. 8.5x11; glossy cover; 90 pages.

Focus and Audience

Looks at the scope of healthcare and healing methods being practiced around the world. Presents information in a non-confrontational, investigative, well-researched way. Employs an easy-to-read, self-help format.

Interests and Word Lengths

- *Nonfiction:* Self-help features and interviews exploring the spiritual, nutritional, mental, physical, psychological, ecological, and environmental aspects of health and healing. Accepts healing success stories, judicial and governmental issues concerning health and healing such as lobbying and litigation, and biographies. 800–1,000 words.
- *Departments:* Speak Out, editorials. Focus, Recipes.

How to Submit

Query with outline, resume, writing samples, and clips. Include SASE. Accepts computer printouts and fax submissions. Simultaneous submissions okay. Reports in 1 month.

Payment and Policies

All rights. No payment.

The Helping Hand

Doris L. Moore, Editor
P.O. Box 12609
Oklahoma City, OK 73157-2609
405-787-7110

AT A GLANCE:
THE HELPING HAND

- Pentecostal, Women
- 35% freelance
- 10% new writers
- Bimonthly
- Circ: 4,000
- Receives 7–10 queries, 5 mss each month.
- Pays: $20 per piece on publication.

From the Editor:
"We are a ministry magazine for women of the Pentecostal Holiness Church."

Best Bet: Articles addressing women's interests and needs.

Sample copy: Free with 8.5x11 SASE. Send #10 SASE for guidelines.

Profile

A bimonthly denominational Christian magazine for women. Published and sponsored by the Pentecostal Holiness Church. Member of the Evangelical Press Association and International Pentecostal Press Association. 8.5x11; self cover; 2-color; 20 pages.

Focus and Audience

Inspirational and motivational articles and stories for women who are members of the Pentecostal Holiness Church.

Interests and Word Lengths

- *Fiction:* Inspirational stories about women and their interests and needs. 500–1,300 words.
- *Departments:* True stories and personal experiences about children, family, single motherhood, working mothers, women of the '90s, time management, self-image, health, and prayer.
- *Poetry:* Open to poetry that reflects the spirit of the magazine.
- *Seasonal:* Submit material 4–5 months in advance. 500–1,300 words.

How to Submit

Query with writing samples or clips, or send complete ms with resume and clips. Include SASE. Accepts photocopies, computer printouts, and faxes. Simultaneous submissions okay. Reports in 3–4 months.

Payment and Policies

Pays on publication. $20 per piece. Authors receive 1 copy of the issue.

Herald of Holiness

Wesley D. Tracy, Editor
6401 The Paseo
Kansas City, MO 64131
816-333-7000

AT A GLANCE:
HERALD OF HOLINESS

- Church of the Nazarene, Lifestyle
- 40% freelance
- Monthly
- Circ: 85,000
- Receives 100 mss each month.
- Pays: $.03–$.05 per word on acceptance.

From the Editor:
"Write in an informal, concrete, conversational style and use anecdotes and examples. Don't preach— show us."

Avoid: Lectures disguised as prose; sermonic writing.

Sample copy: Free with 9x12 SASE. Send #10 SASE for guidelines.

Profile
A monthly denominational magazine of the Church of the Nazarene. 8.5x11; glossy cover; 2-color; 64 pages.

Focus and Audience
Explores Christian lifestyle and social issues as interpreted by the doctrines of Wesleyan Holiness Movement. Audience consists primarily of lay people.

Interests and Word Lengths
- *Nonfiction:* Personal experiences, Christian family life, Christian marriage, social issues, application and interpretation of the Wesleyan Holiness Movement. 2,000 words.
- *Poetry:* Uses little poetry, but looks for short poems with insightful comments, memorable language, demonstration of poets knowledge of metrics, standard poetic forms, and rhetorical devices.
- *Seasonal:* Seasonal articles on Christian holidays and seasons; Advent, Christmas, Epiphany, Lent, Easter, Pentecost, Holy Trinity Sunday, etc. 2,000 words.

How to Submit
Send complete ms with cover letter. Include SASE. Accepts photocopies and computer printouts. Simultaneous submissions okay. Reports in 2 months.

Payment and Policies
One-time rights. Pays on acceptance. Articles, $.03–$.05 per word. Poetry, $.50 plus $1 a line. Authors receive 1 copy of the issue.

Heritage Florida Jewish News

Jill Hayflick, Associate Editor
P.O. Box 300742
Fern Park, FL 32730
407-834-8787

AT A GLANCE:

HERITAGE FLORIDA JEWISH NEWS

- Jewish, Regional
- 5–30% freelance
- 5% new writers
- Weekly
- Circ: 6,000
- Receives 60 mss each month.
- Pays: $.50 per column inch on publication.

From the Editor:
"Articles must have a Jewish connection or relate to the Jewish community."

Best Bet: Articles on Jewish-related cultural issues.

Sample copy: Free. No guidelines.

Profile

A weekly newspaper for the central Florida Jewish community. Tabloid-size; 20 pages.

Focus and Audience

Offers Jewish-related news and events plus special holiday and thematic issues. Readers are 20- to 75-year-old central Florida residents.

Interests and Word Lengths

- *Fiction:* Short stories on Jewish themes. 500–1,000 words. Accepts poetry.
- *Nonfiction:* Features, interviews, essays, and personal experiences on any Jewish-related topic. Special issues focus on Jewish holdays or specific topics like health and fitness. Accepts filler. 500–1,000 words.
- *Departments:* Editorial Page; Viewpoint Column. Interests include politics, Israel, and anti-Semitism.
- *Cartoons:* Political satire and social commentary.
- *Photos:* Submit to Jeff Gaser, Editor/Publisher. B/W prints and line drawings.

How to Submit

Send complete ms with cover letter. Include SASE. Accepts photocopies, computer printouts, Macintosh Microsoft Word disk submissions, and faxes (407-831-8507). No simultaneous submissions. Report time varies.

Payment and Policies

First rights. Pays on publication. $.50 per column inch. Authors receive at least 1 copy the issue.

High Adventure

Marshall Bruner, Editor
1445 Boonville Avenue
Springfield, MO 65802
417-862-2781

AT A GLANCE:
HIGH ADVENTURE

- Christian, Juvenile
- 40% freelance
- 15% new writers
- Quarterly
- Circ: 80,000
- Receives 50 mss each month.
- Pays: $.02–$.03 per word on acceptance.

From the Editor:
"Read the magazine and know the readership. Give attention to writing style. Be accurate and document your references."

Best Bet: Articles that challenge boys to higher ideals and greater spiritual dedication.

Avoid: Not following theme list.

Sample copy: Free with 8.5x11 SASE. Send #10 SASE for guidelines.

Profile

A Christian magazine published quarterly by Royal Rangers for their members. 8.5x11; 4-color; 16 pages.

Focus and Audience

Designed to provide boys, ages 6–17, with worthwhile, enjoyable leisure reading; to challenge them to higher ideals and greater spiritual dedication; and to perpetuate the spirit of the Royal Ranger program.

Interests and Word Lengths

- *Fiction:* Short stories with a Christian emphasis. Interests include adventure, inspirational, salvation, and the Holy Spirit. Up to 1,000 words.
- *Nonfiction:* Articles on adventure, Christian living, the Holy Spirit, salvation, and youth issues with Christian emphasis. Self-help and inspirational pieces. Biographies, missionary stories, news items, and testimonies. Up to 1,000 words.
- *Seasonal:* Submit 6 months in advance.
- *Filler:* Cartoons, jokes, crafts,and puzzles.
- *Photos:* Color prints.

How to Submit

Query with outline and resume, or send complete ms with cover letter. New writers should include personal background and church affiliation. Include SASE. Accepts computer printouts. Simultaneous submissions okay. Reports in 1–2 months.

Payment and Policies

First or all rights. Pays on acceptance. Nonfiction, $.02–$.03 per word. Cartoons, $12–$20. Puzzles, $12. Jokes, $2–$3. Authors receive 1 copy of the issue.

His Garden

Margi Washburn, Editor
216 North Vine Street
Kewanee, IL 61443

AT A GLANCE: His Garden

- Christian, Inspirational
- 90% freelance
- 3 issues a year
- Circ: not available
- Pays: $5 per piece on acceptance.

From the Editor:
"I want to work with new and unpublished writers. Be open to suggestion. Each piece of mail is personally handled and read by me. If I think you have a good thing going, we can work together to see your work published."

Best Bet: Creative, inspirational material that brings light into the world.

Avoid: "Gooey" fiction.

Sample copy: $3.50. Send #10 SASE for guidelines.

Profile
A compilation of inspirational Christian writing. Est.: 1992.

Focus and Audience
Serves as a forum for the work of new and unpublished Christian writers who want to share their creativity and inspiration with others.

Interests and Word Lengths
- *Fiction:* Creative, uplifting stories that have impact but are not overly sentimental. Buys 6–10 per year. 250–2,500 words.
- *Nonfiction:* Personal-experience and inspirational pieces. Buys 3–4 per year. Up to 2,500 words.
- *Departments:* Current Events; Film and Book Reviews. Buys 3–5 per year. 100–2,000 words.
- *Poetry:* Free verse, light verse, and traditional poetry and haiku. Buys 15–25 per year. Up to 5 poems per submission.
- *Seasonal:* Submit seasonal or holiday pieces 6 months in advance.

How to Submit
Fiction and poetry, send complete ms or up to 5 poems. Nonfiction, query first. Include SASE. Accepts reprints. Reports on mss in 2 months; on queries in 3 weeks.

Payment and Policies
All rights. Pays on acceptance. All material, $5 per piece. Authors receive 1 copy of the issue.

The Home Altar

M. Elaine Dunham, Editor
Augsburg Fortress
426 South Fifth Street, Box 1209
Minneapolis, MN 55440
612-330-3140

AT A GLANCE:
THE HOME ALTAR

- Lutheran, Devotions
- 95% freelance
- 10% new writers
- Quarterly
- Circ: 70,000
- Receives 15 queries, 10 mss each month.
- Pays: $10 per piece on acceptance.

From the Editor:
"All meditations are written on assignment. Teaching experience and theological education are desirable qualifications."

Best Bet: Daily devotions for Lutheran families with children.

Avoid: Religious jargon; first-person point-of-view; stereotypes.

Sample copy: Free with 6x9 SAE and postage for 4 ounces. Send #10 SASE for guidelines.

Profile

A devotional booklet of family meditations and Scripture readings. Selections are based on the three-year lectionary as it appears in the *Lutheran Book of Worship*. All work is assigned. 5.25x7.25; glossy cover; 2-color; 64 pages.

Focus and Audience

Publishes daily devotions intended to be read aloud by families. Readers are primarily Lutheran (ELCA) families with children between 5–12 years of age.

Interests and Word Lengths

- *Fiction:* Short-short stories that correspond to Scripture for devotional reading. 150 words.
- *Nonfiction:* Personal experiences adapted to a third-person story format for devotional reading. 150 words.
- *Poetry:* Occasionally uses poetry and prayers.
- *Artwork:* On assignment only.

How to Submit

All meditations are assigned. Request writer's guidelines and sample copy. Submit writing samples only after studying the magazine.

Payment and Policies

All rights. Pays on acceptance. $10 per meditation. Authors receive 4 copies of the issue.

Home Education Magazine

Helen Hegener, Managing Editor
P.O. Box 1083
Tonasket, WA 98855
509-486-1351

AT A GLANCE:

HOME EDUCATION MAGAZINE

- Education, Family
- 60% freelance
- 30% new writers
- Bimonthly
- Circ: 4,700
- Receives 20–30 queries, 30–40 mss each month.
- Pays: $.45 per column inch on publication.

From the Editor:
"We accept only articles of interest to homeschooling families. Please note that we appeal to a wide variety of philosophies and have no particular religious focus."

Best Bet: Considers almost anything related to homeschooling.

Sample copy: $4.50. Send #10 SASE for guidelines.

Profile

A bimonthly publication for homeschooling families. 8.5x11; self cover; 2-color; 64 pages.

Focus and Audience

Advocates a non-structured approach to homeschooling. Interested in a variety of home-education methods, ideas, and choices for parents who are teaching their children at home.

Interests and Word Lengths

- *Nonfiction:* Features, essays, and interviews on all aspects of homeschooling. Prefers non-coercive learning situations or student-led learning. Welcomes resource lists and related sidebars with articles. Also interested in humorous personal experiences about the funny side of homeschooling. Publishes byline and author credits. 750–3,500 words.
- *Photos:* B/W prints that accompany articles.

How to Submit

Send complete ms with cover letter. Include SASE. Accepts photocopies, computer printouts, Macintosh disks, and legible handwritten articles. Reports in 1 month.

Payment and Policies

One-time rights. Occasionaly requests reprint options for anthologies. Pays on publication. Articles, $.45 per column inch. B/W photos, $5. Authors recieve up to 3 copies of the issue upon request.

Home Life

Charlie Warren, Editor
127 Ninth Avenue North
Nashville, TN 37234
615-251-2272

AT A GLANCE:

HOME LIFE

- Southern Baptist, Family
- 50% freelance
- 20% new writers
- Monthly
- Circ: 600,000
- Receives 100 queries, 1,000 mss each month.
- Pays: $75–$225 on acceptance.

From the Editor:
"We are designed to help families and individuals live a fuller, richer life."

Best Bet: Upbeat, positive parenting and marriage articles that present Christian values and lifestyles or a strong biblical presence.

Avoid: Sermons; overly scholarly articles.

Sample copy: $1 with 9x12 SAE and $1 postage. Send #10 SASE for guidelines.

Profile

A family leisure-reading magazine published by The Southern School Board of the Southern Baptist Convention. Uses as doctrinal guidelines the 1963 statement of The Baptist Faith and Message. 8.5x11; glossy cover; 3-color; 66 pages.

Focus and Audience

Advocates a Christ-centered lifestyle and wholesome family values based on biblical truth. Addresses life issues from an optimistic, healthy, and realistic Christian perspective. Most readers are women, ages 25–60.

Interests and Word Lengths

- *Fiction:* Short stories about family crisis, marriage, parenting, grief, overcoming adversity, self-esteem, and nostalgia. Up to 1,400 words.
- *Nonfiction:* Features, interviews with experts, personal experiences, how-tos, humor, and general articles on family issues, concerns, and relationships. Interests include marriage and money management, spiritual development of children, personal growth, and family communication, finances, and recreation. Up to 1,400 words.
- *Poetry:* Short poems that deal with family concerns and relationships. Seasonal poetry on holidays, Mother's Day, Father's Day, etc., are welcome.
- *Artwork:* Cartoons that deal with family living and relationships in a tasteful, humorous way.

How to Submit

Send complete ms with cover letter. Include SASE. Accepts photocopies and computer printouts. Simultaneous submissions okay. Reports within 6 months.

Payment and Policies

First North American serial, one-time, or all rights. Pays on acceptance. $75–$225 per piece. Authors receive 3 copies of the issue.

Homelife

Editor
8855 Dunn Road
Hazelwood, MO 63042-2299

AT A GLANCE:

HOMELIFE

- Pentecostal, Marriage
- 90% freelance
- 40–50% new writers
- 7 issues a year
- Circ: 6,000
- Receives 50–75 mss each month.
- Pays $15–$30 on publication.

From the Editor:
"A good story or article must have conflict and deal with it in a realistic manner. Before writing, make sure you have a good story item. Know where you are taking your reader. Be sensitive, creative, and specific."

Best Bet: Articles and stories relevant to Pentecostal couples.

Avoid: Lengthy articles.

Sample copy: Free with 9x12 SASE. Send #10 SASE for guidelines.

Profile

A denominational magazine directed to young married couples. Published by the General Youth Division of the United Pentecostal Church International. 8.5x11; glossy cover; 4-color; 16 pages.

Focus and Audience

Primary objective is to inspire young married couples by portraying happy, victorious living through faith in God. Readers are Pentecostal.

Interests and Word Lengths

- *Fiction:* Short stories on all aspects of married life—newlyweds, children, parenting, financial issues, etc. 400–800 words for a single-page article; 1,000–1,500 words for a double-page article. Accepts poetry.
- *Nonfiction:* Short articles pertaining to spiritual growth and development; missionary-related stories; character stories; personal testimonies and experiences; and current events, all of interest to and pertaining to young married couples. Use anecdotes and illustrations. In quoting Scripture, use the Cambridge Bible, King James Version. 400–800 words for a single-page article; 1,000–1,500 words for a double-page article.
- *Seasonal:* Publishes one Christmas piece a year. Submit 1 year in advance.

How to Submit

Send complete ms with cover letter. Include SASE. Accepts photocopies and computer printouts. Simultaneous submissions okay. Reports in up to 1 year.

Payment and Policies

All rights. Pays on publication. $15–$30 per piece. Authors receive 1 copy of the issue.

Home Times

Dennis Lombard, Editor
Neighbor News, Inc.
P.O. Box 16096
West Palm Beach, FL 33416
407-439-3509

AT A GLANCE:

HOME TIMES

- Judeo-Christian, Current Events
- 90% freelance
- 70% new writers
- Monthly
- Circ: 8,000
- Receives 50–75 mss each month
- Pays: $5–$25 per piece on publication.

From the Editor:
"Home Times encourages new writers, but is is a unique newspaper. We strongly suggest you read it first. We are conservative, but not ideological. We are pro-Christian, but not religious."

Best Bet: Current events and news from a conservative perspective.

Avoid: Preachiness, Christian clichés, and churchiness.

Sample copy: $1 with 9x12 SAE and 3 first-class stamps. Send #10 SASE for guidelines.

Profile

A monthly conservative newspaper that promotes traditional Judeo-Christian values. Published as an alternative to the liberal press. Tabloid-size; newsprint; 24 pages.

Focus and Audience

Editorial is pro-Christian but not religious or doctrinal. Its viewpoint is conservative, Judeo-Christian, traditional in morals, pro-life and pro-family, patriotic, and positive. Produced by Christians for the general public.

Interests and Word Lengths

- *Fiction:* Creative short stories, short-short stories, and genre fiction related to current affairs, the history and roots of America, and the family. Up to 1,200 words.
- *Nonfiction:* Features, interviews, essays, and personal experiences with a strong focus on current world events, national and local issues, home and family, arts and entertainment, career, and lifestyle. Up to 900 words.
- *Departments:* Movie, TV, book, and music reviews. Open to new ideas for columns. Up to 700 words.
- *Poetry:* Short, traditional poetry.
- *Photos:* B/W or color prints.

How to Submit

Send complete ms with cover letter. Include SASE. Accepts photocopies, computer printouts, and IBM DOS-compatible disks. Simultaneous submissions okay. Reports in 1 week.

Payment and Policies

One-time and reprint rights. Pays on publication. $5–$25 per piece. Authors receive 3 copies of the issue.

Homiletic & Pastoral Review

Rev. Kenneth Baker, S.J., Editor
86 Riverside Drive
New York, NY 10024

AT A GLANCE:
HOMILETIC & PASTORAL REVIEW

- Catholic, Clergy
- 90% freelance
- Monthly
- Circ: 15,000
- Receives 25–50 mss each month.
- Pays: $100 per piece after publication.

From the Editor:
"Ninety-five percent of our readers are Catholic priests. Direct your articles accordingly."

Best Bet: Essays and articles that promote the Catholic faith.

Sample copy: Free. No guidelines.

Profile
A monthly journal of Catholic spiritual and theological thought. 6.5x9.5; glossy cover; 80 pages.

Focus and Audience
Promotes Roman Catholic doctrine and faith for an international audience consisting primarily of Catholic priests.

Interests and Word Lengths
- *Nonfiction:* Essays and articles that explore and promote Roman Catholic theology, doctrine, and spirituality. Up to 6,000 words.

How to Submit
Send complete ms with cover letter. Include SASE. Accepts photocopies and computer printouts. No simultaneous submissions. Reports in 1 month.

Payment and Policies
All rights. Pays 1 month after publication. Articles, $100. Authors receive 3 copies of the issue.

Hospice

Joseph Cerquone, Editor
1901 North Moore Street
Suite 901
Arlington, VA 22209
703-243-5900

AT A GLANCE:

HOSPICE

- Health, Hospice Care
- 70% freelance
- 10% new writers
- Quarterly
- Circ: 7,800
- Receives 5 queries,
  15 mss each month
- Pays on publication.
  Rates vary.

From the Editor:
"We strongly urge
writers to contact the
editor prior to submit-
ting materials. As the
subject matter can be
sensitive, the correct,
compassionate tone is
needed."

Best Bet: Material that
is both informative to
hospice professionals
and volunteers and
understandable to lay-
persons.

Avoid: Overly senti-
mental, academic,
scholarly, or technical
papers; fiction; poetry.

Sample copy: Free.
Send #10 SASE for
guidelines.

Profile

A quarterly publication of the National Hospice Organization. 8.5x11; glossy cover; full-color; 30 pages.

Focus and Audience

Seeks to foster, develop, and highlight professionalism
in hospice care. Focuses on the hands-on, human aspect of caring for terminally ill individuals. Readers are
hospice professionals and volunteers, and interested
lay-people.

Interests and Word Lengths

- *Nonfiction:* First-person accounts of hospice care with
  clear angles and viewpoints. Interviews with and profiles of extraordinary and exemplary people and programs. New methods, ideas, and approaches to serving the terminally ill. Specific hospice disciplines. Subjects include volunteer recruitment; model programs;
  new methods; trial programs; AIDS in hospice; issues
  in caring for children; coping with stress; team-build-
  ing techniques. 1,000–2,000 words.
- *Departments:* Ideas at Work, new successful ideas at
  work in hospice; In My Own Words, humorous personal anecdotes/observations; News Briefs, newsworthy
  national or regional events. Up to 500 words.
- *Poetry:* Universally relevant poems.
- *Photos:* B/W or color photos of exemplary hospice people for Gallery department.

How to Submit

Query with outline, resume, and writing samples, or
send ms with cover letter. Accepts photocopies and
computer printouts. Simultaneous submissions okay. Reports in several months.

Payment and Policies

All rights. Pays on publication. Payment varies based
on amount of time and work invested. Authors receive
3–5 copies of the issue.

Housewife Writer's Forum

Diane D. Wolverton, Editor
P.O. Box 780
Lyman, Wyoming 82937
307-786-4513

AT A GLANCE:
HOUSEWIFE WRITER'S FORUM

- Writers, Inspirational
- Bimonthly
- Circ: 1,000–1,500
- Pays: $.01 per word on acceptance.

From the Editor:
"We rank verve and emotion ahead of linguistic gymnastics. We look for clear, concise and vivid language. Writing style should be lucid and to the point."

Best Bet: Short stories and articles of less than 400 words.

Sample copy: $2.50. Send #10 SASE for guidelines.

Profile
A bimonthly magazine by and for writers who share devotion to the craft of writing in a busy life filled with distractions. 6.5x10; glossy cover; 2-color; 48 pages.

Focus and Audience
Stories by and for writers who juggle writing and family responsibilities. Readers are stay-at-home mothers and fathers, single mothers, working mothers, mothers with grown children, women with no children, and retired women.

Interests and Word Lengths
- *Fiction:* Accepts all genres. Emotional impact—tears or laughter— preferred. Up to 2,000 words.
- *Nonfiction:* Articles on writing and finding time to write; practical tips; interviews/profiles of successful writers; personal experiences/practical advice on overcoming problems or breaking into a market. Lengths range from up to 400 words, up to 750 words, and up to 1,500 words.
- *Departments:* Domestic Humor, the ups and downs of a housewife writer. Confessions of a Housewife Writer, things that happen to housewife writers, up to 500 words. Coffee Break, news about readers' lives.
- *Poetry:* Humorous and literary poems on writing.
- *Filler:* Anecdotes, jokes, writing tips.
- *Artwork:* 5x7 B/W prints; cartoons; line drawings.

How to Submit
Fiction, send complete ms with cover letter. Nonfiction, query with outline. Include SASE.

Payment and Policies
First North American serial or all rights. Pays on acceptance. Articles and stories, at least $.01 per word. Poems, $1. Cartoons, $2. Photos, $3. Authors receive 2 copies of the issue.

Huron Church News

Rev. Roger McCombe, Editor
6 Glenwood Road
Ingersoll, ON N5C 3N6
Canada
519-485-2244

AT A GLANCE:
HURON CHURCH NEWS

- Anglican, Regional
- 40% freelance
- 20% new writers
- Monthly
- Circ: 26,000
- Receives few queries and mss each month.
- No payment. Offers contributor's copies.

From the Editor:
"We emphasize the news and issues of the Southwest Ontario Anglican Diocese so stay regional."

Best Bet: Church-related articles and personal-experience pieces.

Sample copy: Free. No guidelines.

Profile
A monthly newspaper serving the Anglican Diocese of Southwest Ontario. Tabloid-size; 16–32 pages.

Focus and Audience
Emphasizes news and issues of interest to the Southwest Ontario Anglican Diocese.

Interests and Word Lengths
- *Nonfiction:* Articles on Diocesan-related issues and personal experiences. Interests include spirituality, social and world issues, and evangelism. Up to 500 words.
- *Seasonal:* Material for the liturgical calendar.
- *Photos:* B/W prints.

How to Submit
Query with outline, or send complete ms with cover letter. Include SASE. U.S. authors include IRCs. Accepts photocopies. Simultaneous submissions okay. Reports in 1 month.

Payment and Policies
Authors retain rights. No payment. Authors receive as many copies of the issue as needed.

The Hymn

W. Thomas Smith, Executive Director
Texas Christian University
Fort Worth, TX 76129
817-921-7608

AT A GLANCE:
THE HYMN

- Christian, Music
- 100% freelance
- 50% new writers
- Quarterly
- Circ: 3,500
- Receives 10–20 queries, 5–10 mss each month.
- No payment. Offers 3 contributor's copies.

From the Editor:
"*The Hymn* is a journal of research and opinion, containing practical and scholarly articles."

Best Bet: Congregational hymn words and music.

Avoid: Archaic religious language.

Sample copy: Free with 10x12 SASE. Send #10 SASE for guidelines.

Profile

A quarterly journal of congregational song. Published by the Hymn Society in the United States and Canada. 8.5x11; glossy cover; 2-color; 56 pages.

Focus and Audience

Research, opinion, and practical articles on hymnology for church musicians, clergy, scholars, poets, and others interested in congregational music.

Interests and Word Lengths

- *Nonfiction:* Scholarly and practical articles on hymnology that reflect diverse cultural and theological identities, exemplary hymn texts and tunes in various styles. No word-length requirements.
- *Photos:* B/W prints.

How to Submit

Query with outline. Include SASE. Accepts photocopies and computer printouts. Simultaneous submissions okay. Reports in 3 months.

Payment and Policies

Rights are negotiable. No payment. Authors receive 3 copies of the issue.

Ideals

Editorial Department
565 Marriot Drive
Suite 800
Nashville, TN 37214
615-885-8270

Profile

A thematic nostalgia magazine published by Ideals
Publishing Corporation. 8.5x11; glossy cover; full-color;
80 pages.

Focus and Audience

Good-news nostalgic and inspirational material
geared towards women. Each issue centers around one
of the following themes: Valentine, Easter, Mother's
Day, Country Home, Friendship, Thanksgiving, and
Christmas.

Interests and Word Lengths

- *Fiction:* Entertaining, idealistic short stories, short-short
  stories, and drama offering nostalgic looks at one of
  the issue themes. 750–1,000 words.
- *Nonfiction:* Nostalgic features, essays, and personal
  experiences appropriate to issue themes. 750–1,000
  words.
- *Departments:* Legendary Americans; Travel; 50 Years
  Ago Today; and Collectors Corner.
- *Poetry:* Traditional, rhyme verse.
- *Photos:* Illustrations and quality 4x5 transparencies.

How to Submit

Send complete ms with cover letter. Queries accepted.
Submit theme-related pieces 8 months in advance. Include SASE. Accepts photocopies and computer printouts. Simultaneous submissions okay. Reports in 2
months.

Payment and Policies

One-time rights. Requests all rights for illustrations. Pays
on publication. Rates vary. Authors receive 1 copy of
the issue; additional copies are discounted.

In Mission

Richard Schramm, Editor
P.O. Box 851
Valley Forge, PA 19487-0851
215-768-2301

AT A GLANCE:

IN MISSION

- Baptist, Mission
- 8% freelance
- 50% new writers
- Bimonthly
- Circ: 40,000
- Receives 8 queries; 4 mss each month.
- Pays: Up to $150 on publication.

From the Editor:
"All commentary must be based in Scripture with references in the text. Cite specific scriptural passages."

Avoid: Unsubstantiated and unfootnoted writing.

Sample copy: Free with 9x12 SASE. No guidelines.

Profile

A bimonthly American Baptist Church (ABC) mission publication. 8.5x11; self cover; 2-color; 24 pages.

Focus and Audience

Reports on the activities of the American Baptist Church and its mission-related works.

Interests and Word Lengths

- *Nonfiction:* Missionary accounts, travel in mission, 22-minute worship services, and other Scripture-oriented material. 750 words.
- *Departments:* Food for Thought, compilation of interesting tidbits. Newsline, inside ABC personnel. Presidents Perspective; Info Exchange; The Little Scroll; From the Word.

How to Submit

Send complete ms with cover letter. No originals; does not return mss. Accepts photocopies, computer printouts, IBM-compatible disks, faxes, and submissions via modem. Identify simultaneous submissions. Reports in 2 months.

Payment and Policies

First North American serial rights. Pays on publication. Up to $150 honorarium for feature articles. Authors receive 5 copies of the issue upon request.

Inside

Jane Biberman, Editor
226 South 16th Street
Philadelphia, PA 19102
215-893-5700

Profile

A monthly general-interest Jewish magazine published by the Jewish Federation of Greater Philadelphia. 8.5x11; glossy cover; full-color; 150–200 pages.

Focus and Audience

Covers topics of Jewish interest from a cultural, rather
than religious, perspective. Targets a Conservative
and Reformed Jewish readership, ages 30–50.

Interests and Word Lengths

- *Fiction:* Occasionally accepts short stories.
  1,000–2,000 words.
- *Nonfiction:* Features, interviews, and essays that
  center around a particular theme. Favors creative
  topics, profiles of Jewish leaders and personalities,
  and current popular pieces such as "Jews in Holly-
  wood." 1,000–2,000 words. Accepts filler and seasonal material.
- *Departments:* Car & Driver; Interiors, home decorating; Fashion; Dining Out; and Travel.
- *Artwork:* Accepts photos and illustrations.

How to Submit

Query with outline preferred. Accepts complete ms
with cover letter. Include SASE. Accepts photocopies,
computer printouts, and WordPerfect disks. Simultaneous submissions okay. Reports in 2–3 weeks.

Payment and Policies

Pays on publication. $50–$400 per piece. Kill fee,
20–25%. Authors receive 3–4 copies of the issue upon
request.

Insight

Lori Peckham, Associate Editor
55 West Oak Ridge Drive
Hagerstown, MD 21740
301-791-7000

AT A GLANCE:

INSIGHT

- Seventh-day Adventist, Teens
- 75% freelance
- 50% new writers
- Weekly
- Circ: 26,000
- Receives 2–3 queries, 50+ mss each month.
- Pays: $25–$100 on acceptance.

From the Editor:
"We look for writing that is story oriented, concrete, and includes realistic characters. Dialog should sound the way teens talk. The endings should offer hope and practical help."

Best Bet: Stories written from a teen perspective.

Avoid: Adult viewpoints.

Sample copy: Free with 9x12 SAE and $.75 postage. Send #10 SASE for guidelines.

Profile

A weekly magazine of Christian understanding and outreach for Seventh-day Adventist teenagers. Its companion publication, *Insight/Out*, is published for Christian teens of all denominations. 8.5x10.5; glossy cover; 4-color; 16 pages.

Focus and Audience

Covers relevant teen topics in a practical, hopeful way that points teens to Jesus. For Seventh-day Adventist youth, ages 15–19.

Interests and Word Lengths

- *Fiction:* Short stories and parables with realistic, multi-dimensional characters on teenage themes with teenage protagonists. 500–1,800 words.
- *Nonfiction:* Personal experiences, how-tos that incorporate anecdotes, interviews, and news pieces on teen topics. 500–1,800 words.
- *Departments:* Watz Happening, news items related to teens. U Did It!, short stories and poems written by teenagers. Lengths vary.

How to Submit

Send complete ms with cover letter. Include SASE. Accepts photocopies, computer printouts, and 5.25-inch WordPerfect 5.0 disks. Simultaneous submissions okay. Reports in 2–3 months.

Payment and Policies

One-time rights. Pays on acceptance. $25–$100 per piece. Kill fee varies. Authors receive 2–3 copies of the issue.

Insight/Out

Lori Peckham, Associate Editor
55 West Oak Ridge Drive
Hagerstown, MD 21740
301-791-7000

AT A GLANCE:
Insight/Out

- Christian, Teens
- 75% freelance
- 50% new writers
- Monthly
- Circ: 26,000
- Receives 2–3 queries, 50+ mss each month.
- Pays: $25–$100 on acceptance.

From the Editor:
"We look for writing that is story oriented, concrete, and includes realistic characters. Dialog should sound the way teens talk. The endings should offer hope and practical help."

Best Bet: Stories written from a teen perspective.

Avoid: Adult viewpoints.

Sample copy: Free with 9x12 SAE and $.75 postage. Send #10 SASE for guidelines.

Profile
A non-denominational monthly magazine of Christian understanding and outreach for teenagers. Sponsored by the Seventh-day Adventist Church, which also publishes its companion publication, *Insight.* 8.5x10.5; glossy cover; 4-color; 30 pages.

Focus and Audience
Covers relevant teen topics in a practical, hopeful way that points teens to Jesus. For Christian youth ages 15–19.

Interests and Word Lengths
- *Fiction:* Short stories and parables with realistic, multi-dimensional characters on teenage themes with teenage protagonists. 500–1,800 words.
- *Nonfiction:* Personal experiences, how-tos that incorporate anecdotes, interviews, and news pieces on teen topics. 500–1,800 words.
- *Departments:* Watz Happening, news items related to teens. U Did It!, short stories and poems written by teenagers. Lengths vary.

How to Submit
Send complete ms with cover letter. Include SASE. Accepts photocopies, computer printouts, and 5.25-inch WordPerfect 5.0 disks. Simultaneous submissions okay. Reports in 2–3 months.

Payment and Policies
One-time rights. Pays on acceptance. $25–$100 per piece. Kill fee varies. Authors receive 2–3 copies of the issue.

Interchange

Michael Barwell, Editor
Diocese of Southern Ohio
412 Sycamore Street
Cincinnati, OH 45202
513-421-0311

AT A GLANCE:

INTERCHANGE

- Episcopal, Regional
- 10% freelance
- 1% new writers
- 8 issues a year
- Circ: 12,800
- Receives few queries each month.
- Pays: $35–$50 on publication.

From the Editor:
"Contact the editor before submitting a manuscript. *Interchange* is distributed to every Episcopal household in the 40 counties of southern Ohio."

Best Bet: Articles with a southern Ohio angle that show faith in action.

Sample copy: Free with 9x12 SASE. No guidelines.

Profile

A regional newspaper of the Episcopal Church and Anglican Communion in southern Ohio. Tabloid-size; newsprint; 28 pages.

Focus and Audience

Offers Episcopal and Anglican Church-related news and features that show faith in action in southern Ohio-area communities. Prefers pieces with a regional angle.

Interests and Word Lengths

- *Nonfiction:* Feature articles, analyses, news, and commentary on local, national, and international events in the Episcopal and Anglican Church. Priority given to pieces with regional interest. Also accepts general informational articles on topics such as small church ministries and social justice that can be adapted by local churches. 500–2,000 words.
- *Artwork:* Prefers B/W prints or line drawings.

How to Submit

Query with outline and writing samples. Include SASE. Accepts photocopies, computer printouts, Macintosh disks, and fax submissions. Simultaneous submissions okay. Reports in 2 months.

Payment and Policies

All rights. Pays on publication. $35–$50 per piece. Authors receive copies of the issue.

Israel Horizons

Ralph Seliger, Editor
224 West 35th Street, #403
New York, NY 10001

AT A GLANCE:

ISRAEL HORIZONS

- Jewish, Socialist Zionism
- 10–20% freelance
- 10% new writers
- Quarterly
- Circ: 3,000
- Receives 3–5 queries, 2–3 mss each month.
- Pays: $25–$50 on publication.

From the Editor:
"We are Zionist, primarily secularist, and of the liberal and democratic socialist left. We are associated with a political party in Israel's current government and a Kibbutz federation."

Best Bet: Articles on issues of concern to Israel and Jews.

Avoid: Opinion essays by new writers.

Sample copy: $4. No guidelines.

Profile

A quarterly publication of Americans for Progressive Israel—Hashomer Hatzair, an organization dedicated to the advancement of Socialist Zionism and to democratic socialism in general. 8.5x11; self cover; newsprint; 36 pages.

Focus and Audience

Opinion and news analysis of a liberal/left persuasion regarding Israel and Jewish communities everywhere. Readers are primarily secular Jews sympathetic to Socialist Zionism.

Interests and Word Lengths

- *Nonfiction:* Articles, analyses, and reviews on issues of concern to Israel and Jews, including bridge-building toward peace with the Arab world, secular-religious relations, women's issues, concerns about Kibbutz life, and economic justice. 1,000–2,500 words.
- *Poetry:* Submit in triplicate. No payment.
- *Photos:* B/W prints.

How to Submit

Query with outline and writing samples, or send complete ms with cover letter. Include SASE. Accepts photocopies, computer printouts, and 3.5-inch ASCII PC-compatible disk submissions. Simultaneous submissions okay. Reports in 1–3 months.

Payment and Policies

Authors retain rights. Pays on publication. Articles, $50. Book reviews, $25 plus copy of the book. Poetry, no payment. Authors receive 5 copies of the issue; additional copies upon request.

Issues
A Messianic Jewish Perspective

Susan Perlman, Editor
P.O. Box 424885
San Francisco, CA 94142-4885
415-854-2600

AT A GLANCE:
ISSUES

- Jewish, Messianic
- 25% freelance
- 20% new writers
- Bimonthly
- Circ: 30,000
- Receives 10 queries, 5 mss each month.
- Pays: $200–$300 on publication.

From the Editor:
"We want people to ask God the truth about various issues. We have faith in Jesus and want to direct people's attention to Him."

Best Bet: Articles that give a messianic Jewish perspective on a variety of issues.

Avoid: Theological treatises; politics; Christian jargon; preachiness; and profanity.

Sample copy: Free. Send #10 SASE for guidelines.

Profile

Published bimonthly by Jews for Jesus, whose members believe that Jesus is the Messiah promised to the Jewish people by God in the Hebrew scriptures. 8.5x11; color; 8 pages.

Focus and Audience

Evangelistic with the primary purpose of expressing a Jewish/Christian viewpoint on the current spiritual, religious, and social concerns of contemporary American Jews. Most readers are Jewish, more secular than religious, committed to maintaining a Jewish identity but willing to consider the publication's messianic perspective.

Interests and Word Lengths

- *Fiction:* Short-short stories about Jews who have trusted in God.
- *Nonfiction:* Scholarly and popular articles that explain or express the christological significance of common Jewish symbols, rituals, holidays, and traditions. Current themes and topics from the perspective of the Jewish believer in Jesus. 1,200–1,500 words. Also accepts short testimonies from Jewish believers.
- *Poetry:* Occasionally accepts spiritual poetry.
- *Illustrations:* Line drawings.

How to Submit

Articles, query with outline. Fiction and testimonies, send ms with cover letter. Include SASE. Accepts computer printouts, and Macintosh disk submissions. Simultaneous submissions okay. Reports in 2 months.

Payment and Policies

All rights. Pays on publication. $200–$300 for lead articles; $50–$75 for poems. Kill fee, $30. Authors receive 6 copies of the issue.

Jewish Action

Charlotte Friedland, Editor-in-Chief
333 Seventh Avenue
New York, NY 10001
212-563-4000

AT A GLANCE:
JEWISH ACTION

- Jewish, Orthodox
- 75% freelance
- 5% new writers
- Quarterly
- Circ: 50,000
- Receives 10 queries, 15 mss each month.
- Pays: $150 after publication.

From the Editor:
"Cover topics of interest to an international Orthodox Jewish audience."

Best Bet: Fresh approaches to articles that reflect and enhance the Orthodox experience.

Avoid: Issues that are too timely; anything not Orthodox.

Sample copy: Free with 9x12 SASE. Send #10 SASE for guidelines.

Profile

A quarterly magazine reflecting Orthodox Jewish values. Published by the Union of Orthodox Jewish Congregations of America. 8.5x11; glossy cover; full-color; 80–96 pages.

Focus and Audience

Seeks to provide a forum for a diversity of legitimate opinions within the spectrum of Orthodox Judaism. Audience is international, well educated, and Orthodox.

Interests and Word Lengths

- *Nonfiction:* Human interest features, news pieces, interviews, essays, historical pieces, humor, and personal experiences related to current ongoing issues of Jewish life and experience, Israel, and the Holocaust. 1,000–2,000 words.
- *Departments:* Opinion; Student Voice; Jewish Living; Book reviews. 1,000 words.
- *Seasonal:* Jewish holiday material.
- *Poetry:* Reflecting Orthodox Jewish themes.
- *Artwork:* Accepts photos and illustrations.

How to Submit

Prefers queries with outline and clips. Accepts complete ms with cover letter. Include SASE. Accepts photocopies, computer printouts, and ASCII disks. Simultaneous submissions okay. Reports in 6–8 weeks.

Payment and Policies

One-time rights. Pays 6 weeks after publication. Articles, approximately $150. Poetry, $25–$75. Authors receive 2–3 copies of the issue.

Jewish Community Chronicle

Harriette Ellis, Editor
3801 East Willow Street
Long Beach, CA 90815-1791
310-426-7601

Profile

A regional newspaper serving the Jewish community. Published by the Federation of Greater Long Beach and West Orange County. Est.: 1947. Tabloid-size; newsprint; 16–20 pages.

Focus and Audience

Informs and enlightens the Jewish community of Greater Long Beach and West Orange County, CA. Prefers community-oriented straight news stories that encourage hands-on interaction with readers.

Interests and Word Lengths

- *Nonfiction:* News features, interviews, and essays on any aspect of Judaism, local, national, or international. Use a journalistic style: no editorializing. See sample copy for upcoming article deadlines. 500–1,000 words.
- *Departments:* Travel; Entertainment; and Perspective.
- *Seasonal:* Jewish holiday material.
- *Photos:* B/W photos to accompany articles. Caption or identify all photos on a separate piece of paper.

How to Submit

Query with outline and resume preferred. Accepts complete ms with cover letter. Include SASE. Accepts photocopies, computer printouts, and fax submissions. Simultaneous submissions okay. Report time varies.

Payment and Policies

All rights. Pays 30 days after publication. Rates vary. Kill fee, 25%. Authors receive copies of the issue upon request.

Jewish Education

Dr. Alvin I. Schiff, Editor
339 Jordan Street
Oceanside, NY 11572
516-766-8274

AT A GLANCE:
JEWISH EDUCATION

- Jewish, Education
- 80% freelance
- 20% new writers
- 3 issues a year
- Circ: 2,000
- Receives 20 queries,
  15 mss each month.
- No payment. Offers 3
  contributor's copies.

From the Editor:
"*Jewish Education* is transideological. It records educational practices and recommends theories and procedures."

Best Bet: Articles on early childhood education, adult Jewish education, family education, supervision, pedagogy, and the sociology of Jewish education.

Avoid: Fictional ideas and how-to-teach articles.

Sample copy: $5 with $1 postage. Send #10 SASE for guidelines.

Profile

A transideological scholarly journal of Jewish education theories and practices. Published by the Council for Jewish Education. 6.5x10; glossy cover; 48 pages.

Focus and Audience

Provides a forum for the exchange of ideas, opinions, and research on the theory and practice of Jewish education. Aimed at administrators, teachers, rabbis, academicians, and lay leaders of all denominations involved in Jewish education.

Interests and Word Lengths

- *Nonfiction:* Historical studies, research summaries, and personal-experience and opinion pieces on early childhood education, adult Jewish education, supervision, financing of private education, pedagogy, and family education. 2,000–3,000 words.
- *Departments:* One Person's Opinion, 2,000–3,000 words. Book Reviews and Juvenile Literature Reviews, 1,000–2,000 words.

How to Submit

Query with resume, or send complete ms with cover letter. Include SASE. Accepts computer printouts, faxes, and submissions via modem. No simultaneous submissions. Reports in 3 months.

Payment and Policies

Authors retain rights. No payment. Authors receive 3 copies of the issue.

Jewish Exponent

Albert H. Erlick, Managing Editor
226 South 16th Street
Philadelphia, PA 19102
215-893-5700

AT A GLANCE:

JEWISH EXPONENT

- Jewish, Regional
- 10–15% freelance
- 5% new writers
- Weekly
- Circ: 65,000
- Pays on publication. Rates vary.

From the Editor:
"Address the entire Jewish community, secular and non-secular."

Best Bet: Short news pieces of Jewish relevance.

Avoid: Q&A interviews.

Sample copy: Free. No guidelines.

Profile

A weekly regional news tabloid for the Philadelphia-area Jewish community. Published by the non-profit Jewish Federation of Greater Philadelphia. Est.: 1887. Tabloid-size; newsprint; 80 pages.

Focus and Audience

Covers local, national, and international news of interest to the Jewish community in Philadelphia, PA.

Interests and Word Lengths

- *Nonfiction:* Features, essays, news pieces, and personal experiences on topics with Jewish relevance. Up to 1,000 words. Accepts filler.
- *Departments:* Op-Ed; Magazine Section; Recipes; Youth News; Torah Study.
- *Seasonal:* Jewish holiday material.
- *Photos:* B/W and color prints; no negatives or slides.

How to Submit

Query with outline, or send complete ms with cover letter. Include SASE. Accepts photocopies and computer printouts. Occasionally accepts simultaneous submissions. Report time varies.

Payment and Policies

Authors retain rights. Pays on publication. Rates vary. Authors receive tear sheets.

Jewish Leader

Editor
28 Channing Street
New London, CT 06320
203-442-7395

Profile

A biweekly regional publication of Jewish news and events. 8–12 pages.

Focus and Audience

Local, national, and international news and events of interest to Jewish leaders in the Connecticut area.

Interests and Word Lengths

- *Nonfiction:* Short features, interviews, and personal-experience pieces on Israel, cultural and religious concerns, and world and social issues. Interviews with Connnecticut-area Jewish personalities. Accepts filler and seasonal material. Prefers short articles.

How to Submit

Send complete ms with cover letter. Include SASE. Accepts photocopies, computer printouts, and fax submissions. Simultaneous submissions okay. Report time varies.

Payment and Policies

Authors retain rights. No payment. Authors receive copies of the issue upon request.

The Jewish News

Alan Hitsky, Associate Editor
27676 Franklin Road
Southfield, MI 48034
313-354-6060

AT A GLANCE:
The Jewish News

- Jewish, Regional
- 5% freelance
- Weekly
- Circ: 20,000
- Receives 6 mss each month.
- Pays: $40–$100 on publication.

From the Editor:
"We publish 4 or 5 fiction pieces each year. Other articles and stories might be used if there is a strong Detroit angle."

Best Bet: Material with Jewish interest or Jewish themes.

Avoid: Poetry.

Sample copy: $1. Send #10 SASE for guidelines.

Profile
A weekly Jewish newspaper for residents of Detroit, MI, and surrounding areas. Sister publications include the *Baltimore Jewish Times* and the *Atlanta Jewish Times*. 10x13; newsprint; 3-color cover; 132 pages.

Focus and Audience
Covers news of the Jewish community in the Detroit area, across the nation, and around the world.

Interests and Word Lengths
- *Fiction:* Publishes 4–5 stories per year Must be of Jewish interest or on Jewish themes. Up to 1,200 words.
- *Nonfiction:* Considers articles that have a strong Detroit angle and Jewish themes. Occasionally purchases opinion pieces.

How to Submit
Send complete ms with cover letter. Include SASE. Accepts photocopies and computer printouts. Simultaneous submissions okay. Reports in 2 months.

Payment and Policies
One-time rights. Pays on publication. Rates vary depending on quality and length of work. Payment is negotiated upon acceptance. Fiction and articles, $40–$100 per piece. Opinion pieces, $25. Kill fee, 33%. Additional fee paid for pieces used in sister publications. Authors receive 2 copies of the issue.

Jewish Press

Steve Walz, Editor
338 Third Avenue
Brooklyn, NY 11215
718-330-1100

AT A GLANCE:
JEWISH PRESS

- Orthodox Jewish, Regional
- 25% freelance
- 5% new writers
- Weekly
- Circ: 125,000
- Receives 50 queries, 50 mss each month.
- Payment varies.

From the Editor:
"Keep it simple. Read a sample copy and scan each section."

Best Bet: Punchy, to-the-point articles with an Orthodox Jewish angle.

Avoid: Poetry; long-winded analysis.

Sample copy: Free. No guidelines.

Profile
A weekly newspaper for the New York-area Orthodox Jewish community. Tabloid-size; 104 pages.

Focus and Audience
Offers Zionist-oriented national and international news. Readers are New York-area Orthodox Jewish people.

Interests and Word Lengths
- *Nonfiction:* Features, interviews, essays, and personal experiences relevant to Orthodox Jewish people. Interests include regional and national news. 3–4 typed, double-spaced pages.
- *Departments:* Kosher Food; Business; Travel; Fashion; Arts & Entertainment.
- *Photos:* B/W prints and illustrations to accompany articles.

How to Submit
Query with outline or send complete ms with cover letter. Include SASE. Accepts photocopies, computer printouts, and IBM WordPerfect disk submissions. No simultaneous submissions. Reports in 2–4 weeks.

Payment and Policies
All rights. Pays for outstanding articles. Rates vary. Authors receive copies of the issue upon request.

The Jewish Review

Paul Haist, Editor
6800 SW Beaverton-Hillsdale Highway
Suite C
Portland, OR 97225
503-292-4913

AT A GLANCE:
THE JEWISH REVIEW

- Jewish, Regional
- 25% freelance
- 1% new writers
- Biweekly
- Circ: 7,500
- Receives 3–4 queries, 15–20 mss each month.
- Pays: $20–$100 on publication.

From the Editor:
"Tight, straight ahead newspaper writing only. Manuscripts must conform to the *AP Stylebook* or they will be rejected."

Avoid: Messianic Judaism and revisionist history.

Sample copy: Free. No guidelines.

Profile

A newspaper of Jewish lifestyle published biweekly by the Jewish Federation of Portland. Est.: 1959. Tabloid-size; newsprint; 28 pages.

Focus and Audience

Covers Jewish life and lifestyles as well as domestic and international news and issues of interest to Jewish readers in Oregon and southwest Washington.

Interests and Word Lengths

- *Nonfiction:* Articles on Jewish family and religious issues, Israel, Mideast peace efforts, domestic Jewish political issues, and Jewish opinion. Writing must conform to the *AP Stylebook*. 750–1,000 words
- *Seasonal:* Submit Jewish holiday pieces 2 months in advance.
- *Photos:* B/W prints.

How to Submit

Query with outline and clips, or send complete ms. Include SASE. Accepts letter-quality computer printouts and IBM disk submissions. Simultaneous submissions okay. Reports in 1 month.

Payment and Policies

One-time regional rights. Pays on publication. $20–$100 per piece. Contributor's copies not provided.

Jewish Science Interpreter

David Goldstein, Executive Director
54 Sunnyside Boulevard
Suite J
Plainview, NY 11803
516-349-0022

AT A GLANCE:

JEWISH SCIENCE INTERPRETER

- Jewish, Inspirational
- 10–25% freelance
- 5% new writers
- 8 issues a year
- Circ: 1,200
- No payment. Offers 10 contributor's copies.

From the Editor:
"We believe that spirituality and a spiritual viewpoint of life is attainable in a modern world, and can have an impact on all areas of daily living."

Best Bet: Inspirational Jewish works.

Sample copy: Free with 5x8 SAE and $1 postage. No guidelines.

Profile

The official publication of the Society of Jewish Science, which believes in the application of Jewish faith in daily life experience so as to eliminate worry, fear, and tendencies to illness. 8.5x11; self cover; 12 pages.

Focus and Audience

Inspirational articles and essays for those looking for health, happiness, and peace of mind through the Jewish faith. Adheres to Jewish tradition as it discovers a new richness of Judaism.

Interests and Word Lengths

- *Fiction:* Short stories of inspiration, spirit, and Judaism. Accepts poetry.
- *Nonfiction:* Features, articles, interviews, and personal experiences. Subjects include individual uses of Judaism in the modern world, prayer, visualization, meditation, affirmation, healing, inspiration, and spirituality. Accepts filler.
- *Seasonal:* Seasonal and holiday material.

How to Submit

Fiction, query with resume and writing samples. Nonfiction, query with resume and writing samples, or send complete ms with cover letter and resume. Include SASE. Accepts photocopies, computer printouts, and Macintosh disks. Simultaneous submissions okay. Reports in 3 months.

Payment and Policies

All rights. No payment. Authors receive 10 copies of the issue.

Jewish Times

Matthew Schuman, Editor
103 A Tomlinson Road
Huntingdon Valley, PA 19006
215-938-1177

Matthew Schuman, Editor
103 A Tomlinson Road
Huntingdon Valley, PA 19006
215-938-1177

AT A GLANCE:

JEWISH TIMES

- Jewish, Regional
- 30% freelance
- Weekly
- Circ: 35,000
- Receives 10 queries, 6–10 mss each month.
- Pays on publication. Rates vary.

From the Editor:
"Keep articles oriented to Jewish issues, activities, people, or holidays. Clear, crisp, concise writing is a requirement."

Avoid: Pro-PLO viewpoints.

Sample copy: Free with SASE. No guidelines.

Profile

A weekly Jewish newspaper serving the Greater Northeast, Lower Bucks, and Eastern Montgomery counties of Pennsylvania. Tabloid-size; newsprint; 40 pages.

Focus and Audience

Represents a broad spectrum of Jewish views—from liberal to conservative—and a broad range of interests and lifestyles. Most readers are 50 years and older.

Interests and Word Lengths

- *Nonfiction:* Features on Jewish issues and human interest pieces, up to 1,000 words. Personal experience pieces such as first trips to Israel or Poland or accounts of life in concentration camps, 800–1,000 words.
- *Departments:* Op/Ed; Sportsline; Investmentline; Healthline; Entertainment, focuses on Jewish entertainers or productions.
- *Seasonal:* Unique ways of celebrating Jewish holidays.
- *Photos:* 5x7 or 8x10 B/W prints.

How to Submit

Query with outline and writing samples, or send complete ms with cover letter and resume. Include SASE. Accepts computer printouts. Reports in 2 months.

Payment and Policies

First North American serial rights. Pays on publication. Rates vary. Authors receive 2 copies of the issue.

Jewish Vegetarians Newsletter

Shelli Yesenko, Editor
P.O. Box 1463
Baltimore, MD 21203
410-754-5550

AT A GLANCE:

JEWISH VEGETARIANS NEWSLETTER

- Jewish, Vegetarianism
- 100% freelance/membership
- Quarterly
- Circ: 800
- No payment. Offers contributor's copies upon request.

From the Editor: "We focus on Judaism only as it pertains to vegetarian food and the observance of Jewish holidays."

Best Bet: Pleasant and encouraging articles on Jewish vegetarianism.

Avoid: Excessively emphatic pieces on extreme cruelty to animals.

Sample copy: Free with 9x12 SAE and $.52 postage. No guidelines.

Profile

A quarterly newsletter published by Jewish Vegetarians of North America for its members. All material is member written. 8.5x11; self cover; 16 pages.

Focus and Audience

Promotes the practice of vegetarianism within the Judaic tradition, and explores the relationship between Judaism, dietary laws, and vegetarianism.

Interests and Word Lengths

- *Nonfiction:* Articles on vegetarianism, Judaism, and the vegetarian observance of Jewish holidays; nutrition and health; animal rights; true stories of animals; and environmental issues as related to vegetarianism. Also accepts question-and-answer pieces; restaurant and book reviews; and recipes. No word-length requirements.

How to Submit

Submit complete ms with cover letter. Include SASE. Accepts photocopies, computer printouts, and Macintosh disk submissions. Report time varies.

Payment and Policies

First North American serial rights. No payment. Authors receive copies of the issue upon request.

The Jewish Veteran

Howard Metzger, Assistant National Director of Communications
1811 R Street NW
Washington, DC 20009
202-265-6280

AT A GLANCE:

THE JEWISH VETERAN

- Jewish, Seniors
- 5% freelance
- 5% new writers
- 5 issues a year
- Circ: 60,000
- Receives 10–20 queries, 10–20 mss each month.
- No payment. Offers contributor's copies.

From the Editor:
"If it deals with topics of concern to our members, we welcome your manuscript."

Best Bet: Articles on topics of interest to members of The Jewish War Veterans.

Avoid: Travel, cooking, gardening, or gossipy pieces.

Sample copy: Free. No guidelines.

Profile

The official publication of The Jewish War Veterans (JWV). 24 pages.

Focus and Audience

Covers topics of interest to Jewish veterans. Distributed to members of Congress, it serves as an informational resource on policies affecting JWV members.

Interests and Word Lengths

- *Fiction:* Short stories on experiences as Jewish veterans and military members. 500–2,000 words.
- *Nonfiction:* Feature articles, essays, and personal-experience pieces on health, politics, seniors, social and world issues, and worship as experienced by or in some way related to Jewish members of the military. 500–2,000 words.
- *Poetry:* On subjects of interest to JWV members.
- *Seasonal:* On subjects of interest to JWV members.
- *Photos:* 5x7 B/W prints.

How to Submit

Query with outline. Include SASE. Accepts photocopies and computer printouts. Simultaneous submissions okay.

Payment and Policies

Authors retain rights. No payment. Authors receive copies of the issue.

Jewish Weekly News

Kenneth White, Editor
P.O. Box 1569
Springfield, MA 01101-1569
413-739-4771

AT A GLANCE:

JEWISH WEEKLY NEWS

- Jewish, Regional
- 15% freelance
- Weekly
- Circ: 2,000
- Receives 2 queries, 10 mss each month.
- Pays: $.50–$.75 per column inch on publication.

From the Editor:

"We are primarily interested in stories with a local angle, or seasonal material from a fresh angle."

Sample copy: Free with 9x12 SAE with $.65 postage. Send #10 SASE for guidelines.

Profile

An independent journal of Jewish news and opinion. Member of the American Jewish Press Association. Est.: 1945. Tabloid-size; newsprint; 12 pages.

Focus and Audience

Covers local, national, and international issues of Jewish interest. Readers cross all age and Jewish religious demographics.

Interests and Word Lengths

- *Nonfiction:* Interests include regional issues, Judaism, Jewish holidays, Israel, Jewish life in America, politics, and social and world issues. 500–1,000 words.
- *Departments:* Torah Talk, independent commentary and opinion. Jewish Kitchens, cooking. 500–750 words.
- *Artwork:* B/W photos and line drawings.

How to Submit

Send complete ms with cover letter. Include SASE. Accepts photocopies, computer printouts, and Macintosh disks. Simultaneous submissions okay. Reports in 2–3 months.

Payment and Policies

One-time rights. Pays on publication. $.50–$.75 per column inch. Authors receive 1 copy of the issue.

The Jewish World

Laurie J. Clevenson, Associate Editor
1104 Central Avenue
Albany, NY 12205
518-495-8455

AT A GLANCE:

THE JEWISH WORLD

- Jewish, News
- 15% freelance
- 1% new writers
- Weekly
- Circ: 7,000
- Receives 5 queries, 2 mss each month.
- Pays on publication. Rates vary.

From the Editor:
"You can fax or mail copies of your proposal. Exclusivity is not an issue."

Best Bet: News and features about Israel and Jewish people.

Avoid: Flowery writing.

Sample copy: Not provided. No guidelines.

Profile

A weekly Jewish newspaper covering Northeastern New York state, Vermont, and Western Massachusetts. Tabloid-size; newsprint; 24 pages.

Focus and Audience

News, features, and activities about Israel and Jewish people that are more news than rhetoric and religion.

Interests and Word Lengths

- *Nonfiction:* Articles, features, and human interest pieces on people, politics, regional activities, Israel, and social and world issues with emphasis on Jewish people and interests. Word lengths vary.
- *Seasonal:* Jewish holidays and customs.
- *Photos:* B/W or color prints, slides, and line drawings.

How to Submit

Query with resume and writing samples. Include SASE. Accepts fax submissions. Simultaneous submissions okay.

Payment and Policies

One-time rights. Pays on publication. Rates vary. Authors receive copies of the issue.

The Journal of Christian Camping

John Ashmen, Managing Editor
2100 Manchester Road
Suite 605
Wheaton, IL 60189
708-462-0300

AT A GLANCE:
THE JOURNAL OF CHRISTIAN CAMPING

- Christian, Recreation
- 75% freelance
- 50% new writers
- Bimonthly
- Circ: 7,000
- Receives 10 queries, 1–2 mss each month.
- Pays: $.06 per word on publication.

From the Editor:
"*The Journal* is meant to be an informational source. We prefer a query first. It is helpful if an interested freelance writer obtains a copy of our publication and a list of our editorial guidelines before proceeding."

Avoid: Fiction and poetry.

Sample copy: $4.50 with 8.5x11 SASE. Send #10 SASE for guidelines.

Profile

A professional journal that serves as a resource for Christian camp leaders. Member pubication of the Evangelical Press Association. 8.5x11; glossy cover; 3-color; 32 pages.

Focus and Audience

Designed as an informational source for camping professionals. All material geared to equip and enable leaders of Christian camps, conferences, and retreat centers.

Interests and Word Lengths

- *Nonfiction:* Articles that explore camp purposes and objectives; administration and organization; programming; food service; health and safety; marketing and public relations; fundraising. Interests include camping-related articles, personal experiences, or inspirational pieces on the environment, evangelism, family, lifestyle, seniors, and spirituality. 1,000 words.
- *Filler:* Tasteful jokes, quips, and quotes.
- *Photos:* B/W and color prints. Prefers mood/action shots and facial close-ups.

How to Submit

Query with outline and clips. Include SASE. No unsolicited mss. Accepts computer printouts and 3.5-inch WordPerfect or Microsoft Word disks. Simultaneous submissions okay. Reports in 1 month.

Payment and Policies

First North American serial rights. Pays on publication. $.06 per word. Authors receive 2 copies of the issue.

Journal of Christian Nursing

Melodee Yohe, Managing Editor
5206 Main Street
Downers Grove, IL 60515
708-964-5700

AT A GLANCE: JOURNAL OF CHRISTIAN NURSING

- Nursing, Christian
- 25–50% freelance
- 25–50% new writers
- Quarterly
- Circ: 10,000
- Receives 6-8 queries, 15 mss each month.
- Pays: $25–$80 on publication.

From the Editor:
"The few non-nurse authors from whom we accept material must write about Christian nurses who are ministering in a creative way, or address their topic from the nursing viewpoint. Our stance is pro-life and anti-euthanasia."

Best Bet: Very readable, not technical, articles about real people.

Avoid: Research articles; preachy tone; New Age techniques.

Sample copy: Free with 9x12 SAE with $.65 postage. Send #10 SASE for guidelines.

Profile

A professional quarterly journal published by Nurses Christian Fellowship, a division of InterVarsity Christian Fellowship. Issues are thematic. Est.: 1945. Tabloid-size; newsprint; 12 pages.

Focus and Audience

For and about Christian nurses who care about the spiritual needs of patients and want to meet ethical dilemmas in nursing in a consistently biblical way, growing spiritually themselves. Most articles are written by nursing professionals.

Interests and Word Lengths

- *Nonfiction:* Interviews, first-person articles, nurses' mission experiences, didactic material if appropriate to theme, ethical and professional issues affecting nursing and nurses, and articles about interesting nursing experiences. All should explore ways Christian nurses successfully combine their faith and their profession. Incorporate true anecdotes and include illustrations. Occasionally accepts seasonal material. 8-12 double-spaced, typewritten pages.
- *Departments:* The Last Word, guest editorial by nurses involved in interesting jobs/ministries. 4 double-spaced, typewritten pages.
- *Artwork:* B/W or color prints, slides, and drawings to illustrate and accompany manuscripts.

How to Submit

Prefers complete ms with cover letter. Accepts query with outline. Include SASE. Accepts photocopies, computer printouts, and fax submissions. Reports in 1 month.

Payment and Policies

One-time and reprint rights. Pays on publication. $25–$80 per article. Kill fee, 50%. Authors receive 2-8 copies of the issue.

Joyful Noise

William W. Maxwell, Editor
310 North Tulane Drive
Archer, FL 32618
904-486-3232

AT A GLANCE:
JOYFUL NOISE

- African-American, Religion
- Bimonthly
- Circ: not available
- Pays: $50–$250 on acceptance.

From the Editor:
"We will serve a diverse audience and do not seek to make social statements or to pass judgment. We simply want to inform, educate, entertain, and inspire readers. We are their friends."

Best Bet: Easy-to-read, upbeat articles about African-American churches and their members.

Avoid: Academic prose; preachy social statements.

Sample copy: Not available. Send #10 SASE for guidelines.

Profile

A new, non-denominational and interfaith magazine about the African-American experience in religion. First issue not available at time of review. Est.: 1993.

Focus and Audience

Seeks articles with religious themes that relate to some aspect of African-American life and reflects the importance of the church in Black culture. Written for African-Americans, although writers may be of different cultures or races.

Interests and Word Lengths

- *Nonfiction:* First six issues will focus solely on Florida Black churches. Areas of interest include fatherhood; vacation and travel pieces; the best Sunday school programs in Florida; inspirational sermons; new trends in Black gospel music; congregations fighting AIDS and drugs; reviews of religious books of interest to African-Americans; profiles of Black Catholics, Muslims, Unitarians, etc.; prison ministries; pastor burnout; women in ministry; worship styles; and ministering to children. For subsequent issues, seeks general-interest articles on church-related topics such as church landscaping and architecture; organizing a convention or meeting; preparing a special church cookout; purchasing choir robes; financing new construction; finding a reputable builder; and keeping a marriage viable. 700–3,000 words.
- *Artwork:* Accepts photos and illustrations.

How to Submit

Submit complete ms with cover letter, or query with clips and author biography. Include SASE.

Payment and Policies

Pays on acceptance. $50–$250 per piece. Photos, $20–$30.

The Joyful Noiseletter

Cal Samra, Editor
P.O. Box 895
Portage, MI 49081-0895
616-324-0990

AT A GLANCE:
THE JOYFUL NOISE-
LETTER

- Christian, Humor
- 99% freelance
- Monthly
- Circ: 10,000
- Receives many mss each month.
- No payment. Offers 1 contributor's copy.

From the Editor:
"We do not pay for free-lance items. *JN* is written mainly by the editors. Members of the Fellowship of Merry Christians contribute items to us free-of-charge."

Best Bet: Humorous anecdotes and jokes for church-goers.

Sample copy: $2. No guidelines.

Profile

A monthly newsletter of Christian humor, published by and for members of the Fellowship of Merry Christians. 8.5x11; 2-color; folded; 6 pages.

Focus and Audience

Provides humor, jokes, anecdotes, and cartoons to pastors of all denominations and to local church newsletters and bulletins. Most material is contributed by Christian humorists and Merry Christian members.

Interests and Word Lengths

- *Humor:* Short jokes, anecdotes, and cartoons appropriate for sermons or church bulletins. 50–100 words.

How to Submit

Submit complete ms with cover letter. Include SASE. Accepts photocopies and computer printouts.

Payment and Policies

No payment. Authors receive 1 copy of the issue upon request.

The Joyful Woman

Elizabeth Rice Handford, Editor
Shiloh on Shannon
118 Shannon Lake Circle
Greenville, SC 29615
803-234-0289

AT A GLANCE: THE JOYFUL WOMAN

- Christian, Women
- 50% freelance
- Bimonthly
- Circ: 15,000
- Receives 100 mss each month.
- Pays: $.02–$.04 per word on publication.

From the Editor:

"We are committed to the fundamental biblical viewpoint of the authority of God's Word, the need for salvation by grace through faith in Christ's atoning death, personal purity of life, and wise and caring soul winning."

Best Bet: Articles that address the spiritual and temporal needs of Christian women.

Sample copy: $3 with $1 postage. Send #10 SASE for guidelines.

Profile

A nondenominational, fundamental Christian magazine for and about Bible-believing women who want God's best. Member of the Evangelical Press Association. 8.5x11; glossy cover; 2-color; 24 pages.

Focus and Audience

Designed to encourage, stimulate, teach, and develop the Christian woman to reach her full potential, joyful and fulfilled, a useful servant of Christ regardless of her situation.

Interests and Word Lengths

- *Fiction:* Occasionally uses short stories and poetry.
- *Nonfiction:* Purchase approximately 60 freelance articles a year. Accepts articles on every facet of a Christian woman's life. Address emotional, physical, and intellectual needs as well as a woman's spiritual life and ministry to others. 400–2,000 words. Uses filler.
- *Seasonal:* Submit 4 months in advance.

How to Submit

Fiction, send complete ms. Nonfiction, query or send complete ms. Include SASE. Simultaneous submissions okay. Reports on mss in 6 weeks, on queries in 1 week.

Payment and Policies

First or reprint rights. Pays usually on publication, occasionally on acceptance. $.02–$.04 per word. Authors receive 5 copies of the issue.

Jr. High Ministry

Barbara Beach, Departments Editor
2890 North Monroe Avenue
Loveland, CO 80538
303-669-3836

AT A GLANCE:
JR. HIGH MINISTRY

- Christian, Youth Ministry
- 50% freelance
- 5% new writers
- 5 times a year
- Circ: 30,000
- Receives 5 queries, 30 mss each month.
- Pays: $75–$150 on acceptance.

From the Editor:
"We need how-to articles for junior-high group membership building, worship planning, handling specific group problems, improving as a leader, and understanding junior highers."

Best Bet: Practical how-to articles that are fun, experiential, very active–learning oriented.

Avoid: Fiction, poetry, anything preachy.

Sample copy: $1 with 9x12 SASE bearing $1 postage. Send #10 SASE for guidelines.

Profile

An interdenominational magazine for adults who work with junior-high-age Christian young people. 8.5x11; glossy cover; full-color; 40 pages.

Focus and Audience

Supplies ideas, practical help, inspiration, and training for Christian youth leaders.

Interests and Word Lengths

- *Nonfiction:* How-to articles concerning retreats, and special meetings. Other subjects include competition, faith in action, seasonal themes, friendship, specific life situations, and service projects. 500–2,200 words.
- *Departments:* Parents Page, discipline, faith, communication, building a close family, parent self-understanding, practical help, and understanding junior-high values. 150 words.
- *Photos:* State availability of photos with submission; model releases and identification of subjects required.

How to Submit

Query with writing samples, or send ms with cover letter. Include SASE. Accepts photocopies, computer printouts, Macintosh Microsoft Word disks, and fax submissions. Simultaneous submissions okay. Reports in 1 month.

Payment and Policies

All rights. Pays on acceptance. $75–$150 based on article length and type. Kill fee, $25. Authors receive 2 copies of the issue.

Junior Trails

Sinda S. Zinn, Editor
1445 Boonville Avenue
Springfield, MO 65802
417-862-2781

AT A GLANCE:

JUNIOR TRAILS

- Christian, Sunday School
- 95% freelance
- Weekly
- Circ: 65,000
- Pays: $.02–$.03 per word on acceptance.

From the Editor:
"*Junior Trails* is intended to help boys and girls learn how they can act in biblical ways to everyday situations."

Best Bet: Fiction that promotes biblical principles, aimed at 9- to 11-year-old children.

Avoid: Stories about Halloween, Santa Claus, and the like.

Sample copy: Free with SASE. Send #10 SASE for guidelines.

Profile

A weekly Sunday school take-home paper for children. Published by The General Council of the Assemblies of God, Inc. 5.5x8; full-color, stapled; 8 pages.

Focus and Audience

Seeks stories that present realistic characters working out problems according to biblical principles for children, ages 9–11.

Interests and Word Lengths

- *Fiction:* Short stories about 9- to 11-year-old children on subjects including city living and its problems, blended families, temptations faced by Christians and how to overcome them. 1,000–1,500 words.

How to Submit

Send complete ms with cover letter. Include SASE. Accepts computer printouts. Simultaneous submissions okay. Reports in 4–6 weeks.

Payment and Policies

One-time rights. Pays on acceptance. $.02–$.03 per word. Authors receive 3 copies of the issue.

Just Between Us

Managing Editor
P.O. Box 7728
Louisville, KY 40257
502-899-3119

Profile

A quarterly inspirational magazine for wives of evangelical ministers. 8.5x11; 20 pages.

Focus and Audience

Offers ideas, council, and encouragement by and for ministers' wives. Readers are predominantly evangelical Christians.

Interests and Word Lengths

- *Nonfiction:* Personal experiences and articles of interest to ministers' wives. Interests include practical ideas, council, and encouragement. No word-length restrictions. Accepts seasonal material.
- *Photos:* Accepts prints with article.

How to Submit

Query with outline. Include SASE. Accepts photocopies, computer printouts, and IBM-compatible disks with hard copy. Simultaneous submissions okay. Report time varies.

Payment and Policies

One-time rights. No payment. Authors receive copies of the issue.

Kaleidoscope

Darshan Perusek, Editor-in-Chief
326 Locust Street
Akron, OH 44302-1876
216-762-9755

AT A GLANCE:

KALEIDOSCOPE

- Disability, Fine Arts
- 33% freelance
- 2 issues a year
- Circ: 500
- Receives 60 mss each month.
- Pays: $100 per piece on publication.

From the Editor:
"*Kaleidoscope* features writers and artists both with and without disabilities. We are not interested in how-I-overcame or poor-me stories."

Best Bet: Articles that explore disability through the literary and visual arts.

Avoid: Euphemisms such as "physically challenged" or "visually impaired."

Sample copy: Free. Send #10 SASE for guidelines.

Profile

A thematic semiannual journal exploring disability through literature and the fine arts. 8.5x11; glossy cover; 4-color; 16 pages.

Focus and Audience

Examines the experiences of disability through diverse forms of literature and fine art. Strives to challenge and overcome stereotypical, patronizing, and sentimental attitudes about disability: Not an advocacy or rehabilitation magazine. Appeals to those with disabilities, educators, health-care professionals, students, and literature and art enthusiasts.

Interests and Word Lengths

- *Fiction:* Creative, well-written short stories. Up to 5,000 words.
- *Nonfiction:* Informative and entertaining articles relating to the arts, both literary and visual. Accepts interviews and personal experiences. Word lengths vary.
- *Departments:* Book reviews on timely, powerful works about some aspect in the field of disability.
- *Poetry:* High-quality poetry with strong images and evocative language. Up to 5 poems per submission.
- *Artwork:* All media; watercolor, charcoals, collages, and sculpture, usually by an artist with a disability. Photos, 5x7 or 8x10 B/W glossy photos preferred. Accepts 35mm slides and color photos.

How to Submit

Query with outline or send complete ms with cover letter. Include SASE. Accepts photocopies, computer printouts, and fax submissions. Simultaneous submissions okay. Reports in 1–2 months.

Payment and Policies

First North American serial rights. Pays on publication. Articles and stories, $100. Poems, $5. Authors receive 1 copy of the issue.

The Kansas City Jewish Chronicle

Ruth Baum Bigus, Editor
7373 West 107th Street
Overland Park, KS 66212
913-648-4620

AT A GLANCE:
THE KANSAS CITY JEWISH CHRONICLE

- Jewish, Regional
- Weekly
- Circ: 20,000
- Receives 10 mss each month.
- No payment. Offers 5 contributor's copies.

From the Editor:
"Inform the Jewish community about something not found in mainstream media."

Best Bet: News and feature stories of interest to the Kansas City-area Jewish community.

Avoid: Poetry.

Sample copy: Not provided. No guidelines.

Profile

A weekly Jewish newspaper for Kansas City-area residents. Member of the American Jewish Press Association. Est.: 1920. Tabloid-size; newsprint; 28–32 pages.

Focus and Audience

Covers events in the Jewish community—local, national, and international—for readers in Kansas City and surrounding areas.

Interests and Word Lengths

- *Nonfiction:* Features, interviews, and news on current events in the Jewish community. Up to 30 column inches.
- *Seasonal:* Jewish holiday material.
- *Artwork:* Accepts photos and illustrations.

How to Submit

Send complete ms with cover letter. Include SASE. Accepts photocopies, computer printouts, and fax submissions. Simultaneous submissions okay.

Payment and Policies

Authors retain rights. No payment. Authors receive 5 copies of the issue.

Kashrus Magazine

Rabbi Yosef Wikler, Editor
P.O. Box 204, Parkville Station
Brooklyn, NY 11204
718-336-8544

Profile

A trade magazine for the kosher consumer. Published by Yeshivas Birkas Reuven. 8.5x11; glossy cover; 52 pages.

Focus and Audience

Researches and updates the kosher consumer and trade industries about products and technology, and monitors all 150 certifying agencies.

Interests and Word Lengths

- *Fiction:* Humor only.
- *Nonfiction:* Personal experiences of kosher travel, catering, etc. 500–1,500 words. Assigns feature articles and interviews.
- *Departments:* Food Technology; Kosher Travel; Pharmacuticals; Jewish Holidays; New Products; Consumer Alert; Keeping Kosher In. . . ; Exciting Kosher Cuisine; Passover/Rosh Hashanna. 50–1,500 words.
- *Photos:* B/W prints. No photos of women who are not fully clad.

How to Submit

Query with writing samples and clips, or send ms with cover letter and clips. Include SASE. Accepts photocopies, computer printouts, and PC disk submissions. No simultaneous submissions. Reports in 2–4 weeks.

Payment and Policies

One-time rights. Pays on publication. $50–$250 per piece. Kill fee, 50%. Authors receive 2–3 copies of the issue; additional copies at nominal charge.

Keys for Kids

Hazel Marett, Editor
1331 Plainfield NE
Grand Rapids, MI 49505
616-451-2009

AT A GLANCE:
KEYS FOR KIDS

- Juvenile, Devotional
- 100% freelance
- 50% new writers
- Bimonthly
- Circ: 38,000
- Receives 30 queries, 30 mss each month.
- Pays: $12–$16 on acceptance.

From the Editor:
"Study the magazine and guidelines—follow them carefully."

Best Bet: Daily devotionals that illustrate a biblical principle.

Avoid: Overworked topics: the Bible as a map, light, instruction sheet, or plumb line; rules are for your good; "house built on sand" illustrations.

Sample copy: Free with 6x9 SAE and $1.05 postage. Send #10 SASE for guidelines.

Profile
A bimonthly Christian booklet of devotional reading for children and families. 6x9; glossy cover; 96 pages.

Focus and Audience
Writings reflect the beliefs in the inerrancy of the Scriptures, the deity of Jesus, and that salvation is through Him only. Designed to be read by children on their own or with family.

Interests and Word Lengths
- *Devotions:* Devotionals for children or the family on any subject. Stories should draw from everyday life and illustrate a biblical principle. 400 words.

How to Submit
Send complete ms with cover letter. Include SASE. Accepts computer printouts. Simultaneous submissions okay. Reports in 1 month.

Payment and Policies
All rights. Pays on acceptance. $12–$16 per devotional. Authors receive 1 copy of the issue.

The Kiln

Gregory E. Zschomler, Editor
EVT Ministries
P.O. Box 5763
Vancouver, WA 98668

Profile

An evangelical discipleship magazine for teens that addresses social and religious issues and encourages readers in their faith. Published by Earthen Vessel Teen Ministries of Vancouver. 5.5x8; self cover, stapled; 12–16 pages.

Focus and Audience

Proclaims the Gospel of Jesus Christ in a style, format, and methodology designed to effectively reach today's Christian young people, ages 13–19. Does not address typical youth problems such as drugs and sex. Readers are "radical" Christians.

Interests and Word Lengths

• *Nonfiction:* Christian discipleship, missions and evangelism, and religious and social issues such as constitutional rights, racism, abortion, and birth control as they affect ethics, morals, and values in Christian living. Accepts seasonal material. 300–1,500 words.
• *Departments:* Fryer Yuk, religious humor. Quotes.
• *Artwork:* Religious cartoons. Appropriate B/W photos to accompany articles.

How to Submit

Query first. Include SASE. Accepts photocopies, computer printouts, and 3.5-inch Macintosh Microsoft Word 4.0 disks. Format disks as follows: 4.5-inch margin lines, single spaced, block-style, using 12-point New Century Schoolbook. Simultaneous submissions okay. Reports in 1 month.

Payment and Policies

First North American serial rights and reprint rights. Occasionally pays $12 for outstanding articles. Pays an additional $3 for articles submitted on computer disk when formatted as specified. Fryer Yuk jokes and quotes, $1. Authors receive 1 copy of the issue.

Lady's Circle

Mary Bemis, Editor
152 Madison Avenue
Suite 906
New York, NY 10016
212-689-3933

AT A GLANCE:
LADY'S CIRCLE

- Women, Family
- 50% freelance
- Bimonthly
- Circ: 100,000
- Receives 100 queries each month.
- Pays: $125–$200 on publication.

From the Editor:
"Send us a good, solid query. Our guidelines will show you how to do that."

Best Bet: Topical, upbeat, informational articles for homemakers.

Avoid: Unhappy endings; unsolicited manuscripts.

Sample copy: $2.95. Send #10 SASE for guidelines.

Profile

An international bimonthly publication for women. 8.5x11; glossy cover; 68 pages.

Focus and Audience

Upbeat, family-oriented material that caters to the needs of homemakers. Most readers are women from midwestern U.S. and Canada.

Interests and Word Lengths

- *Fiction:* Short stories and short-short stories with happy endings. Themes include family and women's issues. 1,500 words.
- *Nonfiction:* Topical articles on family and women's issues; practical how-to pieces on homemaking, including crafts and recipes; profiles of people involved in the community, volunteer work, and overcoming problems. All must be upbeat with happy endings. 1,500 words.
- *Seasonal*: Submit 4 months in advance.

How to Submit

Query with outline. No unsolicited mss. Include SASE. Accepts photocopies, computer printouts, and fax submissions (212-725-2239). Simultaneous submissions okay. Reports in 1–2 months.

Payment and Policies

First North American serial rights. Pays on publication. $125–$200 per piece. Authors receive 1 copy of the issue.

Language Bridges Quarterly

Eva Ziem, Editor
P.O. Box 850792
Richardson, TX 75085
214-530-2782

AT A GLANCE:
LANGUAGE BRIDGES QUARTERLY

- Polish, Cultural
- 90% freelance
- 4 issues a year
- Circ: 500
- Receives 4 mss each month.
- No payment. Offers contributor's copies.

From the Editor:
"Write for a Polish-American audience. We accept religious and inspirational writing."

Best Bet: Articles that promote bilingualism, Polish culture, and knowledge of Poland within the Polish-American community.

Avoid: Vulgar writing; racism; ethnocentrism.

Sample copy: $5. Send #10 SASE for guidelines.

Profile
A bilingual Polish-English literary magazine for the Polish-American community. Member of the Council of Literary Magazines and Presses. Est.: 1988. 8x10; B/W; heavy bond cover; 24 pages.

Focus and Audience
Offers cultural and inspirational articles of interest to Polish-Americans. Published in both English and Polish.

Interests and Word Lengths
- *Fiction:* Inspirational short stories, and short-short stories dealing with Polish-American culture. No word-length restrictions. Accepts poetry.
- *Nonfiction:* Features and interviews that promote bilingualism, Polish culture, and knowledge of Poland in the Polish-American community. Interests include social, religious, and cultural concerns. No word-length restrictions.
- *Artwork:* B/W ink or pencil drawings.

How to Submit
Accepts text in English or Polish. Send complete ms with cover letter. Include SASE. Accepts photocopies, computer printouts, and IBM-compatible ASCII disks. Simultaneous submissions okay. Reports in 3 months.

Payment and Policies
One-time rights. No payment. Authors receive 5–6 copies of the issue.

Latin America Evangelist

John Maust, Editor
P.O. Box 52-7900
Miami, FL 33152
305-884-8400

AT A GLANCE:

LATIN AMERICA
EVANGELIST

- Christian, Cultural Issues
- 10% freelance
- Quarterly
- Circ: 21,000
- Receives 3–5 mss each month.
- Pays on publication. Rates vary.

From the Editor:
"Study the magazine before you query. Do not send manuscripts."

Best Bet: Reports on the religious situation in Latin America.

Avoid: Inspirational or preachy articles; poetry; fiction.

Sample copy: Free. No guidelines.

Profile

A quarterly magazine exploring the religious beliefs and practices in Latin America. Published by Latin America Mission, Inc. Member of the Evangelical Press Association. 8.5x11; glossy cover; full-color; 22 pages.

Focus and Audience

Reports and reflects on religious developments in Latin America for an adult Christian audience in the U.S.

Interests and Word Lengths

- *Nonfiction:* News and analysis of the religious climate and social conditions in Latin America. 1,000 words.

How to Submit

Query with outline. No unsolicited mss. Include SASE. Accepts photocopies, computer printouts, 3.5-inch Macintosh disks, and fax submissions (305-885-8649). Simultaneous submissions okay. Report time varies.

Payment and Policies

Authors retain rights. Pays on publication. Rates vary. Authors receive 3 copies of the issue.

Leader

Joseph Cookston, Editor
P.O. Box 2458
Anderson, IN 46018
317-642-0255

AT A GLANCE:
LEADER

- Church of God, Leadership
- 70% freelance
- Bimonthly
- Circ: 4,000
- Receives 10 mss each month.
- Pays: $10–$30 on publication.

From the Editor:
"In planning articles, ask yourself these questions: Will what I am saying improve the skills of local church workers? Will the concern expressed foster personal growth through enrichment or challenges in patterns of thinking related to key issues in Christian education today?"

Best Bet: Resources for Church of God leaders.

Avoid: Academic articles.

Sample copy: Free with 9x12 SAE and $.75 postage. Send #10 SASE for guidelines.

Profile
Published by the Board of Christian Education of the Church of God for leaders in all phases of ministry through local congregations. 8.5x11; glossy cover; 2-color; 16 pages.

Focus and Audience
Informs, instructs, and inspires planners and leaders in the Church of God. Material is consistent in philosophy of Christian education. Readers include church school teachers, superintendents and principals, board members, persons serving on program committees in special ministries such as youth, family life, special days, and vacation church school.

Interests and Word Lengths
- *Nonfiction:* Leadership guidance and planning and programming resources in the following areas: administration, children, youth, adult, Sunday school, family, discipling, worship, small groups, and so forth as related to Christian education. Feature articles, 500–800 words. Shorter articles, 300 words.
- *Departments:* Book reviews.
- *Filler:* Poetry, puzzles, and anecdotes.

How to Submit
Send complete ms with cover letter. Include SASE. Accepts computer printouts. Simultaneous submissions okay. Reports in 2 months.

Payment and Policies
One-time rights. Pays on publication. $10–$30 per article. Authors receive 1 copy of the issue.

Leader in the Church School Today

Keith H. Kendall, Editor
P.O. Box 801
Nashville, TN 37202
615-749-6474

AT A GLANCE:

LEADER IN THE CHURCH SCHOOL TODAY

- United Methodist, Religious Education
- 40% freelance
- 25% new writers
- Quarterly
- Circ: 12,000
- Receives 15 queries, 15 mss each month.
- Pays: $.05 per word on acceptance.

From the Editor:
"Be concise and practical. Write to the interest of leaders in your local church's Christian education program or don't write at all."

Best Bet: Practical articles for Christian education leaders.

Avoid: Stereotypical academic style; cutesy articles with simplistic morals.

Sample copy: Not provided. Send #10 SASE for guidelines.

Profile

A practical resource for Christian education leaders in local churches. Published by The United Methodist Publishing House. 8.5x11; glossy cover; 2-color; 64 pages.

Focus and Audience

Nurtures and supports leaders in Christian education with articles to enhance their knowledge and skill. Provides resources, training events, and programs. Audience includes pastors, directors of Christian education, educational assistants, age-level coordinators, chairpersons, counseling teachers, and Sunday school superintendents—all at differing levels of training and experience.

Interests and Word Lengths

- *Nonfiction:* Reports on programs that are working in local churches. These can include youth programs, teacher and leader development training, idea exchanges, planning tips, and resources for ministry. Write actively and in the second person. 1,225 words.
- *Seasonal:* Christmas and Easter dramas. 1,700 words.
- *Photos:* 5x7 B/W prints.

How to Submit

Nonfiction, query with outline. Dramas, send complete ms with cover letter. Include SASE. Accepts computer printouts and XyWrite disks. Simultaneous submissions okay. Reports in 2 months.

Payment and Policies

First North American serial or all rights. Pays on acceptance. $.05 per word. Authors receive 1 copy of the issue.

Leadership

Marshall Shelley, Editor
465 Gundersen Drive
Carol Stream, IL 60187
708-260-6200

AT A GLANCE:

LEADERSHIP

- Protestant, Pastors
- 50% freelance
- 25% new writers
- Quarterly
- Circ: 70,000
- Receives 50 queries, 150 mss each month.
- Pays: $.07–$.10 per word on acceptance.

From the Editor:
"Pastors are smart, well-educated, well-intentioned people. They learn best from the real experiences of their peers."

Best Bet: True stories of people in ministry.

Avoid: Preachiness.

Sample copy: $3. Send #10 SASE for guidelines.

Profile

A practical journal for Protestant church leaders. Published by Christianity Today, Inc. 8.5x11; 3-color; 148 pages.

Focus and Audience

Seeks practical pieces that relate the personal experiences of ministers. Most readers are Protestant pastors, some are lay people active in church ministry. All are trying to make the church both faithful and effective.

Interests and Word Lengths

- *Fiction:* Short stories about church life, temptations faced by ministers. Stories must be believable and the character of the pastor should be generally winsome. 3,000–5,000 words.
- *Nonfiction:* Personal-experience pieces on preaching, counseling, conflict, administration, and vision. Most successful are accounts of a pastor who is doing something right, or who has done some things wrong and is willing to talk about them. Reflects on the transferable principles others can benefit from. 1,200–3,000 words.
- *Departments:* Submit to David Goetz. Ideas that Work, innovative programs or systems. People in Print, reviews of books that apply to church leaders. 500–1,200 words.

How to Submit

Fiction, send complete ms with cover letter. Nonfiction and departments, query with outline. Include SASE. Accepts photocopies, computer printouts, and ASCII disks. Simultaneous submissions okay. Reports in 2 months.

Payment and Policies

One-time rights. Pays on acceptance. $.07–$.10 per word. Authors receive 1 copy of the issue.

Leaves

Rev. Thomas Heier, C.M.M., Editor
P.O. Box 87
Dearborn, MI 48121-0087
313-561-2330

AT A GLANCE:

LEAVES

- Catholic, Devotional
- 40–50% freelance
- Bimonthly
- Circ: 200,000
- Receives few mss each month.
- No payment. Offers 1 contributor's copy.

From the Editor:
"We have no *particular* needs. If we receive a manuscript, we review it based on the needs of that time."

Best Bet: Personal religious experiences, petitions, or thanksgivings.

Sample copy: Free. No guidelines.

Profile

A bimonthly Catholic devotional magazine published by the Mariannhill Mission Society of the American-Canadian Province. 6x9; self cover; 2-color; 24 pages.

Focus and Audience

Promotes devotion to God and His saints and serves as a publication of readers' spiritual experience, petitions, and thanksgivings. Much material is staff-written.

Interests and Word Lengths

- *Nonfiction:* Devotions, letters of petition and thanksgiving, and personal spiritual experiences. 250 words.
- *Poetry:* Short poems in keeping with the magazine's theme.
- *Photos:* B/W photos of readers and their families.

How to Submit

Send complete ms with cover letter. Include SASE. Accepts photocopies and computer printouts. Simultaneous submissions okay. Reports in 3 weeks.

Payment and Policies

All rights. No payment. Authors receive 1 copy of the issue upon request.

Librarian's World

Nancy Dick, Editor
P.O. Box 353
Glen Ellyn, IL 60138
708-668-0519

AT A GLANCE:
LIBRARIAN'S WORLD

- Evangelical, Church Libraries
- 80% freelance
- 50% new writers
- Quarterly
- Circ: 700
- Receives few queries and mss each month.
- Pays: $20–$25 per page on publication.

From the Editor:
"Write for a copy of the magazine before submitting to us."

Best Bet: Instructional articles for church librarians; religious book reviews.

Sample copy: Free. No guidelines.

Profile
The official publication of the Evangelical Church Library Association, a non-profit organization that ministers through church libraries and media centers. Member of the Evangelical Press Association. 8.5x11; self cover; stapled; 52 pages.

Focus and Audience
Provides church librarians with practical information on establishing and maintaining church libraries and religious media centers.

Interests and Word Lengths
- *Nonfiction:* Inspirational or technical articles relating to the organization and operation of libraries, promotional ideas, and other helpful information.
- *Departments:* Reviews of religious, children's, and seasonal books and media appropriate for church libraries. 2 typed, double-spaced pages.

How to Submit
Query with outline. Include SASE. Accepts photocopies and computer printouts. Simultaneous submissions okay. Reports in 1–2 months.

Payment and Policies
Authors retain rights. Pays on publication. $20–$25 per piece. Authors receive 1 copy of the issue.

Life Enrichment

Flo McLaughlin, Publisher
1346 Joan Drive
Southampton, PA 18966-4341
215-322-1346

AT A GLANCE:
LIFE ENRICHMENT

- Inspirational, Personal Experience
- 95% freelance
- 75% new writers
- Quarterly
- Circ: 1,000
- Receives 1 query, 12 mss each month.
- No payment. Offers a free subscription.

From the Editor:
"Beginning writers are most welcome. Bring a smile to our readers with the message that life is to be enjoyed and true riches come from helping others."

Best Bet: Inspirational articles and stories that support, encourage, and inform.

Avoid: Abstract musings; heavy, ponderous writing; too many biblical quotes; dull or depressing material.

Sample copy: $3. Send #10 SASE for guidelines.

Profile

An inspirational quarterly of stories and poetry with an uplifting tone. Welcomes the work of beginning writers. 8.5x11; photocopied; stapled; 8 pages.

Focus and Audience

Presents a forum for people willing to share thoughts or experiences to encourage others. Strives to renew faith in traditional values and the appreciation of common-sense, courtesy, and kindness.

Interests and Word Lengths

- *Fiction:* Short stories and short-short stories about men and women who challenged adversity and won, Positive, upbeat tone is more important than particular subject. 100–1,000 words. Occasionally accepts longer pieces for serialization if of exceptional quality.
- *Nonfiction:* Features, essays, interviews and profiles, personal experiences, how-to articles, nostalgic pieces, and vignettes about travel, volunteer activities, goal setting, and life-changing experiences. 100–1,000 words.
- *Poetry:* Short inspirational and/or humorous poems.
- *Filler:* Accepts filler and seasonal material.

How to Submit

Obtain and read guidelines before submitting. Then, send complete ms with cover letter. Include SASE. Accepts computer printouts and IBM-compatible ASCII files on 3.5- or 5.25-inch disks. Simultaneous submissions okay. Reports in 1 month.

Payment and Policies

One-time rights. No payment. Authors receive a free one-year subscription and 4 copies of the issue.

Lifeglow

Richard J. Kaiser, Editor-in-Chief
4444 South 52th Street
P.O. Box 6097
Lincoln, NE 68506
402-488-0981

AT A GLANCE:

LIFEGLOW

- Christian, Inspirational
- 90% freelance
- 5–10% new writers
- Quarterly
- Circ: 28,000
- Receives varied number of queries and mss each month.
- Pays: $.03–.05 per word on acceptance.

From the Editor:
"Keep in mind that you are writing for a sight-impaired readership."

Best Bet: Manuscripts focusing on the lives and needs of visually impaired persons.

Avoid: Highly controversial topics.

Sample copy: Free with 9x12 SAE and $1.45 postage. Send #10 SASE for guidelines.

Profile

An inspirational, health-related magazine published in an easy-to-read, large-print format for visually impaired Christian adults. 6.5x10; glossy cover; large print; 65–70 pages.

Focus and Audience

Positive-living, health-related pieces that brighten, inspire, and entertain a non-denominational Christian audience. Readers are adults over the age of 25, who are sight impaired or physically unable to hold a book to read ordinary print.

Interests and Word Lengths

- *Nonfiction:* Adventure, biography, career opportunities, devotions and inspirational pieces, experiences of the disabled, health, history, hobbies, holidays, marriage, nature, nostalgia, relationships, sports, and travel. Articles that address the needs of the sight impaired are preferred. 800–1,400 words.
- *Departments:* Healthwatch, current health-related topics.
- *Filler:* 400–600 words.
- *Photos:* Prefers B/W glossy prints. Accepts color transparencies and slides if accompanying a manuscript.

How to Submit

Prefers query first with outline. Will accept complete ms with cover letter. Include SASE. Informational articles should be well documented. Accepts photocopies and computer printouts. Simultaneous submissions okay if noted. Reports in 2–3 months.

Payment and Policies

One-time rights. Pays on acceptance. Articles, $.03–$.05 per word. Photos, $5–$10 each. Authors receive 2 copies of the issue.

Light and Life

Robert B. Haslam, Editor
770 North High School Road
Indianapolis, IN 46214
317-244-3660

AT A GLANCE:

LIGHT AND LIFE

- Free Methodist, Inspirational
- 40% freelance
- 3–5% new writers
- Monthly
- Circ: 32,000
- Receives 5 queries, 50–100 mss each month.
- Pays: $.04 per word on publication.

From the Editor:
"Do your homework before you write, both for your material and in understanding your audience. Be on target for them."

Best Bet: Practical, heart-warming articles for average readers.

Avoid: Radical tirades; academic and deeply theological treatises; fiction.

Sample copy: $1.50. Send #10 SASE for guidelines.

Profile

The official publication of the Free Methodist Church of North America, an evangelical denomination of Wesley-Arminian persuasion. 8.5x11; 32 pages.

Focus and Audience

Exists to meet the spiritual and temporal needs of Free Methodists and serve as an outreach publication. Audience is evangelical but diverse in education, age, environment, vocations, interests, reading ability, and church background.

Interests and Word Lengths

- *Nonfiction:* Inspirational, practical, heart-warming material. First-person stories of God's help in hard times, 1,200 words. First-person, humorous pieces on practical Christian living, 650 words. Spiritual growth articles on doctrine, Christian experience, relationships, human need, social issues, and the church, 1,000–1,200 words. How-to articles on Christian discipleship covering prayer, witnessing, Bible study, worship, and service opportunities, 500–700 words. Devotional pieces, 500–700 words. Social commentary from a Christian perspective on family values, Christian social action, and politics, 1,000–1,200 words. Personal-opinion essays, 700 words.
- *Poetry:* Short seasonal poems.
- *Artwork:* Contact Regine Stotts, Art Director.

How to Submit

Send complete ms with cover letter. Include SASE. Accepts computer printouts and WordPerfect disks with hard copy. Simultaneous submissions okay if sent to another Free Methodist publication. Reports in 6 weeks.

Payment and Policies

First North American serial or one-time rights. Pays on publication. Articles, $.04 per word. Poetry, at least $10. Authors receive 3 copies of the issue.

Liguorian

Rev. Allan Weinert, C.SS.R., Editor-in-Chief
One Liguori Drive
Liguori, MO 63057-9999
314-464-2500

AT A GLANCE:

LIGUORIAN

- Catholic, Spiritual Growth
- 25% freelance
- 15% new writers
- Monthly
- Circ: 400,000
- Receives 10 queries, 100 mss each month.
- Pays: $.10–$.12 per word on acceptance.

From the Editor:
"Your manuscript stands a better chance of acceptance if it is neatly presented, carefully polished, and on a topic of special interest to our readers."

Best Bet: Marriage and parenting; articles that touch a reader's life in a personal way.

Sample copy: Free with 6x9 SAE and 3 first-class stamps. Send #10 SASE for guidelines.

Profile

A monthly Catholic magazine that illustrates and applies Gospel and Church teaching to daily life. 6x9; glossy cover; 2-color; 72 pages.

Focus and Audience

Aims to lead readers to a fuller Christian life by helping them better understand the teaching of the Gospel and the Catholic Church. Readers are Catholics of all ages and stages of development.

Interests and Word Lengths

- *Fiction:* Short stories of interest to Catholic readers. 1,500–2,000 words.
- *Nonfiction:* Practical and inspirational articles on spirituality, prayer, liturgy, and the problems confronting readers as members of families, the Church, and society. Currently needs marriage and parenting articles, and articles with personal impact. Use examples, quotes, and anecdotes. 1,000–2,000 words.
- *Seasonal:* Submit 6 months in advance.
- *Poetry:* Traditional poems, 8–24 lines. Buys 6–12 a year.

How to Submit

Send complete ms with cover letter. Include SASE. No reprints. Accepts photocopies, computer printouts, and fax submissions. No simultaneous submissions. Reports in 1–2 months.

Payment and Policies

All rights. Pays on acceptance. $.10–$.12 per word. Kill fee, 50%. Authors receive 5 copies of the issue.

Lilith
The Independent Jewish Women's Magazine

Susan Weidman Schneider, Editor-in-Chief
250 West 57 Street, # 2432
New York, NY 10107
212-757-0818

AT A GLANCE:
LILITH

- Jewish, Feminist
- 80% freelance
- Quarterly
- Circ: 10,000
- Payment negotiable.

From the Editor:
"Since 1976, our articles have drawn attention to unexplored subjects and areas of concern to Jewish women. We encourage you to read our magazine to judge whether Lilith is the appropriate vehicle for your work."

Best Bet: Nonfiction on people, issues, and developments of interest to Jewish women.

Avoid: Fiction, drama, and poetry, until 1994.

Sample copy: $5. Send #10 SASE for guidelines.

Profile

An independent Jewish women's quarterly. Est.: 1976. 8.5x11; glossy cover; 2-color; 40 pages.

Focus and Audience

Functions as an outreach tool and the center of a network for Jewish feminism. Readers range across the spectrum of Jewish identification, political views, and generations.

Interests and Word Lengths

- *Fiction:* Due to the volume of submissions, new fiction and drama will not be considered until 1994.
- *Nonfiction:* Articles that address the interests and concerns of Jewish women. Interests include autobiography (testimony, letters, journals, memoirs); biographies of women living or dead; interviews; legal, literary, political, or historical analyses of the lives, decisions, and struggles of Jewish women; sociological and historical research; literary criticism; book, film, television, music, and art reviews; investigative reporting; grass roots projects; opinion pieces; and new ceremonies and rituals related to the lives of Jewish women. 1,000–3,000 words.
- *Departments:* Kol Ishah, news pages. Tsena-Rena, resource listings. Letters to the Editor.
- *Poetry:* Due to the volume of submissions, poetry will not be considered until 1994.

How to Submit

Send complete ms with cover letter and brief author biography written in the third person. Include SASE. Accepts photocopies, computer printouts, and Macintosh Microsoft Word disks. Simultaneous submissions okay. Reports in 3 months.

Payment and Policies

One-time rights. Payment negotiable. Authors receive 2 copies of the issue.

The Link & Visitor

Esther Barnes, Editor
12-35 Waterman Avenue
London, ON N6C 5T2
Canada
519-668-3391

AT A GLANCE:
THE LINK & VISITOR

- Baptist, Women
- 70% freelance
- 9 issues a year
- Circ: 5,500
- Pays: $20–$80 (CAN) on publication.

From the Editor:
"Have you wrestled with a difficult issue? Do you have a global perspective? Have you read *The Link & Visitor*? Canadian writers preferred."

Avoid: Warm fuzzies; tirades; charismatic experiences and jargon; U.S. politics and heroes; exclusive language.

Sample copy: Free with 9x12 SAE and $.86 (CAN) postage. Send #10 SASE/IRC for guidelines.

Profile

A practical magazine for Baptist women. Published by the Baptist Women's Missionary Society. 8.5x11; color cover; 16 pages.

Focus and Audience

Mission-oriented material, both Canadian and overseas, from a biblically feminist and Canadian point-of-view. Bent is evangelical with a social conscience. Readers are Canadian Baptist women.

Interests and Word Lengths

- *Nonfiction:* Positive, practical articles on missionary work and issues of concern to women including family, parenting, and education. Prefers Canadian writers. 700–1,500 words

How to Submit

Query with writing samples or send complete ms with cover letter. Include SASE. U.S. authors include IRCs. Accepts photocopies, computer printouts, Macintosh disks, and fax submissions. Simultaneous submissions okay. Reports within 2–12 months.

Payment and Policies

One-time rights. Pays on publication. $20–$80 (CAN) per article. Authors receive 2 copies of issue.

Listen

Lincoln Steed, Editor
1350 North Kings Road
Nampa, ID 83687
208-465-2500

Profile

A monthly drug-prevention magazine for teenagers that promotes positive lifestyles. 8.5x11; glossy cover; 4-color; 32 pages.

Focus and Audience

Teaches high school-age teens life skills, success tips, drug facts, and the advantages of a lifestyle free from alcohol and drugs.

Interests and Word Lengths

- *Fiction:* Short stories that show teens working out day-to-day problems or drug-related problems. No clichéd drunk-driving stories. 1,200–1,500 words.
- *Nonfiction:* Articles that promote a drug-free, alcohol-free lifestyle. Self-help articles, personality profiles, drug- and alcohol-free alternative activities for teens. 1,200–1,500 words.
- *Poetry:* Poems for teens.

How to Submit

Send complete ms with cover letter for fiction. Query with outline or send complete ms with cover letter for nonfiction. Include SASE. Accepts photocopies and computer printouts. Simultaneous submissions okay. Reports in 3 months.

Payment and Policies

First North American serial or one-time rights and reprint rights. Pays on acceptance. $.05–$.10 per word. Contributor's copies are not provided.

Listen

Janet Reeves, Editor
6401 The Paseo
Kansas City, MO 64131

AT A GLANCE:
LISTEN

- Christian, Sunday School
- 80% freelance
- 30% new writers
- Weekly
- Circ: 37,500
- Receives 50 mss each month.
- Pays: $25 or more on publication.

From the Editor:
"We depend on free-lancers for our supply of stories, poems, and activities. However, these must relate to weekly Sunday school themes."

Best Bet: Stories about 5- and 6-year-olds.

Avoid: Precocious or abnormally mature children, flashbacks, symbolism, holidays other than Christmas and Easter, personification of animals and objects, moralizing.

Sample copy: Send #10 SASE for sample and guidelines.

Profile
A Sunday school story paper for 5- and 6-year-old children. 8.5x11; folded; full-color; 4 pages.

Focus and Audience
Publishes stories with strong character and plots that connect Sunday school learning with the daily living experiences and growth of 5- and 6-year-olds.

Interests and Word Lengths
- *Fiction:* Interesting stories about the everyday experiences of kindergarten-age children. Demonstrate character building or scriptural applications. Use dialog and action. Subjects of interest include family life, friendship, understanding basic Christian truths and Easter events, and recognizing God's power. 300–400 words. Also accepts poetry and age-appropriate activities.
- *Photos:* Color slides of active kindergarten-age children.

How to Submit
Send complete ms with cover letter. Include SASE. Accepts photocopies and computer printouts. Reports in 1 month.

Payment and Policies
Multi-use rights. Pays on publication. Fiction, $.05 per word or $25, whichever is greater. Poetry, $.25 per line or $3, whichever is greater. Kindergarten activities, $5–$15. Authors receive 4 copies of the issue.

Liturgy 90

David Phillppart, Editor
1800 North Hermitage Avenue
Chicago, IL 60622-1101
312-486-8970

AT A GLANCE:

LITURGY 90

- Catholic, Liturgy
- 90% freelance
- 10% new writers
- 8 issues a year
- Circ: 5,000
- Receives 5–7 queries, 1–2 mss each month.
- Pays: $25 per manuscript page on publication.

From the Editor:
"Contact the editor before submitting a manuscript. Write for and study our style sheet."

Best Bet: Worship-oriented articles for Catholic clergy.

Avoid: Advocating the ordination of women.

Sample copy: Free. Send #10 SASE for guidelines.

Profile

A worship-oriented magazine for Catholic parish ministers. Published by the Office for Divine Worship of the Archdiocese of Chicago. 8.5x11; glossy cover; 2-color; 16 pages.

Focus and Audience

Concentrates on all aspects of liturgy and worship for ministers. Primarily Roman Catholic, it also addresses other High Liturgical churches such as Methodist, Lutheran, Episcopalian, and Presbyterian. Promotes Vatican II reforms.

Interests and Word Lengths

- *Nonfiction:* Essays concerning all areas of church worship, liturgy, and spirituality. No word-length restrictions.
- *Departments:* Book Reviews; Music Reviews; Q&A column.
- *Poetry:* Worship-oriented poems.
- *Seasonal:* Welcomes holiday pieces and material related to seasons of the church year.
- *Photos:* B/W prints.

How to Submit

Query with outline. No unsolicited mss. Include SASE. Accepts photocopies, computer printouts, WordPerfect disks, and fax submissions. Simultaneous submissions okay. Reports in 3 months.

Payment and Policies

All rights. Pays on publication. Rates vary; averages $25 per manuscript page. Photos, $50. Authors receive 5 copies of the issue.

Live

Editor
1445 Boonville Avenue
Springfield, MO 65802-1894
417-862-2781

AT A GLANCE:
Live

- Assemblies of God,
  Sunday School
- 98% freelance
- Weekly
- Circ: 155,000
- Receives 150–200
  mss each month.
- Pays: $.02–$.03 per
  word on acceptance.

From the Editor:
"Proofread, and edit.
Say something that will
inspire people to be-
lieve in God and the
Bible."

Best Bet: Believable, inspirational, non-con-
demning writing that
applies Christian prin-
ciples to everyday life.

Avoid: Science fiction,
Bible fiction, Santa
Claus, Easter Bunny,
witches, anything
putting authority in a
bad light, swimming,
co-ed dorms etc.

Sample copy: Free with
6x9 SASE. Send #10
SASE for guidelines.

Profile

A weekly Sunday school take-home paper for adults. Published by the General Council of the Assemblies of God. 5.5x8.5; 8 pages.

Focus and Audience

Intent is to inspire readers to live more dedicated, devoted Christian lives through inspirational writing that applies Christian principles to everyday living. Readers are primarily 40–65 years old.

Interests and Word Lengths

- *Fiction:* Short stories of realistic characters who utilize biblical principles and challenge readers to take risks for God and to resolve their problems scripturally. Subjects include family, community, church, nature, volunteer work, relationships, acts of heroism, inventive ministries, witnessing, holidays, and intergenerational and urban themes. 500–2,000 words.
- *Nonfiction:* Inspiring insights and incidents of people solving problems scripturally and living out Christian principles. 500–2,000 words.
- *Departments:* Reflections, short quips or humorous saying on any subject applying to Christian lifestyle.
- *Seasonal:* National and religious holiday stories.
- *Poetry:* 12–25 lines.
- *Filler:* 200–700 words.

How to Submit

Send ms with cover letter. Include SASE. Accepts photocopies, computer printouts, and IBM and Macintosh disk submissions. Simultaneous submissions okay. Reports in 12–15 months.

Payment and Policies

First or second rights. Pays on acceptance. First rights, $.03 per word. Second rights, $.02 per word. Poetry, $.20 per line. Authors receive 2 copies of the issue.

Living

Linda Bartlett, Editor
P.O. Box 819
Benton, AR 72015
501-794-2212

AT A GLANCE:
LIVING

- Christian, Pro-Life
- 50% freelance
- 25% new writers
- Quarterly
- Circ: 2,000
- Receives 1 ms each
  month.
- No payment. Offers
  1–2 contributor's
  copies.

From the Editor:
"We uphold biblical
values and the promise
of John 10:10."

Best Bet: Personal and
factual articles that
promote pro-life Christ-
ian values.

Sample copy: $2 with
8.5x11 SASE. Send #10
SASE for guidelines.

Profile
A pro-life publication promoting strong Christian families. 8x10; 24 pages.

Focus and Audience
Dedicated to providing a loving, joyous Christian attitude on marriage, family, children, and the sanctity of human life. Reaches parents, pastors, and teachers who desire to make a difference based on their pro-life values.

Interests and Word Lengths
- *Fiction:* Personal stories on pro-life issues. 2,000 words and up.
- *Nonfiction:* Personal experience stories, interviews with medical professionals, and feature articles that promote pro-life Christian family values and offer alternatives to abortion, infanticide, and euthanasia. Up to 2,000 words.
- *Departments:* Living in Washington, Medical Ethics, In My Opinion. 1,500 words.
- *Artwork:* Accepts photos and illustrations.

How to Submit
Query with outline, resume, and writing samples; or send complete ms with cover letter and resume. Include SASE. Accepts photocopies and computer printouts. Simultaneous submissions okay.

Payment and Policies
One-time rights. No payment. Authors receive 1–2 copies of issue.

The Living Church

John Schuessler, Managing Editor
816 East Juneau Avenue
Milwaukee, WI 53186
414-276-5420

AT A GLANCE:
THE LIVING CHURCH

- Episcopal, News
- 60% freelance
- Weekly
- Circ: 8,500
- Receives 50 queries, 30 mss each month.
- No payment. Offers 5–10 contributor's copies.

From the Editor:
"While our magazine serves the Episcopal Church, it is independent of the national church and its policies."

Best Bet: Articles on topics related to the Episcopal Church.

Sample copy: Free. No guidelines.

Profile

A weekly magazine published by The Living Church Foundation, a non-profit, independent organization serving the Episcopal Church. Est.: 1878. 8.5x11; glossy paper; 16–20 pages.

Focus and Audience

Reports primarily on news and personalities of the Episcopal Church and the views of its members.

Interests and Word Lengths

- *Nonfiction:* Features and profiles of significant parishes or personalities within the Episcopal Church. 800–1,000 words.
- *Departments:* Observations, viewpoints, and opinion pieces occasionally accepted from freelance writers. 500–600 words.
- *Photos:* Prefers B/W prints. Accepts color photos.

How to Submit

Send complete ms with cover letter. Include SASE. Accepts computer printouts, and fax submissions. Reports in 2 months.

Payment and Policies

No payment. Authors receive 5–10 copies of the issue.

Living Prayer

Sr. Mary Roman, O.C.D., Editor
260 Beckley Hill Road
R.R. 2, Box 4784
Barre, VT 05641
802-476-8362

AT A GLANCE:
LIVING PRAYER

- Prayer, Spirituality
- 90% freelance
- Bimonthly
- Circ: 5,200
- Receives 46 mss each month.
- Pays: $100 for pieces over 5 pages on acceptance.

From the Editor:
"Our imperative is to maintain always an awareness of the Transcendent, which alone brings to life and makes fruitful the prayer hidden in the depths of each one of us."

Best Bet: Articles and essays that explore the life of prayer.

Avoid: Preachy styles; poetry.

Sample copy: Free. Send #10 SASE for guidelines.

Profile
A bimonthly magazine focusing on prayer and the life of prayer. 8.5x8; self cover; 2-color; 40 pages.

Focus and Audience
Dedicated to examining every aspect of life in the light of the reality of God and bearing witness to the vitality of the spiritual life. Readers come from all walks of life, mainly lay people, who desire to build into their lives a more profound sense of the holy.

Interests and Word Lengths
- *Nonfiction:* Articles on how to discover and nurture the contemplative dimension of life. Essays and mediations on the human spirit and its relationship to God through prayer and daily living. Studies of theology, philosophy, psychology, and the arts that offer spiritual insights. Personal spiritual journeys. Essays on timely topics concerning family, spirituality, ecumenism, and peace. 3,000–4,500 words.

How to Submit
Send complete ms with cover letter. Type necessary footnotes and/or bibliographical information on a separate sheet. Include SASE. Accepts photocopies, computer printouts, and disk submissions with hard copy. Simultaneous submissions okay. Reports in 2 weeks.

Payment and Policies
First North American serial rights. Pays on acceptance. $100 per 5-page article. Authors receive 3 copies of the issue.

Living Today

Editor
Scripture Press Publications
Box 62
Glen Ellyn, IL 60187
708-668-6000

Editor
Scripture Press Publications
Box 62
Glen Ellyn, IL 60187
708-668-6000

AT A GLANCE:

LIVING TODAY

- Evangelical, Sunday School
- Little freelance material accepted
- Quarterly
- Circ: not available
- Receives few queries and mss each month.
- Pays on acceptance. Rates vary.

From the Editor:
"Quarterly themes are predetermined and can be requested by perspective writers in advance."

Best Bet: Theme-related Bible studies.

Sample copy: $2.50 with 8.5x11 SASE. Send #10 SASE for theme list. No guidelines.

Profile

A quarterly Sunday school magazine for Christian adults. Published by Scripture Press. Issues are thematic. 7x10; 50 pages.

Focus and Audience

Geared toward adult education programs in conservative Fundamentalist evangelical churches.

Interests and Word Lengths

- *Nonfiction:* Bible studies and features on Christian living, all related to issue themes. Submit all material 1 year in advance. 700–1,500 words.

How to Submit

Request theme list. Then, query with outline, resume, and, if available, writing samples or clips. Include SASE. Accepts photocopies and computer printouts. Notify before sending fax submissions. Simultaneous submissions okay. Reports in up to 1 year.

Payment and Policies

One-time rights. Pays on acceptance. Pays per word; rates vary. Authors receive 1 copy of the issue.

Living with Children

Ellen Oldacre, Editor
127 Ninth Avenue North
Nashville, TN 37234
615-251-2229

AT A GLANCE:
LIVING WITH CHILDREN

- Southern Baptist, Parenting
- 20–30% freelance
- 10–20% new writers
- Quarterly
- Circ: 40,000
- Receives 20 queries, 30–40 mss each month.
- Pays $.055 per word on acceptance.

From the Editor:
"We believe the Bible has God for its author, salvation for its end, and truth, without any mixture of error, for its matter."

Best Bet: Fiction and nonfiction of interest to parents with children ages 6–11.

Sample copy: Free with 8.5x11 SAE and 4 first-class stamps. Send #10 SASE for guidelines.

Profile

A magazine for Christian parents. Published quarterly by the Sunday School Board of the Southern Baptist Convention. Follows as doctrinal guidelines the 1963 statement of The Baptist Faith and Message. 8.5x11; glossy cover; 2-color; 50 pages.

Focus and Audience

Enriches parents' understanding and aids in the guidance of their 6- to 11-year-old children. All material is based on a Christian approach to living.

Interests and Word Lengths

- *Fiction:* Accepts fiction on any subject related to parents of children ages 6–11. Up to 1,200 words.
- *Nonfiction:* Self-help and how-to articles on any subject related to parents of 6- to 11-year-old children. Up to 1,200 words.

How to Submit

Query with outline, or send complete ms with cover letter. Include SASE. Accepts photocopies, computer printouts, and faxes. Simultaneous submissions okay. Reports in 2–3 months.

Payment and Policies

First North American serial, one-time, or all rights. Pays on acceptance. $.055 per word. Authors receive 3 copies of the issue.

Living with Preschoolers

Ellen Oldacre, Editor
127 Ninth Avenue North
Nashville, TN 37234
615-251-2229

AT A GLANCE:

LIVING WITH PRESCHOOLERS

- Southern Baptist, Parenting
- 20–30% freelance
- 10–20% new writers
- Quarterly
- Circ: 110,000
- Receives 20 queries, 30 mss each month.
- Pays $.055 per word on acceptance.

From the Editor:
"We believe the Bible has God for its author, salvation for its end, and truth, without any mixture of error, for its matter."

Best Bet: Stories and articles that aid parents of preschool children.

Sample copy: Free with 8.5x11 SAE and 4 first-class stamps. Send #10 SASE for guidelines.

Profile

A quarterly Christian parenting magazine published by the Sunday School Board of the Southern Baptist Convention. Follows as doctrinal guidelines the 1963 statement of The Baptist Faith and Message. 8.5x11; glossy cover; 2-color; 50 pages.

Focus and Audience

Helps parents enrich their understanding and guidance of preschool children, ages birth to 5 years, and is based on a Christian approach to living.

Interests and Word Lengths

- *Fiction:* Stories on any subject related to parents of preschoolers. Up to 1,200 words.
- *Nonfiction:* Self-help and how-to articles on any subject related to parents of preschoolers. Up to 1,200 words.

How to Submit

Query with outline, or send complete ms with cover letter. Include SASE. Accepts photocopies, computer printouts, and faxes. Simultaneous submissions okay. Reports in 2–3 months.

Payment and Policies

First North American serial, one-time, or all rights. Pays on acceptance. $.055 per word. Authors receive 3 copies of the issue.

Living with Teenagers

Ellen Oldacre, Editor
127 Ninth Avenue North
Nashville, TN 37234
615-251-2229

AT A GLANCE:

LIVING WITH TEENAGERS

- Southern Baptist, Parenting
- 20–30% freelance
- 10–20% new writers
- Quarterly
- Circ: 36,000
- Receives 20 queries, 30 mss each month.
- Pays $.055 per word on acceptance.

From the Editor:
"We believe the Bible has God for its author, salvation for its end, and truth, without any mixture of error, for its matter."

Best Bet: Material of interest to parents of teenagers.

Sample copy: Free with 8.5x11 SAE and 4 first-class stamps. Send #10 SASE for guidelines.

Profile

A quarterly Christian parenting magazine published by the Sunday School Board of the Southern Baptist Convention. Follows as doctrinal guidelines the 1963 statement of The Baptist Faith and Message. 8.5x11; glossy cover; 2-color; 50 pages.

Focus and Audience

Aimed at parents of youth ages 12–17. Designed to enrich parents' understanding and guidance of teenagers based on a Christian approach to living.

Interests and Word Lengths

- *Fiction:* Accepts fiction on any subject related to parents of teens. Up to 1,200 words.
- *Nonfiction:* Self-help and how-to articles on any subject related to parents of teens. Up to 1,200 words.

How to Submit

Query with outline, or send complete ms with cover letter. Include SASE. Accepts photocopies, computer printouts, and faxes. Simultaneous submissions okay. Reports in 2–3 months.

Payment and Policies

First North American serial, one-time, or all rights. Pays on acceptance. $.055 per word. Authors receive 3 copies of the issue.

Logos

A Journal of Eastern Christian Studies

Andriy Chirovsky, Managing Editor
c/o St. Paul University, 223 Main Street
Ottawa, ON K1S 1C4
Canada
613-782-3031

AT A GLANCE:
Logos

- Eastern Christian, Theology
- 90% freelance
- 10% new writers
- 2 issues a year
- Circ: 1,000
- Receives 3 queries, 3 mss each month.
- No payment. Offers contributor's copy.

From the Editor:
"Articles should be well-researched and well-documented. Submissions will be judged by several referees."

Best Bet: Articles dedicated to ecumenical rapprochement between Eastern and Western Christians through an honest, objective, scholarly presentation of facts.

Avoid: Polemics; accusatory and attacking styles.

Sample copy: Not provided. Send #10 SAE/IRCs for guidelines.

Profile

A scholarly journal of Eastern Christian studies. 5.5x8.5; 200 pages.

Focus and Audience

Publishes scholarly articles that treat all aspects of the Eastern churches, both Orthodox and Catholic. Readership includes theologians, church historians, clergy, and lay leaders of Eastern Christian churches.

Interests and Word Lengths

- *Nonfiction:* Interviews with prominent church leaders; scholarly articles on aspects of Eastern Christian churches; in-depth articles on Eastern Christian institutions of higher learning in various countries. Interests include patristics, Eastern Christian theology and spirituality, and the history of Eastern churches and their canonical tradition. 10,000 words.
- *Artwork:* Line drawings of Byzantine icons.

How to Submit

Send complete ms with cover letter. Include SASE. U.S. authors send IRCs. Accepts photocopies, computer printouts, disk submissions, and faxes. No simultaneous submissions. Reports in 3 months.

Payment and Policies

All rights. No payment. Authors receive 1 copy of the issue.

The Lookout

Simon J. Dahlman, Editor
8121 Hamilton Avenue
Cincinnati, OH 45231
513-931-4050

AT A GLANCE:
THE LOOKOUT

- Churches of Christ, Lifestyle
- Weekly
- 60% freelance
- Varied number of new writers
- Circ: 118,000
- Receives 20 queries, 250 mss each month.
- Pays: $.04–$.08 per word on acceptance.

From the Editor:
"We work to address issues important to Christians in a balanced, fair, and informed manner. We prefer to teach through example and anecdote and seek to bring theological subjects down to earth."

Best Bet: Opinon pieces for Outlook department.

Avoid: Subjects that interest only church leaders. Bombastic writing style.

Sample copy: $.50. Send #10 SASE for guidelines.

Profile

A weekly magazine for Christian adults, primarily non-charismatic Pentecostals. 8.5x11; self cover; 4-color; 16 pages.

Focus and Audience

Helps readers grow in faith, encourages them to serve, and informs them of current issues. Most readers are in Churches of Christ, but reaches other fellowships.

Interests and Word Lengths

- *Fiction:* Stories about modern Christians, written from an adult perspective. Topics include family and social issues, and realistic but ultimaterly positive crises of faith. Up to 2,000 words.
- *Nonfiction:* Features, interviews, personality profiles, human interest pieces, personal experiences, humor, and applied Bible studies that address Christian growth, family life, and social issues. Accepts seasonal material. 500–2,000 words.
- *Departments:* Outlook, reader opinion on timely topics. Welcomes differing viewpoints if presented reasonably and with biblical basis. 500–900 words.
- *Photos:* Submit to Richard Briggs. B/W prints, color slides, full-color artwork. Send for guidelines.

How to Submit

Fiction, send complete ms with cover letter. Nonfiction, query with outline, resume, and writing samples, or send complete ms with cover letter and resume. SASE. Submit seasonal material 6 months in advance. Accepts photocopies, computer printouts, and faxes. Simultaneous submissions okay. Reports in 2 months.

Payment and Policies

First North American serial or one-time rights. Pays on acceptance. First rights, $.05–$.08 per word. Reprints, $.04–$.05 per word. Kill fee, 33%. Authors receive 1 copy of the issue; more upon request.

Lotus
Journal for Personal Transformation

Mary NurrieStearns, Editor
4032 South Lamar Boulevard, #500-137
Austin, TX 78704
918-683-4560

AT A GLANCE:
LOTUS

- Spirituality, Inspirational
- 20–30% freelance
- 10% new writers
- Quarterly
- Circ: 20,100
- Receives 20+ queries, 6–8 mss each month.
- Pays $50–$500 on publication.

From the Editor:
"*Lotus* is philosophically based on the belief that society is a reflection of its people. As we are transformed, so is society. It would be helpful to take a look at the journal before submitting."

Best Bet: Articles about personal and spiritual growth.

Avoid: Personal stories.

Sample copy: $6. Send #10 SASE for guidelines.

Profile
A quarterly publication dedicated to providing resources for personal and spiritual development. 8.5x11; glossy cover; 4-color; 96 pages.

Focus and Audience
Seeks to energize, stimulate, and inform readers on their journeys of self-awakening and inspired living. Readers are from several different religious backgrounds; 70 percent are women.

Interests and Word Lengths
- *Nonfiction:* Inspirational and self-help pieces on personal and spiritual growth, psychology, and spirituality. 500–5,000 words.

How to Submit
Send complete ms with cover letter. Include SASE. Accepts photocopies, computer printouts, and Macintosh or IBM disks. Simultaneous submissions okay. Reports in 2–3 months.

Payment and Policies
One-time rights. Pays on publication. $50–$500 per article. Authors receive copies of the issue upon request.

The Lutheran

David Miller, Features Editor
8765 West Higgins Road
Chicago, IL 60473
312-380-2549

AT A GLANCE:
THE LUTHERAN

- Lutheran, News
- 25–50% freelance
- 50% new writers
- Monthly
- Circ: 960,000
- Receives 50 queries,
  100 mss each month.
- Pays: $50–$1,000 on
  acceptance.

From the Editor:
"In general, writers should seek to convey information rather than express personal opinion, though the writer's own personality should be reflected in the article's style."

Best Bet: Features of interest to lay members of the Evangelical Lutheran Church in America.

Avoid: Topics unrelated to the world of religion; fiction; poetry.

Sample copy: Free with 9x12 SASE. Send #10 SASE for guidelines.

Profile
The magazine of the Evangelical Lutheran Church in America (ELCA). Published monthly by Augsburg Fortress. 8.5x11; glossy cover; full-color; 68 pages.

Focus and Audience
Features news and activities of the Evangelical Lutheran Church in America as well as reflections on social, ethical, and religious issues. Readers are ELCA lay people.

Interests and Word Lengths
- *Nonfiction:* Church-at-work articles describing unique aspects of specific church units programs such as a local congregation, an institution, or a churchwide agency. Profiles of individuals whose accomplishments reflect commitment to the Christian faith. Theological, sociological, philosophical, or historical reflection articles that explore important issues related to Christian belief and that encourage readers to think about human values. Personal experiences that describe real-life encounters with adversity, family problems, and the frustrations and opportunities of everyday living and the relevance of Christian faith in dealing with them. 500–2,000 words
- *Departments:* Liteside; Reader's Viewpoint.
- *Photos:* Submit to Jack Lund, Art Director. Request guidelines.

How to Submit
Query with outline, resume, writing samples, and clips. Include SASE. Accepts photocopies, computer printouts, disks, faxes, and modem submissions. No simultaneous submissions. Reports in 3 months.

Payment and Policies
First North American serial rights. Pays on acceptance. $50–$1,000 per piece. Kill fee, 50%. Authors receive 2 copies of the issue.

Lutheran Forum

Leonard R. Klein, Editor
29 South George Street
York, PA 17401
717-854-5589

AT A GLANCE:

LUTHERAN FORUM

- Lutheran, Doctrinal
- 90% freelance
- 20% new writers
- Quarterly
- Circ: 4,000
- Receives 5 mss each month.
- No payment.

From the Editor:
"*Lutheran Forum* has a strong commitment to a catholic/confessional understanding of Lutheranism and critical fidelity toward the Lutheran churches. We are not an open forum for anything and everything."

Sample copy: Not provided. Send #10 SASE for guidelines.

Profile

A quarterly independent Lutheran journal. Published by the American Lutheran Publicity Bureau. Subscription includes *Forum Letter,* a monthly newsletter of Lutheran thought on contemporary societal issues. 8.5x11; self cover; 56 pages.

Focus and Audience

Focus is on Lutheran theological, liturgical, and pastoral issues. Committed to a catholic/confessional Lutheranism. Most readers are Lutheran clergy.

Interests and Word Lengths

- *Nonfiction:* Essays on Lutheran doctrine, theology, liturgy, church life, and worship. Occasionally accepts personal remembrances. 1,000–3,000 words.

How to Submit

Query with outline, writing samples, and clips. Include SASE. Accepts photocopies, computer printouts, and WordPerfect 5.1 disks. No simultaneous submissions. Reports in 1–2 months.

Payment and Policies

Authors retain rights. No payment.

The Lutheran Journal

Rev. Armin U. Deye, Editor
7317 Cahill Road
Minneapolis, MN 55419
612-941-6830

AT A GLANCE:
The Lutheran Journal

- Lutheran, Inspirational
- 60% freelance
- Some new writers
- Quarterly
- Circ: 130,000
- Receives few queries, 50+ mss each month.
- Pays: $.01–$.015 per word on publication.

From the Editor:
"All material must be suitable for a church magazine."

Sample copy: Free with 8.5x11 SAE and $.52 postage. No guidelines.

Profile

A quarterly family magazine distributed free through Lutheran churches and available by subscription to individuals. 8.5x11; glossy cover; full-color; 32 pages.

Focus and Audience

Provides wholesome and inspirational reading material for the enjoyment and enrichment of Lutherans. Most readers are middle-age or older.

Interests and Word Lengths

- *Fiction:* Inspirational stories. 2,000 words.
- *Nonfiction:* Personal experiences, self-help and how-to articles, and inspirational pieces on family life, health and healing, cultural and ethnic issues, lifestyle, seniors, and women's issues. 2,000 words.
- *Photos:* B/W or color prints.

How to Submit

Send complete ms with cover letter for fiction. Query with writing samples or send complete ms with cover letter for nonfiction. Include SASE. Accepts photocopies and computer printouts. Simultaneous submissions okay. Reports in 3–4 months.

Payment and Policies

First North American serial or one-time rights. Pays on publication. $.01–$.015 per word. Authors receive copies of the issue upon request.

The Lutheran Layman

Gerald Perschbacher, Editor
2185 Hampton Avenue
St. Louis, MO 63139-2983
800-944-3450

AT A GLANCE:
THE LUTHERAN LAYMAN

- Lutheran, News
- 10% freelance
- Monthly
- Circ: 80,000
- Pays on publication. Rates vary.

From the Editor:
"Be traditional; this is a conservative audience. We prefer to give assignments to free-lancers. Do not submit articles first—write for information."

Best Bet: Religious news relevant to the Lutheran Hour Ministries.

Sample copy: Free. Send #10 SASE for guidelines.

Profile

A monthly publication of the Lutheran Hour Ministries. 11x11.5; 16 pages.

Focus and Audience

Reports on religious news that relates either directly or indirectly to the Lutheran Hour Ministries. Audience is conservative and traditional. All material must be theologically approved by Lutheran standards.

Interests and Word Lengths

- *Nonfiction:* All material is assigned. Accepts religious news that is national in scope and pertains to the Lutheran Hour Ministries. Occasionally accepts related opinion pieces, essays, and personal experiences. Query for word-lengths.

How to Submit

Query first. No unsolicited mss. Include SASE. Send for writer's guidelines, specs, and sample copy before contacting.

Payment and Policies

All rights. Pays on publication. Rates vary. Authors receive copies of the issue upon request.

Lutheran Partners

Carl E. Linder, Editor
ELCA
8765 West Higgins Road
Chicago, IL 60631

AT A GLANCE:

LUTHERAN PARTNERS

- Lutheran, Ministers
- 50% freelance
- Bimonthly
- Circ: 22,000
- Receives 5–10 mss each month.
- Pays $100–$200 on publication.

From the Editor:
"Most of our articles are written by pastors and ministers, but we do accept articles from concerned lay people that challenge leadership. Know the ELCA audience."

Best Bet: Articles on the issues facing ELCA ministers.

Sample copy: $2 with 9x12 SAE and $2 postage. Send #10 SASE for guidelines.

Profile

A bimonthly magazine for those in the public ministries of the Evangelical Lutheran Church in America (ELCA). Published by Augsburg Fortress. 8.5x11; self cover; 44 pages.

Focus and Audience

Serves as a communications vehicle for pastors and associates to exchange opinions and viewpoints on the interests and concerns most pertinent to ministry in the ELCA. Most articles are written by readers, who are pastors, ministers, prison chaplains, and hospital chaplains.

Interests and Word Lengths

- *Nonfiction:* Christian theology, leadership, mission, and service. Up to 3,000 words.
- *Departments:* Sharing; Second Opinion. 1,200 words. Book and video reviews, works of theology and Christian thought. 700–800 words. Submit to Book or Video Review Editor.
- *Poetry:* Short, inspirational poems that move the spirit and the heart.
- *Filler:* Practical articles of 500 words or less on local church problems and solutions.

How to Submit

Query with outline, or send complete ms with cover letter. Include SASE. Prefers original mss. Accepts computer printouts and IBM-compatible disks, preferably WordPerfect. Identify simultaneous submissions. Reports in 3–4 months.

Payment and Policies

First North American serial rights. Pays on publication. Feature articles, $200. Shorter pieces, $100. Poetry, $50–$75. Offers kill fee, rates vary. Authors receive 2 copies of the issue.

The Lutheran Witness

David Strand, Managing Editor
The Lutheran Church—Missouri Synod
1333 South Kirkwood Road
St. Louis, MO 63122-7295
314-965-9917

AT A GLANCE:
THE LUTHERAN WITNESS

- Lutheran, Doctrinal
- 75% freelance
- 10% new writers
- Monthly
- Circ: 350,000
- Receives 5+ queries, 50+ mss each month.
- Pays $100–$300 on acceptance.

From the Editor:
"Space is limited, but we read everything we receive. Manuscripts are often rejected because they are inappropriate for our audience, too preachy or exhibit poor theology, are poorly written, or too technical in language and syntax."

Best Bet: Stories and non-academic articles with broad appeal.

Avoid: Poetry.

Sample copy: Free. Send #10 SASE for guidelines.

Profile

The official periodical of The Lutheran Church—Missouri Synod (LCMS). Most, but not all, writers are LCMS members. Member of the Associated Church Press. 8.5x11; glossy cover; 26 pages.

Focus and Audience

Provides Missouri Synod lay people with stories and information that complement congregational life, foster personal growth in faith, and help interpret the contemporary world from a Christian perspective.

Interests and Word Lengths

- *Fiction:* Quality fiction from a Christian perspective. 500–1,500 words.
- *Nonfiction:* Features on contemporary and societal issues; personal-experience pieces; internal ministry and missionary stories; biblical, theological, and doctrinal studies. Suggested topics include Learning to Serve, how-to's on ways Christians can serve Christ; Following Him, devotional articles; Lifelines, first-person accounts of faith overcoming adversity; My Growing Faith, faith-related personal experiences; and Missouri Remembers, LCMS history and historical figures. 500–1,500 words. Accepts seasonal material
- *Photos:* B/W or color prints or slides to accompany manuscript. Should be candid and active.

How to Submit

Send complete ms with cover letter, social security number, and author photo. Include SASE. Accepts photocopies and computer printouts. Simultaneous submissions okay if to non-competitor. Reports in 6–8 weeks.

Payment and Policies

First North American serial rights. Pays on acceptance. $100–$300 per piece plus expenses and travel. Kill fee, 50%. Authors receive 6 copies of the issue.

Lutheran Woman Today

Nancy J. Stelling, Editor
8765 West Higgins Road
Chicago, IL 60631-4189
312-380-2743

AT A GLANCE: LUTHERAN WOMAN TODAY

- Lutheran, Women
- 11 issues a year
- Circ: 250,000
- Receives many mss each month.
- Pays: $60–$280 on publication.

From the Editor:
"We seek manuscripts written in a popular style: readable, interesting, and substantive. Generally, use inclusive language and avoid using pronouns when referring to God."

Best Bet: Articles for Devotion department; personal experiences of faith combined with solid theology.

Avoid: Topics covered in previous issues of *Lutheran Woman Today.*

Sample copy: Free. Send #10 SASE for guidelines.

Profile

A monthly devotional magazine for Lutheran women. Developed by the Women of the Evangelical Lutheran Church in America (ELCA) and published by Augsburg Press. Est.: 1988. 5.5x8.5; heavy bond cover; 2-color; 48 pages.

Focus and Audience

Designed for and read by a diverse group of Lutheran women with a variety of lifestyles and interests.

Interests and Word Lengths

- *Fiction:* Short stories with Christian emphasis featuring a woman protagonist. Nothing preachy. 1,250 words.
- *Nonfiction:* Articles by and/or about women that have a spiritual basis and reflect Christian/Lutheran theology. Topics include: family, gifts of the Spirit, love, diversity, peace with justice, life in faith. Up to 1,250 words.
- *Departments:* Devotion, short group or individual devotions, 350 words. Women of the ELCA, profiles of contemporary women of faith. Earthcare, environmental issues. Shortakes, prayers on news items. Forum, guest editorial. Seasons Best, reflections of liturgical seasons. Monthly Bible studies.
- *Poetry:* Poems with a women's and spiritual focus.
- *Artwork:* B/W prints of women subjects reflecting racial, cultural, and age diversity. Cartoons with religious or spiritual content that reflect well on women.

How to Submit

Prefers complete ms with cover letter; accepts query with outline. Include SASE. Reports in 1–2 months.

Payment and Policies

First rights. Pays on publication. Articles and stories, $60–$280. Poetry, $15–$60. Photos, $30–$40. Authors receive copies of the issue upon request.

The Magazine for Christian Youth!

Anthony E. Peterson, Editor
P.O. Box 801
Nashville, TN 37202
615-749-6319

AT A GLANCE:
THE MAGAZINE FOR CHRISTIAN YOUTH!

- Christian, Teens
- 50% freelance
- 30% new writers
- Monthly
- Circ: 30,000
- Receives 12 queries, 25–30 mss each month.
- Pays: $.05 per word on acceptance.

From the Editor:
"Our approach is to provide help for individual youths. Write to teens friend to friend. Instruct with humor and grace, not with judgment. Appreciate the wonders and joys of teen life."

Best Bet: Stories that engage the reader's mind and feelings.

Avoid: Preachy language, simplistic answers, and sentimental resolutions.

Sample copy: $2 with 9x12 SAE and 5 first-class stamps. Send #10 SASE for guidelines.

Profile

A Christian monthly for junior high and senior high youth. Published by The United Methodist Publishing House. 8.5x11; glossy cover; 4-color; 48 pages.

Focus and Audience

Designed to help teenagers develop a Christian identity and live out the Christian faith in contemporary culture. Challenges junior high and senior high students to think, discover, explore, and grow closer to God.

Interests and Word Lengths

- *Fiction:* Short stories, drama, and genre fiction written by teens. Adventures, romance, science fiction, fantasy, relationship stories, and humor. 500–2,000 words.
- *Nonfiction:* Features, essays, personal experiences, profiles and interviews, and self-help and how-to pieces exploring youth groups, missions, animals in service, career and college choices, education, social issues, ethnic and multicultural themes, nature and the environment, family life, sports, the arts, and news. 500–2,000 words.
- *Departments:* Freelance music reviews, 200–500 words. Express Mail, poetry by teens. From You, letter to the editor.
- *Seasonal:* Major Christian or other holidays. Seeks unique angles on holidays such as little known facts or relationships to religious history.
- *Artwork:* Prefers color transparencies. Accepts B/W prints, line drawings, and other artwork.

How to Submit

Send complete ms with cover letter. Include SASE. Accepts photocopies and computer printouts. Simultaneous submissions okay. Reports in 4 months.

Payment and Policies

One-time rights. Pays on acceptance. $.05 per word. Authors receive 2 copies of the issue.

Manna

Roger A Ball, Editor
2966 West Westcove Drive
West Valley City, UT 84119-5940

AT A GLANCE:
MANNA

- Christian, Poetry
- 100% freelance
- 50+% new writers
- 2 issues a year
- Circ: 250
- Receives 15–20 queries, 50 mss each month.
- No payment. Offers prizes for best poems in each issue.

From the Editor:
"We would love to receive a lot of fine inspirational poetry, but we don't. Inspirational poetry is difficult to write and most of what we receive is awful. Request and read a sample and our guidelines carefully."

Best Bet: Short, well-crafted inspirational poetry.

Avoid: Sing-songy poems, greeting card ditties, and sentimental love poetry.

Sample copy: $3.50. Send #10 SASE for guidelines.

Profile

A small but growing Christian magazine of short, non-rhyming poetry written by beginning to intermediate poets. 7x8.5; journal quality; 40 pages.

Focus and Audience

A conservative, but not stuffy or pretentious, magazine that prints the best poetry it can find. Leans heavily toward shorter poetry with clean imagery, strong content, and quality writing. Most readers and contributors are Christians from rural areas.

Interests and Word Lengths

- *Poetry:* Seeks short, well-crafted, inspirational poetry that makes use of concrete imagery and gives a sense of delight in being alive, celebrating, and believing God is part of our everyday lives. No sing-songy rhyming poetry or rehashed hymns. Prefers free-verse inspirational poetry on the human condition and rural or farm concerns. No topic is out of bounds, but be careful and deal sensitively with sex, raw language, love, confession, and violence. Much of the material received is of poor quality.

How to Submit

Send original poetry with #10 SASE. Submit 3–5 poems per batch, each on a single page. Author's name and address should be on each page. No reprints. Accepts photocopies and computer printouts. Reports in 1 month.

Payment and Policies

First North American serial rights. No payment. Offers 3 prizes of $7, $5, and $3 for the best poems in each issue. Contributor's copies are not provided.

Marketplace Métier

Neal Kunde, Editor
6400 Schroeder Road
P.O. Box 7895
Madison, WI 53707-7895
608-274-9001

AT A GLANCE:

MARKETPLACE MÉTIER

- Christian, Business
- Quarterly
- Circ: 15,000
- No payment. Offers copies of the issue.

From the Editor:
"*Métier* is a French word that means vocation, trade, or an area of activity in which one is expert. It comes from the Latin word *ministerium*, which refers to both work and ministry."

Best Bet: Articles for and by those involved in a lay ministry in the marketplace.

Sample copy: Free. Send #10 SASE for guidelines.

Profile

A new publication exploring lay ministry in the marketplace. Published quarterly by Marketplace Ministries, a division of Inter-Varsity Christian Fellowship of the U.S.A. 8.5x11; glossy cover; 2-color; 8 pages.

Focus and Audience

Exists to tell the stories of Christians who are applying their faith to their work, to provide a forum where marketplace issues are discussed, and to suggest resources where readers can get more information on the ministry of the laity.

Interests and Word Lengths

- *Nonfiction:* Faith on the Job, profiles of working men and women who apply their faith to their careers. Marketplace Hero, short accounts of historical figures whose stories inspire today's lay ministers.
- *Departments:* The Campus Connection, college applications of marketplace ministry. In the Lion's Den, Q&A column that addresses specific struggles and issues in the marketplace. Wise Investments, offers resources for marketplace ministries. Laity in Scripture, biblical texts and themes related to marketplace ministry. Financial Column, monetary issues faced by marketplace Christians.
- *Photos:* Prefers B/W prints.

How to Submit

Send complete ms with cover letter. Include SASE. Accepts photocopies, computer printouts, and ASCII disk submissions. Simultaneous submissions okay. Report time varies.

Payment and Policies

No payment. Authors receive copies of the issue upon request.

Marriage Partnership

Annette LaPlaca, Assistant Editor
465 Gundersen Drive
Carol Stream, IL 60188
708-260-6200

AT A GLANCE:
MARRIAGE PARTNER-
SHIP

- Christian, Marriage and Family
- 50% freelance
- 5% new writers
- Quarterly
- Circ: 65,000
- Receives 5–10 queries, 5–10 mss each month.
- Payment varies.

From the Editor:
"We are distinctively Christian—practical but not preachy, inspirational without being overly sentimental. Familiarize yourself with the magazine's voice and overall tone."

Avoid: Writing toward women only. Didactic text and prooftexting with Scripture.

Sample copy: $5 check. Send #10 SASE for guidelines.

Profile

A quarterly magazine dedicated to promoting and strengthening Christian marriages. Published by Christianity Today, Inc. 8x11; glossy cover; 4-color; 80 pages.

Focus and Audience

With candor, hope, and humor, offers realistic and challenging insights as well as practical help in building a healthy Christian marriage. Readers are married, 22–48 years old, have one or more children, work outside the home, and are active in a local church.

Interests and Word Lengths

- *Nonfiction:* Profiles of inspirational couples; advice from marriage or family experts, personality interviews; essays, personal experiences, and short humorous pieces on marriage and family life. 800–1,500 words.
- *Department:* FWO (For Women Only), women's issues, and FMO (For Men Only), men's issues. 400–500 words. Other departments include Q&A, Early Years, Work It Out, American Marriage, Marriage Builders, Stars & Stripes, Heart & Soul, and Lighten Up.
- *Photos:* Submit to Christa Jordan, Assistant Designer. Not encouraged, but accepts B/W and color prints.

How to Submit

Query with an outline and resume. Direct queries to appropriate department or column. Include SASE. Accepts photocopies, computer printouts, and faxes if double spaced. Reports in 2 months.

Payment and Policies

One-time rights. Pays on publication for FWO and FMO. Pays on acceptance for articles. Rates vary according to length. Authors receive 2 copies of the issue.

Martyrdom and Resistance

Dr. Harvey Rosenfeld, Editor
48 West 37th Street
9th Floor
New York, NY 10018
212-564-1865

AT A GLANCE:

MARTYRDOM AND RESISTANCE

- Jewish, Holocaust
- 100% freelance
- Bimonthly
- Circ: 30,000
- Receives 30–40 queries, 25–30 mss each month.
- No payment. Offers up to 12 contributor's copies.

From the Editor:
"Be sure to document your facts."

Best Bet: Writings on the Holocaust and the effects of anti-Semitism.

Sample copy: Free. No guidelines.

Profile

A bimonthly newspaper about the Holocaust and its effects, published by the International Society for Yad Vashem, Inc. Tabloid-size; newsprint; 16 pages.

Focus and Audience

Interested solely in memorializing the Holocaust and its victims. Moderate in approach, it accepts differing points of view. Read by Holocaust survivors, universities, and interested members of the Society of Yad Vashem.

Interests and Word Lengths

- *Nonfiction:* Scholarly articles and other material exploring the pre- and post-Holocaust era (1933–46) and anti-Semitism. No word-length restrictions. Accepts filler, seasonal material, and poetry.
- *Departments:* Survivor's Corner, memoirs of Holocaust experiences. Book Reviews on related topics.
- *Photos:* B/W prints.

How to Submit

Submit complete ms with cover letter. Include SASE. Accepts photocopies, computer printouts, and fax submissions. Simultaneous submissions okay. Reports in 1–2 months.

Payment and Policies

Authors retain rights. No payment. Authors receive up to 12 copies of the issue.

Maryknoll

Joseph R. Veneroso, M.M., Editor
Maryknoll, NY 10545
914-941-7590

AT A GLANCE:

MARYKNOLL

- Catholic, Missions
- 10% freelance
- 15% missionaries
- Monthly
- Circ: 600,000
- Receives 5–10 queries each month.
- Pays: $75–$150 on acceptance.

From the Editor:
"Write from the perspective of a person who is living through the experience."

Best Bet: Concrete articles about real people in real places.

Avoid: General articles about specific problems.

Sample copy: Free. Send #10 SASE for guidelines.

Profile

The monthly magazine for the Catholic Foreign Mission Society of America, Inc., a non-profit organization established to recruit, train, send, and support American missioners in areas overseas. 5.5x8.5; glossy cover; full-color; 66 pages.

Focus and Audience

Informs supporters of the work of the Maryknoll missions overseas. Much material is written by missionaries or those who have recently visited mission sites.

Interests and Word Lengths

- *Nonfiction:* Profiles of missionaries—Maryknoll or other, priests, brothers or sisters, U.S. or foreign, who are making significant contributions to missions or missions training. Documentary analysis of problems that relate the moral, cultural, psychic, and political concerns of those in developing nations. Articles on the customs of other cultures. Humorous articles about missionaries in action. All articles must be concrete and have very human, personal angles. Must be accompanied by photos. 1,000 words.
- *Poetry:* Occasionally uses poetry.
- *Photos:* Clear, compelling, and intimate B/W or color photos to illustrate articles. Editors prefer to have a minimum of 100 good photos from which to choose.

How to Submit

Send brief, concrete query letter stating the availability of photos or artwork. Include SASE. No simultaneous submissions. Reports in 2–4 weeks.

Payment and Policies

First North American serial rights. Pays on acceptance. $75–$150 per piece depending on article length and content. Authors receive 3–5 copies of the issue.

Mature Living

Judy Pregel, Assistant Editor
127 Ninth Avenue North
Nashville, TN 37234
615-251-2274

AT A GLANCE:
MATURE LIVING

- Southern Baptist, Seniors
- 75% freelance
- Monthly
- Circ: 365,000
- Receives 1,200 mss each month.
- Pays: $.055 per word on acceptance.

From the Editor:
"Write simply and with clarity. Document informational articles with references."

Best Bet: Human-interest stories.

Sample copy: Free with 9x12 SAE and $.85 postage. Send #10 SASE for guidelines.

Profile

A leisure-reading magazine for Christian senior adults. Published by The Sunday School Board of the Southern Baptist Convention. Uses as doctrinal guidelines the 1963 statement of The Baptist Faith and Message.

Focus and Audience

Emphasizes material with strong human interest angles on topics of interest to a senior adult Baptist readership.

Interests and Word Lengths

- *Fiction:* Short stories with Christian emphasis of interest to seniors. 425–1,500 words.
- *Nonfiction:* Nostalgia, travel pieces, humor, inspirational and informational articles, crafts, and articles on grandparenting and health-related topics. 425–1,500 words.
- *Seasonal:* Submit 1 year in advance.
- *Photos:* B/W and color photos to accompany articles.

How to Submit

Submit complete ms. Include SASE. No reprints. Accepts photocopies and computer printouts. No simultaneous submissions. Reports in 1 month.

Payment and Policies

First North American serial or all rights. Pays on acceptance. $.055 per word. Authors receive 3 copies of the issue.

The Mennonite

Gordon Houser, Editor
722 Main Street
Newton, KS 67114
316-283-5100

AT A GLANCE:

THE MENNONITE

- Mennonite, Social Issues
- 30% freelance
- 5% new writers
- Bimonthly
- Circ: 9,000
- Receives 2–3 queries, 5 mss each month.
- Pays: $.05 per word on publication.

From the Editor:
"Tell stories, preferably from personal experience, that relate to living day by day as a Christian."

Best Bet: Good Bible studies.

Avoid: Passive voice, academic styles, and inconsistent tenses.

Sample copy: Free. Send #10 SASE for guidelines.

Profile

An official magazine of the General Conference Mennonite Church. A member of Associated Church Press, Evangelical Press Association, and Meetinghouse, a Mennonite and Brethren in Christ editor's group. 8.5x11; 2-color; 24 pages.

Focus and Audience

Seeks to inform and challenge the Christian fellowship. Most readers are Mennonites, but the magazine confronts issues faced by all Christians.

Interests and Word Lengths

- *Nonfiction:* Features, personal experiences and humorous pieces on family life, prayer, social and world issues, evangelism, and peace. Up to 1,000 words.
- *Departments:* Speaking Out, Profile, Bible, Commentary. Seeks good Bible studies. 600–650 words.
- *Seasonal:* Christmas and Easter material. Up to 1,000 words.
- *Artwork:* B/W photos. Also, seeks artists to illustrate articles.

How to Submit

Query with outline, or send complete ms with cover letter. Include SASE. Accepts computer printouts, Macintosh Microsoft Word 4.0 disks, and faxes. Simultaneous submissions okay. Reports in 1 month.

Payment and Policies

One-time rights. Pays on publication. $.05 per word. Authors receive 2 copies of the issue.

Mennonite Brethren Herald

Ron Geddert, Editor
3-169 Riverton Avenue
Winnipeg, MB R2L 2E5
Canada
204-669-6575

AT A GLANCE:

MENNONITE BRETHREN HERALD

- Mennonite, Devotional
- 20% freelance
- Biweekly
- Circ: 14,500
- Receives 30 queries, 30 mss each month.
- Pays on publication. Rates vary.

From the Editor:
"Consider that the audience is Canadian Mennonite Brethren. Articles must be more than simply devotional; they should be provocative."

Best Bet: Material with an evangelical, Anabaptist context.

Sample copy: $1 with a 9x12 SASE/IRC. Send #10 SASE/IRC for guidelines.

Profile

A denominational periodical for Canadian Mennonite Brethren. Also publishes a special edition aimed at non-Christians on practical topics that point toward the Christian faith. 8.5x11; self cover; 32 pages.

Focus and Audience

Purpose is to inform members of church events, to meet members' personal and spiritual needs, to act as a vehicle of communication within the church, to serve conference agencies, and to reflect the history and theology of the Mennonite Brethren Church in Canada.

Interests and Word Lengths

- *Fiction:* Short stories on a variety of topics of interest to church members. 1,200–1,500 words. Accepts poetry.
- *Nonfiction:* Articles on a range of subjects that are provocative as well as devotional in nature. Must be from an evangelical, Anabaptist perspective. 1,200–1,500 words.
- *Departments:* 900 words.
- *Photos:* Submit to Fred Koop.

How to Submit

Send complete ms with cover letter. Include SASE. U.S. authors include IRCs. Accepts photocopies, computer printouts, IBM-compatible disks, and fax submissions. Simultaneous submissions okay. Reports in 6 months.

Payment and Policies

Pays on publication. Rates vary. Authors receive copies of the issue upon request.

Mennonite Family History

Lois Ann Mast, Editor
Ten West Main Street
Elverson, PA 19520
215-286-0258

Profile
A quarterly periodical covering Mennonite, Amish, and Brethren genealogy and family history. Est.: 1982. 8.5x11; glossy cover; 44 pages.

Focus and Audience
Dedicated to preserving the Mennonite, Amish, and Brethren heritage by encouraging the study of genealogy and family history.

Interests and Word Lengths
- *Nonfiction:* Genealogy, family history, and personal research experience stories concentrating on early Swiss and German immigrants who settled in Pennsylvania in the late 1600s and then moved south and west. Also published lists of books for sale or wanted, reviews, Bible records, research in progress, and genealogical queries. Lengths vary.
- *Poetry:* Related to history or genealogy.

How to Submit
Query with outline and resume. Include SASE. Accepts photocopies, computer printouts, Macintosh SE disks, and faxes. Simultaneous submissions okay. Reports in 1 month.

Payment and Policies
Pays on publication. Rates vary. Authors receive 3 copies of the issue.

Mennonite Life

James C. Juhnke, Editor
Bethel College
300 East 27th
North Newton, KS 67117
316-283-2500

AT A GLANCE:

MENNONITE LIFE

- Mennonite, History
- 90% freelance
- Quarterly
- Circ: 650
- Receives less than 10 queries each month.
- No payment. Offers 2 contributor's copies.

Best Bet: Anything connected with Mennonite history.

Sample copy: $4. No guidelines.

Profile

An illustrated quarterly magazine dedicated to Mennonite History. Published by Bethel College. 8.5x11; glossy cover; 36 pages.

Focus and Audience

Publishes anything related to Mennonite history or culture. Readers are those interested in popular history and, in particular, Mennonite history.

Interests and Word Lengths

- *Fiction:* Rare, but considers short stories of historical connection with Mennonite history. No word-length restrictions.
- *Nonfiction:* Features, interviews, profiles, and personal experiences, all dealing with Mennonite history, Mennonite social and theological issues and concerns, and arts-related themes. Photos should accompany articles. No word-length restrictions.
- *Poetry:* Occasionally accepts poetry.
- *Artwork:* Prefers B/W prints. Accepts color photos and illustrations.

How to Submit

Query first. Include SASE. Accepts photocopies, computer printouts, and IBM-compatible WordPerfect disks. No simultaneous submissions. Reports in 1 month.

Payment and Policies

Author retains rights. No payment. Authors receive 2 copies of the issue.

Mennonite Reporter

Ron Rempel, Editor
3-312 Marsland Drive
Waterloo, ON N2J 3Z1
Canada
519-884-3810

AT A GLANCE:

MENNONITE REPORTER

- Mennonite, News
- 15% freelance
- Uses new writers
- Biweekly
- Circ: 11,000
- Receives 4–5 queries each month.
- Pays: $.10 per word on publication.

From the Editor:
"Please query first and be aware that most of our audience is Canadian."

Best Bet: Articles on issues concerning Canadian Mennonites.

Sample copy: Free. Send #10 SASE/IRC for guidelines.

Profile

An independent, inter-Mennonite paper of news and comment. Member of Associated Church Press and Canadian Church Press. Tabloid-size; newsprint; 20 pages.

Focus and Audience

Publishes church-related news and social comment from an Anabaptist and Mennonite perspective. Readers are Canadian Mennonites.

Interests and Word Lengths

- *Nonfiction:* Interviews and profiles, personal experiences, and features on renewal of church life, church at work and worship, worship education, and missions. 1,000–1,500 words. Articles on current issues and news pieces, 500–750 words.
- *Departments:* Reader Forum, opinion pieces about church or social issues.
- *Seasonal:* Articles and photos related to seasons of the church year.
- *Artwork:* B/W or color prints; line drawings.

How to Submit

Query first. Include SASE. U.S. authors include IRCs. Accepts photocopies, computer printouts, and Microsoft Word disks. Identify simultaneous submissions. Reports in 3–4 weeks.

Payment and Policies

First North American serial rights. Pays on publication. $.10 per word. Authors receive clippings of their article.

Mennonite Weekly Review

Robert Schrag, Editor
Box 568
Newton, KS 67114-0568
316-283-3670

AT A GLANCE:
MENNONITE WEEKLY REVIEW

- Mennonite, News
- 5% freelance
- Under 5% new writers
- Weekly
- Circ: 11,000
- Receives less than 10 queries, 10 mss each month.
- Pays: $.05 per word on publication.

From the Editor:
"Familiarity with the Mennonite Church would be helpful to those wishing to write for us."

Best Bet: Mennonite and general religious news and opinion.

Sample copy: $1 with SAE and $.50 postage. No guidelines.

Profile

An independent inter-Mennonite newspaper published by Herald Publishing Company. Tabloid-size; newsprint; 12–16 pages.

Focus and Audience

Publishes general religious news and Mennonite news and opinion. Conservative to moderate in approach. Reaches Mennonite conferences and groups throughout the U.S.

Interests and Word Lengths

- *Nonfiction:* News and feature articles on Mennonite and general religious issues. Priority given to Mennonite writers. 400–500 words.
- *Departments:* Editorials and opinion pieces, all on religious issues. Considers religious opinion pieces by non-Mennonite writers.
- *Photos:* B/W prints.

How to Submit

Send complete ms with cover letter. Include SASE. Accepts photocopies and computer printouts. Simultaneous submissions okay. Reports on request only with SASE, usually within 1 month.

Payment and Policies

Authors retain rights. Pays on publication. $.05 per word. Authors receive 1 copy of the issue; additional copies available upon request.

Message

Stephen P. Ruff, Editor
55 West Oak Ridge Drive
Hagerstown, MD 21740
301-791-7000

Profile

A Christian magazine of contemporary issues from an African-American perspective. Published by the Review and Herald Publishing Association. 8.5x11; glossy cover; full-color; 32 pages.

Focus and Audience

Strives to present contemporary issues in light of the Gospel and to attract readers to a healthy, balanced Christian lifestyle. Most readers are middle-aged African-Americans.

Interests and Word Lengths

- *Fiction:* Message Jr., short, realistic stories for children that are based in Christianity and relate to childhood experiences. Can be a new twist on a Bible story. 400 words.
- *Nonfiction:* Features, interviews, personal experiences, and news stories on family, religion, health, social issues, social ministries, positive role models, African-American issues, and other cultures. 800–1,200 words.
- *Departments:* Healthspan, short health pieces, quizzes, and personal inventories. 400 words.
- *Seasonal:* Submit 6 months in advance.

How to Submit

Send complete ms with cover letter and resume. Include SASE. Accepts photocopies, computer printouts, IBM 3.5-inch WordPerfect 5.1 disks, and fax submission. Simultaneous submissions okay. Reports in 1–2 months.

Payment and Policies

First North American serial rights. Pays on acceptance. $80–$150 per piece. Authors receive 3 copies of the issue.

Message of the Cross

George R. Foster, Editor
6820 Auto Club Road
Minneapolis, MN 55438
612-946-4180

AT A GLANCE:
MESSAGE OF THE CROSS

- Christian, Missions
- 5–10% freelance
- 5–10% new writers
- Quarterly
- Circ: 7,000
- Receives 10 mss each month.
- No payment. Offers 3 contributors copies.

From the Editor:
"We would like to stir Christians to seek an abundant life of victory over sin, effective witness, and commitment to world missions."

Sample copy: Free. No guidelines.

Profile

A quarterly publication of Christian living. Free distribution. 5.5x8; 32 pages.

Focus and Audience

Emphasizes victorious Christian living and fosters a commitment to world missions.

Interests and Word Lengths

- *Nonfiction:* Articles on victorious Christian living; deliverance from harmful habits; insights into Bible passages; and missions experiences. Interests include witnessing, spirituality, and evangelism. No word-length restrictions.
- *Artwork:* Illustrations of victorious living and missions.

How to Submit

Send complete ms with cover letter and resume. Include SASE. Accepts computer printouts and disk submissions. No simultaneous submissions. Reports in 2 months.

Payment and Policies

One-time rights. No payment. Authors receive 3 copies of issue.

Message of the Open Bible

Delores Winegar, Editor
2020 Bell Avenue
Des Moines, IA 50315
515-288-6761

AT A GLANCE:

MESSAGE OF THE OPEN BIBLE

- Open Bible Standard Church, Inspirational
- 10% freelance
- 0–10% new writers
- 10 issues a year
- Circ: 4,200
- Receives 3–4 mss each month.
- No payment. Offers 1–2 contributor's copies.

From the Editor:
"Please know that we exist for our Open Bible readers. We do not pay for articles."

Avoid: Fiction.

Sample copy: Free with 9x12 SAE and $.75 postage. Send #10 SASE for guidelines.

Profile

The official organ of Open Bible Standard Churches. 8.5x11; glossy cover; 20 pages.

Focus and Audience

Inspires, informs, educates, and unifies the Open Bible family. Articles are for Open Bible people, by Open Bible people.

Interests and Word Lengths

- *Nonfiction:* Testimonies of outstanding salvation experiences, the Holy Spirit's moving, healings, miracles, etc. Inspirational pieces, original sermons that teach or challenge: prefers Open Bible authors, but considers other sources. Profiles of outstanding spiritual or numerical growth in churches. Accepts seasonal material. 750–1,600 words.
- *Poetry:* Accepts poems as filler or to accompany articles.

How to Submit

Send complete ms with cover letter and short author biography. Include SASE. Submit seasonal material 2 months in advance. Accepts photocopies and computer printouts. Simultaneous submissions okay. Reports in 1 month.

Payment and Policies

Author retains rights. No payment. Authors receive 1–2 copies of the issue.

Messenger

Jean Bach, News Editor
Box 18068
Covington, KY 41018-0068
606-581-2271

AT A GLANCE:
MESSENGER

- Catholic, Regional
- 40% freelance
- Weekly
- Circ: 16,000
- Receives 3–4 queries each month.
- Pays $1.25 per column inch on publication.

From the Editor:
"We cover national and world issues as well as local news."

Best Bet: Well-founded articles on all topics related to the Catholic Church, including controversial topics.

Avoid: Poetry.

Sample copy: Free. Send #10 SASE for guidelines.

Profile

The official newspaper of the Roman Catholic Diocese of Covington, Kentucky. Tabloid-size; newsprint; 24 pages.

Focus and Audience

Covers local, national, and international issues relevant to the Catholic Church. Most readers are women, age 40 and older.

Interests and Word Lengths

- *Nonfiction:* Features, personality profiles, local Covington-area news, and guest opinions on Church-related issues such as liturgy, the sacraments, and family life. 500–800 words.
- *Seasonal:* Submit 1 month in advance.
- *Photos:* Prefers B/W prints.

How to Submit

Query with resume and writing samples. Include SASE. Accepts photocopies and computer printouts. Simultaneous submissions okay. Reports in 1 week.

Payment and Policies

First North American serial rights. Pays on publication. Features, $1.25 per column inch. No payment for opinion pieces. Authors receive 1 or more copies of the issue.

Michigan Christian Advocate

Kay DeMoss, Editor
316 Springbrook
Adrian, MI 49221
517-265-2075

AT A GLANCE:
MICHIGAN CHRISTIAN ADVOCATE

- United Methodist, Regional
- 20% freelance
- Less than 10% new writers
- Biweekly
- Circ: 13,500
- Receives 1 query, 1 ms each month.
- Pays: $15–$40 on publication.

From the Editor:
"Our outlook is fairly inclusive."

Best Bet: Issue-oriented material on family and social concerns.

Avoid: Negative tones.

Sample copy: Free. Send #10 SASE for guidelines.

Profile

The official publication of the United Methodist Church in Michigan. Tabloid-size; 16 pages.

Focus and Audience

Covers regional and national issue-oriented church and religious news for Michigan-area members of the United Methodist Church. Moderate to liberal in nature.

Interests and Word Lengths

- *Nonfiction:* Issue-oriented feature articles, interviews, personal-experience pieces, and some essays on family and faith life, societal concerns, and timely issues, all with a human-interest angle. Up to 750 words.
- *Departments:* My Experience; It Worked for Us; Book Reviews; Film Reviews.
- *Artwork:* B/W prints and cartoons with religious themes.

How to Submit

Submit complete ms with cover letter including biographical information. Include SASE. Accepts photocopies and computer printouts. Notify before sending faxes or submissions via modem. Simultaneous submissions okay. Reports in 1 month.

Payment and Policies

One-time rights. Pays on publication. Rates vary; generally $15–$40 per piece. Authors receive 10 copies of the issue.

Ministries Today

Barbie Eslin, Associate Editor
Michele Buckingham, Managing Editor
3901 Hield Road NW
Palm Bay, FL 32907
407-724-2999

AT A GLANCE:

MINISTRIES TODAY

- Christian, Leaders
- 30% freelance
- Bimonthly
- Circ: 36,000
- Receives 50–100 mss each month.
- Pays: $100–$500 on publication.

From the Editor:
"Most of our writers are highly educated and are writing to a highly educated audience. Use you article to make a single point. Get to know the magazine before submitting."

Best Bet: Instructional and entertaining articles for Christian leaders.

Avoid: Personal testimonies.

Sample copy: Send $4 to 600 Rinehart Road, Lake Mary, FL 32746 for sample. Send #10 SASE to address listed above for guidelines.

Profile

A non-denominational magazine for pastors and church leaders. Includes a supplement, *Worship Today*. 8.5x11; glossy cover; full-color; 84 pages.

Focus and Audience

Seeks to inspire, inform, and assist Christian leaders in their ministries. Audience includes pastors of mainline, independent, charismatic, Pentecostal, and fundamental churches, as well as church administrators, youth and lay leaders, and music directors.

Interests and Word Lengths

- *Nonfiction:* Biblically based features, interviews, profiles, and practical how-to articles that enhance a leader's ministry life, management skills, relationship to God and church, or personal life. Topics include family life, finances, contemporary issues, women in ministry, and prayer. Use specific, true-life illustrations to make a point. Also accepts practical and ethereal articles exploring worship practices for *Worship Today* supplement. 1,500–3,000 words.
- *Departments:* Soapbox, guest column, 800–1,100 words. Insiders Report, current news of interest to Christian leaders. Spring Boards, practical helps for leaders. Book and video reviews, 150–200 words.
- *Seasonal:* Submit 6 months in advance.

How to Submit

Query with outline, social security number, and anticipated word count. Include SASE. Accepts photocopies, computer printouts, and IBM-compatible disks. Simultaneous submissions okay if noted, but not encouraged. Report time 1–2 months.

Payment and Policies

All rights or one-time rights upon request. Pays on publication. Articles, $200–$500. Columns, $100. Authors receive 2 copies of the issue.

Ministry

David Newman, Editor
12501 Old Columbia Pike
Silver Spring, MS 20904
301-680-6510

AT A GLANCE:

MINISTRY

- Seventh-day Adventist, Clergy
- 50–60% freelance
- 10% new writers
- Monthly
- Circ: 75,000
- Receives 20 queries and mss each month.
- Pays: $50–$200 on acceptance.

From the Editor:
"Our goal is to help prepare pastors to minister to their congregations and present the everlasting Gospel of Jesus Christ and His salvation."

Best Bet: Articles for pastors, by pastors.

Avoid: Sermons, theses, general religious information not aimed specifically at pastors.

Sample copy: $2. Send #10 SASE for guidelines.

Profile

An international journal for clergy. Targeted primarily to leaders in the Seventh-day Adventist Church, six issues each year are distributed to non-Adventist clergy. 8.5x11; glossy cover; 32 pages.

Focus and Audience

Provides practical information and Christ-centered articles for Seventh-day Adventist ministers, evangelists, administrators, and interested lay persons, as well as non-Adventist clergy. All articles must be aimed at pastors and are best written by pastors.

Interests and Word Lengths

- *Nonfiction:* Send for complete guidelines. Christ-centered, cross-centered articles on evangelism and church growth, pastoral care and nurture, preaching and worship, church management, personal growth, personal relationships, theology, and Bible studies. Also accepts practical how-to articles, Bible expositories, devotionals, and health- and music-related articles. 2,000–3,500 words.
- *Departments:* Submit to Ella Rydzewski, Editorial Assistant. Biblio File, reviews of books pertaining to ministers. 1.5 typed, double-spaced pages.
- *Photos:* Head-shot photos of authors.

How to Submit

Query with outline. Include SASE. Accepts photocopies, computer printouts, WordPerfect 5.1 disks with hard copy, and faxes if notified. No simultaneous submissions. Reports in 1–3 months.

Payment and Policies

All rights. Pays on acceptance. $50–$200 per piece. Authors receive 2 copies of the issue.

Miraculous Medal

Rev. John W. Gouldrick, C.M., Editor
475 East Chelten Avenue
Philadelphia, PA 19144
215-848-1010

Profile

A quarterly Catholic digest of religious fiction and poetry. The official organ of the Central Association of the Miraculous Medal. 5.5x8.5; 2-color; 30 pages.

Focus and Audience

Seeks devotional fiction and poetry with religious themes that adheres to Roman Catholic teaching.

Interests and Word Lengths

- *Fiction:* All subjects are accepted provided that they do not contradict Roman Catholic teachings. 1,600–2,400 words.
- *Poetry:* Poems with religious themes, preferably about the Blessed Virgin Mary. Up to 20 lines.

How to Submit

Query with resume and writing samples. Include SASE. No reprints. Accepts computer printouts. Simultaneous submissions okay. Reports in 6 months.

Payment and Policies

First North American serial rights. Pays on acceptance. Fiction, $.02–up per word. Poetry, $.50 per line. Authors receive 1 copy of the issue.

Missiology

An International Review

Darrell L. Whiteman, Editor
Asbury Theological Seminary
Wilmore, KY 40390
606-858-2215

AT A GLANCE:

MISSIOLOGY

- Christian, Missions
- 100% freelance
- 20% new writers
- Quarterly
- Circ: 2,000
- Receives 4 queries, 4 mss each month.
- No payment. Offers 20 contributor's copies.

From the Editor:
"*Missiology* is a forum for the exchange of ideas."

Best Bet: Academic articles combining mission theory and practice.

Avoid: Devotionals; Bible studies; non-academic stories.

Sample copy: Free with 6x9 SASE. Send #10 SASE for guidelines.

Profile

A scholarly, academic missions journal published by the American Society of Missiology. 5.5x9; glossy cover; 128 pages.

Focus and Audience

Designed to serve those involved in cross-cultural ministries. Read by missionaries, professors of mission, anthropologists, and those interested in theology, history of missions, and religious studies.

Interests and Word Lengths

- *Nonfiction:* Scholarly articles that combine missiological theory with missions practice. Address cross-cultural ministries. Interests include evangelism, theology, and Christian apologetics. No word-length restrictions.
- *Photos:* B/W prints to accompany articles.

How to Submit

Submit 3 copies of complete ms with cover letter and resume. Include SASE. Accepts computer printouts and disks. No simultaneous submissions. Reports in 2 months.

Payment and Policies

All rights. No payment. Authors receive 20 copies of the issue.

The Missionary Tidings

Dan Runyon, Editor
770 North High School Road
Indianapolis, IN 46214
317-244-3660

AT A GLANCE:
THE MISSIONARY TIDINGS

- Free Methodist, Missionary
- 75% freelance
- 50% new writers
- Bimonthly
- Circ: 7,000
- Receives 5–10 queries, 5–10 mss each month.
- No payment. Offers 2 contributor's copies.

From the Editor:
"Freelance articles are accepted only from those with experience visiting or working at a Free Methodist Mission site."

Best Bet: Free Methodist mission experiences.

Sample copy: No information provided.

Profile

A bimonthly missions magazine published by Free Methodist World Missions. Most articles are assigned to missionaries. 8.5x11; 2-color; stapled; 32 pages.

Focus and Audience

Articles focus on Free Methodist missionary work and experience. Most subscribers are Free Methodists who support the missions.

Interests and Word Lengths

- *Nonfiction:* Assigns most articles to visiting career, or short term Free Methodist missionaries. Seeks practical articles that equip readers to fulfill their missionary duties. Photos must accompany submissions. No word-length restrictions.
- *Photos:* B/W photos must accompany submissions.

How to Submit

Send complete ms with cover letter. Include SASE. Accepts photocopies and computer printouts. Simultaneous submissions okay. Reports in 2 months.

Payment and Policies

One-time rights. No payment. Authors receive 2 copies of the issue.

Modern Liturgy

Nick Wagner, Managing Editor
160 East Virginia Street
No. 290
San Jose, CA 95112
408-286-8505

AT A GLANCE:
MODERN LITURGY

- Catholic, Liturgy
- 80–85% freelance
- 25% new writers
- 10 issues a year
- Circ: 10,000
- Receives 6–10 mss each month.
- No payment. Offers $40 worth of liturgy products.

From the Editor:
"Our readers are busy people, active in their parishes, who don't have time to waste."

Best Bet: Short, practical, upbeat pieces on planning liturgies.

Avoid: Religious material.

Sample copy: $4. Send #10 SASE for guidelines.

Profile

A resource journal for Roman Catholic liturgy planners. Published by Resource Publications, Inc. 8.5x11; 48 pages.

Focus and Audience

Informational resource of short, practical ideas on enhancing all aspects of Roman Catholic liturgical worship. Independent and progressive in approach.

Interests and Word Lengths

- *Nonfiction:* How-to articles on planning, organizing, and decorating for liturgies, especially for Advent and other seasons of the church year. Prefers short pieces.
- *Photos:* Liturgy-related photos, such as renovated churches, religious art, etc.

How to Submit

Send complete ms with cover letter, resume, and clips. Include SASE. Accepts photocopies, computer printouts, DOS disks with hard copy, and fax submissions. No simultaneous submissions. Reports in 3–4 weeks.

Payment and Policies

First North American rights. No payment. Offers liturgy planning products valuing $40. Authors receive 5 copies of the issue upon request.

Moment

Elizabeth Snider, Assistant Editor
3000 Connecticut Avenue NW
Suite 300
Washington, DC 20008
202-387-8888

AT A GLANCE:

MOMENT

- Jewish, Lifestyle
- 90% freelance
- 50–60% new writers
- Bimonthly
- Circ: 70,000
- Receives 150 queries each month.
- Pays on publication. Rates vary.

From the Editor:
"We like to hear what people have to say. Submit your work but be patient. We have a small staff and it takes a long time to review all the submissions we receive."

Best Bet: Focused articles with a unique hook.

Sample copy: Free. Send #10 SASE for guidelines.

Profile

A bimonthly magazine of general Jewish interest. 8.5x11; glossy cover; full-color.

Focus and Audience

Addresses cultural and religious issues of interest to Jewish people of all denominations. Readers are college-age and older.

Interests and Word Lengths

- *Nonfiction:* Features, interviews, essays, and personal experience pieces on cultural, social, religious, news-related, and sometimes controversial topics of Jewish interest. 2,000–2,500 words.
- *Departments:* Responsa, rabbinic Jewish questions. Guest Commentary, opinion pieces. Book reviews. 1,000–1,500 words.
- *Seasonal:* Jewish holiday pieces. Submit 2–3 months in advance.
- *Photos:* B/W or color prints and slides.

How to Submit

Query with outline and writing samples. Include SASE. Accepts photocopies, computer printouts, and fax submissions. May request computer disk after acceptance. Simultaneous submissions okay. Reports in 4 months.

Payment and Policies

One-time rights. Pays on publication. Rates vary according to subject and length. Authors receive 2–3 copies of the issue; more upon request.

The Montana Catholic

Gerald M. Korson, Editor
515 North Ewing Street
P.O. Box 1729
Helena, MT 59624-1729
406-442-5820

AT A GLANCE: THE MONTANA CATHOLIC

- Catholic, Regional
- 2% freelance
- 16 issues a year
- Circ: 8,300
- Receives 1–2 queries, 7–8 mss each month.
- Payment negotiable.

From the Editor:
"Ours is a Catholic publication for a Catholic audience and maintains a balance between conservative and moderate points of view."

Best Bet: General features with a Catholic angle and Montana tie-in.

Avoid: Overly strident commentaries. Negative views of Catholic and other faith groups.

Sample copy: No information provided.

Profile

Official newspaper of the Roman Catholic Diocese of Helena, Montana. Tabloid size; newsprint; 2-color; 20–24 pages.

Focus and Audience

Covers local news of Catholic interest as well as general Catholic features in special topical supplements. Serves readers in western Montana.

Interests and Word Lengths

- *Nonfiction:* Features with a Catholic angle and a regional connection, especially to western Montana, and articles of general Catholic interest. Special supplement themes include marriage, health care, vocations, colleges, retirement and seniors, death and dying, Lent, and Advent, all with a Catholic angle. Prefers 400–1,000 words. Accepts filler.
- *Departments:* Guest Commentary, essays and meditations on theology, church/politics, and social issues. 500–800 words.
- *Poetry:* Related to special supplement themes.
- *Photos:* Prefers 5x7 B/W prints or line drawings. Accepts color prints.

How to Submit

Query with outline, resume, and writing samples or clips, or send complete ms with cover letter, resume and clips. Include SASE. Accepts photocopies, computer printouts, 3.5-inch ASCII or IBM WordPerfect 5.0 disks, and faxes. Simultaneous submissions okay. Reports in 1 month.

Payment and Policies

One-time rights. Pays on publication. Rates are negotiable. Authors receive 5–10 copies of the issue.

Moody

Andrew Scheer, Managing Editor
820 North La Salle Boulevard
Chicago, IL 60610
312-329-2163

AT A GLANCE:
MOODY

- Evangelical, Lifestyle
- 80% freelance
- 40% new writers
- 11 issues a year
- Circ: 135,000
- Receives 150 queries, 100 mss each month.
- Pays: $.15–.20 per word on acceptance.

From the Editor:
"We're non-denominational, reaching a broad spectrum of conservative, evangelical but non-charismatic laity. Articles must be anchored in Scripture."

Best Bet: Vivid narratives showing the application of scriptural principles. Prefers a "how-I" rather than a "how-to" approach.

Avoid: Exhortational or advocacy articles that point to a problem but show no solutions.

Sample copy: Free with 8.5x11 SAE and $.79 postage. Send #10 SASE for guidelines.

Profile
A conservative envangelical publication that equips Christians to live biblically in a secular culture. 8.5x11; glossy cover; 4-color; 76 pages.

Focus and Audience
Looks for practical, popular-level articles that show the application of scriptural principles in daily living. The average reader is a 35–55-year-old, married, college-educated lay person active in his or her local church.

Interests and Word Lengths
- *Fiction:* Realistic, contemporary short stories that illustrate everyday Christian living. Purchases 3–4 stories per year. 1,400–2,000 words.
- *Nonfiction:* Personal narratives and topical reporting that address and apply everyday Christian living. Narrative should show how the writer applied scriptural principles to a personal problem or situation. 1,400–2,200 words.
- *Departments:* First Person, salvation testimonies written specifically for non-Christians, 800–1,000 words. Just for Parents, anecdotal parenting narratives, 1,300–1,500 words.
- *Seasonal:* Christmas and Easter material.

How to Submit
Query with outline. State working title, suggested length, biblical support, and author's qualifications and experience. No unsolicited mss. Include SASE. Accepts photocopies, computer printouts, and faxes. Reports in 2 months.

Payment and Policies
First North American serial rights. Pays on acceptance. Queried material, $.15 per word. Assigned material, $.20 per word. Authors receive 2 copies of the issue.

Moravian

Hermann Weinlick, Editor
Moravian Church in America
Box 1245
Bethlehem, PA 18016
215-867-0594

AT A GLANCE:

MORAVIAN

- Moravian, Denominational
- Under 10% freelance
- Monthly
- Circ: 25,000
- Receives 6 queries and mss per year.
- No payment. Offers 5 contributor's copies.

From the Editor:
"Writers can call us in advance to ask about monthly themes."

Avoid: Ultra-conservative viewpoints and issues, i.e., right-to-life.

Sample copy: Free. No guidelines.

Profile

The official journal of the Moravian Church in America, a small, mainline Protestant denominational with historical German background. Issues are thematic. 6x9; self cover; 2-color; 32 pages.

Focus and Audience

Reports on church-related themes and issues of interest to Moravians worldwide from a moderate Protestant Christian perspective.

Interests and Word Lengths

- *Nonfiction:* Theme-related articles on evangelism, changing families, church music, retreats, and international Moravian churches. Up to 1,000 words. Accepts filler and seasonal material.
- *Photos:* B/W prints.

How to Submit

Call for monthly themes. Then, query with outline. Include SASE. Accepts photocopies, computer printouts, IBM-compatible WordPerfect 5.1 disks, and fax submissions (215-866-9223). Simultaneous submissions okay. Reports in 1 month.

Payment and Policies

Authors retain rights. No payment. Authors receive 5 copies of issue.

Morning Glory

Arnold Windahl, Editor
314 West Spruce Street
Fergue Falls, MN 56537
218-736-7293

AT A GLANCE:

MORNING GLORY

- Lutheran, Salvation
- 10% freelance
- 10% new writers
- Quarterly
- Circ: 700
- Receives few queries, 20–25 mss each month.
- No payment. Offers 1 contributor's copy.

From the Editor:
"We are very conservative and cover specific topics of concern to Hauge Lutherans."

Best Bet: Writing on experienced salvation, fellowship, and simplicity of worship.

Avoid: Anything liberal or lengthy.

Sample copy: Not provided. No guidelines.

Profile

A salvation-oriented magazine for spiritual edification. Published quarterly by the Hauge Lutheran Innermission Federation. 8.5x11; self cover; 12 pages.

Focus and Audience

Espouses a conservative Christian outlook in accordance with the Hauge Lutheran movement doctrine of salvation, to which all material must adhere.

Interests and Word Lengths

- *Fiction:* Short stories with salvation themes. Up to 300 words.
- *Nonfiction:* Features and interviews that relate specifically to the Hauge Lutheran movement, experienced salvation, Christian fellowship, and simplicity of worship. Up to 300 words.
- *Poetry:* Salvation-related poems.

How to Submit

Send complete ms with cover letter, clips, and author biography stating religious affiliation and spiritual background. Include SASE. Accepts original mss. Reports in 1–4 months.

Payment and Policies

Rights vary. No payment. Authors receive 1 copy of the issue.

The Music Leader

Anne Trudel, Coordinating Editor
127 Ninth Avenue North
Nashville, TN 37234
615-251-2513

AT A GLANCE:
THE MUSIC LEADER

- Southern Baptist,
  Church Music
- 5% freelance
- 5% new writers
- Quarterly
- Circ: 35,000
- Receives 2–3 queries,
  5–10 mss each
  month.
- Pays: $.055 per word
  on acceptance.

From the Editor:
"We try to be creative,
yet practical. Keep in
mind the limited time
that people have to
plan for choir. We
accept freelance sub-
missions for our articles
section only."

Best Bet: Tried and
proven-successful
music activities suit-
able for preschool and
children's choirs.

Avoid: Writing that is
too technical; using a
third-person point of
view.

Sample copy: Free with
9x12 SASE . Send #10
SASE for guidelines.

Profile

A quarterly magazine for music leaders of preschool and children's choirs. Published by The Sunday School Board of the Southern Baptist Convention. Uses as doctrinal guidelines the 1963 statement of The Baptist Faith and Message. 8.5x11; glossy cover; 2-color; 92 pages.

Focus and Audience

Seeks practical ideas and activities for choir leaders to use with preschoolers and children in grades 1–6. Most leaders are volunteers; only a few are professional musicians. Audience is largely Southern Baptist, but curriculum is also used by other Protestant denominations.

Interests and Word Lengths

- *Fiction:* Seasonal dramas including Thanksgiving, Christmas, and spring programs that incorporate all preschool and children's choirs. Include narration and suggest songs, preferably from the curriculum. 7–8 typed, double-spaced ms pages.
- *Nonfiction:* Practical articles on training leaders, planning rehearsals, organizing choirs, and selecting music. Personal-experience, child development, and classroom management articles. Music education trends and their application in church settings. Teaching methods. Musical activities for use with preschoolers, children in grades 1–3 or grades 4–6, or combined grades 1–6. 7–8 typed, double-spaced pages.
- *Poetry:* Inspirational poems for choir leaders.
- *Artwork:* 35-mm B/W or color photos; line drawings.

How to Submit

Send complete ms with cover letter. Include SASE. Accepts computer printouts and Macintosh disks. No simultaneous submissions. Reports in 1–2 months.

Payment and Policies

All or one-time rights. Pays on acceptance. $.055 per word. Authors receive 3 copies of the issue.

My Friend

Sr. Anne Joan, fsp, Editor
50 St. Paul's Avenue
Boston, MA 02130
617-522-8911

AT A GLANCE:
My Friend

- Catholic, Juvenile
- 50% freelance
- 10% new writers
- 10 issues a year
- Circ: 8,000
- Receives 50 queries,
  150 mss each month.
- Pays: $30–$150 before publication.

From the Editor:
"Make sure that the plot and setting of your story are suitable for the age level required to read it."

Best Bet: Science features; true-to-life children's stories.

Avoid: Moralizing; overly pious treatment; poetry; doctrinal articles, which are staff-written.

Sample copy: $1 with 9x12 SAE and $.75 postage. Send #10 SASE for guidelines.

Profile

A Catholic magazine for 6- to 12-year-old children. Published by the Daughters of St. Paul. 8.5x11; glossy cover; 32 pages.

Focus and Audience

Provides wholesome and entertaining reading for young people while imparting Christian values and basic Catholic doctrines. Readers are Catholic children, ages 6–12.

Interests and Word Lengths

- *Fiction:* Short-short stories that show children learning to deal with contemporary situations according to Christian principles. Stories should present realistic child life and events as well as social issues as kids face them, including inner city issues, family relations, and school life. Present problems that are solvable by child characters rather than adults. No moralizing; instead weave the Christian message into the story. Accepts accurate historical fiction. 300–500 words.
- *Nonfiction:* Feature articles, especially science articles on nature, chemistry, electronics, etc. Biographies of Catholic personalities and saints. Self-help pieces on coping with a particular problem. 300–500 words.
- *Filler:* Bible Facts, shorts on Bible words, people, and archaeology. 50–65 words. Accepts jokes and riddles.
- *Artwork:* Submit illustrations to Sr. Mary Joseph; photos to Sr. Annette Margaret.

How to Submit

Send complete ms with resume. Include SASE. Accepts photocopies and computer printouts. No simultaneous submissions. Reports in 1 month.

Payment and Policies

First North American serial rights. Pays prior to publication. Articles, $30–$150. Filler, $3–$20. Kill fee, $10. Authors receive 2 copies of the issue.

Na'amat Woman

Gloria Gross, Assistant Editor
200 Madison Avenue
Suite 2120
New York, NY 10016
212-725-8010

AT A GLANCE:
NA'AMAT WOMAN

- Jewish, Women
- 20% freelance
- 5 issues a year
- Circ: 30,000
- Receives 30 mss each month.
- Pays: $.08 per word on publication.

From the Editor:
"Be coherent, to-the-point, upbeat, and positive."

Best Bet: Positive articles and stories of interest to Jewish women.

Avoid: Negative issues such as death and the Holocaust.

Sample copy: Free. Send #10 SASE for guidelines.

Profile
The membership magazine of Na'amat U.S.A., the Women's Labor Zionist Organization of America. 8.5x11; glossy cover; 2-color; 32 pages.

Focus and Audience
Advocates progressive legislation for women's rights and child welfare, furthers Jewish education, and supports human rights. Readership includes Jewish women worldwide.

Interests and Word Lengths
- *Fiction:* Stories with Jewish themes on issues of concern to women. 2,000–4,000 words.
- *Nonfiction:* Articles of particular interest to the Jewish community and/or on women's issues. 2,000–4,000 words.
- *Photos:* B/W prints.

How to Submit
Send complete ms with cover letter. Include SASE. Accepts photocopies and computer printouts. No simultaneous submissions. Reports in 6 months.

Payment and Policies
One-time rights. Pays on publication. $.08 per word. Authors receive 1 copy of the issue plus 2 tear sheets.

National Catholic Reporter

Thomas Fox, Editor
115 East Armour Boulevard
Kansas City, MO 64141
816-531-0538

AT A GLANCE:
NATIONAL CATHOLIC REPORTER

- Catholic, Current Events
- 44 issues per year
- Circ: 48,000
- Pays on publication. Rates vary.

From the Editor:
"We aim to be *The New York Times* of the Catholic Church."

Best Bet: Features and essays on current controversial or church-related topics.

Profile

An independent weekly newspaper of progressive Catholic thought. Distributed in the U.S. and 93 other countries. Tabloid-size; newsprint; 44–48 pages.

Focus and Audience

Offers progressive, liberal Roman Catholic opinion and commentary on social and church-related issues. Read by an international audience of highly educated, politically liberal Catholics, most of whom are in their 40s and 50s.

Interests and Word Lengths

- *Nonfiction:* Feature articles and essays that reflect on modern Catholic life as they report on controversial or church-related issues. Articles should have general appeal; all topics are considered. Accepts book and film reviews. No word-length restrictions.
- *Departments:* Query with department or column ideas.
- *Artwork:* B/W cartoons.

How to Submit

Query with outline, resume, and writing samples. Include SASE. Accepts photocopies and computer printouts. Notify before submitting disk or fax submissions. Simultaneous submissions okay. Reports in 2 months.

Payment and Policies

Pays on publication. Rates vary. Authors receive 10 copies of the issue.

Sample copy: Information not provided.

National & International Religion Report

Mark Henry, Managing Editor
P.O. Box 21433
Roanoke, VA 24018
703-989-7500

AT A GLANCE:
NATIONAL & INTERNATIONAL RELIGION REPORT

- Christian, News
- 7% freelance
- 2% new writers
- Biweekly
- Circ: 7,000–8,000
- Pays: $50 per piece on publication.

From the Editor:
"We especially like to have coverage of events that wire services and major media have missed."

Best Bet: Original, concise reports on national Christian news.

Avoid: Polemics; promotions; human interest features; articles rewritten from published sources; lengthy and redundant pieces.

Sample copy: Free. Send #10 SASE for guidelines.

Profile
A biweekly newsletter of religious news and event coverage. 8.5x11; folded; 8 pages.

Focus and Audience
Reports on religious news and trends of national significance to Christians and Christianity. Most readers are full-time religious professionals in church or para-church ministry, Protestant, and somewhat conservative.

Interests and Word Lengths
- *Nonfiction:* National news articles about or affecting Christianity. Interests include conflicts, accomplishments, evangelism, missionary work, conferences, social and world issues, and trends in religion that affect Protestant churches and non-profit ministries. 150–400 words.

How to Submit
Query by phone or fax. Then, send ms and resume. Include SASE. Accepts computer printouts and fax submissions (703-989-0189). No simultaneous submissions. Reports in 1–2 months.

Payment and Policies
First North American serial rights. Pays on publication. $50 per piece. Does not provide copies of the issue.

National Review

Editorial Department
150 East 35th Street
New York, NY 10016
212-679-7330

AT A GLANCE:
NATIONAL REVIEW

- Politics, Culture
- 20% freelance
- 1% new writers
- Biweekly
- Circ: 175,000
- Receives 200 queries, 300 mss each month.
- Pays: $200 per magazine page on publication.

From the Editor:
"We want sharp, crisp, witty, well-argued prose. Timeliness is helpful."

Sample copy: Available at newsstands. Send #10 SASE for guidelines.

Profile
A national journal of conservative political thought. 8.5x11; glossy cover; 4-color; 64 pages.

Focus and Audience
Promotes a conservative political, cultural, and social agenda. Readers are religious, conservative, and well educated.

Interests and Word Lengths
- *Nonfiction:* Timely, crisp articles on politics, the economy, family and social issues, and religion, especially issues of religious bias, growing secularization, and assault on religion. 1,000–2,500 words.
- *Artwork:* Submit to Geoffrey Morris. Humorous cartoons. B/W prints. Line drawings and half-tones.

How to Submit
Send complete ms with cover letter. Include SASE. Accepts photocopies and computer printouts. Reports in 4–6 weeks.

Payment and Policies
All rights. Pays on publication. Approximately $200 per magazine page (900 words). Kill fee, 50%. Authors receive 2 copies of the issue.

Nature Friend Magazine

Stanley Brubaker, Editor
22777 State Road, No. 119
Goshen, IN 46526
219-534-2245

AT A GLANCE:

NATURE FRIEND MAGAZINE

- Fundamentalist, Juvenile
- 40% freelance
- 20% new writers
- Monthly
- Circ: 10,000
- Receives 50 mss each month.
- Pays: $.05 per word on publication.

From the Editor:
"Read our guidelines and at least two sample copies before submitting to be aware of our requirements."

Best Bet: Whole, family-oriented material that glorifies God's creation from a Fundamental creationist perspective.

Avoid: Evolution-based material; anything that does not portray traditional family values; negative or scary articles.

Sample copy: $5 with 6x9 SAE for 2 copies and guidelines.

Profile

A non-denominational Fundamental creationist magazine for children. Est.: 1983. 6.5x9.5; 36 pages.

Focus and Audience

Inspires 4- to 14-year-old children to glorify God and His creations in nature. Conservative in approach; promotes wholesome, traditional family values.

Interests and Word Lengths

- *Fiction:* Friendly stories that foster an appreciation of nature. No talking animal stories.
- *Nonfiction:* Essays and personal experiences geared toward children; feature articles that evidence God's hand in creation; projects that build science and nature skills in children. Up to 1,500 words.
- *Poetry:* Original, symmetrical, high-quality poems.
- *Artwork:* B/W photos and illustrations.

How to Submit

Request writer's guidelines before submitting. Then, send complete ms with cover letter. Include SASE. Accepts photocopies and computer printouts. Simultaneous submissions okay. Reports in 3–6 months.

Payment and Policies

One-time rights. Pays on publication. $.05 per word. Authors receive 2 copies of the issue.

NCSE Reports

John R. Cole, Editor
1328 Sixth Street
Berkeley, CA 94710-1404
510-526-1674

Profile

The quarterly membership newsletter of The National Center for Science Education (NCSE) a religious organization that promotes biblical creationism. 8.5x11; self cover; 24 pages.

Focus and Audience

Monitors the creation vs. evolution controversy from a religious viewpoint. Allows members to share information about science education problems. Readers are scientists, teachers, and civil libertarians.

Interests and Word Lengths

- *Nonfiction:* Submit to John R. Cole, Editor, 248 Amherst Road, L-2, Sunderland, MA 01375. Current events, discussion, essays, news, reviews, and commentary on issues in evolution education and the creation/evolution debate. 500–1,000 words.
- *Artwork:* Line drawings. Occasionally accepts B/W prints.

How to Submit

Query with outline, or send complete ms with cover letter. Include SASE. Accepts photocopies and MS-DOS disks, preferably WordPerfect. Simultaneous submissions okay. Reports in 3 months.

Payment and Policies

One-time rights. No payment. Authors receive 5 copies of the issue.

New Church Life

Rev. Donald L. Rose, Editor
Box 277
Bryn Athyn, PA 19009
215-947-6225

AT A GLANCE:

NEW CHURCH LIFE

- Denominational, Theology
- 10% freelance
- 10% new writers
- Circ: 2,000
- Receives 2 queries, 2 mss each year.
- No payment. Offers contributor's copies.

From the Editor:
"*New Church Life* promotes a new revelation of Divine Truth and affirms the value of all religions."

Best Bet: Short essays related to the writings of Emanuel Swedenborg.

Avoid: Putting down the views of others.

Sample copy: $1.25 with 8x10 SAE and $.50 postage. No guidelines.

Profile

A monthly magazine based on the revelations and writings of Emanuel Swedenborg. Published by the General Church of the New Jerusalem. 6x9; heavy bond cover; 48 pages.

Focus and Audience

All material is related to Emanuel Swedenborg's writings on life after death, the nature of God, freedom, the Bible, and Divine Providence.

Interests and Word Lengths

- *Nonfiction:* Essays on Swedenborg's teachings about God's providence and applicable inner meaning in the Bible. 1,000 words.

How to Submit

Send complete ms with cover letter, resume, and clips. Include SASE. Accepts computer printouts and Word-Perfect 5.1 disks. Simultaneous submissions okay. Reports in 2 months.

Payment and Policies

Author retains rights. No payment. Authors receive copies of the issue upon request.

New Covenant

Jim Manney, Editor
200 Noll Plaza
Huntington, IN 46750
313-668-4896

AT A GLANCE:
NEW COVENANT

- Catholic, Charismatic
- 85% freelance
- 10% new writers
- Monthly
- Circ: 42,000
- Receives 5 queries, 20 mss each month.
- Pays: $100–$400 on acceptance.

From the Editor:
"Be practical, anecdotal, and personal. Exhibit a hands-on orthodox faith."

Best Bet: Inspirational articles on prayer and spirituality in light of the Catholic charismatic renewal.

Avoid: Abstract theologizing.

Sample copy: Free with 9x12 SAE and $1.21 postage. Send #10 SASE for guidelines.

Profile
A monthly magazine that serves the charismatic renewal of the Catholic Church. Also committed to the ecumenical renewal of the whole Christian people. 8.5x11; glossy cover; 2-color; 36 pages.

Focus and Audience
Reflects an ecumenical, evangelical, renewal-minded spirituality centered on Jesus Christ, led by the Holy Spirit, and nourished by the sacraments, personal prayer, and charismatic gifts. Readers are Catholics active in the charismatic renewal and other renewal movements.

Interests and Word Lengths
- *Nonfiction:* Features, essays, interviews, profiles, personal experiences, and inspirational pieces on spirituality, prayer, Scripture, evangelism, family topics, and healing. 500–1,500 words.

How to Submit
Query with outline and clips, or send complete ms with cover letter and clips. Include SASE. Accepts photocopies and computer printouts. Simultaneous submissions okay. Reports in 1 month.

Payment and Policies
First North American serial rights. Pays on acceptance. $100–$400 per piece. Kill fee, $50. Authors receive copies of the issue upon request.

The New Era

Richard M. Romney, Managing Editor
50 East North Temple Street
Salt Lake City, UT 84150
801-240-2951

AT A GLANCE:
THE NEW ERA

- Mormon, Teen
- 60% freelance
- 30% new writers
- Monthly
- Circ: 230,000
- Receives 100 queries, 200–300 mss each month.
- Pays: $.03–$.10 per word on acceptance.

From the Editor:
"We talk to teens as though we were older brothers or sisters, giving them encouragement and support to live Gospel principles."

Best Bet: Sharing a first-person experience in a conversational style is the easiest way to get started.

Avoid: Preaching to the reader.

Sample copy: $1 with 9x12 SAE and $.60 postage. Send #10 SASE for guidelines.

Profile

A monthly general-interest magazine for teens that serves as the official publication for youth of The Church of Jesus Christ of Latter-day Saints (LDS). 8.5x11; glossy cover; full-color; 52 pages.

Focus and Audience

Encourages, supports, and reinforces LDS and Gospel principles for Mormon teenagers, ages 12–18.

Interests and Word Lengths

- *Fiction:* Simple, short, and direct stories of all categories and genres. Topics include family relationships, Gospel principles, and relationship with Christ. 500–1,800 words. Accepts poetry.
- *Nonfiction:* Features, interviews, essays, and personal experiences that reinforces LDS principles and lifestyle. 200–1,500 words.
- *Departments:* Everyday Heroes, Mormon youth giving Christian service. Scripture Lifeline, personal experiences and insights into Scripture and living the Gospel. 50–1,000 words.
- *Photos:* Accepts photos of any type on speculation. Illustrations reviewed by assignment only from art director.

How to Submit

Query with outline, or send complete ms with cover letter. Include SASE. Accepts photocopies, computer printouts, WordPerfect disks, and fax submissions. No simultaneous submissions. Reports in 6 weeks.

Payment and Policies

All rights. Reprint rights reassigned to author upon written request. Pays on acceptance. $.03–.$10 per word. Experienced writers and regular contributors given special consideration. Kill fee negotiable. Authors receive 2 copies of the issue.

A New Heart

Aubrey Beauchamp, Editor
P.O. Box 4004
San Clemente, CA 92674-4004
714-496-7655

Profile

A quarterly evangelical Christian journal for health-care givers. Official publication of the Hospital Christian Fellowship, an international and interdenominational organization of health-care workers. 8.5x11; glossy cover; 2-color; 16 pages.

Focus and Audience

Promotes biblical principles in health-care practices. Encourages and strengthens evangelical Christian care-givers in their faith, occupation, and personal life.

Interests and Word Lengths

- *Nonfiction:* True stories with Christian emphasis written from the point-of-view of patients, visitors, or medical professionals. Also accepts articles on bioethical issues. 400–500 words
- *Departments:* Chaplains, Medical News, Medical Missions.
- *Photos:* B/W or color photos.

How to Submit

Query with writing samples. Include SASE. Accepts photocopies, computer printouts, and faxes. Simultaneous submissions okay. Reports 3 months before publication.

Payment and Policies

One-time rights. No payment. Authors receive 1 or more copies of the issue upon request.

The New Press Literary Quarterly

Robert Dunn, Editor
53-35 Hollis Court Boulevard
Flushing, NY 11365
718-229-6782

AT A GLANCE:

THE NEW PRESS LITERARY QUARTERLY

- Fiction, Poetry
- 70% freelance
- 50% new writers
- Quarterly
- Circ: 1,200
- Receives 10 queries, 40 mss each month.
- Pays: $25 per piece on publication.

From the Editor:
"We encourage personal journalism and social criticism."

Best Bet: Imaginative and spiritual fiction. Lyrical and accessible poetry.

Avoid: Concrete poetry; glorifications of or gratuitous violence; hatred.

Sample copy: $4. Send #10 SASE for guidelines.

Profile

A literary quarterly of poetry, fiction, and essays exploring social mores, human relationships, and spirituality. Sponsors an essay contest. 8.5x11; heavy bond cover; 40 pages.

Focus and Audience.

Seeks material that feeds the literary mind, but accepts expressions of sentiment. Values originality of expression and thought and the poetic voice and vision. Readers are poets, writers, and the literate public.

Interests and Word Lengths

- *Fiction:* Short stories, short-short stories, prose poems, monologues, and humor. Prefers imaginative and spiritual fiction. Up to 22 typed, double-spaced pages.
- *Nonfiction:* Essays, including personal journalism, on writers and writing, social criticism, human relations, and revelatory and informative philosophy. Up to 10 typed, double-spaced pages.
- *Poetry:* Lyrical, accessible poetry.
- *Artwork:* B/W reproducible pen & ink line drawings.

How to Submit

Send complete ms with cover letter. Include SASE. Accepts photocopies, computer printouts, and DOS Word-Perfect disks with hard copy. Simultaneous submissions okay. Reports in 2 months.

Payment and Policies

One-time rights. Pays on publication. Prose, $25. Contest, $75 for best essay if entered with a $5 contest fee. Authors receive 3 copies of the issue.

New World Outlook

Christie House, Associate Editor
475 Riverside Drive, No. 1351
New York, NY 10115
212-870-3927

AT A GLANCE: NEW WORLD OUTLOOK

- United Methodist, Missions
- 5% freelance
- Under 5% new writers
- Bimonthly
- Circ: 35,000
- Receives 12 queries, 12 mss each month.
- Pays on publication. Rates vary.

From the Editor:
"We target 8.5 million United Methodist members throughout the U.S."

Best Bet: United Methodist mission- and outreach-related material.

Avoid: Submitting unsolicited manuscripts and original artwork.

Sample copy: $2 with 9x12 SAE and $.52 postage. Send #10 SASE for guidelines.

Profile

A bimonthly United Methodist missions magazine published by the United Methodist Board of Global Ministries. 8.5x11; 48 pages.

Focus and Audience

Focuses solely on United Methodist mission and outreach projects. Church-affiliated, it reaches United Methodist Church members in the U.S.

Interests and Word Lengths

- *Nonfiction:* Accepts all types of articles, essays, interviews, profiles, and personal-experience pieces provided that they relate in some way to United Methodist mission projects. Up to 2,000 words.
- *Artwork:* Full-color photos and illustrations; send copies, not originals.

How to Submit

Query with outline, resume, writing samples, and clips. No unsolicited mss. Include SASE. Accepts photocopies, computer printouts, WordPerfect 5.1 disks, and fax submissions. No simultaneous submissions. Reports in 2 months.

Payment and Policies

One-time rights. Pays on publication. Rates vary depending on author's experience. Authors receive 2 copies of the issue.

Northwestern Lutheran

Rev. James P. Schaefer, Editor
2929 North Mayfair Road
Milwaukee, WI 53222
414-771-9357

AT A GLANCE:

NORTHWESTERN LUTHERAN

- Lutheran, Evange-
  lism
- 80% freelance
- 5% new writers
- Monthly
- Circ: 65.000
- Receives 5–10
  queries, 5–10 mss
  each month.
- Pays: At least $50 on
  publication.

From the Editor:
"We rarely print articles
not written by WELS
members unless they
are about WELS mem-
bers, institutions, or organizations."

Best Bet: Feature articles and religious news
of interest to WELS
members.

Avoid: Anything
preachy; poetry and
fiction.

Sample copy: Free with
10x12 SASE. Send #10
SASE for guidelines.

Profile

The official publication of the Wisconsin Evangelical
Lutheran Synod (WELS), the third largest Lutheran body
in the United States. 8.5x11; glossy cover; 2-color; 36
pages.

Focus and Audience

Designed to inspire and inform the laity of the Wisconsin Evangelical Lutheran Synod. Most material is written by WELS members.

Interests and Word Lengths

- *Nonfiction:* Features, personal experiences, inspirational pieces, Bible study, and religious news about
  and of interest to WELS members. 500–1,500 words.

How to Submit

Query with outline. Include SASE. Accepts photocopies
and computer printouts. Simultaneous submissions
okay. Reports in 1 month.

Payment and Policies

One-time rights. Pays on publication. $5 per 500 words.
Contributor's copies are not provided.

Now and Then

Pat Arnow, Editor
CASS/ETSU
P.O. Box 70556
Johnson City, TN 37614-0556
615-929-5348

AT A GLANCE:
NOW AND THEN

- Regional, Inspirational
- 3 issues a year
- Circ: not available
- No payment. Offers 2 contributor's copies and a free subscription.

From the Editor:
"We are glad for the opportunity to review writing. Previous theme issues have featured women, music, Blacks, Cherokees, health, writers, children, and veterans."

Best Bet: Writing related to the Appalachian region.

Sample copy: $3.50. Send #10 SASE for guidelines.

Profile

A regional of Appalachian history and lifestyle. Published by the Center for Appalachian Studies and Services at East Tennessee State University. Est.: 1984. 8.5x11; glossy cover; 48 pages.

Focus and Audience

Each issue focuses on one aspect of life in the Appalachian region—anywhere hilly from Northern Alabama and Georgia on up. Can be contemporary or show historical perspective.

Interests and Word Lengths

- *Fiction:* Short stories with regional focus. See guidelines for special themes. No word-length restrictions.
- *Nonfiction:* Articles; essays; memoirs; book reviews; interviews with people from the region or with someone who knows about the region. See guidelines for special themes. Upcoming themes include Politics and Appalachia, Celebrations in Appalachia, and Center for Appalachian Studies and Services 10th Anniversary. No word-length restrictions.
- *Poetry:* Submit to Jo Carson. Related to the region. Submit no more than 5 poems at a time.
- *Artwork:* Photos and drawings.

How to Submit

Query with brief author biography. Include SASE. No reprints. Accepts clear photocopies and computer printouts. Simultaneous submissions okay. Reports in 4 months.

Payment and Policies

All rights. Generally, no payment. On occasion will pay some honorarium for articles and stories. Authors receive 2 copies of the issue and a free one-year subscription.

The Oak

Betty Mowery, Editor
1530 Seventh Street
Rock Island, IL 61201
309-788-3980

AT A GLANCE:
THE OAK

- Writing, Inspirational
- 100% freelance
- 50% new writers
- Bimonthly
- Circ: 200
- Receives 50 mss each month.
- No payment. Offers 2 contributor's copies.

From the Editor:
"Write about true feelings, Don't give up, keep submitting!"

Best Bet: Progressive writing. Pieces about good living and living by the golden rule.

Avoid: Violence; preachiness; obvious religion.

Sample copy: $2.00. Send #10 SASE for guidelines.

Profile

An inspirational publication for·adults, many of whom are writers. 8.5x11; folded; photocopied; 16 pages.

Focus and Audience

Offers the opportunity for new and up-coming writers to share their thoughts and feelings through writing that demonstrates good living and living by the golden rule. Many readers are writers.

Interests and Word Lengths

- *Fiction:* Up to 500 words.
- *Nonfiction*: Up to 200 words.
- Poetry: Up to 32 lines.

How to Submit

Send complete ms with cover letter. Include SASE. Accepts photocopies, computer printouts, and hand-written submissions. Simultaneous submissions okay. Reports in 1 month.

Payment and Policies

First North American serial and one-time rights. No payment. Authors receive 2 copies of the issue.

Oblates

Priscilla Kurz, Manuscripts Editor
15 South 59th Street
Belleville, IL 62223-4694
618-233-2238

AT A GLANCE:

OBLATES

- Catholic, Inspirational
- 25% freelance
- Bimonthly
- Circ: 500,000
- Pays: $80 per piece on publication.

From the Editor:
"Focus on sharing a personal insight into a problem such as death or change, but be positive and uplifting."

Best Bet: Reverent, inspirational articles geared toward older readers.

Avoid: Heavy allusions; clever rhyme schemes; and "heavy" modern verse.

Sample copy: Free with 6x9 SASE for sample and guidelines.

Profile

A bimonthly inspirational digest published by the Missionary Oblates of Mary Immaculate. 5.25x8.5; self cover; full-color; 20 pages.

Focus and Audience

Seeks inspirational writings for an audience of mostly older Americans who look for comfort, encouragement, and a positive sense of applicable Christian direction to their lives.

Interests and Word Lengths

- *Nonfiction:* Uplifting articles, preferably personal experiences, that share insight gained by living through a particular problem. 500 words.
- *Poetry:* Traditional meter and rhyme poetry, averaging 16 lines.

How to Submit

Send complete ms with cover letter. Include SASE. Reports in 2 months.

Payment and Policies

First North American serial rights. Pays on acceptance. Articles, $80. Poems, $30 each. Authors receive 3 copies of the issue.

The Observer

Owen Phelps, Editor
921 West State Street
Rockford, IL 61102
815-963-3471

AT A GLANCE:

THE OBSERVER

- Catholic, Regional
- 15% freelance
- 10% new writers
- Bimonthly
- Circ: 30,000
- Receives 1 ms each month.
- Pays on publication. Rates vary.

From the Editor:
"We try to give the Catholic dimension of the news and offer something other papers don't."

Best Bet: Regional and national news of Catholic interest.

Avoid: First-person articles.

Sample copy: Free. No guidelines.

Profile

The official Catholic newspaper of the Diocese of Rockford, IL. Tabloid-size; newsprint; 24 pages.

Focus and Audience

Covers news, personalities, and events of interest to Catholics in eleven counties of northern Illinois.

Interests and Word Lengths

- *Nonfiction:* Assigns most material and ideas. Features, interviews, essays, and profiles of active Catholics involved in ministries. Coverage of regional and national events of Catholic interest. 750 words.
- *Photos:* B/W prints of Catholic events; B/W illustrations.

How to Submit

Call for current needs. Submit complete ms with cover letter. Include SASE. Accepts photocopies and computer printouts. Notify before sending disks or fax submissions. Simultaneous submissions okay. Reports in 1–2 months.

Payment and Policies

All rights. Pays on publication. Rates vary according to author's experience. Authors receive 1 copy of the issue.

On the Line

Mary Clemens Meyer, Editor
616 Walnut Avenue
Scottdale, PA 15683-1999
412-887-8500

AT A GLANCE:
ON THE LINE

- Mennonite, Youth
- 90% freelance
- 10% new writers
- Weekly
- Circ: 8,500
- Receives 3 queries, 100 mss each month.
- Pays $.02–$.04 per word on acceptance.

From the Editor:
"Don't preach, but *teach* with example, humor, and everyday situations. Let the happenings in the story speak for themselves."

Best Bet: Real-life stories that portray Christian values for junior high school students.

Avoid: Fantasy, Bible stories, and moralistic and preachy stories.

Sample copy: Free with 7.5x10.5 SAE and 2 first-class stamps. Send #10 SASE for guidelines.

Profile

A story paper that reinforces Christian values for children ages 10–14. Co-published by the Mennonite Publishing House and the General Conference Mennonite Church. Published monthly in weekly parts. 7x10; folded; 2-color; 8 pages.

Focus and Audience

Helps upper elementary and junior high school children understand and appreciate God, the created world, themselves, and others. Nurtures a desire for world peace and provides tools for peaceful living. Read by children in the U. S. and Canada.

Interests and Word Lengths

- *Fiction:* Short stories that reflect everyday life of junior high school students. Subjects include school, pets, friends, parents, church, and resolving typical problems. Use contemporary language. 1,000–1,500 words.
- *Nonfiction:* Feature articles about nature, food, science, history, world cultures, and religious heroes. 300–500 words.
- *Poetry:* Light verse. Up to 24 lines.
- *Filler:* Jokes, riddles, how-to craft pieces, and puzzles—biblical, seasonal, or general interest.
- *Photos:* Submit to Debbie Cameron, Photo Secretary. 8x10 B/W prints showing junior high children from many ethnic backgrounds.

How to Submit

Send complete ms with cover letter. Include SASE. Accepts photocopies, computer printouts, faxes, and submissions via modem. Simultaneous submissions okay. Reports in 1 month.

Payment and Policies

One-time rights. Pays on acceptance. $.02–$.04 per word. Authors receive 2 copies of the issue.

Open Hands

Mary Jo Osterman, Editor
3801 North Keeler Avenue
Chicago, IL 60641
312-736-5526

AT A GLANCE:
OPEN HANDS

- Christian, Gay/
  Lesbian
- 95% freelance
- 80% new writers
- Quarterly
- Circ: 1,800
- Receives 2–3 queries,
  1–2 mss each month.
- No payment.

From the Editor:
"Each issue is based on
a theme, so it is best to
call or write for a list of
upcoming themes."

Best Bet: Theme-
related pieces that
address issues of con-
cern to gay and
lesbian Christians.

Sample copy: Free.
Send #10 SASE for
guidelines/theme list.

Profile

A quarterly Christian magazine addressing ministry
with gay, lesbian, and bisexual persons. Published by
the United Methodist Reconciling Congregation Program in conjunction with other mainline churches.
8.5x11; self cover; 2-color; 32 pages.

Focus and Audience

Serves as a resource for congregations and individuals seeking to be in ministry with lesbian, bisexual,
and gay persons. Each issue focuses on a specific
area of concern within the church. Audience is primarily United Methodist, but is becoming increasingly
ecumenical.

Interests and Word Lengths

- *Fiction:* Interested in theme-related sermons and
  parables. 800–1,000 words.
- *Nonfiction:* Publishes 1–2 theological essays per issue
  plus several personal experience pieces. All are
  theme related. Past themes include combatting the
  Religious Right; worship resources for gay and lesbian ministries; and celebrating lesbian and gay
  pride. 800–3,000 words.
- *Poetry:* Open to all styles. Must fit theme.

How to Submit

Send for theme list before submitting material. Then,
query with outline or send complete ms with cover letter. Include SASE. Accepts photocopies, computer
printouts, IBM-compatible disks, and fax submissions.
Simultaneous submissions okay. Reports if interested.

Payment and Policies

One-time rights. No payment. Does not provide copies
of the issue.

Opening the Word

Ray Crooks, Editor
7405 Metcalf
P.O. Box 4060
Overland Park, KS 66204
913-432-0331

AT A GLANCE:
OPENING THE WORD

- Evangelical, Devotions
- Quarterly
- Circ: 5,000
- No payment. Offers gift certificates.

From the Editor:
"Our daily devotions are all easy reading. Most Christians could enjoy and benefit from them. Each devotional is intended to be uplifting and challenging."

Best Bets: Write for assignment.

Avoid: Unsolicited manuscript submissions.

Sample copy: Not available. Send #10 SASE for guidelines.

Profile

An evangelical quarterly of daily devotions. Correlated with The Way, Truth, and Life Series Sunday school curriculum. All material is assigned. 5x8; 4-color cover; 80 pages.

Focus and Audience

Inspirational and challenging devotional readings intended for evangelical Christians.

Interests and Word Lengths

- *Nonfiction:* Inspirational daily devotions on a variety of topics. Writers are assigned specific topics. 200–250 words.

How to Submit

Weekly topics are assigned by editors. To receive a writing assignment, send for guidelines and devotion outline. Include SASE. Accepts computer printouts and 3.5- and 5.25-inch disks. Simultaneous submissions okay.

Payment and Policies

Author retains rights. No payment. Offers gift certificates to Christian bookstores. Authors receive 1 copy of the issue.

Oregon Association of Christian Writers Newsletter

Tom Luther, Managing Editor
1625 SW 87th Avenue
Portland, OR 97225
503-297-2987

AT A GLANCE:

OREGON ASSOCIATION OF CHRISTIAN WRITERS NEWSLETTER

- Christian, Writing
- 80% freelance
- 40% new writers
- 3 issues a year
- Circ: 400
- No payment. Offers contributor's copies.

From the Editor:
"We exist primarily as a communication vehicle for OACW members."

Best Bet: Tips and information of interest to OACW members.

Sample copy: Free with #10 SAE and $.52 postage. No guidelines.

Profile

The membership newsletter of the Oregon Association of Christian Writers (OACW). 8.5x11; folded; 6–8 pages.

Focus and Audience

Offers inspirational, motivational, and practical information for Christian writers seeking to publish their work. Non-denominational in nature. Members include novice and established writers.

Interests and Word Lengths

- *Nonfiction:* Membership information on upcoming events, marketing updates, awards, and other useful material of interest to writers.
- *Artwork:* B/W line drawings.

How to Submit

Query or send complete piece. Include SASE. Accepts computer printouts, computer disks, and fax submissions. Modemed submissions must be pre-arranged. Simultaneous submissions okay. Reports in 1 month.

Payment and Policies

One-time rights. No payment. Authors receive copies of the issue upon request.

Orthodox Observer

Jim Golding, Editor-in-Chief
Eight East 79th Street
New York, NY 10021
212-628-2590

AT A GLANCE:
ORTHODOX OBSERVER

- Greek Orthodox, Church News
- Very little freelance
- Monthly
- Circ: 130,000
- No payment. Offers 1 contributor's copy.

From the Editor:
"We follow conservative, Greek Orthodox teaching."

Best Bet: Religious articles, parish news, and book and movie reviews.

Sample copy: $.50. Send #10 SASE for guidelines.

Profile
A newspaper of Greek Orthodox Church issues, published monthly for the Greek Orthodox Archdiocese of North and South America. Tabloid-size; newsprint; 20 pages.

Focus and Audience
Covers national and international church and parish news for conservative Greek Orthodox readers of all ages.

Interests and Word Lengths
- *Nonfiction:* Articles on Greek Orthodox religious and parish news. Accepts commentary and opinion pieces, book and movie reviews, articles on culture and heritage, youth-related pieces, and contemporary life. Up to 2 typed, double-spaced pages.
- *Photos:* B/W prints.

How to Submit
Send complete ms with cover letter and resume. Include SASE. Accepts photocopies, computer printouts, and fax submissions. No simultaneous submissions. Does not respond; if interested, will publish ms.

Payment and Policies
Rights vary. No payment. Authors receive 1 copy of the issue.

The Other Side

Doug Davidson, Managing Editor
300 West Apsley Street
Philadelphia, PA 19144
215-849-2178

AT A GLANCE:
THE OTHER SIDE

- Christian, Peace and Social Justice
- 80% freelance
- 5% new writers
- Bimonthly
- Circ: 13,000
- Receives 10 queries, 200+ mss each month.
- Pays: $50–$300 on acceptance.

From the Editor:
"Because we cherish God's spirit, we oppose racism, sexism, homophobia, prisons, economic exploitation, militarism, and violence."

Best Bet: High-quality writing, creative insights, and fresh thinking for Christians who share a passion for peace and justice.

Sample copy: $4.50. Send #10 SASE for guidelines.

Profile

A bimonthly magazine focusing on peace, justice, and the ways of Jesus from a radical Christian perspective. Prefers to work with established authors. Est.: 1965. 8.5x11; glossy cover; 4-color; 64 pages.

Focus and Audience

Encourages readers toward solidarity with Jesus. Offers spiritual nurturing, forgotten voices, prophetic challenge, artistic vision, and hopeful expectation to Christians committed to peace and justice.

Interests and Word Lengths

- *Fiction:* Jennifer Wilkins, Fiction Editor. Short stories, humor, and satire. 1,200–4,000 words.
- *Nonfiction:* Features, interviews, profiles of committed Christians, Bible study, personal experiences, opinion pieces, politics, spirituality, social and world issues, all consistent with the magazine's commitments. 1,200–4,000 words.
- *Poetry:* Rod Jellema, Poetry Editor. Short, creative though-provoking poetry. No more than 3 poems submitted at a time.
- *Artwork:* Cathleen Benberg, Art Director, 1807 S. Spring, Sioux Falls, SD 57105. B/W or color photos or original art.

How to Submit

Send complete ms with cover letter to appropriate editor. Include SASE. Accepts photocopies and computer printouts. Reports in 1–3 months.

Payment and Policies

First North American serial rights. Pays on acceptance. Fiction and nonfiction, $50–$300. Poetry, $15. Authors receive 4 contributor's copies.

Our Family

Fr. Nestor Gregoire, Editor
Box 249
Battleford, SK S0M 0E0
Canada
306-937-7771

AT A GLANCE:
OUR FAMILY

- Catholic, Family
- 50% freelance
- 10% new writers
- Monthly
- Circ: 10,000
- Receives 15 queries,
  100–150 mss each
  month.
- Pays: $.07–$.12 per
  word on acceptance.

From the Editor:
"Our strong concern is
to make the connec-
tion between our faith,
the Sunday liturgy,
and daily life."

Avoid: Fiction and science fiction. Fringe is-
sues of religion. Articles
that do not have a reli-
gious focus.

Sample copy: $2.50.
Send #10 SASE for
guidelines/theme list.

Profile
A monthly magazine exploring family and moral issues from a Catholic perspective. 8.5x11; glossy cover; 40 pages.

Focus and Audience
Articles on peoples' lived experiences of family and faith, marriage, Scripture study, and parish life that connects faith with daily living. No fiction. Readers are average Catholics.

Interests and Word Lengths
- *Nonfiction:* Articles on and personal experiences of family life, marriage, marriage as sacrament, children, blended families, sexual abuse, growing faith life, Scripture study, Sunday liturgy, parish life, prayer experiences; all expressing the Catholic experience and approach to life. 500–3,000 words. Projected themes for 1994 include improving communication in marriage, Catholics rediscovering spirituality, and caring for the earth. Send for theme list. Publishes an annual Lenten issue. Accepts filler and seasonal material.
- *Artwork:* Cartoons.

How to Submit
Send complete ms with cover letter. Include SASE. Accepts photocopies, computer printouts, and fax submissions. Simultaneous submissions okay. Reports in 1 month.

Payment and Policies
First North American serial rights. Pays on acceptance. $.07–$.12 per word. Authors receive 2 copies of the issue.

Our Little Friend

Aileen Andres Sox, Editor
P.O. Box 7000
Boise, ID 83707
208-465-2500

AT A GLANCE:
OUR LITTLE FRIEND

- Seventh-day Adventist, Juvenile
- 75% freelance
- 50% new writers
- Weekly
- Circ: 45,000–50,000
- Receives 75 mss each month.
- Pays: $25–$50 on acceptance.

From the Editor:
"Stories that are humorous, yet teach a lesson, rate high in this office. Tickle the child's funny bone to make a point."

Best Bet: True stories that help children understand and develop a personal relationship with God.

Avoid: Stories of talking animals, hunting, and fishing; fantasy and Halloween stories.

Sample copy: Free with 9x12 SAE and 2 first-class stamps. Send #10 SASE for guidelines.

Profile

A spiritually oriented Sabbath school magazine for Seventh-day Adventist children. Published weekly by Pacific Press Publishing Association. 8.5x11; self cover; 2-color; 8 pages.

Focus and Audience

Its mission is to teach Christian beliefs and values and present God's love to children in a way that will help them love Him. Written for 1- to 6-year-old children who attend Sabbath school at a Seventh-day Adventist Church. Stories must be consistent with Seventh-day Adventist beliefs and practices.

Interests and Word Lengths

- *Nonfiction:* True stories that portray a loving God. Characters should be good children setting good examples, being kind, and making right choices. Speak to the experience, lifestyle, needs, and vocabulary of today's child. Special interests include stories about personal Godliness; coping with peer pressure; mission experiences, sibling rivalry and fair fighting; prayer; nature; and basic social skills. 650–900 words.
- *Seasonal:* Christmas, Thanksgiving, and Mother's, Father's, and Grandparent's Days. Submit 7 months in advance.
- *Filler:* Bible- or nature-based games and puzzles. Short poems with spiritual themes.

How to Submit

Submit complete ms with cover letter. Include SASE. Accepts photocopies, computer printouts, and fax submissions. Simultaneous submissions okay. Reports in 3 months.

Payment and Policies

One-time rights. Pays on acceptance. $25–$50 per piece. Authors receive 3 copies of the issue.

Our Sunday Visitor

Tricia Hempel, Editor
200 Noll Plaza
Huntington, IN 46750
219-356-8400

AT A GLANCE:
OUR SUNDAY VISITOR

- Catholic, Spirituality
- 80% freelance
- 5% new writers
- Weekly
- Circ: 130,000
- Receives 40–50 queries, 50–75 mss each month.
- Pays: $100–$250 on acceptance.

From the Editor:
"Be familiar with official Church teaching and the issues of urgency to Catholics."

Avoid: Fiction; poetry; manuscripts over 1,500 words.

Sample copy: Free. Send #10 SASE for guidelines.

Profile

A national weekly Catholic newspaper of opinion and commentary on church, family, amd social issues. Tabloid-size; newsprint; 4-color; 24 pages.

Focus and Audience

Adheres to the official teaching of the Catholic Church.

Interests and Word Lengths

- *Nonfiction:* News pieces; Q&A interviews; feature articles; profiles; opinions and editorials. All must relate to issues faced by Catholics. 700–1,500 words.

How to Submit

Query with outline, resume, writing samples, and clips, or send complete ms with cover letter. Include SASE. Accepts photocopies and computer printouts. No simultaneous submissions. Reports in 2–3 months.

Payment and Policies

First North American serial rights. Pays on acceptance. $100–$250 per piece. Authors receive 2 copies of the issue.

Parabola

Editor
656 Broadway
New York, NY 10012
212-505-6200

AT A GLANCE:

PARABOLA

- Comparative Religion, Mythology
- 70–80% freelance
- 10% new writers
- Quarterly
- Circ: 40,000
- Receives 15 queries, 20 mss each month.
- Pays: $200–$400 per piece on publication.

From the Editor:
"Each issue is organized around a theme—submissions must be directed to it. Send for guidelines and theme list before submitting your work."

Avoid: Excessively academic or scholarly writing; jargon.

Sample copy: $6. Send #10 SASE for guidelines and theme list.

Profile

A quarterly journal devoted to the quest for meaning as expressed in the myths and symbols of the world's religious traditions. Issues are thematic. 6.5x10; glossy cover; perfect bound; 128 pages.

Focus and Audience

Seeks to reach new understandings of universal human themes as expressed in myth, legend, symbol, sacred art, folklore, and ritual. Emphasizes the relationship between traditional wisdom and contemporary life.

Interests and Word Lengths

- *Nonfiction and Fiction:* Articles and stories directed toward a particular theme. Send for theme list and guidelines. Past themes include Healing, Death, Sacrifice and Transformation, Obstacles, Words of Power, Pilgrimage, Disciples and Discipline, Solitude and Community, and Forgiveness. 2,000–4,000 words.
- *Departments:* Epicycles, retellings of traditional stories. Tangents, reviews related to the issue theme. Up to 2,000 words. Book reviews, 500 words.
- *Poetry:* Occasionally uses poetry related to theme.
- *Photos:* B/W prints. Send with manuscripts or submit separately to Art Research Editor.

How to Submit

Query with outline and resume, or send complete ms with cover letter and resume. Include SASE. Accepts photocopies, computer printouts, and legible fax submission. Accepts disks; prefers IBM WordPerfect or Microsoft Word, but accepts Macintosh Microsoft Word. Identify simultaneous submissions. Reports in 1–2 months.

Payment and Policies

First North American serial or one-time rights. Pays on publication. Articles and stories, $200–$400. Epicycles, $75. Kill fee, $100. Authors receive 2 copies of the issue.

Parent Care

Betty Robertson, Editor
Box 216
Bethany, OK 73008
405-787-7272

AT A GLANCE:
PARENT CARE

- Caregiving, Seniors
- 90% freelance
- 75% new writers
- Monthly
- Circ: 100+
- Pays: $3–$5 per piece on acceptance.

From the Editor:
"Do not write to us unless you have actually been a caregiver."

Best Bet: Practical pieces for and by those who care for elderly parents.

Sample copy: $2.50. Send #10 SASE for guidelines.

Profile

A monthly newsletter for adult children caring for aging parents. Published by Creative Christian Ministries. 8.5x11; 16 pages.

Focus and Audience

Serves as an inspirational and informational guide and resource written for and by adults who care for their aging parents.

Interests and Word Lengths

- *Nonfiction:* Personal experience pieces and feature articles on the issues surrounding senior care. 750–1,200 words. Devotionals, 450 words. Writers should have experience as caregivers.
- *Departments:* Ideas Exchange, practical advice and tips on caring for older adults. 50–100 words.

How to Submit

Send complete ms with cover letter and resume. Include SASE. Accepts photocopies and computer printouts. Simultaneous submissions okay. Reports in up to 3 months.

Payment and Policies

One-time rights. Pays on acceptance. Personal experiences and feature articles, $3–$5. No payment for Ideas Exchange pieces or devotionals. Authors receive 1 copy of the issue.

Parenting Treasures

Toni Blackwood, Editor
400 West Boulevard South
Elkhart, IN 46514
216-522-1491

AT A GLANCE:

PARENTING TREASURES

- Lutheran, Parenting
- 95% freelance
- 50% new writers
- Quarterly
- Circ: 400
- Receives 1–2 queries, 1–2 mss each month.
- No payment. Offers a free subscription.

From the Editor:
"As long as writers query with an idea that fits in our theme, there is a 95 percent chance we will publish the article, with editing."

Best Bet: Articles that address parental frustrations and joys; creative ideas that relate to the theme list.

Avoid: Non-Christian viewpoints; Christian jargon that non-Christians will not understand.

Sample copy: $1 with 10x12 SASE. Send #10 SASE for guidelines.

Profile

A quarterly magazine that supports and teaches Christian parents. Published by the Trinity Lutheran Church. 8.5x11; glossy cover; 24 pages.

Focus and Audience

Challenges parents of newborn through college-age children to apply their Christian faith to everyday attitudes and actions.

Interests and Word Lengths

- *Nonfiction:* Send for theme list. Non-preachy features, interviews, personal testimonies, and family experiences on Christian living, parenting, and understanding children as they grow together spiritually and emotionally. 1,000–1,500 words.
- *Departments*: A Time to Laugh, anything relating to the funny things kids say or do. Letters to the Editor. 200–500 words.
- *Filler.* Anecdotes, facts, poetry.
- *Photos*: Original B/W prints.

How to Submit

Query with outline and writing samples, or send complete ms with cover letter. Include SASE. Accepts photocopies, computer printouts, and faxes. Simultaneous submissions okay. Reports in 1–2 months.

Payment and Policies

One-time rights. No payment. Offers a free subscription. Authors receive 4 copies of the issue.

Parents of Teenagers

Gloria Chisholm, Managing Editor
P.O. Box 850
Sisters, OR 97759-0850
503-549-8261

Profile
An interdenominational service magazine for Christian parents with teenagers. 8.5x11; glossy cover; full-color; 40 pages.

Focus and Audience
Supplies practical ideas to help Christian parents in their relationships with teenagers.

Interests and Word Lengths
- *Nonfiction:* Feature articles, interviews, personality profiles, and personal experiences on family, parenting, and teenage issues. 1,400–1,800 words.
- *Departments:* Departments are assigned. Query first.
- *Photos:* Submit B/W photos to Ben Alex.

How to Submit
Query with outline, or send complete ms with cover letter and clips. Include SASE. Accepts photocopies and computer printouts. Simultaneous submissions okay. Reports in 1–2 months.

Payment and Policies
First North American serial rights. Pays on acceptance. $.10–$.15 per word. Kill fee, $50. Authors receive 1–2 tear sheets.

Parish Teacher

Carol A. Burk, Editor
429 South Fifth Street
Box 1209
Minneapolis, MN 55440
612-330-3423

AT A GLANCE:

PARISH TEACHER

- Lutheran, Religious Education
- 30–40% freelance
- 5–10% new writers
- 10 issues a year
- Circ: 50,000
- Receives 3–5 mss each month.
- Pays: $50 per piece on publication.

From the Editor:
"*Parish Teacher* is largely a Lutheran publication. We adhere to the basic doctrine of Christianity as expressed by the Lutheran Church."

Best Bet: Articles of practical interest to teachers in church education programs.

Avoid: Articles that emphasize a law-oriented view of faith and condemn rather than forgive.

Sample copy: Free with 9x12 SAE and 3 first-class stamps. Send #10 SASE for guidelines.

Profile

A practical periodical for Lutheran religion educators. Published monthly during the school year. 8.5x11; glossy cover; 12 pages.

Focus and Audience

Provides practical skills and teaching methods for volunteer teachers and leaders in congregational programs of Christian education. Adheres to the doctrines of the Lutheran Church.

Interests and Word Lengths

- *Nonfiction:* Articles on Christian education, teaching skills, and classroom ideas. Interests include Bible storytelling, faith development of children, seasons of the church year, and craft ideas. Articles, 500–800 words. Ideas, 100–200 words.
- *Photos:* Related B/W prints.

How to Submit

Send complete ms with cover letter. Include SASE. Accepts photocopies, computer printouts, and fax submissions. Simultaneous submissions okay. Reports in 1–2 months.

Payment and Policies

First North American serial rights. Pays on publication. Articles, average $50. Authors receive 1–4 copies of the issue.

Pastor's Tax & Money

Daniel D. Busby, Editor
P.O. Box 50188
Indianapolis, IN 46250

AT A GLANCE:
PASTOR'S TAX & MONEY

- Clergy, Finances
- 50% freelance
- 10% new writers
- Quarterly
- Circ: 6,000
- Receives 1–2 mss each month.
- Pays: $50 on publication.

From the Editor:
"We report on the latest developments in clergy and church money and management."

Best Bet: Cutting-edge ideas to help ministers manage their personal finances.

Avoid: Long paragraphs and sentences—keep it short.

Sample copy: $1 with #10 SAE and $.50 postage. No guidelines.

Profile
A quarterly newsletter for clergy who manage finances. 8.5x11; 2-color; folded; 10 pages.

Focus and Audience
Provides practical support, ideas, and guidance to ministers and pastors in their management of church and personal finances, taxes, and money.

Interests and Word Lengths
- *Departments:* Computers; Personal Finances; Church Finances; Minister's Taxes. 600–800 words.

How to Submit
Send complete ms with cover letter. Include SASE. Accepts photocopies, computer printouts, and fax submissions. Reports in 3 months.

Payment and Policies
One-time rights. Pays on publication. $50 per piece. Authors receive 5 copies of the issue.

Pastoral Life
The Magazine for Today's Ministry

Anthony L. Chenevey, Editor
Canfield, OH 44406-0595
216-533-5503

AT A GLANCE:
PASTORAL LIFE

- Catholic, Ministry
- 90% freelance
- 30% new writers
- Monthly
- Circ: 3,500
- Receives 15–20 queries, 10–12 mss each month.
- Pays: $.04 per word on publication

From the Editor:
"Articles should be eminently pastoral in approach and content."

Best Bet: Articles related to any aspect of Catholic pastoral work.

Avoid: Merely academic treatments on abstract and/or too controversial subjects.

Sample copy: Free with 6x9 SAE and $.98 postage. Send #10 SASE for guidelines.

Profile
A monthly review that addresses issues relevant to the Catholic priesthood. Published by the Society of St. Paul. Est.: 1953. 5.5x8.5; glossy cover; 68 pages.

Focus and Audience
Designed to focus on the current problems, needs, issues, and all important activities related to all phases of pastoral work and life. Aimed at Catholic priests.

Interests and Word Lengths
- *Nonfiction:* Articles that are eminently pastoral in approach and content. Areas of interest include communications, counseling, education, liturgy and sacraments, ministries, moral and social issues, preaching, priestly and ministerial life, prayer, and spirituality. Features pastoral homilies for Sundays and Holy days. Long articles should include appropriate subheadings. Up to 3,500 words.

How to Submit
Prefers queries with outline and brief author biography. Accepts complete ms with cover letter. Include SASE. Accepts photocopies, computer printouts, faxes, and submissions via modem. No simultaneous submissions. Reports in 2–4 weeks.

Payment and Policies
One-time rights. Pays on publication. $.04 per word. Authors receive 2 copies of the issue.

Pathway I.D.

Lance Colkmire, Editor
1080 Montgomery Avenue
P.O. Box 2250
Cleveland, TN 37320-2250

AT A GLANCE:

PATHWAY I.D.

- Pentecostal, Teen
- 5–10% freelance
- Weekly
- Circ: 18,000
- Receives 10–15 mss each month.
- Pays: $20–$40 on acceptance.

From the Editor:
"Write from a Pentecostal perspective for 15- to 17-year-olds."

Best Bet: Personal testimonies of teens living Spirit-filled lives.

Avoid: Fiction and poetry.

Sample copy: Free with guidelines for a #10 SASE.

Profile

A weekly take-home paper for Pentecostal teens. Published by Pathway Press. 5.5x7.5; folded; 8 pages.

Focus and Audience

Its mission is to demonstrate how Pentecostal teenagers, ages 15–17, can and do live a distinctively Christian life.

Interests and Word Lengths

- *Fiction:* Not accepting fiction submissions at this time. Query for future issues.
- *Nonfiction:* Feature articles and first-person pieces that offer testimonies about Holy Spirit-filled living and show teens living a Spirit-filled life, involved in ministry, and overcoming great odds to follow Christ. 400–800 words.
- *Seasonal:* Submit 1 year in advance.

How to Submit

Send complete ms with cover letter and resume. Include SASE. Accepts photocopies, computer printouts, and fax submissions. Simultaneous submissions okay. Reports in 1 month.

Payment and Policies

First North American serial or one-time rights. Pays on acceptance. $20–$40 per piece. Authors receive 4 copies of the issue.

Pax Christi USA

Sister Marlene Bertke, O.S.B., Publications Coordinator
348 East Tenth Street
Erie, PA 16503
814-453-4955

AT A GLANCE:
PAX CHRISTI USA

- Catholic, Peace
- 5% freelance
- Quarterly
- Circ: 11,500
- Receives 3 queries, 10 mss each month.
- Pays: $25 per published page on publication.

From the Editor:
"We focus on peace, nonviolence, and justice. Our members ground their peacemaking in prayer, study, and action on the message of Jesus Christ."

Avoid: Anything that is not pro-life, e.g., in favor of abortion, war, or the death penalty.

Sample copy: Information not provided. Send #10 SASE for guidelines.

Profile
A quarterly magazine of Pax Christi USA, the national division of the international Catholic peace movement. 8x11; heavy bond cover; 40 pages.

Focus and Audience
Tries to touch the average Catholic Christian with an across-the-board pro-life stance. Primary objective is to work with all people for peace for all humankind, always witnessing to the peace of Christ. Priorities are the Christian vision of disarmament, a just world order, primacy of conscience, education for peace, and alternatives to violence.

Interests and Word Lengths
- *Nonfiction:* Feature articles and columns on economic conversion, nonviolence, peace, spirituality, a just world order, ecology, and pro-life and women's issues. Use inclusive language. Features, 750–1,500 words. Columns, 800 words.
- *Photos:* Prefers B/W; accepts color if sharp.

How to Submit
Send complete ms. Include SASE. Accepts computer printouts, Macintosh disks, faxes, and submissions via modem. Simultaneous submissions okay. Reports in 2–3 months.

Payment and Policies
All rights. Pays on publication. $25 per printed page. Authors receive 5 copies of the issue.

Peace Newsletter

PNL Committee
Syracuse Peace Council
924 Burnet Avenue
Syracuse, NY 13203
315-472-5478

AT A GLANCE:
PEACE NEWSLETTER

- Social Justice, Politics
- 100% freelance
- 25% new writers
- Monthly
- Circ: 4,500
- Receives 2–3 queries, 20–30 mss each month.
- No payment. Offers contributor's copies.

From the Editor:
"*PNL* challenges the existing unjust power relationships among nations, among people, and between ourselves and the environment. As members, we work to replace inequality, hierarchy, domination, and powerlessness with mutual respect, personal empowerment, cooperation, and a sense of community."

Sample copy: Free. No guidelines.

Profile

A monthly newsletter published by The Syracuse Peace Council (SPC), an anti-war, social justice organization that is community-based, autonomous, and funded by private contributions. Est.: 1936. 8.5x11; newsprint; 24 pages.

Focus and Audience

Serves as a forum for the discussion of issues concerning the peace movement. As official organ of the SPC, it strives to educate, agitate, and organize for a world where war, violence, and exploitation in any form will no longer exist. Founded by Quakers, it is read by those active in the peace movement, primarily the politically left and some anarchists.

Interests and Word Lengths

- *Nonfiction:* Articles that reflect personal experience with issues of social justice, politics, and grass-roots activism. Up to 2,000 words.
- *Departments:* Opinion pieces on any aspect of peace and social justice issues.
- *Artwork:* B/W photos on Syracuse, NY-area subjects. Accepts cartoons and comics.

How to Submit

Send complete ms with cover letter. Include SASE. Accepts photocopies, computer printouts, IBM-compatible disks, faxes, and submissions via modem. Simultaneous submissions okay. Reports in 2 months.

Payment and Policies

Authors retain rights. No payment. Authors receive copies of the issue.

The Pegasus Review

Art Bounds, Editor
P.O. Box 134
Flanders, NJ 07836-0314
201-927-0749

AT A GLANCE:
THE PEGASUS REVIEW

- Fiction, Poetry
- 100% freelance
- 5% new writers
- Bimonthly
- Circ: 100
- Receives 25–30 queries, 25 mss each month.
- No payment. Offers 2 contributor's copies.

From the Editor:
"It is a good idea to read an issue to understand our format and need for brevity. All material appears in calligraphy."

Best Bet: Short fiction and poetry in keeping with issue themes.

Avoid: The common place—approach subjects from new angles.

Sample copy: $2. Send #10 SASE for guidelines/theme list.

Profile

A small, thematic magazine of poetry and prose. Welcomes the work of unpublished writers. 5.5x8.5; calligraphy; 10–12 pages.

Focus and Audience

Offers new and established poets and authors the opportunity to present their work in a unique setting. Readers are from the U.S. and Canada.

Interests and Word Lengths

- *Fiction:* Send for theme list. Short short stories that fit issue themes. Past themes include Education, Childhood, Civilization, Heroes, and Belief. Up to 2.5 typed, double-spaced pages.
- *Poetry:* Up to 24 lines. Must relate to issue theme.

How to Submit

Send complete ms with cover letter. Include SASE. Accepts computer printouts. Simultaneous submissions okay. Reports within 2 months.

Payment and Policies

One-time rights. No payment. Authors receive 2 copies of the issue.

Pentecostal Evangel

Richard G. Champion, Editor
1445 Boonville Avenue
Springfield, MO 65802
417-862-2781

AT A GLANCE:

PENTECOSTAL EVANGEL

- Assemblies of God, Charismatic
- 70–80% freelance
- Weekly
- Circ: 270,000
- Receives 200–250 mss each month.
- Pays: Up to $.06 per word on acceptance.

From the Editor:
"Become familiar with the magazine's content and editorial style. Know the readership and slant material accordingly. Be accurate with facts, document quotations. Pray about your writing; it is a ministry."

Avoid: Preachiness.

Sample copy: Free with 8.5x11 SAE and $58 postage. Send #10 SASE for guidelines.

Profile

The official magazine of the Assemblies of God designed to inspire lay people to live for Christ. Member of the Evangelical Press Association and the International Pentecostal Press Association. 8.5x11; glossy cover; full-color; 32 pages.

Focus and Audience

Written for a Pentecostal/Charismatic readership that espouses a conservative theology and traditional family and personal values. Slanted primarily toward lay persons. Designed to promote denominational programs and inform readers about issues and trends impacting society and the church.

Interests and Word Lengths

- *Nonfiction:* General features; personality profiles of Assemblies of God members; current issues and trends; home and family; evangelism; personal experiences; sanctity of human life; spirituality; healing; and doctrine. Accepts seasonal material. Up to 1,200 words.
- *Photos:* Submit to Cindy Replogle, Layout Coordinator. B/W prints, preferably 8x10; 35-mm color transparencies; or color prints (no Polaroids). Cover photos, 2.25x2.25 transparencies.

How to Submit

Send complete ms with cover letter and resume. Include SASE. Accepts photocopies, computer printouts, and fax submissions. No simultaneous submissions. Reports in 2–3 months.

Payment and Policies

First North American serial rights and reprint rights. Pays on acceptance. Up to $.06 per word. Authors receive 6 copies of the issue.

The Pentecostal Messenger

Peggy Allen, Managing Editor
4901 Pennsylvania, P.O. Box 850
Joplin, MO 64804
417-624-7050

AT A GLANCE:
THE PENTECOSTAL MESSENGER

- Pentecostal, Spiritual Growth
- 50% freelance
- Monthly
- Circ: 8,000
- Receives 10–25 mss each month.
- Pays: $.015 per word on publication.

From the Editor:
"We prefer articles that show the power of God sufficient in all circumstances of life."

Best Bet: Articles that deal with the issues facing the church and society.

Avoid: Articles that contain "worldly" activities, dress, or language.

Sample copy: Free with $1.05 postage. Send #10 SASE for guidelines.

Profile
Official publication of the Pentecostal Church of God. Member of the Evangelical Press Association and the International Pentecostal Press Association. 8.5x11; glossy cover; full-color; 32 pages.

Focus and Audience
Interested in contributing to the spiritual growth of adult members and ministers of the Pentecostal Church of God.

Interests and Word Lengths
- *Nonfiction:* Articles on church-related and societal issues. Inspirational feature articles and personal experience pieces that foster spiritual growth and exhibit reliance on the power of God. Accepts seasonal material. 900–2,400 words.
- *Photos:* 5x7 or larger color prints.

How to Submit
Send complete ms with cover letter. Include SASE. Accepts photocopies, computer printouts, disks, faxes, and submissions via modem. Simultaneous submissions okay. Reports in 1 month.

Payment and Policies
One-time rights. Pays on publication. $.015 per word. Authors receive 2 copies of the issue.

People Who Care

Susan Scheck, Publisher
P.O. Box 310
Old Bethpage, NY 11804-0310
516-520-0433

AT A GLANCE:

PEOPLE WHO CARE

- Volunteerism, Social Issues
- 25–50% freelance
- 25% new writers
- Quarterly
- Circ: 100
- Receives 5 queries each month.
- No payment. Offers 5 contributor's copies.

From the Editor:
"Know in your heart that good ultimately triumphs over evil, and find stories that epitomize that philosophy. Then send them to us!"

Best Bet: Upbeat, solution-oriented articles profiling a person or group working actively to make their community a better place to live.

Avoid: Overtly religious references; trying to convert readers to your religion; gloom-and-doom views of social issues.

Sample copy: Free with guidelines for a #10 SASE.

Profile

A quarterly newsletter that profiles volunteers and social activists. Focus is on the Northeast region, but themes can be applied nationally. Published by New Life Publications. 8.5x11; folded; 8 pages.

Focus and Audience

Explores social issues such as prejudice, child welfare, homelessness, and hunger with profiles of those who confront them. Espouses no particular religious philosophy, but embraces a spirituality of good ultimately triumphing over evil. Readers are primarily volunteers who actively combat social problems.

Interests and Word Lengths

- *Nonfiction:* Interviews and profiles, essays, features, and how-to articles that address social issues such as homelessness, AIDS, hunger, prejudice, child welfare, domestic violence, etc. No gloom-and-doom stories; instead find people who are confronting and impacting frightening social problems. Profiles of interesting volunteer opportunities, unusual fund drives, or activities benefiting charities. 500–1,200 words.
- *Departments:* Book Nook, reviews of current works pertaining to social issues, volunteerism, or activism. 500–750 words.
- *Artwork:* B/W photos and line drawings no larger than 8.5x11.

How to Submit

Query with outline, writing samples, and clips. Include SASE. Accepts photocopies, computer printouts, and Macintosh Microsoft Word or WordPerfect disks. Simultaneous submissions okay. Reports in 1 month.

Payment and Policies

First North American or one-time rights. No payment. Authors receive 5 copies of the issue.

Perspectives on Science and Christian Faith

Dr. J. W. Haas, Jr., Editor
P.O. Box 668
Ipswich, MA 01938
508-356-4375

AT A GLANCE:
PERSPECTIVES ON SCIENCE AND CHRISTIAN FAITH

- Christian, Science
- 99% freelance
- 50% new writers
- Monthly
- Circ: 3,000
- Receives 2–3 mss each month.
- No payment. Offers 2 contributor's copies.

From the Editor:
"The pages of *Perspectives* are open to any contribution dealing with the interaction between science and Christian faith in a manner consistent with science and theological integrity."

Sample copy: Free with 9x12 SASE bearing $1.05 postage. Send #10 SASE for guidelines.

Profile
A peer-reviewed scholarly journal exploring the relationship between science and Christianity from an evangelical perspective. Published by the American Scientific Affiliation. An Evangelical Press Association member publication. 8.5x11; perfect bound; 72 pages.

Focus and Audience
Open to any scholarly exploration of the interaction of science and Christian faith in a manner consistent with scientific and theological integrity. Contributors and readers are evangelical Christians who are professional scientists.

Interests and Word Lengths
- *Nonfiction:* Regular Papers are treatments of particular subjects relating science and the Christian position, 10–20 typed, double-spaced pages. Communications are brief treatments of a wide range of subjects related to the interaction of science and Christian faith, no longer than 9 typed, double-spaced pages.
- *Departments:* Dialogue debates relevant issues. Book Reviews encourages readers to review books in their scientific fields which have implications for the Christian faith. Send for guidelines.
- *Artwork:* Related figures or diagrams, B/W line ink drawings or glossy photos.

How to Submit
Send original plus two copies of ms. Include an abstract of no more than 100 words with Regular Papers. Include SASE. Accepts photocopies, computer printouts, and fax submissions. No simultaneous submissions. Acknowledges submissions within 1 month, reviews within 6 months.

Payment and Policies
All rights. No payment. Authors receive 2 copies of the issue.

Plenty Good Room

J-Glenn Murray, Editor
1800 North Hermitage Avenue
Chicago, IL 60622-1101
312-486-8970

AT A GLANCE:
PLENTY GOOD ROOM

- Catholic, African-American
- 6 issues a year
- Circ: not available
- Pays $25 per manuscript page.

From the Editor:
"*Plenty Good Room* is a new magazine. Please send for guidelines."

Best Bet: Worship-oriented articles for and about the African-American Catholic community.

Sample copy: Free. Send #10 SASE for guidelines.

Profile
A new magazine for and about African-American Catholic parishes. Published by Liturgy Training Publications. Est.: 1993. 6.5x11.5; glossy cover; 2-color; 12 pages.

Focus and Audience
A forum on the spirit and truth of African-American worship in the Catholic Church.

Interests and Word Lengths
- *Nonfiction:* Essays, interviews, and personal experiences that address the African-American experience in the Catholic Church. Material should be inspirational and worship-oriented. Accepts seasonal material.
- *Departments:* Elders & Ancestors, profiles of people who have made great contributions to the spiritual growth of others. Cry Holy, music column. Round My Way, conference and event listings.
- *Photos:* B/W prints.

How to Submit
Query with outline. Include SASE. Accepts photocopies, computer printouts, WordPerfect disks, and fax submissions. Reports in 3 months.

Payment and Policies
All rights. Pays $25 per manuscript page on average. Authors receive 5 copies of issue.

The Plowman

Tony Scavetta, Editor
510 Athol Street
Whitby, ON L1N 5S4
Canada
416-668-7803

AT A GLANCE:
The Plowman

- Christian, Poetry
- 100% freelance
- 75% new writers
- Quarterly
- Circ: 15,000
- Receives 100 queries,
  100 mss each month.
- No payment. Offers 2
  contributor's copies.

From the Editor:
"Write what you feel.
We see the poet as a
philosopher and lean
towards poems of so-
cial commentary."

Best Bet: Work that
deals with social and
environmental issues.

Avoid: Sending more
than five poems per
submission.

Sample copy: Free.
Send #10 SASE for
guidelines.

Profile

An eclectic collection of poetry and other writing that
offers social commentary from a Christian perspective.
Submissions from subscribers given first consideration.
Est.:1988. Tabloid-size; newsprint; 56 pages.

Focus and Audience

Interested in material, especially poetry, that deals with
important societal issues. Subscribers are Christian
writers.

Interests and Word Lengths

- *Fiction:* Drama, plays, and novellas.
- *Nonfiction:* Bible study, comparative religion, cultural
  and ethnic issues, religious education, philosophy,
  prayer, and theology.
- *Poetry:* Topics include: holocaust, religion, love, eth-
  nicity.
- *Artwork:* Calligraphy, artwork, and photos related to
  submissions.

How to Submit

Query with writing samples and clips, or send complete ms with clips. Include SASE. Accepts photocopies
and computer printouts. Simultaneous submissions
okay. Reports in 1 month.

Payment and Policies

One-time or all rights. No payment. All submissions eligible to win cash prizes. Authors receive 2 copies of the
issue.

Plus

The Magazine of Positive Thinking

Bob Chuvala, Managing Editor
66 East Main Street
Pawling, NY 12564-1409
914-855-5000

AT A GLANCE:

Plus

- Christian, Inspirational
- 1% freelance
- 10 issues a year
- Circ: 700,000
- Pays: Up to $750 on publication.

From the Editor:
"We are story-tellers, weaving practical advice on living out one's faith within the story. Read the magazine before you send us anything."

Best Bet: Well-developed, well-structured *true* stories about practical Christianity written in a warm, personal style.

Avoid: Lectures and sermons.

Sample copy: Not provided. Send #10 SASE for guidelines.

Profile

A nondenominational Christian magazine of inspirational writing. Published by the Peale Center for Christian Living. 4x6; glossy cover; full-color; 36 pages.

Focus and Audience

Upbeat, practical articles about people who perservere through faith in Jesus Christ.

Interests and Word Lengths

- *Nonfiction:* Inspirational, practical articles featuring people who have overcome or are overcoming obstacles by living out their faith in Jesus Christ. Use anecdotes and a personal writing style. Up to 2,000 words.

How to Submit

Query with outline and writing samples, or send complete ms with cover letter. Include SASE. Accepts photocopies, computer printouts, and fax submission. No simultaneous submissions. Reports in 1–2 months.

Payment and Policies

One-time rights. Pays on publication. Up to $750 per article. Kill fee, $250. Authors receive 3 copies of the issue.

Pockets

Lynn W. Gilliam, Associate Editor
1908 Grand Avenue
P.O. Box 189
Nashville, TN 37202
615-340-7333

AT A GLANCE:
POCKETS

- Christian, Children
- 50% freelance
- 11 issues a year
- Circ: 70,000
- Receives few queries, 200 mss each month.
- Pays: $.12 per word on acceptance.

From the Editor:
"Please send for a theme list before submitting. New themes are available each December. In your stories, use lots of action, believable dialog, and inclusive language."

Best Bet: Realistic stories about how children express their faith.

Avoid: Preachy or didactic stories. Tired, overdone plots such as how a child wins over a crotchety old neighbor.

Sample copy: Free with 7x9 SAE and 4 first-class stamps. Send #10 SASE for guidelines, theme list, and contest rules.

Profile

A devotional magazine for children. Published by The Upper Room. Each issue focuses on a theme. 7x9; glossy cover; full-color; 32 pages.

Focus and Audience

Designed to help 6- to 11-year-old children pray, be in relationship to God, and carry out Jesus' teachings in daily life. Emphasizes God's love and the call to community

Interests and Word Lengths

- *Fiction:* Short stories and short-short stories about children in everyday life from a faith perspective. Can be communicated through adventure, legend, history, present day, etc. Sponsors an annual Fiction Contest; deadline is September 1. 1,000–1,600 words.
- *Nonfiction:* Christian role models especially profiles of children involved in environmental and justice activities. Retold Old and New Testament Scripture stories. Theme-related articles about the Bible, church history, and different cultures. 600–1,200 words.
- *Departments:* Family communications activities; recipes.
- *Poetry:* Short poems, under one page.
- *Seasonal:* Material on holidays and the liturgical year; seasonal religious activities.
- *Games:* Hidden pictures, word puzzles, and mazes.

How to Submit

Send complete ms with cover letter. Include SASE. Accepts photocopies and computer printouts. Simultaneous submissions okay. Reports in 1 month.

Payment and Policies

First North American serial rights. Pays on acceptance. Fiction and nonfiction, $.12 per word. Poetry, $1–$2 per line. Games, $25–$50. Recipes, $25. Fiction Contest award, $1,000. Authors receive 5 copies of the issue.

Poetry Forum Short Stories

Gunvor Skogsholm, Editor
5713 Larchmont Drive
Erie, PA 16509
819-866-2543

AT A GLANCE:

POETRY FORUM SHORT STORIES

- Poetry, Fiction
- 90% freelance
- 60% new writers
- 4 issues a year
- Circ: 500
- Receives 150 queries, 180 mss each month.
- No payment.

From the Editor:
"Start with a good lead—the opening paragraph must catch the reader's interest. The middle must contain the telling of the story. The ending must round out the story without introducing a new element."

Best Bet: Fiction and poetry on the human condition.

Avoid: Dialog and action that does not fit the character you've created.

Sample copy: $3. Send #10 SASE for guidelines.

Profile

A quarterly compilation of mainstream, semi-literary prose and poetry. Interdenominational in nature, open to all religions, colors, and creeds. 5.5x8.5; self cover; folded and stapled; photocopied; 24 pages.

Focus and Audience

Encourages writing that depicts the human condition as honestly as possible. Focus is on good writing: Do not make the message more important than the words. Readership is diverse.

Interests and Word Lengths

- *Fiction:* General-interest, mainstream, enlightening short stories. Dialog and action should be appropriate to characters. 800–3,000 words.
- *Nonfiction:* Essays on poetry and the connection between healthy bodies and healthy minds. 100–800 words.
- *Poetry:* Inspiring poems.
- *Artwork:* Line drawings.

How to Submit

Send complete ms with short cover letter. Include SASE. Accepts photocopies, computer printouts, disk submissions, and faxes (814-866-2543, 8–10 a.m. and 5–8 p.m.). Simultaneous submissions okay. Reports in 1–3 months.

Payment and Policies

One-time rights. No payment.

Portland

The Magazine of the University of Portland

Brian Doyle, Editor
5000 North Willamette Boulevard
Portland, OR 97203
503-283-7202

AT A GLANCE:

PORTLAND

- Education, Catholic
- 30% freelance
- 10% new writers
- Quarterly
- Circ: 23,000
- Receives 8–10 queries, 1–2 mss each month
- Pays: $100–$500 on publication.

From the Editor:
"*Portland* is not an alumni magazine but a University magazine. It links the University and its constituents and reaches out to those who do not know the University's mission of teaching, faith, and service."

Best Bet: Articles on the University and its people, Catholicism, spirituality, education, and the Pacific Northwest.

Sample copy: Free with 9x12 SAE and $1 postage. Send #10 SASE for guidelines.

Profile

A quarterly magazine of news, ideas, and issues affecting the University of Portland, its students, and its alumni. 9x12; glossy cover; 2-color; 40 pages.

Focus and Audience

Serves as a communications vehicle for readers—University of Portland students, faculty, staff, and alumni. As such, it is primarily concerned with University personalities, ideas, and events, although material on Roman Catholicism and spirituality is welcome.

Interests and Word Lengths

- *Nonfiction:* Feature articles on the Roman Catholic faith, spirituality, higher education, and the Pacific Northwest region. Occasionally features a profile of University of Portland alumni, staff, or friends. 2,000–3,000 words.
- *Departments:* On the Bluff, reportorial essays on an issue, event, program, or trend at the University of Portland. 800–1,000 words.

How to Submit

Request sample copy and guidelines before submitting. Then, query with outline and at least 3 writing samples or clips. Include SASE. Accepts photocopies and computer printouts. No simultaneous submissions. Reports in 3 months.

Payment and Policies

First North American serial rights. Pays on publication. Feature articles, $100–$500 depending on length of work, research involved, and author's history with the publication. Authors receive up to 20 copies of the issue.

A Positive Approach

Patricia Johnson, Editor
P.O. Box 910
Millville, NJ 08332-0910
609-451-4777

AT A GLANCE:
A POSITIVE APPROACH

- Christian, Disabilities
- 95% freelance
- 75% new writers
- 4 issues a year
- Circ: 200,000
- Receives 400+ queries, 350+ mss each month.
- No payment. Offers 10 contributor's copies.

From the Editor:
"We guide new writers and give them the exposure they need to obtain writing assignments elsewhere."

Best Bet: Positive, upbeat articles that encourage and inform those with physical disabilities.

Avoid: Referring to a person with a disability as wheelchair bound, crippled, or ill; wheelchairs are for mobility.

Sample copy: $2 with 9x12 SASE. Send #10 SASE for guidelines.

Profile

A non-profit, inspirational magazine for Christians with physical disabilities. Member of the Christian Council on Persons with Disabilities. 8.5x11; glossy cover; 2-color; 64 pages.

Focus and Audience

Upbeat, encouraging articles for Christians with disabilities who want to be more mobile and help others grow from their experiences. Focus is on positive growth, not pain and suffering. Does not publish publicity pieces nor product or service reviews.

Interests and Word Lengths

- *Nonfiction:* Interviews with and profiles of men, women, or children who go beyond their physical strength and are inspired by God to do their best. Interests include careers, driving, art, photography, physical fitness, chronic pain, and ministries working with disabilities. 500–1,000 words
- *Departments:* All assigned. Includes Travel, Chronic Pain, Computers, Careers, Incontinence, Driving, ADA, Art/Photography. 500–1,000 words.
- *Artwork:* B/W or color slides or drawings to accompany articles.

How to Submit

Send complete ms with cover letter for articles/interviews. Query with outline for departments. Include SASE. Accepts computer printouts and faxes. Simultaneous submissions okay. Reports in 1 month.

Payment and Policies

One-time rights. No payment. Authors receive 10 copies of the issue.

Power and Light

Beula Postlewait, Editor
6401 The Paseo
Kansas City, MO 64131
816-333-7000

AT A GLANCE:
POWER AND LIGHT

- Church of the Nazarene, Preteen
- 30% freelance
- 10–15% new writers
- Weekly
- Circ: 30,000
- Receives 20–25 queries, 10–15 mss each month.
- Pays: $.05 per word on publication.

From the Editor:
"Write in accordance with the Church of the Nazarene theology and practices."

Best Bet: Short fiction for preteens that correlates with the Church of the Nazarene Sunday school curriculum.

Avoid: Focusing on American culture and holidays.

Sample copy: Free with 5x7 SAE and $1 postage. Send #10 SASE for guidelines.

Profile

A weekly Church of the Nazarene take-home paper the connects Sunday school learning with the daily life of preteens. 5.5x8.5; folded; full-color; 8 pages.

Focus and Audience

Focuses on the needs and issues facing today's 11- to 12-year-old preteens. All themes and outcomes should conform to the theology and practices of the Church of the Nazarene and other Holiness denominations.

Interests and Word Lengths

- *Fiction:* Short-short stories on the issues faced by preteens today. All stories should involve preteens as main characters. 600–800 words.
- *Filler:* Single-frame, humorous cartoons for preteens.
- *Artwork:* By assignment only. B/W line art or color illustrations. Submit portfolio with resume for consideration.

How to Submit

Send complete ms with cover letter. Include SASE. Accepts photocopies and computer printouts. Simultaneous submissions okay. Reports in 1–3 months.

Payment and Policies

Multi-use rights. Pays on publication. $.05 per word. Kill fee, $15 for assigned work. Authors receive 4 copies of the issue.

Power for Living

Roy Irving, Editor
P.O. Box 632
Glen Ellyn, IL 60138
708-668-6000

AT A GLANCE:
POWER FOR LIVING

- Christian, Adult Sunday School
- 50–70% freelance
- Weekly
- Circ: not available
- Receives 40–55 mss each month.
- Pays: $.05–$.10 per word on acceptance.

From the Editor:
"Copy must show in a compelling way, without sermonizing, how adults put God's Word into practice or how Christ's power makes a difference in their lives."

Best Bet: Personality profiles of unique Christians or personal conversion experiences.

Avoid: Tales of accidents, illness, handicaps, and hospitals—currently overstocked.

Sample copy: Free with 6x9 SAE and $.29 postage. Send #10 SASE for guidelines.

Profile
A Sunday school take-home paper for adults. Part of the Scripture Press *Power/Line Papers*, it is correlated with the Scripture Press *Bible for Today* curriculum. 5.5x8.5; folded; 3-color; 8 pages.

Focus and Audience
Designed to help Christian adults become more Christlike by showing them how to apply biblical truths to everyday life and to convince non-Christians of their need to receive Christ as savior. Evangelical in nature.

Interests and Word Lengths
- *Nonfiction:* Personality Profiles, well-rounded portrayals of colorful, living evangelical Christians who serve the Lord in unique ways. Also considers profiles of Christian groups. Personal Experiences, dramatic or humorous true accounts of how believers have applied biblical truths to their lives or have been changed or challenged by the Lord. All material must be Christ-centered. Prefers timely topics—avoid as focal events any incidents that occurred more than five years ago. Up to 1,500 words.

How to Submit
Query for all submissions over 750 words. May send complete ms if less than 750 words. Include SASE. Accepts photocopies and computer printouts. No simultaneous submissions. Reports in 4–6 weeks.

Payment and Policies
First or reprint rights. Pays on acceptance. First rights, $.07–$.10 per word. Reprint rights, $.05–$.07 per word. Authors receive 4 copies of the issue.

Praying

Art Winter, Editor
115 East Armour Boulevard
Kansas City, MO 64129
816-531-0538

AT A GLANCE:

PRAYING

- Catholic, Prayer
- 5% freelance
- 10% new writers
- Bimonthly
- Circ: 15,000
- Receives 20 queries, 20 mss each month.
- Pays: $50–$150 on publication.

From the Editor:
"Write personally out of your own experience, based on post-Vatican II spirituality."

Best Bet: Creative and personal stories of a lived-awareness of God's presence.

Avoid: Religious jargon; fundamentalism; Catholic Church hassles; "the world is evil" or "me and Jesus only" viewpoints; religion concerned only with heaven.

Sample copy: Free with 10x12 SASE.

Profile

A Catholic magazine of prayer and spirituality for everyday living. Published by The National Catholic Reporter Publishing Company, Inc. 8x10.5; self cover; 2-color; 40 pages.

Focus and Audience

Works to help people to respond to God's presence in their daily lives in the world through prayer and action. Writings should be based on post-Vatican II theology and spirituality.

Interests and Word Lengths

- *Fiction:* Creative stories about Christian living or spirituality that demonstrate an awareness of God working in the world and in people's lives. 2,000 words.
- *Nonfiction:* Articles, especially personal experiences, on prayer, spirituality, and Scripture. 2,000 words.
- *Departments:* Our Way, personal accounts of how an individual writer prays or performs Christian activities on a continuing basis. 750 words.
- *Photos:* B/W photos that tell a story or lead to reflection.

How to Submit

Send complete ms with cover letter. Include SASE. Accepts photocopies, computer printouts, and IBM disk submissions. No simultaneous submissions. Reports in 1 month.

Payment and Policies

One-time rights. Pays on publication. $50–$150 per piece. Kill fee, 33% if assigned. Authors receive 2 copies of the issue.

The Preacher's Magazine

Randal Denny, Editor
10814 East Broadway
Spokane, WA 99206
509-226-3464

AT A GLANCE:
THE PREACHER'S MAGAZINE

- Holiness Ministers
- 25% freelance
- 10% new writers
- Quarterly
- Circ: 18,000
- Receives 20–30 queries, 20–30 mss each month.
- Pays: $.035 per word on publication.

From the Editor:
"We attempt to encourage, support, enlighten, and inspire ministers. When thinking of manuscript length, please keep in mind that less is better."

Best Bet: Practical and scholarly articles on all aspects of ministry.

Sample copy: Not provided. Send #10 SASE for guidelines.

Profile

A quarterly trade journal for Christian ministers of the Holiness Movement. Each issue focuses on one theme. 80 pages.

Focus and Audience

Seeks to provide insights and resources for lifelong ministerial development and apply biblical truths to modern-day ministry. Theological association is Wesleyan-Arminian.

Interests and Word Lengths

- *Nonfiction:* Scholarly and practical articles pertaining to the issue theme. Contents are divided into major sections such as Church Administration, Church Growth, Pastoral Care, Evangelism, Theology, Staff Ministries, The Minister's Mate, Pastor's Personal Growth, Pastor's Professional Growth, Holiness Heritage, Preaching, Biblical Studies, Church Music, and Finance. 700–2,500 words

How to Submit

Send complete ms with cover letter. Include SASE. Identify all Scripture quotations including the version quoted. Footnote other sources. Obtain and include with article permission to use copyrighted material of more than 120 words. Accepts photocopies and computer printouts. Simultaneous submissions okay. Reports in 3–6 weeks.

Payment and Policies

First North American serial or one-time rights. Pays on publication. $.035 per word. Authors receive 1 copy of the issue.

Preaching

Dr. Michael Duduit, Editor
P.O. Box 7728
Louisville, KY 40257-0728
502-899-3119

AT A GLANCE:
PREACHING

- Christian, Clergy
- 80% freelance
- 25% new writers
- 6 issues a year
- Circ: 10,000
- Receives 5–10 queries, 30–50 mss each month.
- Pays: $35–$50 per piece on publication.

From the Editor:
"All material must be directed to the professional needs of preachers."

Best Bet: How-to articles on preaching-related topics.

Avoid: Specific theological or denominational viewpoints; articles by persons not active as preachers.

Sample copy: $2.50. Send #10 SASE for guidelines.

Profile

A professional journal for ministers. Published bimonthly by Preaching Resources, Inc. 8.5x11; glossy cover; 64 pages.

Focus and Audience

Devoted entirely to preaching and worship leadership. Non-denominational in nature. All material is written by preachers.

Interests and Word Lengths

- *Nonfiction*: How-to articles offering practical, helpful, guidance for pastors on various areas of preaching; general ministry-related topics must have slant that ties them to the pulpit. 1,250–1,500 words.
- *Sermons*: Sermons that have actually been preached prior to submission. Should offer worthy models for other pastors and reflect the interdenominational, evangelical stance of the publication. 1,000–1,250 words.
- *Departments*: Children's Sermons, original sermons that tell a biblical message at a child's level, 150–200 words. Sermons in Brief, partially developed sermon outlines, up to 2 typed, double-spaced pages.

How to Submit

Query with outline. Include SASE. Accepts photocopies and computer printouts. No simultaneous submissions. Reports in 2–4 months.

Payment and Policies

First North American serial and reprint rights. Pays on publication. Feature articles, $50. Sermons, $35. Authors receive copies of issue.

The Presbyterian Outlook

Robert H. Bullock, Jr., Editor
3711 Saunders Avenue
Richmond, VA 23227
804-359-8442

Profile

An independent newsmagazine serving the Presbyterian Church (U.S.A.). 8.5x11; self cover; stapled; 16 pages.

Focus and Audience

Attempts to be a fair and open forum for Presbyterian ministers and informed lay people who care about their denomination.

Interests and Word Lengths

- *Nonfiction:* Material that relates directly to the Presbyterian Church (U.S.A.). Ideas must be queried and discussed with editor in advance. 500–1,000 words.
- *Departments:* News; opinion and editorials, book and movie reviews; church issues; ministerial and church professional changes. Must be queried and discussed with editor in advance. Up to 500 words.

How to Submit

Query with outline. Include SASE. Accepts photocopies, computer printouts, and fax submissions. No simultaneous submissions. Reports promptly.

Payment and Policies

One-time rights. No payment. Authors receive 1 copy of the issue upon request.

Presbyterian Record

Rev. John Congram, Editor
50 Wynford Drive
North York, ON M3C 1J7
Canada
416-441-1111

AT A GLANCE:

PRESBYTERIAN RECORD

- Presbyterian, Opinion
- 50% freelance
- 11 issues a year
- Circ: 63,000
- Pays: $25–$75 per piece on publication.

From the Editor:
"We emphasize things Reformed (Presbyterian) and Canadian."

Best Bet: Articles and stories of interest to church members.

Sample copy: Free with 9x12 SASE/IRCs. Send #10 SASE/IRC for guidelines.

Profile

A national magazine of The Presbyterian Church in Canada, under the General Assembly. Member of The Canadian Church Press and Associated Church Press. 8x10.5; glossy cover; 52 pages.

Focus and Audience

Covers issues of general Christian faith as well as those of particular concern to members of The Presbyterian Church in Canada.

Interests and Word Lengths

- *Fiction:* Short stories. Up to 1,500 words.
- *Nonfiction:* Christian faith and life issues, denominational and national concerns, opinion, and current and timely news analyses. Up to 1,500 words.
- *Departments:* An Everyday God, Suggestion Box, You Were Asking?, People and Places, Meditation. Up to 750 words.
- *Poetry:* Submit to Tom Dickey, Poetry Editor.
- *Artwork:* Submit to Editor.

How to Submit

Query with outline or send complete ms with cover letter. Include SASE. U.S. authors include IRCs. Accepts photocopies, computer printouts, and fax submissions. Simultaneous submissions okay. Reports in 2 months.

Payment and Policies

First North American serial rights or one-time rights, as well as reprint and simultaneous rights. Pays on publication. $25–$75 per piece. Authors receive 2 copies of the issue.

Presbyterian Survey

Kenneth Little, Editor
100 Witherspoon Street
Louisville, KY 40202-1396
502-569-5637

AT A GLANCE:

PRESBYTERIAN SURVEY

- Presbyterian, Spirituality
- 70% freelance
- 30% new writers
- 10 issues a year
- Circ: 112,000
- Receives 10 queries, 55 mss each month.
- Pays: $100 on scheduling for publication.

From the Editor:
"We are a denominational magazine, published primarily for the members and associates of the Presbyterian Church (USA)."

Best Bet: Articles that are related to the Presbyterian Church.

Avoid: Personal testimonies and preachy articles.

Sample copy: Free. Send #10 SASE for guidelines.

Profile

A denominational magazine of the Presbyterian Church (USA), published for its members. Member of the Associated Church Press. 8.5x11; glossy cover; full-color; 44 pages.

Focus and Audience

Covers the work of the Presbyterian Church (USA), discusses contemporary issues, and assists church members with everyday Christian living. Readers are primarily adult Presbyterian lay people.

Interests and Word Lengths

- *Nonfiction:* Articles on issues relating to the the Presbyterian Church, including current social issues and practical Christian living. Avoid excessive use of the first person. Up to 1,500 words; prefers 1,000–1,200 words.
- *Departments:* As I See It, op-ed page for reader response. 600–650 words.
- *Photos:* B/W or color prints or slides. No size requirements. Submit photos with manuscript or to managing editor upon acceptance.

How to Submit

Send complete ms with cover letter. Include SASE. Prefers original copy. Accepts photocopies, computer printouts, and Macintosh Microsoft Word 3.5-inch disk submissions. Identify simultaneous submissions. Reports in 4–6 weeks.

Payment and Policies

One-time rights. Pays when scheduled for publication. Rates vary; usual fee is $100. Authors receive 2 copies of the issue.

The Priest

Robert A. Willems, Associate Editor
200 Noll Plaza
Huntington, IN 46750
219-356-8400

AT A GLANCE:
THE PRIEST

- Catholic, Clergy
- 50–75% freelance
- Uses new writers
- Monthly
- Circ: 10,000
- Receives 20–30 mss each month.
- Pays: $175–$300 on acceptance.

From the Editor:
"We ask that all material follow the Magisterium of the Catholic Church."

Best Bet: Articles on the problems confronting Catholic priests.

Avoid: Tirades against the Church or its present laws.

Sample copy: Free. Send #10 SASE for guidelines.

Profile
A monthly publication designed to edify and enlighten Catholic priests. Published by Our Sunday Visitor Publishing. 8.5x11; glossy cover; 48 pages.

Focus and Audience
Addresses the pastoral, spiritual, psychological, and theological problems and challenges inherent in daily ministry. Adheres to the tenets of Catholicism. Read by Catholic priests, permanent deacons, and seminarians.

Interests and Word Lengths
- *Nonfiction:* Feature articles and opinion pieces on anything related to the daily life of priests, seminarians, or permanent deacons. Interests include inspirational and devotional pieces; articles on evangelism, liturgy, the sacraments, prayer, spirituality, theology, and worship. Features, up to 3,500 words. Viewpoints, up to 1,000 words.

How to Submit
Send complete ms with cover letter. Include SASE. Accepts computer printouts. No simultaneous submissions. Reports in 1 month.

Payment and Policies
First North American serial rights. Pays on acceptance. $175–$300. Authors receive 2 copies of the issue.

Primary Days

Janice K. Burton, Editor
P.O. Box 632
Glen Ellyn, IL 60138
708-668-6000

AT A GLANCE:
PRIMARY DAYS

- Christian, Juvenile
- 50% freelance
- Uses new writers
- Weekly
- Circ: not available
- Receives 10–20 mss each month.
- Pays $.05–$.10 per word on acceptance.

From the Editor:
"We seek to honor Jesus Christ in all our publishing efforts, and to help children come to know the Lord and be discipled in His ways. We are an evangelical publishing house."

Avoid: Subjects that are more appropriate for older readers such as abuse, AIDS, abortion, eating disorders, dating, sex, suicide, etc.

Sample copy: Free with 4.5x9.5 SAE and $.29 postage. Send #10 SASE for guidelines.

Profile
A Sunday school take-home paper for children. Correlated with the Scripture Press *Bible for Today* curriculum. 7x10; 4-color; folded; 4 pages.

Focus and Audience
Designed to help children, ages 6–8, apply Scripture lessons to everyday life situations and come to know Jesus Christ. Evangelical in nature.

Interests and Word Lengths
- *Fiction:* Short stories on topics such as response to authority, accepting responsibility, cheating, divorce, interpersonal relationships, family, friends, justice, lying, peer pressure, prayer, prejudice, salvation, trusting God, and witnessing. 600–700 words. Avoid stories on subjects more appropriate for older readers.
- *Nonfiction:* Personal experiences, interviews, and true stories with photos if possible. See *Fiction* for subjects of interest. 600–700 words.
- *Filler:* Puzzles and creative activities that reflect a spiritual truth. Must be solvable in both the *King James* and *New International* Bible versions.
- *Photos:* B/W or color slides to accompany material.

How to Submit
Send complete ms with cover letter. Include SASE. Accepts photocopies and computer printouts. No simultaneous submissions. Reports in 4–6 weeks.

Payment and Policies
First North American, one-time, or all rights. Pays on acceptance. $.05–$.10 per word depending on rights offered and editing required. Authors receive 2 copies of the issue.

Primary Treasure

Aileen Andres Sox, Editor
P.O. Box 7000
Boise, ID 83707
208-465-2500

AT A GLANCE:

PRIMARY TREASURE

- Seventh-day Adventist, Juvenile
- 75% freelance
- 50% new writers
- Weekly
- Circ: 35,000
- Receives 75 mss each month.
- Pays: $25–$50 on acceptance.

From the Editor:
"Story plots, vocabulary, and main characters should fit the age level for whom the story is written."

Best Bet: True stories that help children understand and develop a personal relationship with God.

Avoid: Stories of talking animals, hunting, and fishing; fantasy and Halloween stories.

Sample copy: Free with 9x12 SAE and 2 first-class stamps. Send #10 SASE for guidelines.

Profile

A spiritually oriented Sabbath school magazine for Seventh-day Adventist children. Published weekly by Pacific Press Publishing Association. 8.5x11; self cover; 2-color; 16 pages.

Focus and Audience

Its mission is to teach Christian beliefs and values and present God's love to children in a way that will help them love Him. Written for 7- to 9-year-old children who attend Sabbath school at a Seventh-day Adventist Church. Stories must be consistent with Seventh-day Adventist beliefs and practices.

Interests and Word Lengths

- *Nonfiction:* True stories that portray a loving God. Characters should be good children setting good examples, being kind, and making right choices. Speak to the experience, lifestyle, needs, and vocabulary of today's child. Special interests include stories about personal Godliness; coping with peer pressure; mission experiences, sibling rivalry and fair fighting; prayer; nature; and basic social skills. Write to a third-grade reading level. Up to 1,200 words.
- *Seasonal:* Christmas, Thanksgiving, and Mother's, Father's, and Grandparent's Days. Submit 7 months in advance.
- *Filler:* Bible- or nature-based games and puzzles. Short poems with spiritual themes.

How to Submit

Submit complete ms with cover letter. Include SASE. Accepts photocopies, computer printouts, and fax submissions. Simultaneous submissions okay. Reports in 3 months.

Payment and Policies

One-time rights. Pays on acceptance. $25–$50 per piece. Authors receive 3 copies of the issue.

Priority Parenting

Tamra B. Orr, Editor
P.O. Box 1793
Warsaw, IN 46581-1793
219-268-1415

Tamra B. Orr, Editor
P.O. Box 1793
Warsaw, IN 46581-1793
219-268-1415

AT A GLANCE:

PRIORITY PARENTING

- Parenting, Family
- 90% freelance
- 80% new writers
- Monthly
- Circ: 150
- Receives 2–8 queries, 2–5 mss each month.
- No payment. Offers 2–5 contributor's copies.

From the Editor:
"Writers should know the upcoming themes and stick to them. New writers are always needed and appreciated."

Best Bet: Theme-related first-person pieces on natural childcare.

Avoid: Articles promoting family separation or modern-style childcare; third-person or expert pieces.

Sample copy: $2 with 6x9 SAE and $.29 postage. Send #10 SASE for guidelines.

Profile

A small monthly publication focusing on alternative parenting and childrearing methods. Issues are thematic. 5.5x8; folded; photocopied; 20 pages.

Focus and Audience

Encourages and supports parents who believe in quality, natural childcare and do not follow the "mainstream" on issues of child nurturing.

Interests and Word Lengths

- *Nonfiction:* Theme-related first-person experience essays. Topics include at-home moms, breastfeeding, home birth, home education, family beds, and peaceful homes. Past themes include Child Abuse—Emotional, Physical, and Sexual; Parenting the Older Child Naturally; Education Alternatives; and Husbands, Fathers, and Men. 750–1,000 words.
- *Departments:* Viewpoint, opinion pieces on any aspect of natural/alternative parenting. 500–750 words.
- *Poetry:* Welcomes theme-related poems.
- *Artwork:* B/W drawings.

How to Submit

Request theme list before submitting material. Then, send complete ms with cover letter. Include SASE. Accepts photocopies and computer printouts. Simultaneous submissions okay. Reports in under 1 month.

Payment and Policies

One-time rights. No payment. Authors receive 2–5 copies of the issue upon request.

Probe

Cecelia Lavan, Editor
National Assembly of Religious Women (NAR)
529 South Wabash, #404
Chicago, IL 60605
312-663-1980

Profile

A progressive newspaper published by the National Assembly of Religious Women (NAR). Issues are thematic. Tabloid-size; newsprint; 12 pages.

Focus and Audience

A forum for progressive, social justice and feminist thought. Serves as a networking tool for NAR members, who are women of faith working for social transformation of society and church. It is rooted in the Catholic tradition, but readership is ecumenical.

Interests and Word Lengths

- *Fiction:* Short stories that help women understand and connect with social justice issues. 2,000 words. Accepts poetry.
- *Nonfiction:* Personal experiences of NAR members. Analysis of the ways in which women are oppressed. Accounts of women's lived experiences with insight into how to bring about social change. Articles that promote social action and help women to take action—include resources. Interviews, profiles, and how-to articles. Up to 2,000 words. Accepts seasonal material.
- *Departments:* Resources, theme-related events and activities.
- *Poetry:* Poems related to issue theme.
- *Artwork:* B/W or color photos. Illustrations, any type.

How to Submit

Query with outline. Include SASE. Accepts photocopies, computer printouts, IBM WordPerfect disks, faxes, and submissions via modem. Identify simultaneous submissions. Report time varies.

Payment and Policies

One-time rights. No payment. Authors receive a free one-year subscription and copies of the issue.

Progress Magazine

Susan Collard, Managing Editor
10121 Grandview Road
Box 9609
Kansas City, MO 64134
816-763-7800

AT A GLANCE:

PROGRESS MAGAZINE

- Christian, Evangelical
- 10% freelance
- Few new writers
- Bimonthly
- Circ: 30,000
- Receives 10+ mss each month.
- No payment. Offers up to 50 contributor's copies.

From the Editor:
"If you are not familiar with Stonecroft Ministries, write for our guidelines before submitting."

Best Bet: Personal experiences and testimonies showing how Jesus Christ is working in your life.

Avoid: Anything controversial or critical; Christian clichés.

Sample copy: Free with 6x9 SASE. Send #10 SASE for guidelines.

Profile

An interdenominational evangelistic magazine published bimonthly by Stonecroft Ministries, an association of Christian organizations dedicated to spreading the Christian faith. 5.5x8.5; glossy cover; full-color; 64 pages.

Focus and Audience

Sole focus is to introduce people to Jesus Christ through personal testimonies of living faith in today's world. Read primarily by women and families involved in Stonecroft Ministries.

Interests and Word Lengths

- *Nonfiction:* Light, insightful feature articles, 300–600 words. Salvation stories, personal testimonies of how you came to know and follow Jesus Christ. Include information on your life before conversion and how Jesus is working in your life today. 1,500–2,000 words.
- *Departments:* Coping Series, first-person articles showing how faith helped an individual cope with crisis or stress. 1,000–1,500 words. Ministry in the Marketplace, articles encouraging Christians to share their faith in the workplace. Offer a Christian perspective on work-related issues such as time management, handling stress and competition, and dealing with failure. 1,000–1,500 words.
- *Photos:* Color slides or prints.

How to Submit

Send complete ms with cover letter. Include SASE. Accepts photocopies, computer printouts, and fax submissions. No simultaneous submissions. Reports in 1 month.

Payment and Policies

First North American serial rights. No payment. Authors receive up to 50 copies of the issue.

Protestant Challenge

Jonas Shepherd, Editor
600 Woodview Road
Burlington, ON L7N 3A3
Canada
416-639-3318

AT A GLANCE:

PROTESTANT CHALLENGE

- Protestant, Evangelical
- 5% freelance
- Bimonthly
- Circ: 3,000
- Receives 6–7 queries, 6–7 mss each month.
- No payment. Offers up to 10 contributor's copies.

From the Editor:
"The Canadian Protestant League consists primarily of extremely conservative, evangelical Protestant churches."

Best Bet: Educational, historical, scriptural, and evangelical views of Protestantism.

Sample copy: Free. No guidelines.

Profile

A bimonthly magazine of conservative, evangelical Protestant thought. Published by the Canadian Protestant League. 8.5x11; 8 pages.

Focus and Audience

Concerned with preserving and upholding the basic tenets of the Protestant Reformation. Most readers are conservative, evangelical Protestants.

Interests and Word Lengths

- *Nonfiction:* Articles on educational, historical, scriptural, and evangelical aspects of the Protestant movement. 5–8 typed, double-spaced pages.
- *Photos:* Occasionally accepts B/W prints.

How to Submit

Send complete ms with cover letter, resume, and clips. Include SASE. U.S. authors include IRCs. Accepts photocopies, computer printouts, and 5.25-inch IBM-compatible disk submissions. Simultaneous submissions okay. Reports in 2 months.

Payment and Policies

Authors retain rights. No payment. Authors receive up to 10 copies of the issue.

Purpose

James E. Horsch, Editor
105 North Chestnut Street
Scottdale, PA 15683
412-887-8500

Profile

A story paper that encourages readers to live a faithful Christian life. Published monthly in weekly parts by the Mennonite Publishing House. 5x8; folded; 2-color; 8 pages.

Focus and Audience

Action-oriented, discipleship-living material that models the resolution of issues through Christian principles. Readers are committed young adult and adult Christians who want to apply their faith in daily life.

Interests and Word Lengths

- *Fiction:* Short stories with Christian discipleship themes that show people putting their faith to work; stress church loyalty and community duties; and inspire interest in other people and cultures. 900 words.
- *Nonfiction:* Inspirational, family, lifestyle, and first-person pieces that show Christians practicing their faith; highlight biographical and historical information of Christian figures and places; and emphasizes hobbies, nature, travel, art, science, and seasonal topics from a Christian perspective. 900 words.
- *Poetry:* Verse up to 12 lines.
- *Photos:* B/W photos.

How to Submit

Send complete ms with cover letter and resume. Include SASE. Accepts photocopies and computer printouts. Simultaneous submissions okay. Reports in 2–4 months.

Payment and Policies

One-time rights. Pays on publication. $.05 per word. Authors receive 2 copies of the issue.

Pursuit

Susan Brill, Assistant Editor
901 East 78th Street
Minneapolis, MN 55420
612-853-8491

Profile

A non-denominational evangelistic magazine published by The Evangelical Free Church of America (EFCA). Issues are thematic. 8.5x11; glossy cover; full-color; 32 pages.

Focus and Audience

Aims to help non-Christians in daily life management while stimulating thought about spiritual answers to human problems. Offers a Christian worldview, but portrays Christian truths in a non-religious manner. Written for non-Christians from different age groups, economic levels, professions, and heritages.

Interests and Word Lengths

- *Fiction:* Stories that convey a Christian message. No word limit. Accepts poetry.
- *Nonfiction:* Feature articles on family-related and life-management issues such as stress, a sense of belonging, hope, and humor. Focus on practical ideas and answers that are compatible with Christian beliefs. Also accepts personality profiles of prominent Christians in any endeavor such as sports, media, or business. Include testimony of God's role in the person's life. 500–1,500 words. Accepts filler and seasonal material.
- *Artwork:* Accepts photos and illustrations.

How to Submit

Query with outline and clips, or send complete ms with cover letter and clips. Include SASE. Accepts photocopies, computer printouts, 3.5-inch ASCII or Macintosh disks, and fax submissions. Simultaneous submissions okay. Reports in 4–6 weeks.

Payment and Policies

One-time rights. Pays on publication. First rights, $.07 per word. Reprints, $.03 per word. Authors receive 3 copies of the issue.

Quarterly Review
A Journal of Theological Resources for Ministry

Dr. Sharon J. Hels, Editor
1001 19th Avenue South
Nashville, TN 37202
615-340-7383

AT A GLANCE:
QUARTERLY REVIEW

- United Methodist, Ministry
- 95% freelance
- 25% new writers
- Quarterly
- Circ: 3,000
- Receives 5–10 queries, 5–10 mss each month.
- No payment. Offers 1 contributor's copy and offprints.

From the Editor:
"The United Methodist tradition behind *Quarterly Review* stresses a combination of knowledge and vital piety."

Best Bet: Short essays with a sound, up-to-date academic perspective.

Avoid: Extremes of technical academic writing and popular, journalistic treatments.

Sample copy: Not provided. Send #10 SASE for guidelines.

Profile

A quarterly journal for United Methodist ministers. Published by the United Methodist Board of Higher Education and Ministry. 6x9; 112 pages.

Focus and Audience

Reflects the theological concerns and meets the educational needs for those in ministry, particularly United Methodist ordained and diaconal ministers worldwide. Stresses learning with a bias toward practical application in Christian life.

Interests and Word Lengths

- *Nonfiction:* Short, academically sound essays exploring theology, Bible study, and religious education with practical Christian application. Values originality of thought and expression. 15–18 typed, double-spaced pages.
- *Seasonal:* Theological reflections—seasonal or situational—on aspects of church life.

How to Submit

Send complete ms with cover letter and resume. Include SASE. Accepts computer printouts and MS-DOS, ASCII disk files. No simultaneous submissions. Reports in 3 months.

Payment and Policies

One-time rights. No payment. Authors receive 1 copy of the issue and 25 offprints.

Queen of All Hearts

Rev. Roger M. Charest, S.M.M., Managing Editor
26 South Saxon Avenue
Bay Shore, NY 11706
516-665-0726

AT A GLANCE:
QUEEN OF ALL HEARTS

- Catholic, Devotions
- Bimonthly
- Circ: 6,000
- Receives 20 mss each month.
- Pays: $40–$60 on acceptance.

From the Editor:
"We are dedicated to Mary, Mother of Jesus as seen in Sacred Scripture, tradition, and Church history."

Best Bet: Stories, articles and poems about the Blessed Mother and/or some aspect of Marian spirituality.

Sample copy: $2. Send #10 SASE for guidelines.

Profile

A Roman Catholic devotional magazine dedicated to Mary, the mother of Jesus. 8x11; 48 pages.

Focus and Audience

Concentrates solely on the person of Mary and Marian spirituality as seen in Sacred Scriptures, Roman Catholic tradition, and the history of the Church. Directed toward Catholic readers interested in Marian devotions.

Interests and Word Lengths

- *Fiction:* Religious short stories about some aspect of Marian spirituality. 1,500–2,500 words.
- *Nonfiction:* Essays and inspirational, personal-experience, and religious articles on some aspect of Mary and Marian devotion: Mary in Scripture, tradition, Church history as seen by early Christian writers and as affecting the lives of saints, poetry, art, music, spiritual writers, apparitions, shrines, and ecumenism. 750–2,500 words. Accepts seasonal and holiday material.
- *Poetry:* Poems about Mary, her shrines and devotions.

How to Submit

Send complete ms with cover letter. Include SASE. Accepts photocopies and fax submissions. No simultaneous submissions. Reports in 6 weeks.

Payment and Policies

One-time rights. Pays on acceptance. Articles, $40–$60. Poems, paid in contributor's copies. Authors receive 6 copies of the issue.

Quiet Revolution

Cornelius Jones, Editor
1655 St. Charles Street
Jackson, MS 39209
601-353-1635

AT A GLANCE:
QUIET REVOLUTION

- Christian, Service
- 10% freelance
- Quarterly
- Circ: 3,000
- Receives 1 query, 1 ms each year.
- No payment. Offers 1 contributor's copy.

From the Editor:
"Keep your writing conservative and holistic. Offer positive attitudes."

Best Bet: Articles that address some aspect of ministering to the poor.

Sample copy: Free. No guidelines.

Profile

The magazine of Voice of Calvary Ministries, an inter-denominational, inter-racial ministry to the poor. 8.5x11; 7 pages.

Focus and Audience

Explores all aspects of Christian ministries to the poor from a conservative, evangelical perspective. Distributed to donors, volunteers, and people interested in Voice of Calvary Ministries.

Interests and Word Lengths

- *Nonfiction:* Feature articles, interviews, essays, and personal-experience pieces that address service and inter-racial ministries to the poor. No word-length requirements.
- *Artwork:* B/W photos and illustrations.

How to Submit

Submit complete ms with cover letter and short author biography. Include SASE. Accepts photocopies, computer printouts, and fax submissions. Identify simultaneous submissions. Reports in 1 month.

Payment and Policies

One-time rights. No payment. Authors receive 1 copy of the issue.

RADAR

Margaret Williams, Editor
8121 Hamilton Avenue
Cincinnati, OH 45231
513-931-4050

AT A GLANCE:
RADAR

- Christian, Sunday School
- 70–80% freelance
- 0–5% new writers
- Weekly
- Circ: 112,000
- Pays: $.03–$.07 a word on acceptance

From the Editor:
"Keep current with where elementary-aged children are today—their interests, sports, and problems."

Best Bet: Features and stories that correlate with Sunday school lesson themes.

Avoid: Science fiction; talking animal stories.

Sample copy: Free with 6x9 SASE. Send #10 SASE for guidelines and quarterly theme list.

Profile

A Sunday school take-home paper for children. Published quarterly in weekly parts by The Standard Publishing Company. Issues are thematic. 6x7.5; folded and stapled; full-color; 12 pages.

Focus and Audience

Helps children in grades 3–6 integrate biblical teachings into their daily lives. Material is correlated with Sunday school lesson themes.

Interests and Word Lengths

- *Fiction:* Stories with believable plots and 11- or 12-year-old protagonists that involve one or more of the following: mystery, animals, sports, adventure, school, travel, and relationships with parents, friends, and others. Make prayer, church attendance, and Christian living a natural part of the story without preaching. Send for theme list. 900–1,000 words. Two-part story, 2,000 words.
- *Nonfiction:* Articles on hobbies, animals, nature, life in other lands, sports, science, etc. Should have a religious emphasis. Send for theme list. 400–500 words.
- *Poetry:* Biblical or seasonal poetry.
- *Seasonal:* Submit 1 year in advance.
- *Filler:* Bible puzzles that correlate with theme list. Cartoons that appeal to children.

How to Submit

Send for quarterly theme list. Then, send complete ms. Include SASE. Accepts photocopies and computer printouts. Identify simultaneous submissions. Reports within 1–2 months.

Payment and Policies

One-time rights. Pays on acceptance. Fiction and nonfiction, $.03–$.07 per word. Poetry, $.50 per line. Cartoons, $15–$20. Authors receive 2 copies of the issue.

Radix

Editor
2600 Dwight Way
P.O. Box 4307
Berkeley, CA 94704
510-548-5329

AT A GLANCE:

Radix

- Christian, Cultural Issues
- 2% freelance
- 10% new writers
- Quarterly
- Circ: varies
- Receives a varied number of queries and mss each month.
- No payment. Offers 2–5 contributor's copies.

From the Editor:
"We rarely publish any unsolicited material. If you do send an unsolicited submission, be sure to be familiar with the tone of the magazine."

Best Bet: Focused pieces on social and cultural issues from a Christian perspective.

Avoid: Personal pieces on inner thoughts on life; preachy or sentimental poetry.

Sample copy: $3 with postage. No guidelines.

Profile

A quarterly magazine offering social commentary from a Christian perspective. 8x11; 32 pages.

Focus and Audience

Evangelical in nature, with an emphasis on the interaction of Christian faith and culture. Most material is assigned.

Interests and Word Lengths

- *Nonfiction:* Focused articles with Christian emphasis on social, world, and cultural issues. Assigns most articles. No personal-experience pieces.
- *Departments:* Reviews of books on timely topics by authors with expertise on book theme.
- *Poetry:* Poems with a Christian worldview, but not preachy or sentimental.
- *Illustrations:* Clear line drawings related to articles.

How to Submit

Send complete ms with cover letter. Include SASE. Accepts photocopies, computer printouts, and Macintosh disks. No simultaneous submissions. Reports in 2 months.

Payment and Policies

One-time rights. No payment. Authors receive 2–5 copies of the issue.

The Reader's Review

A Bookseller's Guide to New Books in Print

Bill Monday, Review Editor
6984 McKinley Street
Sebastopol, CA 95472
707-887-7752

AT A GLANCE:

THE READER'S REVIEW

- Book Reviews, Comparative Religion
- 10% freelance
- 35 issues a year
- Circ: 3,800
- Receives 1–2 queries, 1–2 mss each month.
- Pays: $.05 per word on publication.

From the Editor:
"We want a 3–10 sentence summary of what is of value about the title to be reviewed. Be brief, terse, clever, and vivid."

Best Bet: Book reviews of new religious titles and other recent releases.

Avoid: Sectarian biases; simplistic comparisons between religions; contentious criticism.

Sample copy: Free with guidelines for a #10 SAE and $.52 postage.

Profile

A newsletter for booksellers of reviews and market analyses of recent book releases. Devotes 3–5 issues per year to religious titles. 8.5x11; folded; 8 pages.

Focus and Audience

Specializes in reviewing religious titles and other trade market books. Distributed to booksellers.

Interests and Word Lengths

- *Reviews:* Reviews of religious titles of all types: Christian, Buddhism, Hinduism, Islam, Sufism, conservative and liberal theologies and philosophies, inter-religious studies, alternative religious studies. Other review interests include women's studies, cultural criticism, ethnic studies, cookbooks, how-to books, and art and architecture, history, ecology, popular science, and biographies and autobiographies. Fiction interests include children's books, novels and short stories, postmodern fiction, European and Latin American fiction, and Americana. Up to 500 words.
- *Nonfiction:* Accepts review essays on 3–10 inter-related titles and interviews with authors. 1,000–1,500 words.
- *Artwork:* Scanable B/W line drawings.

How to Submit

Query with writing samples. Include SASE. Accepts photocopies, computer printouts, and ASCII disks. Simultaneous submissions okay. Reports in 2–4 months.

Payment and Policies

One-time and reprint rights. Pays on publication. $.05 per word; $25 per piece maximum. Authors receive 5 copies of the issue.

Reconstructionist

Editor
c/o Church Road and Greenwood Avenue
Wyncote, PA 19095
215-887-1988

AT A GLANCE:

RECONSTRUCTIONIST

- Jewish, Opinion
- Quarterly
- Circ: 10,000
- Pays: $36 per piece
  on publication.

From the Editor:
"We review the significance of Jewish civilization in all of its facets, past and present. We strive to be innovative and, when necessary, controversial."

Best Bet: Explorations of Reconstructionist ideas, practices, and institutions.

Sample copy: No information provided.

Profile

A quarterly journal of creative Jewish thought. Published by the Federation of Reconstructionist Congregations and Havurot. 8.5x11; glossy cover; 32 pages.

Focus and Audience

Serves as a medium for the continuing development of Reconstructionist ideas, practices, and institutions. Explores modes of spiritual growth for the individual Jew and for Jewish communities.

Interests and Word Lengths

- *Fiction:* Stories on topics of Jewish interest. 1,500 words. Accepts poetry.
- *Nonfiction:* Religious, political, social, and moral issues of contemporary Jewish life. 1,500 words.
- *Seasonal:* Jewish holidays.

How to Submit

Send complete ms. Include SASE. Accepts photocopies, computer printouts, and IBM-compatible disks. Simultaneous submissions okay. Report time varies.

Payment and Policies

Rights vary. Pays on publication. $36 per piece.

Reformed Worship

Dr. Emily R. Brink, Editor
2850 Kalamazoo Avenue SE
Grand Rapids, MI 49560
616-246-0752

AT A GLANCE:
REFORMED WORSHIP

- Protestant, Worship
- 75% freelance
- 67% new writers
- Quarterly
- Circ: 3,000
- Receives 1–2 queries,
  1–2 mss each month.
- Pays: $30 per printed
  page on publication.

From the Editor:
"Articles must be practical in nature and address practitioners of worship."

Best Bet: Material on planning and conducting worship.

Sample copy: $5 with 9x12 SASE. Send #10 SASE for guidelines.

Profile
Published quarterly by CRC Publications, a ministry of the Christian Reformed Church in North America. 8.5x11; glossy cover; 2-color; 48 pages.

Focus and Audience
Provides worship leaders and committees with practical assistance in planning, structuring, and conducting congregational worship in the Reformed tradition.

Interests and Word Lengths
- *Nonfiction:* Interviews; resources for pastors, organists, choir directors, and other worship planners. Word lengths vary.

How to Submit
Send complete ms with cover letter. Include SASE. Accepts photocopies, computer printouts, and MS-DOS ASCII disks, preferably WordPerfect 5.1. No simultaneous submissions. Reports in 3 months.

Payment and Policies
All rights. Pays on publication. $30 per printed page. Authors receive 1 copy of the issue.

Rejoice!

Katie Funk Wiebe, Editor
836 Amidon
Wichita, KS 67203-3112
316-269-9185

AT A GLANCE:
REJOICE!

- Mennonite, Devotionals
- 95–100% freelance
- 10–15% new writers
- Quarterly
- Circ: 17,000
- Pays: $.04–$.05 per word on acceptance.

From the Editor:
"All writing is assigned after we see samples. Be in touch with the Bible, Anabaptist doctrine, Mennonite life and spirituality, and with life as it is lived."

Best Bet: Daily devotionals for Mennonite readers.

Avoid: Controversial topics; clichéd religious language and thought; preachiness; heavy theological language.

Sample copy: Not provided. Send #10 SASE for guidelines.

Profile

A quarterly devotional publication for families and individuals. Co-published by the Mennonite Church, General Conference Mennonite Church, and Mennonite Brethren Church. All devotionals are assigned and based on Uniform Lesson series. 5x7; heavy bond cover; saddle-stitched; 100 pages.

Focus and Audience

Publishes devotional writing that inspires a greater love of God, is universal in appeal, and reflects Mennonite constituency and Anabaptist theology. Nearly all writers are members of a Mennonite congregation. Readers include individuals of all ages and families of all situations.

Interests and Word Lengths

- *Devotionals:* Daily inspirational meditations based on Uniform Lesson series. Include a short prayer that captures the context of the devotional. A good devotional will: establish a link between Scripture and daily life; focus on one idea per piece; balance theology and experience; and, above all, direct the reader toward God. 300 words.

How to Submit

Send resume and writing sample to be considered for an assignment. Include SASE. Accepts photocopies and computer printouts. No simultaneous submissions. Reports in 4–5 months.

Payment and Policies

One-time rights. Pays on acceptance. $.04–.05 per word. Authors receive 1 copy of the issue.

Religion Teacher's Journal

Gwen Costello, Editor
185 Willow Street
Mystic, CT 06355
203-536-2611

AT A GLANCE:
RELIGION TEACHER'S JOURNAL

- Catholic, Education
- 25% freelance
- 10% new writers
- 7 issues a year
- Circ: 35,000
- Receives 25 mss each month.
- Pays: $15 per ms page on publication.

From the Editor:
"Our material is for teachers, not for children. Address our readers directly and give complete directions."

Best Bet: Personal experiences of teaching religion.

Avoid: Scholarly articles; fiction and poetry.

Sample copy: $1 with 9x12 SAE and 3 first-class stamps. Send #10 SASE for guidelines.

Profile

A professional journal for Catholic lay religion teachers. Published by Twenty-Third Publications. 8.5x11; glossy cover; 40 pages.

Focus and Audience

Provides practical ideas and projects for Catholic religion classrooms. Readers are parochial-school teachers and catechists, and articles should address them directly, not students.

Interests and Word Lengths

- *Nonfiction:* Non-technical articles based on personal experiences of teaching or directing religious education classes or programs. Address religion teachers directly and provide complete directions. Up to 1,500 words.
- *Departments:* Submit to Susan Peowski, Associate Editor. Trading Post, short accounts of activities that have worked with religion classes. 100–200 words.
- *Seasonal:* Submit 3 months in advance.
- *Photos:* Prefers B/W or color slides; accepts prints.

How to Submit

Query with outline or send complete ms with 2-line biography. Include SASE. Accepts computer printouts and Macintosh disks. No simultaneous submissions. Reports in 1 month.

Payment and Policies

First North American serial rights. Pays on publication. $15 per typed, double spaced ms page. Authors receive 3 copies of the issue.

Renegade

Michael Nowicki, Editor
P.O. Box 314
Bloomfield Hills, MI 48303

AT A GLANCE:

RENEGADE

- Literature, Poetry
- 99% freelance
- 60% new writers
- Semi-annual
- Circ: 60
- Receives 20 queries, 100 mss each month.
- No payment. Offers 2 contributor's copies.

From the Editor:
"We publish the best material we can find. Have friends read your writing. Take their advice cautiously and apply what works, then submit your work."

Avoid: Pornography.

Sample copy: $3. Send #10 SASE for guidelines.

Profile

A small magazine publishing primarily fiction and poetry. 8.5x11; glossy cover; B/W; 24 pages.

Focus and Audience

Open to all types of prose and poetry. Readers like variety and prefer pieces that come close to literature.

Interests and Word Lengths

- *Fiction:* All genres of stories on any subject except pornography. 100–4,000 words.
- *Nonfiction:* All categories of writing on any subject except pornography. 100–4,000 words.
- *Poetry:* Poems of any form.
- *Artwork:* B/W illustrations no larger than 5.5x8.5.

How to Submit

Send complete ms with cover letter. Include SASE. Accepts photocopies and computer printouts. No simultaneous submissions. Reports in 3 weeks to 6 months.

Payment and Policies

Author retains rights. No payment. Authors receive 2 copies of the issue.

Renewal News

Tammy Jones, Managing Editor
115 Richardson Boulevard
P.O. Box 429
Black Mountain, NC 28711
704-669-7373

AT A GLANCE:
RENEWAL NEWS

- Charismatic, Renewal
- 5% freelance
- Quarterly
- Circ: 12,000
- Receives 1–2 mss each month.
- No payment. Offers contributor's copies.

From the Editor:
"Freelance writers interested in writing on assignment should send a letter of inquiry and samples of their work."

Best Bet: Theme-related how-to articles for Charismatic ministers.

Sample copy: Free. Send #10 SASE for theme list.

Profile

A quarterly publication that serves as a teaching tool for Charismatic ministers. Published by Presbyterian Renewal Ministries. Issues are thematic. Interested in hearing from writers who want to work on assignment. 2-color; 16 pages.

Focus and Audience

Focused solely on the power and gifts of the Holy Spirit and related Charismatic themes. Aimed toward a scholarly audience of both clergy and laity.

Interests and Word Lengths

- *Nonfiction:* Assigns most articles. Considers articles providing practical advice for Charismatic ministers and pastors. Personal testimonies on the gifts of the Holy Spirit. Must relate to issue theme. Up to 1,000 words.
- *Seasonal:* Submit 2 months in advance.
- *Poetry:* Poems of all types. Must relate to issue theme.
- *Artwork:* Seeks B/W line art. Accepts B/W and color prints.

How to Submit

To be considered for an assignment, send a letter of inquiry and writing samples. Accepts theme-related unsolicited mss with cover letter. Include SASE. Accepts photocopies and computer printouts. Simultaneous submissions okay. Reports in 2 weeks if interested.

Payment and Policies

First North American serial rights. No payment. Authors receive copies of the issue upon request.

Report from the Capital

Larry Chesser, Editor
200 Maryland Avenue NE
Washington, DC 20002
202-544-4226

AT A GLANCE:

REPORT FROM THE CAPITAL

- Baptist, Politics
- 10% freelance
- 10 issues a year
- Circ: 7,000
- Receives 2–3 queries, 2–3 mss each month.
- No payment. Offers up to 10 contributor's copies.

From the Editor:
"Articles on church-state issues must reflect a separatist view."

Sample copy: No information available.

Profile

A public affairs magazine of the Baptist Joint Committee on Public Affairs, a religious liberty agency maintained in the nation's capital by several Baptist denominations. 8.5x11; self cover; 16 pages.

Focus and Audience

Focuses on First Amendment issues, particularly church and state issues. Readers are members of nine Baptist denominations who are separatist in nature.

Interests and Word Lengths

- *Nonfiction:* Political and denominational articles on church-state issues that are separatist in nature. Word lengths vary.

How to Submit

Query with outline, resume, and writing samples, or send complete with cover letter and resume. Include SASE. Accepts photocopies, computer printouts, disks, fax submissions, and submissions via modem. Simultaneous submissions okay. Reports in 2–3 months.

Payment and Policies

Authors retain rights. No payment. Authors receive up to 10 copies of the issue.

The Reporter

Women's American ORT

Dana B. Asher, Editor
315 Park Avenue South
New York, NY 10010
212-505-7700

AT A GLANCE:

THE REPORTER

- Jewish, Women
- 80% freelance
- 40% new writers
- Quarterly
- Circ: 125,000
- Receives 15 queries, 15 mss each month.
- Pays: $400–$450 per piece on publication.

From the Editor:
"We seek clear, concise, professional writing geared toward Jewish women."

Sample copy: Not provided. Send #10 SASE for guidelines.

Profile

A membership publication of the Women's American ORT, a Jewish women's organization of rehabilitation through training. 8.5x11; glossy cover; full-color; 32 pages.

Focus and Audience

Provides intellectual, intelligent, and professional writings for ORT members and Jewish women in general.

Interests and Word Lengths

- *Fiction:* Stories and viewpoint pieces of interest to Jewish women on topics such as Jewish holiday memories, family experiences, and relationships. 500 words.
- *Nonfiction:* Features, essays, and personal experiences of interest to Jewish women on education, technology, religion, civil and social issues, and culture. Must include photos. Interviews with artists, educators, individuals in high-tech fields, musicians, and writers. 2,000 words.
- *Departments:* Voices, a humorous look at some aspect of Judaism from a woman's point-of-view. 500 words.
- *Photos:* Photo submissions required with features.

How to Submit

Query with outline and writing samples or clips, or send complete ms with cover letter. Include SASE. Accepts photocopies, computer printouts, computer disks, and fax submissions. Simultaneous submissions okay. Reports in 1 month.

Payment and Policies

Pays on publication. $400–$450 per piece. Authors receive copies of the issue.

Response

A Contemporary Jewish Review

Bennett Lovett-Groff, Editor
27 West 20th Street, Ninth Floor
New York, NY 10011
212-675-1168

AT A GLANCE:

RESPONSE

- Jewish, Literary
- 40% freelance
- 60% new writers
- Quarterly
- Circ: 1,600
- Receives 10 queries,
  15 mss each month.
- No payment. Offers
  contributor's copies.

From the Editor:

"There will be no words of divine inspiration here, only practical advice. The work of the writer should be the work of a craftsperson."

Best Bet: Jewish issues, themes, and characters of contemporary interest.

Avoid: Academic prose, shallow Holocaust pieces, and "I Remember Mama's Kitchen" stories.

Sample copy: $4 with 7x10 SAE and $1 postage. Send #10 SASE for guidelines.

Profile

A progressive Jewish journal published quarterly. Student writers receive preferential treatment. Est.: 1966. 64 pages.

Focus and Audience

Contemporary Jewish fiction, nonfiction, and poetry. All material is Jewish in theme or character, progressive, and often of contemporary interest.

Interests and Word Lengths

- *Fiction:* Novel and novella chapters and short stories with Jewish themes or characters and of contemporary interest. Up to 30 typed, double-spaced pages.
- *Nonfiction:* Articles, memoirs, polemics, essays, meditations, interviews, and journal and diary selections dealing with Israel, American Jewry, World Jewry, Jewish history, anthropology, religious thought, sociology, philosophy and other Jewish interests. Up to 30 typed, double-spaced pages.
- *Departments:* Book Reviews. Up to 2,000 words.
- *Poetry:* Any style; Jewish themes. Up to 120 lines.
- *Photos:* B/W prints up to 6x9.

How to Submit

Send complete ms with cover letter. Accepts query with outline for nonfiction. Include SASE. Accepts photocopies, computer printouts, and Macintosh disk submissions. No simultaneous submissions. Reports in 2 months.

Payment and Policies

First North American serial rights. No payment. Authors receive 5 copies of the issue.

Response

Dana E. Jones, Editor
475 Riverside Drive
New York, NY 10115
212-870-3755

AT A GLANCE:

RESPONSE

- United Methodist, Women
- 50% freelance
- 25% new writers
- 11 issues a year
- Circ: 75,000
- Pays on publication. Rates vary.

From the Editor:
"We focus on issues and concerns of women, youth, and children."

Profile
The official publication of United Methodist Women. Published by the Women's Division, General Board of Global Ministries of The United Methodist Church. 8x10.5; glossy cover; full-color; 48 pages.

Focus and Audience
Goals are to educate for mission, to interpret the purpose of United Methodist Women, and to strengthen the organization.

Interests and Word Lengths
- *Nonfiction:* Features, interviews, and essays on mission work, especially of United Methodist women, and the impact of national and world issues on women, youth, and children. 1,000 words.
- *Photos:* B/W or color prints.

How to Submit
Query with outline, resume, and writing samples or clips. Include SASE. Accepts computer printouts, disk submissions, and faxes. No simultaneous submissions.

Payment and Policies
All rights. Pays on publication. Rates are negotiable. Authors receive 5 copies of the issue.

Sample copy: Free. No guidelines.

Review for Religious

David L. Fleming, S.J., Editor
3601 Lindell Boulevard
St. Louis, MO 63108-3393
314-535-3048

Profile

A bimonthly journal for Catholic religious. Published by the Jesuits of the Missouri Province. 6x9; glossy cover; perfect bound; 160 pages.

Focus and Audience

Aims to be a forum for shared reflection on the lived experience of all who find that the Catholic Church's rich heritages of spirituality support their personal and apostolic Christian lives. Read primarily by Catholic priests and consecrated sisters and brothers.

Interests and Word Lengths

- *Nonfiction:* Articles on prayer, prayer practice, vowed life, evangelization, ministry, retreats, Christian ministries, religious formation, and spirituality. All should relate to consecrated Catholic vocations. 1,200–1,500 words.

How to Submit

Send complete ms with cover letter and resume. Include SASE. Accepts computer printouts. No simultaneous submissions. Reports in 2 months.

Payment and Policies

First North American serial rights. Pays on publication. $6 per printed page. Authors receive 4 copies of the issue.

Royal Service

Edna M. Ellison, Editor
P.O. Box 830010
Birmingham, AL 35242'
205-991-8100

AT A GLANCE:

ROYAL SERVICE

- Southern Baptist,
  Women's Missions
- 95% freelance
- 20% new writers
- Monthly
- Circ: 290,000
- Receives 20–30
  queries and varied
  number of mss each
  month.
- Pays: $.055 per word
  on publication.

From the Editor:
"Evidence of good writing can result in assignments. Verification of all facts must accompany manuscripts."

Best Bet: Articles on missions enterprises involving Southern Baptist women.

Avoid: Feminist writing; humor; mushy devotionals; poetry; and fiction.

Sample copy: Not provided. No guidelines.

Profile

A monthly missions magazine for Southern Baptist women. Published by Women's Missionary Union, Auxiliary to Southern Baptist Convention. 8.5x11; glossy cover; 48 pages.

Focus and Audience

Reports on missions enterprises involving Southern Baptists. Written and read by conservative Southern Baptist women over 35.

Interests and Word Lengths

- *Nonfiction:* Features, interviews, personal experiences, and missions action ideas. Subjects include women and family issues, Bible study, prayer, and current world and social issues. Up to 600 words.

How to Submit

Send complete ms with cover letter. Include SASE. Accepts photocopies, computer printouts and 3.5-inch IBM-compatible disk submissions. No simultaneous submissions. Reports in 12–18 months.

Payment and Policies

All rights. Pays on publication. $.055 per word. Does not provide copies of the issue.

The Sabbath Sentinel

Sydney Cleveland, Editor
172 Suncrest Drive
Greenwood, IN 46143
317-885-8122

AT A GLANCE:
THE SABBATH SENTINEL

- Sabbath-keeping Christians, Bible Study
- 75% freelance
- 25% new writers
- Monthly
- Circ: 1,000
- Receives 5 queries, 5 mss each month.
- No payment. Offers 5 contributor's copies.

From the Editor:
"*The Sabbath Sentinel* is a conservative religious magazine targeting Sabbath-keeping individuals."

Best Bet: Christ-centered theological articles and general articles dealing with Christianity.

Sample copy: Free with 9x12 SASE. Send #10 SASE for guidelines.

Profile

A religious journal published by The Bible Sabbath Association, a non-sectarian organization for Sabbath-keeping Christians. 8.5x11; self cover; 2-color; 12 pages.

Focus and Audience

Serves as a forum to promote the understanding of and sharing of items of interest to groups and individuals who keep a seventh-day (Saturday) Sabbath. Conservative in nature.

Interests and Word Lengths

- *Nonfiction:* Articles on legal, historical, theological, and human-interest issues as they relate to Sabbath-keeping churches. 500–1,000 words. Accepts filler and poetry.
- *Departments:* Quoteables, quotations for, about, or by Sabbath-keepers. To Repeat. News. Up to 500 words.
- *Photos:* B/W or color prints.

How to Submit

Submit complete ms with cover letter and clips. Include SASE. Accepts photocopies, computer printouts, and ASCII disk submissions. Simultaneous submissions okay. Reports in 1–2 months.

Payment and Policies

One-time rights. No payment. Authors receive 5 copies of the issue.

The Sacred Name Broadcaster

Elder Jacob O. Meyer, Editor
190 Frantz Road
P.O. Box C
Bethel, PA 19507
717-933-4518

Profile
A denominational magazine of the Assemblies of Yahweh. 8.5x11; 28 pages.

Focus and Audience
Devoted to the study of Sacred Scripture, both Old and New Testaments, according to the teaching of the Assemblies of Yahweh. Reaches an international audience in over 100 countries.

Interests and Word Lengths
- *Nonfiction:* Practical and scholarly Bible studies that explore the New and Old Testament in harmony. Must adhere scripturally and doctrinally with the Assemblies of Yahweh teachings. Accepts personal experiences and seasonal material. 2 typed, double-spaced pages.
- *Poetry:* Accepts poetry on occasion.

How to Submit
Query with outline, resume, and writing samples; or send complete ms with cover letter and resume. Include SASE. Prefers original mss. Accepts photocopies and computer printouts. Report time varies.

Payment and Policies
All rights. No payment. Authors receive copies of the issue.

St. Anthony Messenger

Fr. Norman Perry, O.F.M., Editor
1615 Republic Street
Cincinnati, OH 45210-1298
513-241-5615

AT A GLANCE:
ST. ANTHONY MESSENGER

- Catholic, Family
- Monthly
- Circ: 331,481
- Receives 80–85 ms each month.
- Pays: $.14 per word on acceptance.

From the Editor:
"We always look for lots of examples, anecdotes, and fresh quotes in evaluating articles from freelancers."

Best Bet: Articles that offer concrete, practical, and specific applications. Stories about people that offer hope.

Avoid: Retold Bible stories; overly sentimental or pietistic stories; articles about surviving painful diseases (overstocked with these); essays or academic-style writing.

Sample copy: $1.75. Send #10 SASE for guidelines.

Profile

A general-interest, family-oriented Catholic magazine for people living in families or the family-like situations of church and community. Published by the Franciscan Friars of St. John the Baptist Province. Member of the Catholic Press Association. 8.5x11; glossy cover; full-color; 59 pages.

Focus and Audience

Aims to help readers better understand the teaching of the Gospel and the Catholic Church, and how they apply to life and the problems faced by families, the Church, and society. Most readers are women, ages 30–70 years.

Interests and Word Lengths

- *Fiction:* Stories about family relationships that show people struggling with problems, triumphing in adversity, persevering in faith, overcoming doubt or despair, and coming to spiritual insights. Make characters and resolutions believable. 2,500–3,000 words.
- *Nonfiction:* Church and religion, including Scripture, Catholic doctrine and theology; marriage, family, and parenting; social problems and movements; inspiration and practical spirituality; psychology; and profiles of or interviews with well-known Catholics. Up to 3,000 words.
- *Seasonal:* Christmas, Easter, Lent, Mother's Day, etc. Submit 5–6 months in advance.

How to Submit

Fiction, send complete ms with social security number. Nonfiction, query first, stating subject, sources, and author qualifications. Include SASE. No simultaneous submissions. Reports in 6–8 weeks.

Payment and Policies

First North American serial rights. Pays on acceptance. $.14 per word.

St. Willibrord Journal

C.E. Harrison, D.C., Editor
Box 271751
Houston, TX 77277-1751

AT A GLANCE:
St. Willibrord Journal

- Catholic, Doctrine
- 5% freelance
- 1% new writers
- Quarterly
- Circ: 500
- Receives 1–3 queries,
  1–2 mss each month.
- No payment. Offers 1
  contributor's copy.

From the Editor:
"Our thrust is to explain
the faith of the true
Church. Read the
works of Thomas Mer-
ton and Bishop Karl
Pruter to understand
our slant."

Best Bet: Essays on
Catholic doctrine and
theology.

Avoid: Situational
ethics; writing that is
"cute".

Sample copy: $2. No
guidelines.

Profile

An independent quarterly journal of Catholic doctrine. 40 pages.

Focus and Audience

Exists to explain Catholic faith and doctrine with an
ultimate goal of spreading the Gospel of Christ. Primary audience consists of independent Catholic and Orthodox Christians, both clergy and laity. Adheres to
the strict traditional Catholic approach to daily living.

Interests and Word Lengths

- *Nonfiction:* Interviews and essays on Catholic doctrine, liturgy, theology, and Bible personalities. Up to
  1,000 words.
- *Departments:* Question Box, Q&A column of doctrinal and biblical questions.
- *Illustrations:* Original pen and ink cartoons that are
  religious in nature.

How to Submit

Send complete ms with cover letter. Include SASE. Accepts photocopies and computer printouts. No simultaneous submissions. Reports in 2 months.

Payment and Policies

One-time rights. No payment. Authors receive 1 copy
of the issue.

Saints Herald

Roger Yarrington, Editor
3225 South Noland Road
Independence, MO 64055
816-252-5010

Profile

The denominational magazine of the Reorganized Church of Jesus Christ of Latter-day Saints (RLDS). 8.5x11; glossy cover; 3-color; 40 pages.

Focus and Audience

Offers membership news for and about RLDS members and friends.

Interests and Word Lengths

- *Nonfiction:* News and features about RLDS members and congregations. Subjects include family, health, lifestyle, missionary work, personal experience, religious education, social and world issues, worship, and environment. 600–1,200 words.
- *Photos:* B/W prints, 4-color slides for covers. All photos should relate to articles.

How to Submit

Send complete ms with cover letter. Include SASE. Accepts photocopies and computer printouts. No simultaneous submissions.

Payment and Policies

All rights. No payment. Authors receive 2 copies of the issue.

Salt

Mary Lynn Hendrickson, Managing Editor
205 West Monroe Street
Chicago, IL 60606
312-236-7782

AT A GLANCE:
SALT

- Christian, Social Justice
- 50% freelance
- 5% new writers
- 10 issues per year
- Circ: 11,000
- Receives 10 queries, 10 mss each month.
- Pays: $200–$400 on acceptance.

From the Editor:
"Our readers are Christians who are interested in peace and social justice—liberals, conservatives, and moderates, but *ordinary* Christians, not activists or experts. Articles without a social-justice dimension will not be considered."

Best Bet: Lively, interesting features; fresh, original opinion pieces.

Avoid: Journalistic reporting.

Sample copy: Free. Send #10 SASE for guidelines.

Profile
A magazine for Christians who are concerned with social justice. Biblically based on the Gospels—the Beatitudes and the Corporal Works of Mercy; spiritually based on the need for personal and communal prayer. Est.: 1870. 8.5x11; 2-color; 32 pages.

Focus and Audience
Serves as a catalyst to help individuals respond to opportunities for justice in their daily lives. Aspires to be a forum that unites people and allows groups to share ideas and social-justice strategies. Concentrates on domestic rather than worldwide issues. Readers are primarily lay people, many but not all of whom are Catholic.

Interests and Word Lengths
- *Nonfiction:* Features covering social-justice issues such as poverty, prisons, hunger, women's rights, and what Christians are doing to help. 2,000–3,500 words. First-Person Profiles of men and women incorporating social action into their daily living. Should be ordinary lay people, not social-service professionals. 1,200 words. Opinion Pieces—direct, reflective, or humorous—on an aspect of Christian faith and justice 1,000 words. Also accepts Q&A interviews on justice-related topics and articles on the spirituality of social action.
- *Artwork:* Candid B/W photos.

How to Submit
Query with outline and writing samples, or send complete ms with cover letter and clips. Include SASE. Accepts photocopies. Reports in 1–2 months.

Payment and Policies
First North American serial rights. Pays on acceptance. Features, $400 and up. First -Person Profiles, $250 and up. Opinion Pieces, $200. Offers a kill fee. Authors receive 5 copies of the issue.

SCP Journal

Tal Brooke, President
2606 Dwight Way
Berkeley, CA 94704
510-540-0300

AT A GLANCE:
SCP JOURNAL

- Christian, Apologetics
- 20–60% freelance
- Quarterly
- Circ: 18,000
- Receives varied number of queries each month.
- Pays on publication. Rates vary.

From the Editor:
"Most of the material we publish is generated internally. We do use the work of outside authors on occasion. Most, however, are known to us by reputation or personal contact. Most have been published and have advanced degrees from top-ranked universities."

Best Bet: Christian alternatives to new spiritual trends.

Avoid: Fiction.

Sample copy: $5. Send #10 SASE for guidelines.

Profile

A quarterly journal of comment on new religious and spiritual trends. Published by Spiritual Counterfeits Project (SCP), a privately-funded association that interprets social, cultural, and spiritual trends from a biblical viewpoint. Member of the Evangelical Press Association. 8.5x11; glossy cover; 55 pages.

Focus and Audience

Devoted to analyzing and discerning the inside workings of various spiritual and cultural trends and offering convincing Christian apologetics. Aims high intellectually and stylistically to reach an audience of demanding non-Christians as well as interested Christians.

Interests and Word Lengths

- *Nonfiction:* In-depth, esoteric analysis, critical review, and Christian answers to spiritual and cultural movements and phenomena such as deep ecology, witchcraft, UFOs, visualization, parapsychology, cults, spiritism, new age, and inner healing. No word-length restrictions.
- *Photos:* Only those germaine to the article.

How to Submit

Query by phone before proceeding. Does not respond to unsolicited ms or queries by mail. If assignment is offered, may submit photocopies, computer printouts, or IBM or Macintosh disks. Simultaneous submissions okay.

Payment and Policies

Rights are negotiable. Pays on publication. Rates negotiated by phone. Authors receive copies of issue.

Se La Vie Writer's Journal

Rosalie Avara, Editor
P.O. Box 371371
El Paso, TX 79937

Profile

A quarterly publication showcasing the work of new writers and artists. 5.5x8; photocopied; stapled; 64–84 pages.

Focus and Audience

Dedicated to encouraging novice writers, poets, and artists by giving them a chance to publish their work. Sponsors monthly, quarterly, and thematic writing contests; entry fee required. All works are judged on originality, clarity of thought, and ability to evoke emotional response.

Interests and Word Lengths

- *Quarterly Contest:* All entries should reflect a life theme. Winning poems, essays, and short stories will be published. Fiction, short stories on any subject in good taste with a surprise ending. 500 words. Essays, should relate to writing. 500 words. Poetry, on any subject and in any style. Up to 30 lines. See guidelines for deadlines.
- *Monthly Contest:* Poetry only of any subject or style. Up to 16 lines. Deadlines are the last day of each month.
- *Special Theme Contest:* Poetry only on specified topics. Up to 16 lines. See guidelines for themes. Past themes include Vacation America and Back to School.

How to Submit

Send complete ms with entry fee. Poems, $3 each. Essays and stories, $4 each. Include SASE. Accepts photocopies and computer printouts. No simultaneous submissions. Reports in 4–6 weeks.

Payment and Policies

First North American serial rights. Offers cash prizes. Essays and stories, $10. Poems, $5–$25. Contest winners receive 1 copy of the issue.

Second Stone

Jim Bailey, Editor
Box 8340
New Orleans, LA 70182
504-899-4014

Profile

A national ecumenical news journal for gay and lesbian Christians, their friends, families, and supporters. Est.: 1988. Tabloid-size; newsprint; 20 pages.

Focus and Audience

Provides gay and lesbian Christians with news and information of gay/lesbian issues in church and society, as well as inspiring, enriching features and interviews.

Interests and Word Lengths

- *Nonfiction:* Interviews featuring men and women who are actively and personally involved in justice-seeking activities related to gay/lesbian issues in church and society. 1,000–2,000 words. First–person reflections on a timely issue or personal struggle. Up to 1,500 words. Editorial/opinion pieces, thoughts on any issue impacting gay and lesbian Christian communities. Up to 1,000 words.
- *Poetry:* Poems up to 40 lines.
- *Photos:* 5x7 B/W photo essays.

How to Submit

Send complete ms with cover letter. Include SASE. Accepts photocopies, computer printouts, and Macintosh disks. Simultaneous submissions okay. Reports in 2 months.

Payment and Policies

One-time rights. Pays on publication. Articles, $50–$100. No payment for opinion pieces. Authors receive copies of the issue upon request.

The Secret Place

Kathleen Hayes, Editor
P.O. Box 851
Valley Forge, PA 19482-0851
215-768-2240

AT A GLANCE:
THE SECRET PLACE

- Christian, Devotional
- 100% freelance
- 25% new writers
- Quarterly
- Circ: 120,000
- Receives 1 query,
  60–80 mss each
  month.
- Pays: $15 per piece
  on publication.

From the Editor:
"Be concise and focus on one theme. Use inclusive (nonsexist) language, and appeal to all races, ages, and cultures."

Best Bet: Original, creative, and spiritually insightful devotionals.

Avoid: Preaching; condemnation; over-used Scriptures; excessive nature, gardening, and travelling imagery.

Sample copy: Free with 6x9 SAE and $.52 postage. Send #10 SASE for guidelines.

Profile

A Christian devotional magazine published by the American Baptists and Disciples of Christ. Est.: 1943. 5x7; 64 pages.

Focus and Audience

Non-denominational in nature and designed to reach a broad audience interested in devotionals that can be used at any time of day or night. Readers are of all ages, mostly American Baptist and Disciples of Christ.

Interests and Word Lengths

- *Devotionals:* Devotionals include a suggested Scripture reading of 5–10 verses, a "Thought Today," a related original meditation of 100–200 words, and a brief concluding prayer. Suggested subjects include: urban/suburban and rural/nature experiences; outreach, mission and service; and meditations on less familiar Bible passages.
- *Poetry:* Up to 1 page.
- *Photos:* 4x6 or larger B/W and color prints.

How to Submit

Send complete devotion with cover letter. Include SASE. Accepts photocopies, computer printouts and fax submissions. No simultaneous submissions. Reports in 3–6 months.

Payment and Policies

All rights. Pays on publication. $15 per devotional. Authors receive 1 copy of the issue.

Seek

Eileen Wilmoth, Editor
8121 Hamilton Avenue
Cincinnati, OH 45231
513-931-4050

AT A GLANCE:

SEEK

- Christian, Inspirational
- 100% freelance
- 25% new writers
- Weekly
- Circ: 35,000
- Receives 25 queries, 150–200 mss each month.
- Pays: $.05 per word on acceptance.

From the Editor:
"We look for wholesome, alive, and vibrant writing."

Best Bet: Current, relevant articles that demand to be read.

Avoid: Preachiness and patronizing; poetry.

Sample copy: Free with 6x9 SAE and $.59 postage. Send #10 SASE for guidelines.

Profile

A weekly take-home paper for adults. Published by Standard Publishing. 5.5x8.5; folded; 3-color; 8 pages.

Focus and Audience

Designed to appeal to and inspire modern adults and older teens.

Interests and Word Lengths

- *Fiction:* Short stories, inspirational, devotional, personal, and human interest. 400–1,200 words.
- *Nonfiction:* Essays, personal experiences, first-person testimonies, Christian life experiences, true-to-life happenings. 400–1,200 words.
- *Photos:* 8x10 B/W glossy prints.

How to Submit

Send complete ms with cover letter. Accepts photocopies and computer printouts. No simultaneous submissions. Reports in 2–3 months.

Payment and Policies

First North American serial rights. Pays on acceptance. $.05 per word. Authors receive 5 copies of the issue.

The Senior Musician

Editor
Church Music Department, MSN 170
127 Ninth Avenue, North
Nashville, TN 37234

AT A GLANCE:
THE SENIOR MUSICIAN

• Southern Baptist, Music
• Quarterly
• 100% freelance
• Circ: 32,000
• Pays: $.055 per word on acceptance.

From the Editor:
"Be natural. Write with sincerity, conviction, and enthusiasm. Try to put warmth and feeling into what you write. Let the real 'you' come through."

Best Bet: Informational and inspirational articles and church music for senior adult choir members.

Avoid: Slang, jargon, and overly technical terms.

Sample copy: Free. Send #10 SASE for guidelines.

Profile
A quarterly magazine of choir music and choir-related articles. Published by the Sunday School Board of the Southern Baptist Convention. Uses as doctrinal guidelines the 1963 statement of The Baptist Faith and Message. 7x10.5; glossy cover; 2-color; 26 pages.

Focus and Audience
Provides music for choir directors and senior adult choirs and articles that assist and inspire senior adult choir members.

Interests and Word Lengths
• *Nonfiction:* Articles that focus on senior adults and music. Leisure reading such as testimonials, inspirational pieces, and material on personal growth and development. Music training such as note reading, hymnology quizzes, and notation puzzles. Choir projects for personal growth.
• *Music:* Selections that are easy for senior choirs to use in worship, ministry, and recreation. Lengths vary.
• *Photos:* Prefers B/W glossy prints. Accepts color prints with negatives. Photos must be captioned.

How to Submit
Send complete ms. Include SASE. Accepts typed, double spaced mss on white bond paper. No more than 25 lines per page. See guidelines for additional submissions requirements. Simultaneous submissions okay.

Payment and Policies
First North American serial rights. Pays on acceptance. $.055 per word. Authors receive 2 copies of the issue.

The Shantyman

Margaret Sharpe, Managing Editor
6981 Millcreek Drive, Unit 17
Mississauga, ON L0P 1C0
Canada
416-821-1175

AT A GLANCE:
THE SHANTYMAN

- Evangelistic, Testimonies
- 95% freelance
- 75% new writers
- Bimonthly
- Circ: 15,000
- Receives 5 queries, 20–30 mss each month.
- Pays: $25–$50 on publication.

From the Editor:
"Write clearly with a straightforward honest style. Focus on the facts."

Best Bet: Strong testimonies to God's grace and love in bringing people to faith in Jesus Christ and His continuing work in the lives of believers.

Avoid: Denominational issues, biblical doctrine, and preachiness.

Sample copy: Free with #10 SAE and 2 first-class stamps (CAN). Send #10 SAE/IRCs for guidelines.

Profile
A non-denominational evangelical paper designed to reach rural non-Christians. 8.5x11; 16 pages.

Focus and Audience
Offers strong testimonies of Christian faith to non-Christians living in remote areas of Canada and northern U.S., including miners, loggers, fishermen, Native Americans, and inmates.

Interests and Word Lengths
- *Fiction:* Short stories for children with biblical themes that portray Christian morality and God's faithfulness. 500–800 words.
- *Nonfiction:* Personal testimonies and first-person experiences that show God's faithfulness during times of trial. Testimony of salvation, conversion, and growth in faith. Biographies of faithful Christians. All designed to reach and inspire non-Christians to embrace Christian faith.
- *Poetry:* Short inspirational poems.
- *Seasonal:* Short seasonal pieces to use as filler. Up to 100 words.
- *Photos:* Accepts B/W prints that accompany articles.

How to Submit
Send complete ms with cover letter. Include SASE. U.S. authors include IRCs. Accepts photocopies, computer printouts, and 5.25-inch disks. Simultaneous submissions okay. Reports in 1 month.

Payment and Policies
One-time rights. Pays on publication. Articles and stories, $25–$50. Authors receive 3 copies of the issue.

Share

Catholic Daughters of the Americas

Editor
Mercury Publishing Services
12230 Wilkins Avenue
Rockville, MD 20852

AT A GLANCE:

SHARE

- Catholic, Women
- 10% freelance
- 5% new writers
- 3 issues a year
- Circ: 140,000
- Receives 3 queries, 1 ms each month.
- No payment. Offers 1 contributor's copy.

From the Editor:
"Catholic Daughters are interested in their own spiritual development as well as helping others in charitable activities."

Best Bet: Material emphasizing spiritual growth, sanctity of life, and family values.

Avoid: Preachy or political pieces; criticism of the Catholic Church or the Pope.

Sample copy: $1 with 9x12 SAE and $1 postage. No guidelines.

Profile

The membership magazine of the Catholic Daughters of the Americas, the nation's largest Catholic women's organization dedicated to participating in the religious, charitable, and education apostolates of the Church. 8.5x11; self cover; glossy paper; full-color; 32 pages.

Focus and Audience

Designed to enhance the spiritual growth of members and encourage service to others. Reports on Catholic Daughters members and activities. Embraces the principle of faith working through love in the promotion of justice, quality, and human rights. Supports traditional theological teachings of the Catholic Church.

Interests and Word Lengths

- *Nonfiction:* Feature articles and personal experiences that help readers develop spiritually and in prayer, become closer to God, and advocate the sanctity of life and the preservation of family values. Preference given to members of Catholic Daughters. 500–1,000 words.
- *Departments:* Prayer, original short personal meditations and prayers on God's beauty.
- *Photos:* B/W and color slides.

How to Submit

Query with outline, resume, and one writing sample. Include SASE. Accepts photocopies and computer printouts. Identify simultaneous submissions. Reports in 3 months.

Payment and Policies

First North American serial rights. No payment. Authors receive 1 copy of the issue.

Sharing
A Journal of Christian Healing

Rusty Rae, Editor
Box 1974
Snoqualmie, WA 98065
206-391-9510

AT A GLANCE:
SHARING

- Christian, Healing
- 100% freelance
- 75% new writers
- 10 issues a year
- Circ: 10,000
- Receives 5–10 queries, 10–20 ms each month.
- No payment. Offers contributors copies.

From the Editor:
"Remember that the sole focus is on healing—physically, spiritually, or emotionally."

Best Bet: First-hand accounts and witness stories of healing.

Avoid: Stories that are not Christ-centered.

Sample copy: Free. Send #10 SASE for guidelines.

Profile
An interdenominational, international Christian publication and the official journal for the Order of St. Luke the Physician. 5.5x8.5; self cover; 2-color; 32 pages.

Focus and Audience
Devoted solely to all aspects of Christian healing. Readership encompasses a wide variety of age groups and denominations.

Interests and Word Lengths
- *Fiction:* Occasionally accepts fiction related to Christian healing. 300–2,000 words.
- *Nonfiction:* Essays about the theology of the healing ministry of Jesus. First-person witness stories about those involved in healings. All must be Christ-centered. 300–2,000 words.
- *Poetry:* Accepts 2–3 poems each issue. Open to all styles.
- *Photos:* Small B/W prints.

How to Submit
Send complete ms with cover letter. Include SASE. Accepts photocopies, computer printouts, PageMaker disks, and fax submissions. Simultaneous submissions okay. Report time varies.

Payment and Policies
All rights. No payment. Authors receive copies of the issue upon request.

Shining Star

Rebecca Daniel, Editor
Box 299
Carthage, IL 62321
800-435-7234

AT A GLANCE:
SHINING STAR

- Christian, Education
- 99% freelance
- 10% new writers
- Quarterly
- Circ: 20,000
- Receives 60 queries, 10 mss each month.
- Pays: $10–$50 on publication.

From the Editor:
"Read our magazine to get a sense of what we publish."

Best Bet: Reproducible activities for use in Christian classrooms.

Avoid: Poetry.

Sample copy: $4 with 9x12 SASE. Send #10 SASE for guidelines.

Profile

A quarterly collection of classroom ideas and reproducibles for Christian educators. 8.5x11; glossy cover; 4-color; 80 pages.

Focus and Audience

Provides a variety of activities for Christian educators to use in their classrooms. Focus is on *how* to teach Scripture, not *what* to teach. Readers include teachers of Sunday school classes, church clubs, and Christian day schools.

Interests and Word Lengths

- *Fiction:* Bible-based short stories. 100–500 words. Also accepts seasonal plays.
- *Nonfiction:* Seasonal articles. 100–500 words.
- *Activities:* Bible-based and seasonal puzzles, crafts, bulletin boards, and rebuses that teach Christian truths.

How to Submit

Send complete ms with cover letter. Include SASE. Accepts photocopies, computer printouts, disks, faxes, and submissions via modem. Simultaneous submissions okay. Reports in 1–2 months.

Payment and Policies

All rights. Pays on publication. $10–$50 per piece. Authors receive 3 copies of the issue.

Shofar

Gerald H. Grayson, Managing Editor
43 Northcote Drive
Melville, NY 11747
516-643-4598

AT A GLANCE:
SHOFAR

- Jewish, Juvenile
- 95% freelance
- 75% new writers
- 8 issues a year
- Circ: 16,000
- Receives varied number of queries and mss each month.
- Pays: $.10 per word on publication.

From the Editor:
"The love of Judaism comes from the knowledge and experience of Jewish living. All material must be on a Jewish theme."

Sample copy: Free with 9x12 SAE and $.98 postage. Send #10 SASE for guidelines.

Profile

A magazine for Jewish children. 8.5x11; glossy cover; full-color; 28 pages.

Focus and Audience

Aims to increase the joys in being Jewish for 8- to 13-year-old children.

Interests and Word Lengths

- *Fiction:* Stories with a Jewish theme. 500–700 words. Accepts poetry.
- *Nonfiction:* Cultural, ethnic, lifestyle and other articles with Jewish themes. 500–700 words.
- *Seasonal:* Submit holiday theme pieces at least 4 months in advance.
- *Filler:* Puzzles, games, and cartoons.
- *Photos:* B/W and color prints.

How to Submit

Prefers complete ms with cover letter. Accepts query with outline. Include SASE. Accepts photocopies and computer printouts. Simultaneous submissions okay. Reports in 2–3 months.

Payment and Policies

First North American serial or first serial rights. Pays on publication. $.10 per word. Authors receive 5 copies of the issue.

Signs of the Times

Greg Brothers, Editor
1350 North Kings Road
Nampa, ID 83687
208-465-2577

AT A GLANCE:

SIGNS OF THE TIMES

- Seventh-day Adventist, Outreach
- 50% freelance
- 10% new writers
- Monthly
- Circ: 263,000
- Receives 50 queries, 100 mss each month.
- Pays: $.20 per word on acceptance.

From the Editor:
"Read the magazine and acquaint yourself with Seventh-day Adventist beliefs."

Best Bet: Religious articles for a non-religious public.

Avoid: Religious Right views and all Christian jargon.

Sample copy: Free with 9x12 SAE and $.87 postage. Send #10 SASE for guidelines.

Profile
A monthly magazine sponsored by the Seventh-day Adventist (SDA) Church and published by Pacific Press Publishing Association. 8.5x11; glossy cover; full-color; 32 pages.

Focus and Audience
Sponsored by the Seventh-day Adventist Church as a means of outreach to the general public.

Interests and Word Lengths
- *Nonfiction:* Send for complete guidelines. Articles on better living and lifestyles, and spirituality; testimonies; in-depth articles on doctrine; and self-help and how-to pieces.
- *Photos:* Submit to Merwin Stewart.

How to Submit
Send complete ms with cover letter. Include SASE. Accepts photocopies and disk submissions. Simultaneous submissions okay. Reports in 1 month.

Payment and Policies
First North American serial rights. Pays on acceptance. $.20 per word. Kill fee, $50–$100. Authors receive 2–3 copies of the issue.

Silver Wings

Jackson Wilcox, Editor
P.O. Box 1000
Pearblossom, CA 93553-1000
805-264-3726

AT A GLANCE:
SILVER WINGS

- Christian, Poetry
- 97% freelance
- 35% new writers
- Quarterly
- Circ: 450
- Receives 20 queries, 100 mss each month.
- No payment. Offers free subscription.

From the Editor:
"Poems should have a spiritual quality. Poets should not expect immediate publication of accepted writing. Nothing is returned without a self-addressed, stamped envelope."

Best Bet: Short poetry that is spiritual, understandable, and grammatically correct.

Avoid: Profanity, loose sex, negatives about the church and faith.

Sample copy: $2. Send #10 SASE for guidelines.

Profile

A quarterly journal of Christian poetry. 5.5x8.5; 32 pages.

Focus and Audience

Seeks poetry with spiritual qualities to lift the soul of humankind to God. Ecumenical in spirit.

Interests and Word Lengths

- *Poetry:* Inspirational and devotional poetry on the Bible, evangelism, healing, missionary work, prayer, spirituality, and worship. Open to all forms. Up to 24 lines.

How to Submit

Send complete poems, one per 8.5x11 page. Include SASE. Accepts photocopies and computer printouts. Simultaneous submissions okay. Reports in 2 months.

Payment and Policies

One-time rights. No payment. Offers free one-year subscription. Authors receive 1 copy of the issue.

Single Adult Ministries Journal

Jerry Jones, Editor
P.O. Box 60430
Colorado Springs, CO 80960
719-597-6471

AT A GLANCE:
SINGLE ADULT
MINISTRIES JOURNAL

- Christian, Leadership
- 10–20% freelance
- 5–10% new writers
- 8 issues a year
- Circ: 5,000–6,000
- Pays on publication. Rates vary.

From the Editor:
"We work with writers on assignment. Usually these people are personally involved in a singles ministry leadership position."

Sample copy: $2 with 8.5x11 SASE. No guidelines.

Profile
A transdenominational magazine for those involved in single adult ministry leadership. Published by Singles Ministry Resources. All material is assigned. 8.5x11; self cover; 24 pages.

Focus and Audience
Dedicated to providing practical helps, ideas, and encouragement to those involved in ministry with single adults. This includes single parents and divorced and widowed individuals.

Interests and Word Lengths
- *Nonfiction:* Articles on lifestyle, psychology, leadership, and religious education. How-to pieces offering practical guidance and encouragement for those involved in ministry to singles. By assignment only.

How to Submit
Send letter of introduction including involvement in single adult ministry and writing interests.

Payment and Policies
One-time rights. Pays on publication. Rates vary. Authors receive 2 copies of the issue.

Sisters Today

Sister Mary Anthony Wagner, O.S.B., Editor
St. John's Abbey
Collegeville, MN 56321
612-363-7065

AT A GLANCE:
SISTERS TODAY

- Catholic, Women
- 75% freelance
- Uses new writers
- Bimonthly
- Circ: 8,000
- Receives 10–30 queries, 10–30 mss each month.
- Pays: $5 per printed page on publication.

From the Editor:
"We invite articles and poems that elaborate on our goal and use inclusive language."

Best Bet: Serious, insightful articles, poems, or book reviews that explore the vision of women and the Church.

Avoid: Fiction; "cute" reminiscences about nuns.

Sample copy: $3.50 with 6x9 SASE. Send #10 SASE for guidelines.

Profile
A bimonthly magazine for and about Catholic religious sisters dedicated to exploring the vision of women and the Church today. Published by The Liturgical Press. 6x9; heavy bond cover; 80 pages.

Focus and Audience
Celebrates universal sisterhood by probing and proclaiming the ministry of women everywhere. Audience is primarily religious women, but includes lay men and women, librarians, and clergy.

Interests and Word Lengths
- *Nonfiction:* Serious articles and essays with a theological, spiritual, or psychological message related to prayer, Christian life, or the expanding role of women in the church. Use inclusive language. 8–10 typed, double-spaced pages.
- *Departments:* Voices of the Young, articles from young readers/writers. Assigns book reviews; send query to Sister Stefanie Weisgram.
- *Poetry:* Submit to Sister Mary Virginia Micka. Down-to-earth, compelling poems and haiku. Up to 25 lines; prefers 16–20 lines.
- *Photos:* Vertical 35-mm color transparencies of contemporary religious women for cover. Accepts B/W and color photos accompanying articles. Include captions.

How to Submit
Send complete ms with cover letter. Query for book reviews. Include SASE. Accepts computer printouts. No simultaneous submissions. Reports in 1–2 months.

Payment and Policies
First North American serial rights. Pays on publication. Articles, $5 per printed page. Poetry, $10 per poem. Cover photo, $50. Inside photos, $25 each. Authors receive 2 copies of the issue.

Skipping Stones
A Multicultural Children's Quarterly

Arun Narayan Toké, Editor
P.O. Box 3939
Eugene, OR 97403
503-342-4956

AT A GLANCE:
SKIPPING STONES

- Youth, Multicultural
- 80% freelance
- 80% new writers
- Quarterly
- Circ: 2,500
- Receives 10 queries, 25–40 mss each month.
- No payment. Offers 2 contributor's copies.

From the Editor:
"If you have an unusual background, if you're from underrepresented populations, we encourage you to submit original work that will be thought-provoking for our readers."

Best Bet: Multicultural and multi-ethnic work.

Avoid: Fiction not related to magazine's theme; poetry by adults.

Sample copy: $4 with 9x12 SAE and $.98 postage. Send #10 SASE for guidelines.

Profile

A non-profit children's magazine of multicultural and multi-ethnic writings. Issues are thematic. Upcoming themes are printed in the magazine. Most work is written by young authors. 8.5x11; recycled paper; 36 pages.

Focus and Audience

Encourages cooperation, creativity and celebration of cultural and liguistic richness of our world. Also explores the ecological, sustainable relationships between human beings and nature. Readers are 7–14 years of age.

Interests and Word Lengths

- *Fiction:* Accepts stories by 7- to14-year-old young authors. Occasionally accepts fiction from adults with unusual backgrounds or experiences. Must relate to theme. Bilingual pieces welcome. 500–700 words.
- *Nonfiction:* Multicultural, multi-ethnic articles and ecological, environmental, social, and family issues as they relate to children and teenagers. Bilingual pieces welcome. 500–700 words
- *Departments:* Include Noteworthy NEWS, Taking Action, Book Reviews, Cultural College, Rhymes and Riddles, Letters to the Editor. Prefers 50–75 words. Accepts up to 100 words.

How to Submit

Query with outline, or send complete ms with cover letter. Include SASE. Accepts photocopies, computer pintouts, and Macintosh disks. Simultaneous submissions okay. Reports in 3–5 months.

Payment and Policies

First North American serial rights. No payment. Authors receive 2 copies of the issue.

Skylark

Pamela Hunter, Editor-in-Chief
2200 169th Street
Hammond, IN 46323
219-989-2262

AT A GLANCE:
SKYLARK

- Fiction, Poetry
- 90% freelance
- 30% new writers
- Annually
- Circ: 600
- Receives some queries, 100 mss each month.
- No payment. Offers 1 contributor's copy.

From the Editor:
"We do run some religious poetry and fiction, but the religious theme should not be obtrusive. In other words, the religious theme should inform the work but not be blatant."

Avoid: Sentimentality; confessions; self-consciousness; moralizing; pornography; and science fiction.

Sample copy: $4 with 9x12 SASE. Send #10 SASE for guidelines.

Profile
A college-produced literary annual, published by Purdue University Calumet. 8.5x11; heavy bond cover; 100 pages.

Focus and Audience
Aims to be a literary showcase for poets, writers, and artists. Each issue carries a special section devoted to one theme. Readers are those interested in literary art and artistic design.

Interests and Word Lengths
- *Fiction:* Open to any subject that is treated well. Short stories, 4,500 words; short-short stories, up to 700 words; and plays of no more than ten minutes.
- *Nonfiction:* Open to any subject that is treated well. Essays, up to 3,000 words; interviews, up to 2,000 words; satire and personal experiences, up to 3,000 words.
- *Poetry:* Up to 30 lines.
- Artwork: B/W illustrations, graphics, and photographs.

How to Submit
Submissions are read from December 31 to May 31. Query with outline and resume, or send ms with resume. Include SASE. Accepts photocopies and computer printouts. Identify simultaneous submissions. Reports in 3 months.

Payment and Policies
One-time rights. No payment. Authors receive 1 copy of the issue and discount on additional copies.

Social Justice Review

Rev. John H. Miller, C.S.C., Editor
3835 Westminster Place
St. Louis, MO 63108
314-371-1653

AT A GLANCE: SOCIAL JUSTICE REVIEW

- Catholic, Social Justice
- 90% freelance
- 60% new writers
- Bimonthly
- Circ: 1,550
- Receives 15–20 mss each month.
- Pays: $.02 per word on publication.

From the Editor:
"Be concise, avoid using obtuse words, don't be ashamed to be clear. Make your paragraphs flow one from the other. And have *something to say*."

Best Bet: Social commentary from a Catholic Christian perspective.

Sample copy: Free with 9x12 SASE. Send #10 SASE for guidelines.

Profile

A bimonthly journal of Christian social commentary. Published by the Catholic Central Union. Est.: 1908. 8x11; self cover; 32 pages.

Focus and Audience

Promotes a Christian philosophy of life that supports the dignity of human beings, the sanctity of marriage and the family, the social well-being of society including its political, economic, and educational opportunities and principles. Must be compatible with the teaching of the Magisterium.

Interests and Word Lengths

- *Nonfiction:* Interests include theology, philosophy, social sciences, family, and timely current events. Material must be in accord with Papal teaching, though writers need not be Catholic. Up to 3,000 words.

How to Submit

Send complete ms with cover letter and resume. Include SASE. Accepts photocopies and computer printouts. Reports in 1 week.

Payment and Policies

One-time rights. Pays on publication. $.02 per word. Authors receive 3 copies of the issue.

Sojourners

Karen Lattea, Manuscripts Editor
2401 15th Street NW
Washington, DC 20009
202-328-8842

AT A GLANCE:
SOJOURNERS

- Christian, Social Justice
- 15–20% freelance
- 50% new writers
- 10 issues a year
- Circ: 35,000
- Receives 40 queries, 40 mss each month.
- Pays: $100–$200 on publication.

From the Editor:
"We are interested in quality fiction. Unfortunately, we don't receive enough."

Best Bet: Articles on issues of social justice and everyday Christian faith.

Avoid: Technical or academic writing.

Sample copy: Free. Send #10 SASE for guidelines.

Profile

An independent Christian magazine dealing with issues of faith, politics, and culture serving members of the ecumenical Sojourners Community. 8.5x11; glossy cover; 50 pages.

Focus and Audience

Encourages personal, social, and spiritual transformation through grass roots Gospel living. Readers are people of faith interested in being a member of an ecumenical community of contemplatives and activists, clergy, and laypeople from both mainstream and alternative Christian communities.

Interests and Word Lengths

- *Fiction:* Actively seeking quality fiction on appropriate themes. 3,000 words. Accepts poetry.
- *Nonfiction:* Feature articles on issues of everyday faith, especially situations and events that promote social transformation and confront injustices such as racism and sexism. Profiles of and interviews with individuals or groups working for social justice. Scripture studies and commentary. 3,000 words.
- *Departments:* Under Review, cultural reviews. The Times, news and analysis. 1,200 words.
- *Seasonal:* Meditations. Submit 3 months in advance.
- *Photos:* Send to Art Director. B/W or color prints or slides.

How to Submit

Query first. Include SASE. Accepts photocopies, computer printouts, and disk submissions. No simultaneous submissions. Reports in 6 weeks.

Payment and Policies

All or one-time rights. Grants reprint rights upon request. Pays on publication. 2–3 pages, $100. 4–5 pages, $150. 6 pages–up, $200. Authors receive 5 copies of the issue.

Spes Nostra—Our Hope

Antonella Di Piazza, Editor
531 East Merced Avenue
West Covina, CA 91790
818-917-0040

AT A GLANCE:

SPES NOSTRA

- Catholic, Family
- Bimonthly
- Circ: 6,000
- Pays on publication. Rates vary.

From the Editor: "We emphasize Mary's presence and role in the Church and in the lives of individuals."

Best Bet: Pieces that address real-life issues in light of Catholic doctrine and spirituality.

Avoid: Radical feminist or new age ideology; inclusive language.

Sample copy: Information not provided.

Profile

A non-profit Marian missionary magazine devoted to Catholic formation of youth and families. Published bimonthly by the Fr. Kolbe Missionaries of the Immaculata. 8.5x11; self cover; 2-color; 12 pages.

Focus and Audience

Advocates Catholic doctrine and Marian spirituality in accordance with the Church's tradition and the post-Vatican II Magisterium. Aimed at Catholic families.

Interests and Word Lengths

- *Fiction:* Short stories centering on religion and family life. Word lengths discussed upon assignment.
- *Nonfiction:* Features, interviews, and essays on current social and family issues. Word lengths discussed upon assignment.

How to Submit

Prefers queries with outline, resume, and writing samples or clips. Occasionally accepts unsolicited ms with cover letter. Include SASE. Accepts photocopies, computer printouts, and fax submissions. Reports in 2 months.

Payment and Policies

All rights. Pays on publication. Rates are negotiated on an individual basis. Authors receive copies of the issue.

Spirit

Joan Mitchell, Editor
1884 Randolph Avenue
St. Paul, MN 55105
612-690-7012

AT A GLANCE:
SPIRIT

• Catholic, Teen
• 50% freelance
• 20% new writers
• 26 issues a year
• Circ: 30,000
• Receives 2 queries,
  30 mss each month.
• Pays: $135 per piece
  on publication.

From the Editor:
"We are a Roman
Catholic publication
that does not stress the
born-again conversion
idiom."

Best Bet: Realistic fiction with believable
teenager characters
and conflicts.

Avoid: Short stories
with easy answers or
pious endings; born-
again language.

Sample copy: Free with
SASE and postage.
Send #10 SASE for
guidelines.

Profile

A story paper of realistic Gospel commentary for contemporary Roman Catholic teens. 8x11; 4 pages.

Focus and Audience

Functions as a catalyst for faith reflection and
discussion among Catholic teenagers, ages 14–18, on
the themes of the Sunday liturgy cycles and Gospel
readings.

Interests and Word Lengths

• *Fiction:* Realistic short stories relating to Sunday
  Gospel readings. Incorporate believable conflicts
  and resolutions experienced by real-life teens.
  1,000–2,000 words.
• *Nonfiction:* Interviews with and feature articles on
  contemporary persons that model Christian values
  for teenagers. 1,000–2,000 words.

How to Submit

Fiction, send complete ms with cover letter. Nonfiction, query with outline. Include SASE. Accepts computer printouts. Simultaneous submissions okay. Reports in 3 months.

Payment and Policies

All rights. Pays on publication. Articles and stories,
$135. Authors receive 5 copies of the issue.

Spiritual Life

Steven Payne, O.C.D., Editor
2131 Lincoln Road NE
Washington, DC 20002
202-832-8489

AT A GLANCE:

SPIRITUAL LIFE

- Catholic, Spirituality
- 80–90% freelance
- 25–50% new writers
- Quarterly
- Circ: 13,000
- Receives 10 queries, 20–30 mss each month.
- Pays: $10 per typed page on acceptance.

From the Editor:
"Articles should be addressed to readers interested in moving beyond the basics in their spiritual journey."

Best Bet: Special attention is given to Carmelite themes and figures.

Avoid: Fiction; poetry; sentimental pieces; and personal conversion or miracle stories.

Sample copy: $1 with 7x10 SAE and 4 first-class stamps. Send #10 SASE for guidelines.

Profile

A quarterly Catholic journal of spirituality published by the Discalced Carmelites of the Washington Province. 6x9; glossy cover; 64 pages.

Focus and Audience

Based heavily, though not entirely, on the teachings of St. John of the Cross and the Carmelite tradition. Reflects the experience of God today, and the contemporary significance of the Church's rich spiritual heritage for readers interested in moving beyond the basics.

Interests and Word Lengths

- *Nonfiction:* Serious articles, essays, and book reviews on prayer and spirituality. Special, although not exclusive, attention is given to Carmelite themes and figures. 3,000–5,000 words.

How to Submit

Send complete ms with cover letter and author biography. Include SASE. Accepts photocopies and computer printouts. Identify simultaneous submissions. Reports in 6–8 weeks.

Payment and Policies

First North American serial rights. Pays on acceptance. $10 per typed page. Authors receive 6 copies of the issue.

Sports Spectrum

Dave Branon, Managing Editor
Box 3566
Grand Rapids, MI 49501
616-954-1276

Profile

A Christian outreach magazine that evangelizes through the example of Christian sports figures. 8.5x11; 32 pages.

Focus and Audience

Designed to lead non-Christians to Christian faith by presenting and sharing the Gospel through the experiences of top Christian athletes.

Interests and Word Lengths

- *Nonfiction:* Feature articles using interview-based research featuring leading Christian athletes, coaches, and sports figures. 2,000 words.
- *Departments:* Leaderboard, examples of how Christian athletes help others and display leadership. 300–500 words. Front Row, close-up looks at the world of sports. 1,000 words.
- *Photos:* Accepts sports photos on assignment only.

How to Submit

Query with outline, resume, and clips. Include SASE. Accepts computer printouts, Macintosh Microsoft Word disks, and fax submissions. No simultaneous submissions. Reports in 1 month.

Payment and Policies

First North American serial rights. Pays on acceptance. $.13–$.15 per word. Authors receive 5 copies of issue.

Standard

Everett Leadingham, Editor
6401 The Paseo
Kansas City, MO 64131
816-333-7000

AT A GLANCE:
STANDARD

- Wesleyan-Arminian, Inspirational
- 100% freelance
- Weekly
- Circ: 165,000
- Receives 300 mss each month.
- Pays: $.02–$.035 per word on acceptance.

From the Editor:
"Keep your writing crisp and entertaining by using action verbs, avoiding the passive voice, and keeping sentences concise."

Best Bet: Fictional and true experiences that demonstrate Christianity in ordinary lives.

Avoid: Moralizing; specifically American scenarios and references.

Sample copy: Free with guidelines for a #10 SASE.

Profile
An international publication of inspirational Christian reading for adults. Member of the Evangelical Press Association. 8.5x11; 2-color; folded; stapled; 8 pages.

Focus and Audience
Seeks to present quality Christian material based on biblical truth and the Wesleyan-Arminian tradition. Read by a diverse group of adults: college through retirement age, single, married, widowed, divorced, parents, grandparents, and adult children.

Interests and Word Lengths
- *Fiction:* Short stories and other styles of fiction dealing with Christian living and moral issues. Up to 1,700 words.
- *Nonfiction:* True-experience pieces that demonstrate Christian living and address moral issues. Also accepts informational and instructional articles, devotionals, and humorous anecdotes. Interests include marriage and family relationships, single adult concerns, lessons learned through crisis, personal spiritual growth, Christian issues such as suffering and servanthood, and social issues. Up to 1,700 words.
- *Poetry:* Short poems on Christian themes.
- *Filler:* Crossword, fill-ins, seek & find, and cryptogram puzzles with Christian themes.
- *Artwork:* B/W prints and line drawings.

How to Submit
Send complete ms. Include rights offered and SASE. Accepts photocopies and computer printouts. Simultaneous submissions okay. Reports in 2–3 months.

Payment and Policies
One-time rights. Pays on acceptance. Original articles and stories, $.035 per word. Reprints, $.02 per word. Poetry, $.25 per line. Authors receive 5 copies of the issue.

The Star of Zion

Dr. Morgan W. Tann, Editor
401 East Second Street
P.O. Box 31005
Charlotte, NC 28231
704-377-4329

AT A GLANCE:

THE STAR OF ZION

- African Methodist Episcopal, News
- 10% freelance
- Weekly
- Circ: 8,000
- No payment. Offers 5 contributor's copies.

From the Editor:
"We are known as the 'Freedom Church,' therefore we support all civil rights issues."

Avoid: Profanity; vulgarisms; stereotypes.

Sample copy: Not provided. No guidelines.

Profile

The official organ of the African Methodist Episcopal Zion Church. Published weekly. Est.: 1876. Tabloid-size; newsprint; 12–16 pages.

Focus and Audience

Principally an ethnic publication that is moderate in political approach and conservative in biblical matters. Devoted to topics of interest to its membership.

Interests and Word Lengths

- *Fiction:* Short stories. Up to 600 words.
- *Nonfiction:* Articles, interviews, and personal experiences of interest to the African Methodist Episcopal Zion Church and its educational community. Topics can include health, sociology, seniors, AIDS, travel, missions, and evangelism. Up to 600 words. Accepts seasonal material.
- *Poetry:* Poetry with African-American themes.
- *Filler:* Humor and cartoons.
- *Photos:* B/W and color prints.

How to Submit

Fiction, query with writing samples or send complete ms with resume. Nonfiction, send complete ms with resume. Include SASE. Accepts photocopies. Considers fax submissions if urgent. Reports in 2 months.

Payment and Policies

No payment. Authors receive 5 copies of the issue.

StarLight

Allen W. Harrell, Editor
408 Pearson Street
Wilson, NC 27893-1850
919-237-1591

AT A GLANCE:

STARLIGHT

- Christian, Inspirational
- 80% freelance
- 30–60% new writers
- Quarterly
- Circ: 1,000
- Receives 30–100+ queries, 50+ mss each month.
- No payment. Offers 3 contributor's copies.

From the Editor:
"We want the total impact of each issue to be that Jesus is made real in the lives of writers and readers, too. Show in prose or poetry how Jesus, God, and the Holy Spirit helped you handle a problem."

Best Bet: Fresh, real, God-honoring stories, articles, and poetry.

Avoid: Telling readers what they should do; fictional characters that smoke, drink, or curse.

Sample copy: $4. Send #10 SASE for guidelines.

Profile

An inspirational Christian magazine that showcases the work of unpublished authors. 5.5x7.5; heavy bond cover; 64–70 pages.

Focus and Audience

A primary goal is to give voice to new writers who wish to lift up Jesus in their writing. All material must be strongly Christian in concept and in line with biblical principles. Readers—children and adults—are interested in the reality of living a Christian life, not in research or preaching.

Interests and Word Lengths

- *Fiction:* Stories for children or adults that are true-to-life and scripturally sound. A God-honoring message should be an integral part of the plot, not just tacked on. No word-length restrictions.
- *Nonfiction:* Testimonies, devotionals, Bible studies, prophecies, prayers, and visions and dreams that show what God has done in your life. Show how you have overcome life problems through faith. Be real, scripturally sound, and God-honoring. No word-length restrictions.
- *Poetry:* Submit 5–7 poems at a time, each on its own page. Rhyme is fine if it fits the poem, but not for its own sake.
- *Artwork:* B/W photos and line drawings.

How to Submit

Send complete ms. Include SASE. Accepts photocopies and computer printouts. No simultaneous submissions. Reports in at least 2 months.

Payment and Policies

First North American serial rights. No payment. Authors receive 3 copies of the issue plus 40% discount on additional copies.

Story Friends

Marjorie Waybill, Editor
616 Walnut Avenue
Scottdale, PA 15683
412-887-8500

AT A GLANCE:
STORY FRIENDS

- Mennonite, Children
- 40% freelance
- Weekly
- Circ: 9,500
- Receives 200–300 mss each month.
- Pays $.03–$.05 per word on acceptance.

From the Editor:
"Story characters should mirror the questions children have today. Provide answers as part of the story—a good story doesn't need a moral tacked on."

Best Bet: Fresh, clean copy and interesting story lines that speak to today's children.

Avoid: Moralistic stories; tired story lines such as children who don't have enough money to buy a parent a gift, etc.

Sample copy: Free with 9.5x12 SAE and 2 first-class stamps. Send #10 SASE for guidelines.

Profile
A story paper that reinforces Christian values for children, ages 4–9. Published monthly in weekly parts by the Mennonite Publishing House. 8x10; folded; 4-color; 4 pages.

Focus and Audience
Seeks to speak to the needs of all children, reinforce the values taught by the church family, and portray Jesus as friend and helper.

Interests and Word Lengths
- *Fiction:* Short stories that model positive ways to express love and caring, introduce children to a variety of cultures, focus on God's creation and how to care for it, and emphasize the uniqueness of each person. Characters should mirror the joys, fears, temptations, and successes experienced by children. 500–900 words.

How to Submit
Send complete ms. Include SASE. Accepts photocopies, computer printouts, and fax submissions. Simultaneous submissions okay. Reports in 1 month.

Payment and Policies
One-time rights. Pays on acceptance. $.03–$.05 per word. Authors receive 1 copy of the issue.

Story Mates

Miriam R. Shank, Editor
P.O. Box 1126
Harrisonburg, VA 22801
703-434-0768

AT A GLANCE:
STORY MATES

- Mennonite, Juvenile
- 95% freelance
- Monthly
- Circ: 5,200
- Pays: $.015–$.03 per word on acceptance.

From the Editor:
"Writers should know our publication and the Mennonite way of life. We interpret the New Testament in a way different from many other churches."

Best Bet: Stories that model Mennonite values for children.

Avoid: Fantasy and patriotic stories; characters that watch TV, wear jewelry, play organized sports or musical instruments; girls wearing slacks; stories about circuses, Santa, or the Easter Bunny.

Sample copy: Free with 6x9 SAE and $.52 postage. Send #10 SASE for guidelines and theme list.

Profile

A Sunday school take-home paper for Mennonite children. Published monthly in weekly parts. 8.5x11; folded; 40 pages.

Focus and Audience

Intended to help 4- to 8-year-old Mennonite children reverence God as Father and Creator, accept His authoritative Word, appreciate His great plan of salvation, and grow in virtues.

Interests and Word Lengths

- *Fiction:* Short stories, picture stories, and rebuses that model the virtues of obedience, honesty, unselfishness, etc. Up to 800 words.
- *Filler:* Original Bible puzzles and full-page activities.

How to Submit

Send complete ms with cover letter. Include SASE. Accepts photocopies and computer printouts. No simultaneous submissions. Reports in 2 month.

Payment and Policies

First North American serial, all, or reprint rights. Pays on acceptance. All rights, $.03 per word. First rights, $.02 per word. Reprint rights, $.015 per word. Authors receive 1 copy of the issue; more available upon request.

Straight

Carla J. Crane, Editor
8121 Hamilton Avenue
Cincinnati, OH 45231
513-931-4050

AT A GLANCE:

STRAIGHT

- Christian, Sunday School
- 66% freelance
- 10% new writers
- Weekly
- Circ: 55,000
- Receives 3–5 queries, 15–40 mss each month.
- Pays: $.03–$.07 per word on acceptance.

From the Editor:
"Get to know our publication *and* today's teens. Request our quarterly topics list."

Best Bet: Stories and articles dealing with contemporary issues facing teens from a Christian point of view.

Avoid: Historical fiction; science fiction; moralizing.

Sample copy: Free with guidelines for a #10 SASE.

Profile

A take-home paper distributed through church Sunday schools and aimed at teenagers. 6x7; full-color; folded; 12 pages.

Focus and Audience

Deals with contemporary issues using biblical principles and concentrating on the positive changes that result from being Christian. Readers are 13- to 19-year-old Christian teenagers.

Interests and Word Lengths

- *Fiction:* Humorous and real-life fiction. Request quarterly topics list. 1,100–1,500 words.
- *Nonfiction:* Features, interviews, and personal experiences. Examples of what real teens or youth groups are currently doing. 900–1,500 words.
- *Photos:* B/W and color photos. Model releases required. Illustrations are assigned.

How to Submit

Send complete ms with cover letter. Include SASE. Accepts photocopies and computer printouts. Simultaneous submissions okay. Reports in 1–2 months.

Payment and Policies

First North American serial rights, or one-time rights, and reprint rights. Pays on acceptance. $.03–$.07 per word. Authors receive 5 copies of the issue.

Student Leadership

Jeffrey Yourison, Editor
P.O. Box 7895
Madison, WI 53707-7895
608-274-9001

AT A GLANCE:
STUDENT LEADERSHIP

- Christian, Youth
- 80% freelance
- 50% new writers
- 4 issues a year
- Circ: 8,000
- Receives 3–4 queries, 8–10 mss each month.
- Pays: $25–$125 on acceptance.

From the Editor:
"We welcome submissions aimed thoughtfully at our audience. Ask yourself over and over, 'Am I really in touch with this audience? Is what I'm saying worth reading? If not, how can I make it so?'"

Best Bet: Lively writing on leadership, personal spiritual growth, and ideas for leaders.

Avoid: Legalisms. Articles aimed at the general college student, rather than leaders.

Sample copy: $3. Send #10 SASE for guidelines.

Profile
A training tool for Christian college students who lead campus fellowship groups. Published by the Campus Ministries Division of InterVarsity Christian Fellowship. 8x11; glossy cover; 4-color; 32 pages.

Focus and Audience
Aims to motivate leaders of large and small Christian campus groups and those who plan and coordinate outreach events. Audience is largely InterVarsity Christian Fellowship leaders.

Interests and Word Lengths
- *Fiction:* Short stories, parables, drama, and humor about campus life; leading today's hurting students; home life; commuter-student issues; and biblical characters. 800–1,700 words.
- *Nonfiction:* Features, interviews, issue analysis, personal experiences, surveys/overviews. Includes large-group leadership, small-group Bible studies, caring for people, one-to-one discipling, evangelism, choosing new leaders, biblical models. 800–1,700 words.
- *Departments:* Student Leadership Network, ideas and news. Chapter Strategy, how-tos. Leader to Leader, opinion pieces. Under Review, book and video reviews. 100–800 words.
- *Poetry:* Short, quality poems, usually free verse.
- *Photos:* Student and campus photos of any type.

How to Submit
Query with outline and writing samples, or send complete ms with cover letter. Include SASE. Accepts photocopies, computer printouts, and ASCII or WordPerfect disks. Reports in 1–3 months.

Payment and Policies
First North American serial rights or one-time rights. Occasionally requests reprint rights. Pays on acceptance. $25–$125. Kill fee negotiable. Authors receive 2 copies.

Sunday Digest

Christine Dallman, Editor
850 North Grove Avenue
Elgin, IL 60120

AT A GLANCE:

SUNDAY DIGEST

- Christian, Sunday School
- 70% freelance
- Weekly
- Circ: 100,000
- Receives 200 mss each month.
- Pays on acceptance. Rates vary.

From the Editor:
"Know that being able to write is a gift from God, whether or not your work is published. May God bless your writing and your ministry through it."

Best Bet: Concrete, positive articles and poems that inspire, encourage, and motivate.

Avoid: Issues that may be areas of differing opinion among Christian denominations.

Sample copy: Free with 6x9 SAE and 2 first-class stamps. Send #10 SASE for guidelines and theme list.

Profile

A non-denominational take home paper for Christian adults, often in Sunday school classes. Published quarterly in weekly parts by David C. Cook Publishing Co. 5.5x8.5; full-color; folded; 8 pages.

Focus and Audience

Approaches readers from a positive Christian perspective, aiming to inform, inspire, encourage, and motivate without preaching. Typical readers are 30- to 55-year-old married women with high school educations.

Interests and Word Lengths

- *Fiction:* Send for theme list. Inspiring short stories with Christian emphasis. Up to 1,600 words.
- *Nonfiction:* Send for theme list. Personal experience pieces that encourage and offer subtle suggestions for practical application. How-to articles on timely topics pertinent to Christian faith. Features about Christians in ministry. Topics include prayer, marriage, family, spiritual gifts, parenting, and evangelism. Accepts interviews. Articles can be 300–400 words, 1,000–1,200 words, or 1,400–1,600 words.
- *Seasonal:* Fresh, original approaches to old but timeless themes. Submit 15 months in advance.
- *Poetry:* Up to 20 lines.
- *Filler:* Anecdotes, 400–500 words.

How to Submit

Send complete ms with cover letter. State the rights offered. Accepts reprints; state where the piece was published previously. Include SASE. Accepts photocopies and computer printouts. No simultaneous submissions. Reports in 2 months.

Payment and Policies

Pays on acceptance. $80–$220 for first North American serial rights. $50–$120 for reprint rights. Authors receive 1 copy of the issue.

Sunstone

Elbert Peck, Editor
331 Rio Grande Street, Suite 206
Salt Lake City, UT 84101
801-355-5926

AT A GLANCE:

SUNSTONE

- Mormon, Theology
- 80% freelance
- 5% new writers
- 6 issues a year
- Circ: 10,000
- Receives 20 queries, 25 mss each month.
- No payment. Offers 5 contributor's copies.

From the Editor:
"Most articles deal with Mormon issues, however, we would like to feature more interviews and interfaith pieces."

Best Bet: Mormon history and theology and comparative-religion pieces.

Avoid: Articles that are entirely about another religion, without comparative features or general applicability.

Sample copy: $5. Send #10 SASE for guidelines.

Profile

An intellectual religious magazine for Mormons. Published by the Sunstone Foundation, a non-profit corporation with no official connection to The Church of Jesus Christ of Latter-day Saints. 8.5x11; glossy cover; 64 pages.

Focus and Audience

Explores the history, theology, and contemporary issues relevant to Mormonism and general Christianity. Readers are college-educated generalists.

Interests and Word Lengths

- *Fiction:* Sponsors the D.K. Brown Contest. Deadline is June 1st. Short stories, 6,000 words. Short-short stories, 1,000 words. Open to all subjects, but stories must in some general way deal with a religious worldview.
- *Nonfiction:* Interviews, personal essays, and scholarly pieces on Mormon and general Christian history and theology. Interested specifically in comparative religion pieces. Also accepts news stories. 5,000 words.
- *Departments:* Turning the Time Over to . . ., guest commentary. Mormons and their Neighbors; Voice from Abroad. 2,000 words.
- *Poetry:* Poems and limericks that deal with religious values in some general way.
- *Artwork:* Religious cartoons.

How to Submit

Submit stories for annual fiction contest by June 1st of each year. Query with outline, resume, and writing samples for nonfiction. Include SASE. Accepts photocopies, computer printouts, and IBM WordPerfect disks. No simultaneous submissions. Reports in 2 months.

Payment and Policies

One-time rights. No payment for articles. Fiction contest winners receive cash prizes. Cartoons, $25. Authors receive 5 copies of the issue.

Take Five

Tammy Bicket, Youth Editor
1445 Boonville
Springfield, MO 65802-1894
417-862-2781

AT A GLANCE:
TAKE FIVE

- Assemblies of God, Devotionals
- 80% freelance
- 33% new writers
- Quarterly
- Circ: 30,000
- Receives 5 queries, 3 mss each month.
- Pays: $15 per piece on acceptance.

From the Editor:
"To be considered for assignments, send a resume to the youth editor and express interest. A sample assignment will be sent and your work will be evaluated. We seek Assemblies of God writers who can communicate biblical truth on a practical level for teens."

Avoid: Anything that contradicts Assemblies of God beliefs and practices.

Sample copy: Free with 5x7 SAE and 3 first-class stamps. Send #10 SASE for guidelines.

Profile
A daily devotional guide for teenagers in grades 7–12. Produced by the Assemblies of God. All material is assigned. 4x5.5; 112 pages.

Focus and Audience
Seeks to be an easy-to-read youth-oriented devotional guide that represents the beliefs and practices of the Assemblies of God and other pentecostal and charismatic churches. Communicates biblical beliefs on a practical level for teenagers. Most writers are Assemblies of God members.

Interests and Word Lengths
- *Devotionals:* Assigns devotions to interested Assemblies of God writers. Query for sample assignment.
- *Poetry:* Poems of interest to Christian teens. Publishes several in each issue.
- *Photos:* Submit to Karen Messner, Sunday School Curriculum and Literature. 35mm color slides and glossy B/W prints of teenagers, preferably of various ethnic backgrounds.

How to Submit
Query with resume for an assignment. To be considered, writers must submit a non-paid sample assignment. Include SASE. Reports in 3 months.

Payment and Policies
All rights. Pays on acceptance. $15 per assigned devotion. No payment for sample devotion. Authors receive 2 copies of the issue.

TAL (Torah Art and Literature)

Y. David Shulman, Editor
318 Avenue F
Brooklyn, NY 11218
718-871-1105

AT A GLANCE:

TAL

- Jewish, Literary
- 50% freelance
- 30% new writers
- Issued irregularly
- Circ: 500
- No payment. Offers 6 contributor's copies.

From the Editor:
"Cut away the schmaltz and submit the crispest visions of the heart and the most luminous insights of the mind."

Best Bet: Torah-related literature.

Sample copy: $1 with 8x11 SAE and $1 postage. Send #10 SASE for guidelines.

Profile
A journal of Torah-based literature. 7x8.5.

Focus and Audience
Seeks to presents high-level literary material that expresses Torah-related experiences for people involved with the Torah.

Interests and Word Lengths
- *Literature:* Accepts insightful, high-quality fiction, essays, translations, and folktales on Torah-related spiritual themes. Up to 3,000 words. Accepts poetry.

How to Submit
Send complete ms with cover letter. Include SASE. Accepts photocopies, computer printouts, and WordPerfect disks. Simultaneous submissions okay. Reports in 1 month.

Payment and Policies
First North American serial rights. No payment. Authors receive 6 copies of the issue.

Teachers in Focus

Charles W. Johnson, Editor
420 North Cascade Avenue
Colorado Springs, CO 80903
719-531-3400

AT A GLANCE:

TEACHERS IN FOCUS

- Judeo-Christian, Education
- 75% freelance
- 50% new writers
- Monthly
- Circ: 45,000
- Receives 10–15 queries, 10 mss each month.
- Pays: $150–$200 per piece on acceptance.

From the Editor:
"We want to communicate traditional moral values with a minimum of religious jargon."

Best Bet: Practical articles using appropriate humor and classroom anecdotes.

Avoid: Teacher bashing. Academic and stuffy articles.

Sample copy: Free with 10x13 SAE and $1 postage. Send #10 SASE for guidelines.

Profile

A monthly magazine that helps teachers provide Judeo-Christian values-based education to students in grades K–12. Prefers to work with writers with professional experience in education. 8x11; glossy cover; full-color; 16 pages.

Focus and Audience

Articles designed to encourage and support public and private educators who are maintaining and modeling traditional Judeo-Christian values.

Interests and Word Lengths

- *Nonfiction*: Articles in the following areas of interest: classroom success stories, discipline and control, contemporary students and their families, special needs students, social issues and schools, professional relationships and organizations, child development, holidays, and curriculum. 800–1,500 words.

How to Submit

Query with outline and writing samples. Include SASE. Accepts photocopies, computer printouts, and fax submissions. No simultaneous submissions. Reports in 1–2 months.

Payment and Policies

One-time rights. Pays on acceptance. $150–$200 per piece. Authors receive 5 copies of the issue.

Teachers Interaction

Jane Haas, Editor
3558 South Jefferson Avenue
St. Louis, MO 63118-3968
314-268-1000

AT A GLANCE:

TEACHERS INTERAC-TION

- Lutheran, Teachers
- 10% freelance
- 10% new writers
- Quarterly
- Circ: 20,000
- Receives 10 queries, 25 mss each month.
- Pays: $10–$75 per printed page on publication.

From the Editor:
"Our writers' theology must be approved by doctrinal reviewers of the Lutheran Church—Missouri Synod."

Best Bet: Practical how-to articles that keep the needs of volunteer church school teachers first in mind.

Avoid: Moralizing.

Sample copy: $1. Send #10 SASE for guidelines.

Profile

A magazine for Lutheran volunteer church teachers. Published quarterly by Concordia Publishing House for the Lutheran Church—Missouri Synod. Correlates with Concordia's Sunday school curriculum. 8.5x11; glossy cover; 32 pages.

Focus and Audience

Offers techniques, methods, and background for teaching the Lutheran faith to children, youth, and adults. Readers are Sunday school, vacation Bible school, and weekday volunteer church teachers.

Interests and Word Lengths

- *Fiction:* Short stories that weave practical advice or inspiration for volunteer teachers into them. 750–1,200 words. Accepts Bible verse poetry and Bible stories.
- *Nonfiction:* How-to articles helpful to volunteer church school teachers. Interests include theology, education, teaching methods, psychology, evangelism, doctrine, and inspiration. Personal-experience pieces of volunteer church teachers in the classroom. All must reflect the Lutheran Church—Missouri Synod theology. Accepts seasonal material. 750–1,200 words.
- *Filler:* Puzzles.
- *Photos:* 8.5x11 B/W glossy prints.

How to Submit

Send complete ms with cover letter. Include SASE. Accepts computer printouts. No simultaneous submissions. Reports in 3 months.

Payment and Policies

All rights. Pays on publication. $10–$75 depending on quality and use. Authors receive 1 copy of the issue.

Teen Power

Amy J. Cox, Editor
1825 College Avenue
Wheaton, IL 60187
708-668-6000

AT A GLANCE:
TEEN POWER

- Evangelical, Teens
- 90% freelance
- 25% new writers
- Weekly
- Circ: not available
- Receives 75–120 mss each month.
- Pays: $.06–$.10 per word on acceptance.

From the Editor:
"Read an issue to see what kind of stories and articles we're looking for. Observe young teens. Know what issues they are dealing with; how they talk and react."

Best Bet: Stories and articles with a clear, conservative, evangelical Christian slant.

Avoid: Preaching, moralizing, sermonizing, or talking down to readers.

Sample copy: Free with SASE. Send #10 SASE for guidelines.

Profile

An evangelical Christian Sunday school take-home paper for young teens, ages 11–15. 5x8.5; 3-color; newsprint; folded; 8 pages.

Focus and Audience

Designed to show how biblical principles for Christian living can be applied to everyday life. Each feature has a "take away value" teens can apply to their lives.

Interests and Word Lengths

- *Fiction:* True-to-life stores about everyday issues such as standing up for Christ, friendship, family, daily devotions, honesty, and prayer. Humor works well with this age group. Up to 1,200 words.
- *Nonfiction:* Personal experiences, interviews, profiles, self-help, and how-to's. True stories by and about teens. Also accepts short articles on prayer, friendship, family, school, and other topics of interest to young teens. Up to 800 words.
- *Seasonal:* Submit 6 months in advance. Avoid specific American holidays as readership extends outside the U.S.
- *Photos:* Submit B/W prints to Rod Karmenzind.

How to Submit

Send complete ms with cover letter. Include SASE. Accepts photocopies and computer printouts. No simultaneous submissions. Reports in 2–3 months.

Payment and Policies

One-time rights. Pays $.06–$.10 per word on acceptance. Authors receive 4 copies of the issue.

Teens Today

Carol Gritton, Editor
6401 The Paseo
Kansas City, MO 64131
816-333-7000

AT A GLANCE:

TEENS TODAY

- Church of the Nazarene, Teens
- 75% freelance
- 25% new writers
- Weekly
- Circ: 50,000
- Receives 200 mss each month
- Pays: $.03–$.035 per word on acceptance.

From the Editor:
"Our greatest need is fiction showing teens living out their faith in the everyday world. Emphasize grace."

Best Bet: Stories written from the perspective of a 16- to 18-year-old boy.

Avoid: Drawn out points; preachiness and poor language. Stories featuring dancing.

Sample copy: Free with guidelines for a #10 SASE.

Profile

A Sunday school take-home paper of leisure reading for teens. Published weekly by the Department of Youth of the Church of the Nazarene. 8.5x11; folded; 2-color; 8 pages.

Focus and Audience

Models Christian living for junior high school and senior high school students.

Interests and Word Lengths

- *Fiction:* Stories showing teens living out their faith in the everyday world. 1,200–1,500 words.
- *Nonfiction:* Real-life stories showing teens living out faith, struggling with faith, and triumphing through faith. 1,200–1,500 words.
- *Photos:* Submit to Rosemary Postel. 8x10 B/W prints. Must feature junior or senior high youth.

How to Submit

Send complete ms with cover letter. Include SASE. For future assignments, send resume with true story sample. Accepts photocopies and computer printouts. Simultaneous submissions okay. Reports in 6 weeks.

Payment and Policies

First North American serial rights. Pays on acceptance. Original material, $.035 per word. Reprints, $.03 per word. Authors receive 3 copies of the issue.

Tickled By Thunder

Larry Linder, Editor
7385-129th Street
Surray, BC V3W 7B8
Canada
604-591-6095

AT A GLANCE:
TICKLED BY THUNDER

- Writers, Fiction
- 90% freelance
- 75% new writers
- 3–4 issues a year
- Circ: 100–150
- Receives 1 query, 20–40 mss each month.
- No payment. Offers 1 contributor's copy.

From the Editor:
"We are not a religious publication, but are willing to publish religious material if it is *good*. We want to help writers get published—in our pages or somewhere else."

Best Bet: Creative, organized writing that is in touch with the magazine.

Avoid: Pornography, graphic violence, and mushiness.

Sample copy: $2 (CAN) with 9x12 SASE/IRC. Send #10 SASE/IRC for guidelines.

Profile
A writers roundtable and news publication. 5.5x8.5; self cover; folded; 16 pages.

Focus and Audience
Aims to be a forum for writers; to publish their work or help them get their work published elsewhere.

Interests and Word Lengths
- *Fiction:* Open to any subject, especially fantasy stories and stories about writers and writing. 2,000 words. Accepts poetry.
- *Nonfiction:* Personal experience, self-help, and how-to articles about writing only. 2,000 words.
- *Departments:* Markets, market listings and information for writers.

How to Submit
Send complete ms with cover letter. Include SASE. U.S. authors include IRCs. Accepts photocopies, computer printouts, Macintosh disks, and fax submissions. Simultaneous submissions okay. Reports in 1–4 months.

Payment and Policies
One-time rights. No payment. Authors receive 1 copy of the issue.

Time of Singing

Charles Waugaman, Editor
P.O. Box 211
Cambridge Springs, PA 16403
814-382-5911

AT A GLANCE:

TIME OF SINGING

- Christian, Poetry
- 95% freelance
- 3 issues a year
- Circ: 300
- Receives few mss each month.
- No payment. Offers 1 contributor's copy.

From the Editor:
"I do not feel it is fair to print a poem and let it die. I publish special editions filled with reissued poetry because I feel these poems should live on."

Best Bet: Devotional and inspirational Christian poetry.

Sample copy: $4. Send #10 SASE for guidelines.

Profile

A collection of Christian poetry. Magazine is church-published, non-denominational, and thematic. 40 pages.

Focus and Audience

Distinctly Christian but non-sectarian, it is dedicated to showcasing the work of new and young Christian poets and reissuing previously published poems to give them new life. Willing to work with unpolished writers who show promise.

Interests and Word Lengths

- *Poetry:* Publishes 40–50 poems per issue, originals and reprints. Biblical, devotional, inspirational, and seasonal poetry and poems on nature. Accepts rhymed poems, free verse, and quality haiku. Sponsors a poetry contest: Contact editor for deadlines and themes. Prefers shorter poems.

How to Submit

Prefers 3–5 poems per submission. Include SASE. Accepts photocopies, computer printouts, and legible handwritten submissions. Simultaneous submissions okay. Reports in 3 months.

Payment and Policies

First North American serial and reprint rights. No payment. Authors receive 1 copy of the issue; additional copies available at reduced rates.

Today's Better Life

Laura Barker, Managing Editor
5301 Wisconsin Avenue NW
Suite 620
Washington, DC 20015
202-364-8000

AT A GLANCE:
TODAY'S BETTER LIFE

- Christian, Lifestyle
- 5–10% freelance
- 5% new writers
- Quarterly
- Circ: 100,000
- Receives 7–10 queries, 10–15 mss each month.
- Pays: $.10 per word on publication.

From the Editor:
"All articles must reflect conservative theology and should not conflict with traditional Christian values."

Best Bet: Positive articles on faith, health, relationships, and finances.

Avoid: Any topic that conflicts with traditional Christian values.

Sample copy: No sample. Send #10 SASE for guidelines.

Profile
A Christian lifestyle magazine published quarterly by Thomas Nelson Inc. 8.5x11; glossy cover; full-color; 112 pages.

Focus and Audience
Dedicated to helping readers attain health in every area of their lives—spiritual, physical, and emotional. Geared toward Christian adults concerned with faith, family, and fitness. Articles reflect a conservative theology.

Interests and Word Lengths
- *Nonfiction:* Features on fitness, finance, faith, family, health, and relationships. Personal-experience articles that teach a valuable lesson in spiritual and personal growth. 1,500–2,500 words.
- *Photos:* Color slides, transparencies, or prints to accompany an article.

How to Submit
Query with outline, resume, and writing samples. Include SASE. Accepts photocopies, computer printouts, and fax submissions. No simultaneous submissions. Reports in 1–2 months.

Payment and Policies
First North American serial or all rights. Pays on publication. $.10 a word on average. Authors receive 1 copy of the issue.

Today's Catholic Teacher

Stephen Brittan, Editor
330 Progress Road
Dayton, OH 45449
513-847-5900

AT A GLANCE:
TODAY'S CATHOLIC TEACHER

- Catholic, Educators
- 60% freelance
- 20–25% new writers
- 8 issues a year
- Circ: 60,000
- Receives 60 queries, 45–50 mss each month.
- Pays: $80–$200 on publication.

From the Editor:
"We want practical materials and articles written in an informal style."

Best Bet: Classroom-ready activity pages and teaching supplements for grades K–12 and especially grades 3–8.

Avoid: College religion term papers; educational jargon.

Sample copy: $3. Send #10 SASE for guidelines.

Profile
An internationally circulated publication directed toward educators and all others concerned with nonpublic education in general and Catholic education in particular. 8.5x11; glossy cover; full-color; 55 pages.

Focus and Audience
Focuses on any topic of practical help, concern, or genuine interest to the Catholic educator. Readers are primarily classroom teachers, both religious and lay, but caters to all those concerned with nonpublic education.

Interests and Word Lengths
- *Fiction:* Short plays that teachers can use with students in the classroom. 800–2,000 words.
- *Nonfiction:* Activities, teaching materials, and lesson plans for K–12 classrooms: observations on the teaching of curricular subjects (language arts, math, science, art, etc.); new developments in curriculum; testing; computer education; faculty relationships; parent-teacher relationships; guidance; school problems; school and community needs; school boards; creative teaching; lesson plans; etc. 600–800 words, 1,000–1,200 words, or 1,200–2,000 words. Accepts some filler.
- *Photos:* B/W prints, slides, or line art.

How to Submit
Query with outline or send ms with cover letter. Include SASE. Prefers typed originals, accepts photocopies, computer printouts, Microsoft Word 5.0 for Macintosh disks, and modemed and fax submissions. Simultaneous submissions okay. Reports in 3–4 months.

Payment and Policies
First North American serial rights. Pays on publication. $80–$200 per piece. Authors receive 3–4 copies of the issue upon request.

Today's Christian Woman

Julie Talerico, Editor
465 Gundersen Drive
Carol Stream, IL 60188
708-260-6200

AT A GLANCE:

TODAY'S CHRISTIAN WOMAN

- Christian, Women's Issues
- 85% freelance
- 10% new writers
- Bimonthly
- Circ: 250,000
- Receives 150–200 queries each month.
- Pays: $.15–$.20 per word on publication.

From the Editor:
"Read at least six issues of *Today's Christian Woman* before submitting a query."

Best Bet: Anecdotal, articles for Christian women with a personal tone and universal appeal.

Avoid: Overdone subjects such as co-dependency, dysfunctional families, anorexia, and bulimia.

Sample copy: $3.50 with 9x12 SAE and 5 first-class stamps. Send #10 SASE for guidelines.

Profile

A contemporary Christian women's magazine. Published by Christianity Today, Inc. 8.5x11; glossy cover; full-color; 80 pages.

Focus and Audience

Publishes positive and practical material on issues affecting Christian women of all ages. Readers are single, married, stay-at-home moms, and career women who seek to improve their relationships with spouses, children, friends, co-workers, self, and God.

Interests and Word Lengths

- *Nonfiction:* Articles on marriage, parenting, practical spiritual life, self image, friendship, and women's issues. Should be highly anecdotal, personal in tone, universal in appeal, and from a strong Christian perspective. Quotes from Christian experts are helpful. 1,500–2,000 words.
- *Departments:* One Woman's Story, true-life dramatic personal stories of a particular life incident or event that led to a spiritual turning point.
- *Filler:* Heart-to-Heart, true humorous anecdotes about children or inspirational anecdotes from women. 50–100 words.

How to Submit

Fiction, query with outline and writing samples. Nonfiction, query with outline. Include SASE. Accepts photocopies and computer printouts. No simultaneous submissions. Reports in 1 month.

Payment and Policies

First North American serial rights. Pays on publication. Articles and filler, $.15–$.20 per word. One Woman's Story, $150. Authors receive 2 copies of the issue.

Today's Family

Valerie Hockert, Managing Editor
27 Empire Drive
St. Paul, MN 55103
612-227-4367

AT A GLANCE:

TODAY'S FAMILY

- Family
- 65% freelance
- Quarterly
- Circ: 51,000
- Receives 75 queries, 50 mss each month.
- Pays: $10–$15 on publication

From the Editor:
"Emphasize the positive. Use an anecdote or two to illustrate an idea or point, and to give the article credibility."

Best Bet: Articles that meet editorial needs as presented in issue-specific guidelines.

Avoid: Personal tales of how a family survived a crisis; emphasizing the negative.

Sample copy: $4 with 9x12 SASE. Send #10 SASE for guidelines.

Profile

A quarterly publication for contemporary families. Each issue focuses on 2–3 themes. 8.5x11; glossy cover; full-color; 44 pages.

Focus and Audience

Educational and instructional articles directed towards the family of today with traditional values—this includes the single parent, the step-parent, and the adoptive parent.

Interests and Word Lengths

- *Nonfiction:* Articles on family and school issues, activities, health, children, education, travel, parenting, family styles; and interviews. Send for issue-specific guidelines and topics. Past topics include teaching non-violence; parents involvement with education; selecting family toys; vacations with children; dealing with depression; and nutritious foods. 750–2,000 words.
- *Photos:* 4x5 or 5x7 B/W glossies or 35mm color slides.

How to Submit

Send complete ms with cover letter and one paragraph author biography listing appropriate credentials. Include SASE. Accepts photocopies and computer printouts. Simultaneous submissions okay. Reports in 1 month.

Payment and Policies

First North American serial rights. Pays on publication. $10–$15 per piece. Authors receive 1 copy of the issue.

Total Health

Editor
6001 Topanga Canyon Boulevard
Suite 300
Woodland Hills, CA 91367
818-887-6484

AT A GLANCE:
TOTAL HEALTH

- Judeo-Christian, Health
- 70% freelance
- 15–20% new writers
- Bimonthly
- Circ: 90,000
- Receives 15 queries, 24 mss each month.
- Pays: $50–$75 on publication.

From the Editor:
"We will look at articles on speculation. State availability of visuals—B/W or color—with articles."

Best Bet: How-to articles that explore total health of the body, mind, and spirit.

Avoid: Personal testimonies; fiction; poetry.

Sample copy: $1 with 9x12 SAE with $1.21 postage. Send #10 SASE for guidelines/editorial calendar.

Profile
A bimonthly magazine of wholistic health for individuals and families. Rooted in Judeo-Christian values. 8.5x11; 70 pages.

Focus and Audience
Advocates healthy lifestyles and wholeness of body, mind, and spirit based on the Judeo-Christian concept that the body is the temple of the Lord. The average reader is a 40-year-old woman, college educated, politically conservative, married with two children and conscious of her health and that of family members.

Interests and Word Lengths
- *Nonfiction:* Articles on family and individual fitness, exercise, diet, weight control, and mental and spiritual health. Past issues have explored arthritis prevention, skin care and aging, allergies and asthma, breast cancer, recipes for picnics, water exercises for fitness, guiding teen's behavior, eastern herbs, and eating disorders. 1,400 words.
- *Photos:* B/W and color photos to accompany articles.

How to Submit
Send complete ms. Include SASE. Accepts photocopies and disk submissions. Reports in 2 months.

Payment and Policies
All rights. Pays on publication. $50–$75 per piece. Authors receive 1 copy of the issue.

Touch

Carol Smith, Managing Editor
1333 Alger SE, Box 7259
Grand Rapids, MI 49510
616-241-5616

AT A GLANCE:
TOUCH

- Calvinist, Juvenile
- 75% freelance
- 10% new writers
- 10 issues a year
- Circ: 16,000
- Receives 200+ queries, 200 mss each month.
- Pays: $.025 per word on acceptance.

From the Editor:
"Articles should not be preachy, necessarily religious, or Pollyanna-like. Focus on girls and issues that relate to them."

Best Bet: Realistic stories and articles that touch girls where they are in life.

Sample copy: Free with 8.5x11 SASE. Send #10 SASE for *Update* theme list and guidelines.

Profile

Published by Calvinettes, a United Calvinist Youth girl's club emphasizing Bible study, badge work, service projects, and crafts. Issues are thematic. *Update*, a bi-annual theme list, is available upon request. 8.5x11; 2-color; stapled; 24 pages.

Focus and Audience

Its intent is to show girls how God is at work in their lives and in the world. Readers are Christian girls, ages 9–14.

Interests and Word Lengths

- *Fiction:* Thematic according to issues; send for theme list. 3–4 stories per issue. 900–1,200 words.
- *Nonfiction:* Features, essays, and personal experiences corresponding to issue theme. 400–800 words.
- *Departments:* Puzzles, games, and crafts for fun page. 20–200 words.
- *Poetry:* 2–3 short poems per issue.
- *Artwork:* B/W slides and 5x7 or 8x10 prints.

How to Submit

Send complete ms with cover letter. Include SASE. Accepts clear photocopies and computer printouts. Simultaneous submissions okay. Reports in 2 weeks. May request to hold mss up to 5 months.

Payment and Policies

First North American serial rights. Pays on acceptance. $.025 per word. $15–$20 for poems and puzzles. Authors receive 2 copies of the issue.

Touchstone

James Kushiner, Editor
3300 West Cullom Avenue
Chicago, IL 60618

AT A GLANCE:
TOUCHSTONE

- Christian, Opinion
- 25% freelance
- 10–15% new writers
- Quarterly
- Circ: 1,500
- Receives 2 mss each month.
- No payment. Offers 2–10 contributor's copies.

From the Editor:
"Our goal is to articulate for our day the faith of the historical church."

Best Bet: Conservative Christian commentary and unique insights on current social issues.

Avoid: Being schmaltzy, too trite, or too popular.

Sample copy: Free with 10x12 SAE and $1.67 postage. Send #10 SASE for guidelines.

Profile
An ecumenical Christian journal of news and opinion. 8.5x11; 44 pages.

Focus and Audience
Offers commentary on contemporary social issues from a conservative, historical Christian perspective. Puts forth the positive aspects of conservatism and the joy and confidence of orthodoxy to an ecumenical audience of clergy and lay people.

Interests and Word Lengths
- *Fiction:* Seldom publishes fiction. May consider timely and unique short stories with theological significance. Approximately 3,000 words or 30,000 characters. Accepts poetry.
- *Nonfiction:* Articles, interviews, and essays that offer historical and biblical analysis of contemporary social and church issues. Also personal-experience pieces, critiques of Christian art, and book reviews on Christian literature. Accepts seasonal material. Approximately 2,400 words or 24,000 characters.
- *Illustrations:* Humorous cartoons.

How to Submit
Query with outline, resume, writing samples, and clips; or send complete ms with cover letter and resume. Include SASE. Accepts photocopies, computer printouts, and 3.5-inch WordPerfect 5.1 disks. Simultaneous submissions okay. Reports within 3 months.

Payment and Policies
Authors retain rights. No payment. Authors receive 2–10 copies of the issue.

21st Century Christian

Billie Silvey, Associate Editor
2809 12th Avenue South
Nashville, TN 37204
615-292-4739

AT A GLANCE:

21ST CENTURY CHRISTIAN

- Christian, Inspirational
- 75% freelance
- 10% new writers
- Monthly
- Circ: 10,000
- Receives 1 query, 1 ms each month.
- No payment. Offers 5+ contributor's copies.

From the Editor:
"Focus on New Testament Christianity for contemporary readers."

Sample copy: Free. Send #10 SASE for guidelines.

Profile

A monthly digest focusing on New Testament Christianity. 5.5x8.5; glossy cover; full-color; 32 pages.

Focus and Audience

Strives to make practical application of New Testament Christianity for today's reader.

Interests and Word Lengths

- *Nonfiction:* Submit to Billie Silvey, 4710 West 152nd Street, Lawndale, CA 90260. Religious and inspirational articles on practical Christian living and spirituality. No word-length restrictions. Accepts filler.
- *Poetry:* Inspirational poems.
- *Photos:* Submit to Billie Silvey, 4710 West 152nd Street, Lawndale, CA 90260. B/W and color photos.

How to Submit

Send complete ms with cover letter. Include SASE. Accepts photocopies, computer printouts, and fax submissions. No simultaneous submissions.

Payment and Policies

One-time rights. No payment. Authors receive 5+ copies of the issue.

Twin Cities Christian

Doug Trouten, Editor
1619 Portland Avenue South
Minneapolis, MN 55404
612-339-9579

AT A GLANCE: TWIN CITIES CHRISTIAN

- Christian, Regional
- 10% freelance
- 5% new writers
- Biweekly
- Circ: 7,500
- Receives 8 queries, 6 mss each month.
- Pays: $.05 per word after publication.

From the Editor:
"Examine the publication before submitting articles. A strong local hook is required, so it is unlikely that persons outside Minnesota will be able to publish with us."

Best Bet: Christian news features with a Twin Cities angle.

Avoid: General-interest material.

Sample copy: $1 with $1 postage. Send #10 SASE for guidelines.

Profile

A community newspaper for Christians in the Minneapolis and St. Paul-area. Tabloid-size; 36 pages.

Focus and Audience

Looks for material with a Twin Cities angle and strong news appeal with a clear tie to the Christian community. Audience is varied, but tends toward conservative, evangelical readers.

Interests and Word Lengths

- *Nonfiction:* Feature articles on local personalities, ministries, real-life dramas, and local news that is Christian and timely. Accepts personal experiences and opinion pieces. Topics of interest include family issues, politics, and religious education. 500–1,000 words.
- *Photos:* Prefers B/W prints.

How to Submit

Query with outline and clips. No unsolicited mss. Include SASE. Accepts photocopies, computer printouts, IBM-compatible ASCII disk files, faxes, and submissions via modem. Reports within 3 months.

Payment and Policies

One-time rights. Pays after publication. Rates are negotiable depending on articles; generally pays $.05 per word. Authors receive 4 copies of the issue.

The United Methodist Christian Advocate

Charles Rountree, Editor
898 Arkadelphia Road
Birmingham, AL 35204-3498
205-226-7971

AT A GLANCE:
THE UNITED METHODIST CHRISTIAN ADVOCATE

- United Methodist, Regional
- 5% freelance
- 2% new writers
- Biweekly
- Circ: 7,000
- Receives 15 queries, 5 mss each month.
- No payment. Offers 1–2 contributor's copies.

From the Editor:
"We publish church-related news and feature articles of Christian interest."

Avoid: Being anti-religious.

Sample copy: Not provided. No guidelines.

Profile

A biweekly regional newspaper for members of the North Alabama and West Florida Conferences of the United Methodist Church. Tabloid-size; newsprint; 12–16 pages.

Focus and Audience

Serves as a vehicle for church news—local, state, national, and international. Readers are United Methodist clergy and lay people in Alabama and West Florida.

Interests and Word Lengths

- *Fiction:* Short stories that are uplifting, creative, and motivating. No word-length restrictions.
- *Nonfiction:* Interviews and profiles, personal-experience pieces, and features on Christian living, missionary outreach, religious education, and topics of interest to United Methodist members. Prefers short pieces of no more than 2–3 typed, double-spaced ms pages.
- *Poetry:* Occasionally accepts poetry.
- *Photos:* Prefers B/W prints; accepts color prints.

How to Submit

Send complete ms with cover letter. Include SASE. Accepts photocopies and computer printouts. Identify simultaneous submissions. Report time varies.

Payment and Policies

One-time rights. No payment. Authors receive 1–2 copies of the issue; additional copies available upon request.

The United Methodist Review

Rev. Tom Hughes, Editor
Office of Communications
P.O. Box 3767
Lakeland, FL 33802
813-688-5563

AT A GLANCE:
THE UNTIED METHODIST REVIEW

- United Methodist, Regional
- 5% freelance
- Biweekly
- Circ: 17,000
- Receives few queries and mss each month.
- No payment. Offers contributor's copy.

Best Bet: Short, timely articles that enhance church programs.

Avoid: Long articles.

Sample copy: Free. No guidelines.

Profile
A regional newspaper published by the United Methodist Florida Conference. Tabloid-size; newsprint; 12 pages.

Focus and Audience
News and activities of interest to Florida-area United Methodists.

Interests and Word Lengths
- *Nonfiction:* Features, interviews, and personal experiences related to the United Methodist Church and its programs. Up to 250 words. Accepts seasonal and holiday material.
- *Photos:* B/W prints and line drawings.

How to Submit
Send complete ms with cover letter. Include SASE. Accepts photocopies, computer printouts and fax submissions. Simultaneous submissions okay. Reports in 2 weeks.

Payment and Policies
Authors retain rights. No payment. Authors receive 1 copy of the issue upon request.

United Synagogue Review

Lois Goldrich, Editor
155 Fifth Avenue
New York, NY 10010
212-533-7800

AT A GLANCE:
UNITED SYNAGOGUE REVIEW

- Jewish, Conservative
- 10% freelance
- Less than 10% new writers
- 2 issues a year
- Circ: 255,000
- Receives 5 queries, 20 mss per issue.
- No payment. Offers up to 20 contributor's copies.

From the Editor:
"Try to be educational. This can include humorous and human-interest material."

Best Bet: Issues that affect members as Conservative Jews.

Avoid: Press releases; advertorials; personal-experience pieces with no general impact.

Sample copy: Not provided. No guidelines.

Profile

A leading publication of Conservative Jewish thought. Sponsored by The United Synagogue of Conservative Judaism. 8.5x11; glossy cover; full-color; 32–40 pages.

Focus and Audience

Focuses on trends in the Jewish world, particularly Conservative trends in Judaism. Conservative, but not parochial in nature. Readers are synagogue members of the Association of Conservative Congregations.

Interests and Word Lengths

- *Nonfiction:* Informative, human-interest, and humorous articles and essays based on synagogue-related rather than solely independent experience. Interviews with leading Conservative Jewish thinkers. All must impact Conservative Judaism. Accepts filler and seasonal material. 1,200–1,500 words.
- *Departments:* Living a Conservative Jewish Lifestyle, personal experiences with impact on the Conservative Jewish population. Prefers pieces by congregation members. Perspective, opinion pieces generally written by Jewish leaders in a particular field. Up to 1,000 words.
- *Poetry:* Considers poetry of exceptional merit.
- *Photos:* Outstanding color photos for cover. B/W photos to accompany articles.

How to Submit

Query with outline, or send complete ms with cover letter. Include SASE. Prefers IBM-compatible WordPerfect 5.1 disk submissions. Accepts photocopies, computer printouts, and fax submissions. Identify simultaneous submissions. Reports in 2 months.

Payment and Policies

Rights vary. No payment. Authors receive up to 20 copies of issue upon request.

Unity

Phil White, Editor
Janet McNamara, Associate Editor
Unity Village, MO 64081
816-524-3550

AT A GLANCE:
UNITY

- Christian, Meta-
  physics
- 90% freelance
- 10% new writers
- Monthly
- Circ: 50,000
- Receives 10 queries,
  200+ mss each
  month.
- Pays: $.20 per word
  on acceptance.

From the Editor:
"Thoroughly proofread submissions, and cite all references and quotes. We do not publish material critical of other religions, ways of life, or life decisions."

Best Bet: Personal experiences, Bible interpretation, and practical Christianity.

Avoid: Pro or con articles on controversial subjects. Too much intellectual speculation.

Sample copy: Free with 6x9 SAE and $.80 postage. Send #10 SASE for guidelines.

Profile

A monthly magazine that seeks to discern truths of Christianity as taught by the Unity School of Christianity. Est.: 1889. Digest-size; glossy cover; full-color; 64 pages.

Focus and Audience

Articles cater to a varied adult readership and focus on metaphysical Christianity, new thought, and spiritual development.

Interests and Word Lengths

- *Nonfiction:* First-person stories relating unique religious, metaphysical, or spiritual experience in a positive manner. Articles demonstrating the metaphysics behind a particular human need such as health, prosperity, or human relationships. Bible interpretation relating a biblical incident or story to the unfolding of life experience and consciousness of humankind. Articles emphasizing practical Christianity in everyday life. Articles on church history, new thought in history, and Unity history. 1,000–1,800 words.
- *Departments:* From the World of Holistic Health.
- *Poetry:* Simple spiritual poetry.
- *Photos:* Prefers color transparencies. Accepts B/W prints.

How to Submit

Send complete ms with a brief author biography. Include SASE. Accepts computer printouts, 3.5-inch IBM-compatible disks, and fax submissions. No simultaneous submissions. Reports in 2 months.

Payment and Policies

First North American serial rights. Pays on acceptance. Articles, $.20 per word. Poetry, at least $25 per poem. Authors receive 3 copies of the issue.

The Upper Room

Janice Grana, Editor
1908 Grand Avenue, P.O. Box 189
Nashville, TN 38202-0189
615-340-7252

AT A GLANCE:
THE UPPER ROOM

- Christian, Devotional
- 100% freelance
- Bimonthly
- Circ: not available
- Receives 420 mss each month
- Pays: $15 per piece on publication.

From the Editor:
"Obtain and follow guidelines—specifically length and form."

Best Bet: Meditations based on the Old Testament books of law, history, and prophecy.

Avoid: Psalms and proverbs.

Sample copy: Free with 9x12 SAE and $.52 postage. Send #10 SASE for guidelines.

Profile
A bimonthly nondenominational devotional magazine for Christians. 4x6; glossy cover; 72 pages.

Focus and Audience
Daily meditations for adult Christians.

Interests and Word Lengths
- *Nonfiction:* Each meditation should include a suggested Scripture reading, an anecdote/illustration tied to the text, a "Thought for the Day," a prayer, and title. Up to 250 words
- *Photos:* Contemporary and classic religious art for front and back covers.

How to Submit
Send complete meditation. Include SASE. Accepts photocopies and computer printouts. Clearly identify simultaneous submissions. Reports in 1 year.

Payment and Policies
First North American and translation rights. Pays on publication. $15 per piece. Authors receive 1 copy of the issue.

U.S. Catholic

Patrice Tuohy, Managing Editor
205 West Monroe Street
Chicago, IL 60606
312-236-7782

AT A GLANCE: U.S. CATHOLIC

- Catholic, Opinion
- Monthly
- Circ: 50,000
- Receives 50–75 mss each month.
- Pays: $250–$500 on acceptance.

From the Editor:
"We try to make sense of the traditions of the Church for modern Catholics. We want to tap into the cultural diversity of the Church and encourage women, Hispanic, and African-American authors to write to us."

Best Bet: Features and opinion pieces that give readers the opportunity to consider all sides of an issue.

Avoid: Fiction with overtly religious messages.

Sample copy: Free. Send #10 SASE for guidelines.

Profile
A general-interest magazine for lay Catholic readers. Published monthly by the Claretians. Member of the Catholic Press Association, and the Associated Church Press. 8.5x11; glossy cover; 2-color; 52 pages.

Focus and Audience
Serves as a forum for lay Catholic thought and opinion as it addresses the issues that effect the faith life of everyday Catholics. Encourages open discussion and honest exploration of controversial topics of interest to all faiths, not just Catholic/Christian. Especially open to the experiences of women and culturally diverse writers within the Church.

Interests and Word Lengths
- *Fiction:* Short stories with strong characters and interesting plots. Messages or lessons should be subtle but compelling and woven naturally into the story. 2,000–3,000 words.
- *Nonfiction:* Feature articles that can include reporting pieces, interviews with experts, and strongly worded opinion pieces on controversial topics. Interests include family and parish life, current events, social issues, sacraments, theology, Scripture, and prayer. 4,000 words. Reflective essays on personal and spiritual growth. 1,300–1,800 words.

How to Submit
Query with outline and writing samples. Include SASE. Accepts photocopies, computer printouts, disks, and fax submissions upon acceptance. Identify simultaneous submissions. Reports in 2 weeks.

Payment and Policies
First North American serial rights. Pays on acceptance. Short stories, $300–$400. Features, $500. Opinion pieces, $250. Authors receive 5 copies of the issue, plus copies for article sources.

Venture

Deborah Christensen, Editor
764 Kimberly Drive
Carol Stream, IL 60188
708-665-0630

AT A GLANCE:

VENTURE

- Christian, Juvenile
- 75% freelance
- 5% new writers
- Bimonthly
- Circ: 19,000
- Receives 2–3 queries, 50–75 mss each month.
- Pays: $.05–$.10 per word on publication.

From the Editor:
"Know Christianity. It affects the whole life and is more than a prayer to get out of trouble or difficulty. Read our guidelines."

Best Bet: Articles that help boys integrate faith in God with everyday living.

Avoid: Female perspectives; sex; adult reminiscences; poetry; history; fantasy; and Bible stories.

Sample copy: $1.85 with 9x12 SAE and $.98 postage. Send #10 SASE for guidelines.

Profile

A Christian magazine for boys that promotes wholesome entertainment and a positive image of Christian manhood. Official publication of the Christian Service Brigade, a service organization ministering to evangelical and Fundamental churches. 8.5x11; glossy cover; 3-color; 32 pages.

Focus and Audience

Speaks to the concerns of 10- to 15-year-old boys from a biblical perspective with the goal of "building men to serve Christ." Most readers are active in the Christian Service Brigade or Battalion groups.

Interests and Word Lengths

- *Fiction:* Stories dealing with contemporary teen questions and problems like relationships with parents, peer pressure, drugs, cheating, lying, fear, and careers. Also stories about Christian living involving witnessing, prayer, and doubts about faith. Adventures that include more than a token prayer for help, mysteries, and humorous stories that relate to boys' bizarre sense of humor. 1,000–1,500 words.
- *Nonfiction:* True stories about men and teenagers involved in unique activities. Articles that demonstrate God's creativity in nature. 500–1,000 words.
- *Photos:* A good selection of 8x10 B/W photos can help sell a submission. Send for guidelines.

How to Submit

Send complete ms with cover letter. Include SASE. Accepts photocopies, computer printouts, and fax submissions. Simultaneous submissions okay. Reports in 1 week.

Payment and Policies

First North American serial and reprint rights. Pays on publication. $.05–$.10 per word. Photos, $35–$100. Kill fee, $35. Authors receive 2 copies of the issue.

Vibrant Life

Barbara Jackson-Hall, Editor
55 West Oak Ridge Drive
Hagerstown, MD 21740
301-791-7000

AT A GLANCE:
VIBRANT LIFE

- Health, Lifestyle
- 10% freelance
- Bimonthly
- Circ: 50,000
- Receives 20 queries, 25–30 mss each month.
- Pays: $80–$250 on acceptance.

From the Editor:
"Use an informal, interesting, easy-to-read style. We stress readability and prefer the person-oriented approach."

Best Bet: Positive, practical, non-academic articles that offer a spiritual view of healthy living.

Avoid: Articles focused on a specific disease; medical or religious jargon; overly spiritual or religious material.

Sample copy: $1. Send #10 SASE for guidelines.

Profile

A bimonthly health magazine that promotes a healthful lifestyle in a Christian context. Published by the Review and Herald Publishing Association, a Seventh-day Adventist publishing house. Est.: 1885. 8.5x11; glossy cover; full-color; 32 pages.

Focus and Audience

Seeks practical articles that stress disease prevention, promote better health and a happier family, and present a happy, healthy, Christian outlook on life. Readers are men and women 30–45 years of age.

Interests and Word Lengths

- *Nonfiction:* Articles that offer a spiritual view of healthy living and report on the latest breakthroughs in medicine, health, nutrition, and exercise. Areas of interest include health—physical, mental, and emotional; exercise, nutrition, self-improvement; family and parenting; personal experiences of overcoming crisis through faith; informational articles on home and family safety; and interviews with health experts and well-known personalities. Up to 5 typed, double-spaced pages.
- *Photos:* To accompany articles. Prefers 35mm color slides. Accepts 5x7 or larger B/W glossy prints.

How to Submit

Send complete ms with cover letter, resume, and clips. Accepts reprints. Include SASE. Accepts photocopies, letter-quality computer printouts, and fax submissions. Simultaneous submissions okay. Reports in 1–2 months.

Payment and Policies

First North American serial rights. Pays on acceptance. $80–$250 per piece. Authors receive 3 copies of the issue.

Vintage Northwest

Editor
P.O. Box 193
Bothell, WA 98041
206-822-2411

AT A GLANCE:
VINTAGE NORTHWEST

- Seniors, Disability
- 60–70% freelance
- 2 issues a year
- Circ: 550
- Receives 8–15 mss each month.
- No payment. Offers 1 contributor's copy.

From the Editor:
"Keep a positive outlook."

Best Bet: Inspirational fiction, essays, and poetry for and by seniors.

Avoid: Overtly religious or political views.

Sample copy: $2.75 with 8.5x11 SAE and $.58 postage. Send #10 SASE for guidelines.

Profile
A non-profit literary magazine for and by senior writers over 50 and the physically disabled. 7x8.5; 64 pages.

Focus and Audience
Works to enhance the value and importance of the viewpoints of seniors and those with disabilities. Inspirational in nature, not overtly religious.

Interests and Word Lengths
- *Fiction:* Short stories of interest to seniors on family and lifestyle issues. Up to 1,000 words.
- *Nonfiction:* Essays and personal-experience pieces of interest to seniors on family and lifestyle issues. Up to 1,000 words.
- *Poetry:* Inspirational poems.
- *Illustrations:* Small B/W illustrations.

How to Submit
Send complete ms with cover letter. Include SASE. Accepts photocopies and computer printouts. Simultaneous submissions okay. Reports in 3–4 months.

Payment and Policies
One-time rights. No payment. Authors receive 1 copy of the issue.

Virtue

Marlee Alex, Editor
P.O. Box 850
Sisters, OR 97759
503-549-8261

AT A GLANCE:

VIRTUE

- Christian, Women
- 25% freelance
- 5% new writers
- 6 issues a year
- Circ: 130,000
- Receives 200 queries, 100 mss each month.
- Pays: $.15–$.25 per word on publication.

From the Editor:
"We want well-developed ideas and well-kneaded writing."

Avoid: Preachy writing styles.

Sample copy: Available at newsstands. Send #10 SASE for guidelines.

Profile

A lifestyle magazine for Christian women. Member of the Evangelical Press Association and the Evangelical Christian Publishers Association. 8.5x11; glossy cover; full-color; 80 pages.

Focus and Audience

Seeks to encourage, inspire, and address current issues of interest to Christian women.

Interests and Word Lengths

- *Fiction:* Short-short stories. Accepts poetry.
- *Nonfiction:* Features, essays, personal experiences, inspirational and lifestyle pieces, and practical how-to articles on the family, prayer, social and world issues, spirituality, and women's issues. Accepts seasonal material. 1,200–1,500 words.
- *Departments:* Real Men, In My Opinion, and One Woman's Journal, 1,200 words. Equipped for Ministry, 400 words.

How to Submit

Query with outline and writing sample. Include SASE. Accepts photocopies and computer printouts. Simultaneous submissions okay. Reports in 2–3 months.

Payment and Policies

First North American serial rights. Pays on publication. $.15–$.25 per word. Kill fee, $50. Does not provide contributor's copies.

Vista

Brenda Bratton, Editor
6060 Castleway Drive
P.O. Box 50434
Indianapolis, IN 46250-0434
317-576-8144

AT A GLANCE:

VISTA

- Wesleyan-Arminian, Family
- 80% freelance
- 10% new writers
- Weekly
- Circ: 75,000
- Receives 100 mss each month.
- Pays: $.04 per word on acceptance.

From the Editor:
"Keep in mind that this is an evangelical, Wesleyan-Arminian church take-home paper. Please submit a brief cover letter with information about you and your article, including its word length."

Best Bet: Articles that reflect an evangelical, Wesleyan-Arminian view.

Avoid: Controversial or activist viewpoints.

Sample copy: Free with 8.5x11 SASE. Send #10 SASE for guidelines.

Profile

A weekly take-home Sunday school publication for adults. Published by Wesley Press. 8.5x11; self cover; 2-color; 8 pages.

Focus and Audience

Contents reflect an evangelical, Wesleyan-Arminian view. Readers are adult church-attenders.

Interests and Word Lengths

- *Fiction:* Stories geared toward readers ages 50 and up. Subjects include challenges of retirement, empty-nest syndrome, losing a spouse, life alone again, etc. 1,000–1,200 words.
- *Departments:* Family, the joys and struggles of marriage, parenting, and homemaking—geared toward baby-boomers. Perspective, insights, opinions, how-to articles, self-improvement with God's help. Discipleship, testimonials, Christians helping each other become more like Christ. 550–625 words. Primetime, articles geared toward and of interest to readers over 50. 1,000–1,200 words. Accepts Amazing Facts (i.e., Did you know . . .?) with documentation.

How to Submit

Send complete ms with cover letter. Include SASE. Place name, address, phone number and social security number on cover letter and first ms page. Accepts photocopies, computer printouts, 5.25- or 3.5-inch Microsoft Word disks, and faxes. Simultaneous submissions okay. Reports in 2 months.

Payment and Policies

First North American serial rights. Pays on acceptance. $.04 for first rights, $.02 for reprint rights. Authors receive 2 copies of the issue.

Voice

Editor
3150 Bear Street
Costa Mesa, CA 92626
714-757-1400

AT A GLANCE:
VOICE

- Christian, Men's Issues
- 20% freelance
- 80% new writers
- Monthly
- Circ: 300,000
- No payment. Offers 10 contributor's copies.

From the Editor:
"Voice is a testimonial magazine designed for evangelist outreach to men only."

Best Bet: First-person testimonies of Christian men.

Avoid: How-to articles; fiction; and poetry.

Sample copy: Not provided. Send #10 SASE for guidelines.

Profile
A Christian outreach magazine for men. Published by the Full Gospel Business Men's Fellowship. 5.5x7.5; 4-color; 40 pages.

Focus and Audience
Presents first-person testimonies of conversion and salvation written by men and directed toward business men. Reaches an international audience.

Interests and Word Lengths
- *Nonfiction:* Inspirational personal salvation experiences of men. Designed for evangelistic outreach to men and to promote spiritual growth. No how-to articles. Up to 2,000 words.
- *Photos:* Color prints.

How to Submit
Submit complete ms with cover letter. Accepts original mss only. Simultaneous submissions okay. Reports in 1 month.

Payment and Policies
All or one-time rights. No payment. Authors receive 10 copies of the issue.

The Voice of the Gospel

Symeon Ioannidis, Greek Managing Editor
6815 Shallowford Road
Chattanooga, TN 37421-1755
615-894-6060

Profile
A non-profit, non-denominational, but primarily Protestant Christian magazine published in Greek for a Greek-speaking audience. 7x9.5; 54 pages.

Focus and Audience
Aimed at helping people in their Christian lives. Distributed internationally among Greek-speaking readers in Greece, the U.S., Australia, and other countries. Material should be evangelical in content and appeal to a wide range of Christian readers.

Interests and Word Lengths
- *Fiction:* Short stories with Christian content for children. Must be written in Greek. No word-length restrictions.
- *Nonfiction:* Feature articles, interviews, and other formats with Christian content. Interests include Bible studies, evangelism, and missionary work. Must be written in Greek. No word-length restrictions.
- *Photos:* B/W prints of any size.

How to Submit
Query with outline and resume, or send complete ms with cover letter and resume. Include SASE. Accepts photocopies and computer printouts. No simultaneous submissions. Reports within 9 months.

Payment and Policies
Authors retain rights. No payment. Does not provide copies of the issue.

Vox Benedictina

Dr, Margot King, Editor
17 Woodside Avenue
Toronto, ON M6P 1L6
Canada
416-604-3111

AT A GLANCE:
VOX BENEDICTINA

- Christian, Feminine Spirituality
- 75% freelance
- 0–25% new writers
- 2 issues a year
- Circ: 500
- No payment. Offers 5–10 contributor's copies.

From the Editor:
"Substance and contribution to the field are more important than personal point of view."

Best Bet: Explorations of Christian feminine monastic spirituality.

Avoid: Extreme subjectivism—consider the original cultural milieu of the text when interpreting.

Sample copy: $5 with 6x9 SASE. No guidelines.

Profile
A Christian journal of translations and original articles on the heritage of feminine monastic spirituality. Published by Peregrina Publishing Co. 5x8; 200 pages.

Focus and Audience
Encourages a broad perspective on the original focus of feminine and monastic spirituality and is not strictly "feminist" in a narrow sense. While the perspective is Christian and monastic, lay women and men from all faiths are represented, as are men and women from non-monastic religious orders. Subscribers include women's scholars, universities, religious houses, and seminaries.

Interests and Word Lengths
- *Nonfiction:* Scholarly articles and translations from non-English sources on monastic and women's spirituality from the time of Christ to the present. Material should be of intellectual substance and adequately documented. Up to 1,000 words.

How to Submit
Query with outline and resume. Include SASE. Accepts photocopies, computer printouts, and fax submissions. Simultaneous submissions okay. Reports in 3 months.

Payment and Policies
Original material, first North American serial rights. Translations, first rights publication option retained by Peregrina Publishing Co. No payment. Authors receive 5–10 copies of the issue.

The War Cry

Colonel Henry Gariepy, Editor-in-Chief
615 Slaters Lane
Alexandria, VA 22313
703-684-5518

AT A GLANCE:
THE WAR CRY

- Salvationist, Inspirational
- 5% freelance
- 1% new writers
- Biweekly
- Circ: 500,000
- Receives 100 mss each month.
- Pays: $.15 per word on acceptance.

From the Editor:
"We reach a general readership as well as members and friends of The Salvation Army."

Best Bet: Short, inspirational articles and holiday material.

Sample copy: Free. Send #10 SASE for guidelines.

Profile
An inspirational magazine published biweekly by The Salvation Army. 8.5x11; 24 pages.

Focus and Audience
Provides informational and inspirational writing for both Salvation Army members and other interested readers.

Interests and Word Lengths
- *Nonfiction:* Short, inspirational articles, personal experiences, devotions, and how-to's on family life, women's interests, current events and social issues, and the environment. 400–900 words.
- *Seasonal:* Christmas and Easter material. 400–900 words.

How to Submit
Submit complete ms with cover letter. Accepts photocopies. No simultaneous submissions. Reports in 2 months.

Payment and Policies
One-time rights. Pays on acceptance. $.15 per word. Authors receive 4 copies of the issue.

Washington Jewish Week

Robin Schwartz-Kreger, Assistant Editor
12300 Twinbrook Parkway
Suite 250
Rockville, MD 20852
301-230-2222

AT A GLANCE:
WASHINGTON JEWISH WEEK

- Jewish, Regional
- 25% freelance
- 5% new writers
- Weekly
- Circ: 17,000
- Receives 8–10 queries, 15–20 mss each month.
- Pays: $50–$150 on publication.

From the Editor: "Writing must be focused and word choice precise. Don't be indirect or wordy; instead be factual and descriptive."

Best Bet: Tightly written feature articles on community, national, or international topics of Jewish interest.

Sample copy: $1 with 9x13 SASE. No guidelines.

Profile

A regional independent Jewish newspaper covering world and local news. Est.: 1965. Tabloid-size; newsprint; 56–64 pages.

Focus and Audience

Covers international, national, and community topics of interest to Jewish readers in Washington, DC.

Interests and Word Lengths

- *Nonfiction:* News pieces and features on subjects of Jewish interest—local, national, or international. 800–1,200 words.
- *Seasonal:* Material related to Jewish holidays.
- *Photos:* Photos to accompany articles. Prefers B/W; accepts color if sharp.

How to Submit

Send complete ms with cover letter. Include SASE. Accepts photocopies, computer printouts, ASCII or WordPerfect 5.1 disks, and submissions via modem. No simultaneous submissions. Reports in 1–2 months.

Payment and Policies

First North American serial rights. Pays on publication. $50–$150 per piece. Kill fee, 50%. Authors receive 2 copies of the issue.

Welcome Home

Pam Goresh, Editor-in-Chief
8310 A Old Courthouse Road
Vienna, VA 22182
703-827-5903

AT A GLANCE:
WELCOME HOME

- Family, Inspirational
- 50–75% freelance
- 25% new writers
- Monthly
- Circ: 15,000
- Receives 50–100 mss each month.
- No payment. Offers 3 contributor's copies.

From the Editor:
"*Welcome Home* is for smart women or men who have actively chosen to devote their skills and mind to the nurturing of her or his family."

Best Bet: Thoughtful, humorous, and helpful essays for all parents who value time spent with the family.

Avoid: Stereotypes; overtly religious references; criticizing a woman's choice to work outside the home.

Sample copy: $2.50 with 5x7 SAE and $.80 postage. Send #10 SASE for guidelines.

Profile
A non-profit monthly magazine devoted to family and parenting issues. 32 pages.

Focus and Audience
Aimed at stay-at-home parents, primarily women, this magazine provides an opportunity to share feelings, insights, and enthusiasm with others who face the same challenges.

Interests and Word Lengths
- *Nonfiction:* First-person articles, personal experiences, interviews, humor, essays, and self-help pieces on families, husbands, children, friendships, education, marriage, household tips, and exploring the potential for personal growth to be realized through mothering. Accepts filler and seasonal material. Up to 2,500 words. Prefers 300–1,500 words.
- *Departments:* Early Years; Middle Years; Teen Years; Making Money at Home; Hearthwarming; Problems & Solutions; New Dimensions; Time to Care; Resource Review. All offer insights into the struggles and successes of family life and mothering and affirm the critical importance of nurturing. 300–1,500 words.
- *Photos:* Submit to Cathy Gardner, Art Director. Simple pen & ink drawings. Prefers B/W, accepts color. Accepts B/W and color prints of any size.

How to Submit
Send complete ms with cover letter, author biography, and, if available, clips. Include SASE. Accepts computer printouts. No simultaneous submissions. Reports in 3 months.

Payment and Policies
One-time rights. No payment. Authors receive 3 copies of the issue.

Wellsprings

Baila M. Olidort, Editor
770 Eastern Parkway
Brooklyn, NY 11213
718-774-4000

Profile

A quarterly journal of Chassidic Jewish thought and spirituality. 8.5x11; glossy cover; 4-color; 40 pages.

Focus and Audience

Devoted to exploring the inner dimensions of Jewish life and the Torah. Readers are Jewish, encompassing non-affiliated, Reform, Conservative, and Orthodox. Writings, though, should be in keeping with a Torah-Chassidic perspective.

Interests and Word Lengths

- *Fiction:* Short-short stories on Jewish themes from a Chassidic angle. 1,250 words.
- *Nonfiction:* Feature articles and personal experience pieces on Jewish lifestyle and other issues pertaining to Chassidic Jewish philosophy and spirituality. 2,000–4,000 words.

How to Submit

Query with outline, resume, and writing samples; or send complete ms with cover letter and resume. Include SASE. Accepts computer printouts and IBM-compatible ASCII or Microsoft Word disk submissions. Reports in 2 months.

Payment and Policies

First North American serial rights. Requests credit line in case of reprint. Pays on publication. Rates vary. Authors receive 3 copies of the issue.

Wherever

Jack Kilgore, Editor
400 South Main Place
Carol Stream, IL 60188
708-653-5300

AT A GLANCE:

WHEREVER

- Christian, Youth Missions
- 95% freelance
- 3 issues during school year
- Circ: 15,000
- Receives 10 queries, 1–2 mss per issue.
- Pays: $50–up on publication.

From the Editor:
"Send for our writer's guidelines. We require very specific material. So far we have not used over-the-transom material. Our writer's guidelines include issue themes, story ideas, and deadlines."

Avoid: Devotional jargon.

Sample copy: Free with 9x12 SAE and $.75 postage. Send #10 SASE for guidelines and theme list.

Profile

An evangelical missions magazine for young adults. Each issue focuses on a theme. Published by The Evangelical Alliance Mission (TEAM). 8.5x11; glossy cover; 2-color; 16 pages.

Focus and Audience

Directed toward college-age adults and young professionals who may be considering some type of overseas missions work.

Interests and Word Lengths

- *Fiction:* Submit to Dana Felmly, Editorial Coordinator. Considers fiction that fits the issue's theme. Send for guidelines. 1,000–1,500 words.
- *Nonfiction:* Submit to Dana Felmly, Editorial Coordinator. Articles on mission work. Must fit the issue's theme. Send for guidelines. 1,000–1,500 words.
- *Photos:* Submit to Dana Felmly, Editorial Coordinator. Prefers slides, but accepts prints.

How to Submit

Send for guidelines and theme list before submitting. Then, query with outline and writing samples. Include SASE. Accepts photocopies, letter-quality computer printouts, and ASCII, Word Star 4.0, or WordPerfect disks with hard copy. No simultaneous submissions. Reports in 2 months.

Payment and Policies

First North American serial rights. Pays on publication. 1 page, $50. 2 pages, $125. 3 pages and up, negotiable. Authors receive 2 copies of the issue.

Whisper

Anthony Boyd, Editor
509 Enterprise Drive
Rohnert Park, CA 94928

AT A GLANCE:

WHISPER

- Fiction, Poetry
- 90% freelance
- 10% new writers
- 2 issues a year
- Circ: 250
- Receives 20 queries each month.
- No payment. Offers 1 contributor's copy.

From the Editor:
"This is not a religious magazine, but as a Christian, I do consider well-written, thoughtful work to blend in with more general-interest material. Please include a short cover letter so I know something about you. Be persistent and professional."

Avoid: Clichéd, contrived, preachy religious poetry.

Sample copy: $3. Send #10 SASE for guidelines.

Profile

A small, independent journal of poetry, fiction, and reviews. 8.5x11; heavy bond cover; 16 pages.

Focus and Audience

Promotes the work of new and established poets, artists, and short-story writers. Most material is of general interest, but welcomes thoughtful religious writing.

Interests and Word Lengths

- *Fiction:* Short stories, especially science fiction and fantasy. Up to 1,200 words.
- *Nonfiction:* Interviews with anyone, musicians, politicians, parents, homeless people, etc. Up to 1,200 words.
- *Poetry:* Poems of 50 lines or less. No "bar" poems or clichéd religious poetry. Each poet is showcased on one page, which includes 2 or 3 poems, a photo of the author, and an author biography.
- *Photos:* 5x7 B/W prints.

How to Submit

Send complete ms or 2–5 poems with cover letter or brief author biography and photo. Include SASE. Accepts photocopies and computer printouts. Reports in 1 month.

Payment and Policies

First North American serial or one-time rights. No payment. Authors receive 1 copy of the issue.

Whole Earth Newsletter

Helen M. Hayes, Managing Editor
700 Prospect Avenue
Cleveland, OH 44115
216-736-3208

AT A GLANCE:
WHOLE EARTH NEWSLETTER

- United Church of Christ, Missions
- Uses little freelance
- 3 issues a year
- Circ: 11,000,000
- No payment.

From the Editor:
"We are non-profit and seldom use outside writers. We do not pay nor do we take advertising."

Best Bet: Specialized articles that report on UCC missionary work.

Sample copy: Not provided. No guidelines.

Profile
A non-profit missionary publication of the United Church of Christ (UCC), a liberal mainline Protestant denomination. 8.5x11; self cover; 12 pages.

Focus and Audience
Highlights the work and workings of the United Church Board for World Ministries, the missionary arm of the United Church of Christ. Reaches a specialized audience of UCC pastors and personalities involved in UCC missions.

Interests and Word Lengths
- *Nonfiction:* Articles with emphasis on existing UCC missions, partnerships, or historical institutions as well as profiles of missionary personalities.
- *Photos:* B/W prints.

How to Submit
Query with outline or send complete ms with cover letter. Include SASE. Accepts photocopies and computer printouts.

Payment and Policies
Authors retain rights. No payment.

The Wisconsin Jewish Chronicle

Andrew Muchin, Editor
1360 North Prospect Avenue
Milwaukee, WI 53202
414-271-2992

AT A GLANCE:
THE WISCONSIN JEWISH CHRONICLE

- Jewish, Regional
- 5% freelance
- Weekly
- Circ: 5,000
- Receives 5 mss each month
- Pays: $25–$50 on publication.

From the Editor:
"We're a hard-edged, hard-nosed newspaper seeking to expand our lifestyle and trend offerings."

Best Bet: Cultural, offbeat, or religious oriented features.

Avoid: Writing in the first-person.

Sample copy: $.50 with 8x10 SAE and $.52 postage. Send #10 SASE for guidelines.

Profile
A general interest Jewish newspaper distributed weekly throughout Wisconsin. Tabloid-size; newsprint; 20 pages.

Focus and Audience
Publishes local and world news in relation to and of interest to Jewish readers in the Wisconsin area.

Interests and Word Lengths
- *Nonfiction:* Features, interviews, and essays. Subjects include: religion, culture, politics, and social and world issues. 750–1,000 words.
- *Departments:* Recipes, Book Reviews, Record Reviews, Op-Ed.
- *Photos:* B/W or color prints no larger than 8x10.

How to Submit
Query with outline, resume, and clips. Include SASE. Accepts photocopies, computer printouts, Macintosh disks, faxes, and submissions via modem. Simultaneous submissions okay. Reports in 1 month.

Payment and Policies
One-time rights. Pays on publication. $25–$50 per piece. Authors receive 1 copy of the issue.

With

Carol Duerksen and Eddy Hall, Co-editors
Box 347
Newton, KS 67053
316-283-5100

AT A GLANCE:

WITH

- Mennonite, Teen
- 80% freelance
- 10% new writers
- 8 issues a year
- Circ: 6,100
- Receives 3 queries,
  75 mss each month.
- Pays: $.02–$.05 per
  word on acceptance.

From the Editor:
"We require high-quality writing, but invest time working with writers who demonstrate that they can deliver. If you are funny, humor is a good way to break into With. Our how-to format is very specific, so ask for our guidelines and theme list and query us before submitting."

Best Bet: Humorous pieces; how-to articles related to themes.

Avoid: Christian jargon.

Sample copy: Free with 9x12 SAE and 4 first-class stamps. Send #10 SASE for guidelines and theme list.

Profile
A thematic magazine for high school-age youth in Mennonite and Anabaptist churches. Published by the Mennonite Publishing House and Faith and Life Press. 8.5x11; glossy cover; 2-color; 32 pages.

Focus and Audience
Produced to help teenagers understand the complex issues that impact them and to make choices that reflect Anabaptist-Mennonite understanding of living by the Spirit of Christ.

Interests and Word Lengths
- *Fiction:* Realistic fiction in which the high school-age protagonists learn and grow through resolution of conflict. Uses some fiction with an "unreliable narrator" where the protagonist doesn't learn, but the reader does. 800–2,000 words. Accepts parables, allegorical stories, and fantasies. 100–1,800 words.
- *Nonfiction:* First-person and as-told-to pieces, 800–1,800 words. How-to articles, 500–1,500 words. Humor, 100–1,500 words. Meditations, 100–1,200 words. All must relate to issue themes.
- *Poetry:* Poems that relate to themes and lend themselves to illustrations. Up to 50 lines.
- *Artwork:* 8x10 B/W prints. Humorous cartoons.

How to Submit
Fiction, humor, and meditations, send ms with cover letter. First-person pieces and how-to's, send for guidelines, then query with outline. Include SASE. Accepts photocopies and computer printouts. Simultaneous submissions okay. Reports in 1–2 months.

Payment and Policies
First North American serial or one-time rights. Pays on acceptance. Assigned pieces, $.05–up per word. Unsolicited pieces, $.04 per word. Reprints, $.02 per word. Authors receive 2 copies of the issue.

Woman's Touch

Sandra G. Clopine, Editor
1445 Boonville Avenue
Springfield, MO 65802-1894
417-862-2781

AT A GLANCE:
WOMAN'S TOUCH

- Assemblies of God,
  Women
- 65% freelance
- Bimonthly
- Circ: 18,000
- Receives 100 mss
  each month.
- Pays: $.03 per word
  on acceptance.

From the Editor:
"We are only able to use around ten percent of what is sent to us."

Best Bet: Inspirational uplifting pieces and articles that provide biblical teaching on subjects of interest to women.

Avoid: Fiction.

Sample copy: Free. Send #10 SASE for guidelines.

Profile

An inspirational magazine for women, published by the Assemblies of God Women's Ministries Department. Also issues a leadership edition for those who lead local women's ministry groups. 8.5x11; 28 pages.

Focus and Audience

Publishes uplifting articles and biblical teachings on subjects of interest to Assemblies of God women.

Interests and Word Lengths

- *Nonfiction:* Feature articles and personal experiences of healing, struggling with faith, Bible studies on current issues, faith at work during holidays, the Christian family, women's issues, education, and reflection. 500–1,200 words.
- *Filler:* Short pieces, 50–500 words. Accepts some poetry.
- *Seasonal:* Easter, Thanksgiving, Christmas, and some other holiday pieces.

How to Submit

Send complete ms with cover letter. Include SASE. Accepts computer printouts. Simultaneous submissions okay. Reports in 3–6 months.

Payment and Policies

One-time rights. Pays on acceptance. $.03 per word. Authors receive 3 copies of the issue.

Women Alive!

Aletha Hinthorn, Editor
P.O. Box 4683
Overland Park, KS 66204
913-649-8583

AT A GLANCE:
WOMEN ALIVE!

- Christian, Women
- 50% freelance
- 40% new writers
- Bimonthly
- Circ: 5,000
- Receives 20 mss each month.
- Pays: $15–$40 per piece on publication.

From the Editor:
"Most Christian women understand what they should do but need role models of godly women to pattern after. It's easier to follow a pattern than an idea."

Best Bets: Articles showing Scripture applied to daily living, and spiritual growth, through prayer, Bible study, and developing a Christ-like character.

Sample copy: Free with 9x12 SAE and 4 first-class stamps. Send #10 SASE for guidelines.

Profile

A Christian women's magazine that seeks to show women how to apply Scripture to their daily living. Edited from a Wesleyan-Arminian perspective. 8.5x11; glossy cover; 2-color; 20 pages.

Focus and Audience

Provides a forum for women, and models how to live victorious Christian lives. Readers are women intent on spiritual growth.

Interests and Word Lengths

- *Fiction:* Occasionally accepts relevant fiction. 900–2,000 words.
- *Nonfiction:* Send for annual theme list. Topics for 1993 include Scripture applied to daily living, developing a deeper relationship with God; Bible knowledge; mothering; improving marriage; self-consciousness; improving communication; coping with a strong-willed husband; controlling weight; handling finances; temptations known only to singles; reinforcement techniques for single mothers; how to reach non-Christians; and feature articles for older women. 900–2,000 words.
- *Departments:* Senior Savvy, a helpful, encouraging page for older women. 900–1,200 words.

How to Submit

Send complete ms with resume. Include SASE. Accepts photocopies, computer printouts, and fax submissions. Simultaneous submissions okay. Reports in 1–2 months.

Payment and Policies

One-time rights plus translation rights. Pays on publication. $15–$40 per piece. Authors receive 1 copy of the issue.

Wonder Time

Lois Perriga, Editor
Children's Ministries
6401 The Paseo
Kansas City, MO 64131

AT A GLANCE:
WONDER TIME

- Christian, Juvenile
- 100% freelance
- 40% new writers
- Weekly
- Circ: 41,000
- Receives 10 queries, 30 mss each month.
- Pays: $25 per piece on publication.

From the Editor:
"*Wonder Time* correlates directly with the WordAction Sunday School curriculum. Send for the guidelines."

Best Bet: Contemporary, true-to-life portrayals of 6- to 8-year-old children, related to a lesson in the WordAction curriculum.

Avoid: Fantasy, science fiction; precocious children; personification of animals; extensive cultural or holiday references.

Sample copy: Free with guidelines for a #10 SASE.

Profile
An evangelical weekly Sunday school story paper for first and second graders. Published by WordAction Publishing Company. Full-color; 4 pages.

Focus and Audience
Designed to connect Sunday school learning with the daily growth of the primary child. Readers are first and second graders of the Church of the Nazarene, Evangelical Friends, Free Methodist, Wesleyan, and other Bible-believing evangelical churches.

Interests and Word Lengths
- *Fiction:* Stories that show character-building strength or scriptural application and portray contemporary, true-to-life children, 6–8 years old. Themes should conform to evangelical theology and practice. 250–350 words. Accepts poetry.
- *Puzzles:* Keep it simple; include concise instructions and answer sheet. All correlate to weekly primary Sunday school lessons.
- *Artwork:* Portfolio submissions for future assignment consideration.

How to Submit
Send ms with cover letter. Include SASE. Accepts photocopies and computer printouts. Simultaneous submissions okay. Reports in 6 weeks.

Payment and Policies
Multi-use rights. Pays on publication. $25 for stories; $10–$15 for puzzles; $3 for poems. Authors receive 4 copies of the issue.

The Word in Season

Editor
426 South Fifth Street
Box 1209
Minneapolis, MN 55440-1209

AT A GLANCE: THE WORD IN SEASON

- Lutheran, Devotional
- 100% freelance
- 25% new writers
- Quarterly
- Circ: 140,000
- Receives 5–6 mss each month.
- Pays: $15 per piece on acceptance.

From the Editor:
"We prefer Lutheran writers familiar with ELCA doctrine. Write for guidelines and instructions on submitting a sample devotion. If we like your sample, we will give you an assignment."

Sample copy: $4. Send #10 SASE for guidelines and submissions instructions.

Profile

A daily devotional guide for members of the Evangelical Lutheran Church in America (ELCA). Published quarterly by Augsburg Fortress. 4x6; glossy cover; 2-color; 96 pages.

Focus and Audience

Offers daily devotional reading for ELCA members. All work is assigned. Prefers to work with ELCA writers.

Interests and Word Lengths

- *Devotions:* Devotions and mediations corresponding with prescribed Scriptures and formats. Authors should write for assignments. Each devotion is approximately 1,300 characters long.

How to Submit

Write to receive guidelines and instructions on submitting a sample devotion. Include SASE. Following the prescribed format, submit sample devotion with a brief author biography. Accepts photocopies and computer printouts. No simultaneous submissions. Reports in 2–3 weeks.

Payment and Policies

All rights. Grants reprint rights upon request. Pays on acceptance. $15 per devotion. Author receives 6 copies of the issue plus a 25% discount on additional copies.

The World
Journal of the Unitarian Universalist Association

Linda Beyer, Editor
25 Beacon Street
Boston, MA 02108
617-742-2100

AT A GLANCE:
THE WORLD

- Unitarian, Denominational
- 50% freelance
- 0–5% new writers
- Bimonthly
- Circ: 107,500
- Receives less than 5 queries, 10–20 mss each month.
- Pays: $250–$500 for assigned articles on publication.

From the Editor:
"*The World* is a special-audience magazine designed to promote Unitarian Universalist values."

Best Bet: Articles that educate about the history, personalities, and congregations that comprise Unitarian Universalism.

Avoid: General-interest pieces.

Sample copy: Free with 9x12 SAE and $.58 postage. Send #10 SASE for guidelines.

Profile
A bimonthly denominational journal of the Unitarian Universalist Association. 56 pages.

Focus and Audience
Promotes and inspires Unitarian Universalist (UU) self-reflection and informs readers about the wide range of UU values, purposes, activities, aesthetics, and spiritual attitudes. Offered as part of a paid membership in a Unitarian congregation.

Interests and Word Lengths
- *Nonfiction:* Essays on UU values, history, personalities, and congregations, as well as commentary reflecting UU opinions on issues such as abortion, euthanasia, denominational and congregational growth and diversity, the environment, feminist theology, homophobia, social action, and ethics. 700–2,000 words.
- *Departments:* Submit to Jenna Leight, Manuscript Editor. Among Ourselves News: conference and convocation reports, church business, settlements, etc. 300–900 words.
- *Photos:* Submit to Sheila Jimenez, Production Manager. B/W and color photos of any size or style.

How to Submit
Prefers query with outline, writing samples, and clips. Accepts unsolicited mss with cover letter and clips. Include SASE. Accepts photocopies, computer printouts, and 1.6 megabyte IBM-compatible disks. Simultaneous submissions okay. Reports in 2 months.

Payment and Policies
One-time rights. Pays on publication for assigned articles resulting from a query. No payment for unsolicited mss. $250–$500 per piece. Authors receive 1–5 copies of the issue.

World Vision

Larry Wilson, Managing Editor
919 West Huntington Drive
Monrovia, CA 91016
818-357-7979

AT A GLANCE:

WORLD VISION

- Christian, Missionary
- 80% freelance
- 10–20% new writers
- Bimonthly
- Circ: 100,000
- Receives 2–5 queries, 2–5 mss each month.
- Pays: $.20–$.25 per word on acceptance.

From the Editor:
"Learn to tell stories. Definitely use anecdotal leads—and sprinkle articles with good human interest. Don't preach. Know what you want to say and incorporate your statement within the first few paragraphs."

Avoid: Sermons; poetry; views supporting abortion.

Sample copy: Free with 8x11 SASE. Send #10 SASE for guidelines.

Profile

A non-denominational Christian magazine that supports the various interests of World Vision, a non-profit Christian relief and development organization. 8.5x11; glossy cover; full-color; 24 pages.

Focus and Audience

Addresses the issues and concerns of the poor in the Third World and the United States, and aims to demonstrate that, from a Christian perspective, change is possible, and God is at work among the poor. Readers include donors to World Vision and Christian leaders across the U.S.

Interests and Word Lengths

- *Nonfiction:* News features on various topics; interviews with Christian leaders and thinkers; personal experiences of relief work, and how God is working among the poor. Other topics include Third World poverty; U.S. poverty, children and poverty; the environment; justice and the poor; how to help the poor. 1,000–2,000 words.
- *Departments:* Turning Points, personal stories that show how an event or experience turned a person's life toward ministering to the poor. 700–1,000 words.

How to Submit

Query with outline and writing samples or send complete ms with cover letter. Include SASE. Accepts photocopies, computer printouts, Macintosh WordPerfect disks, and faxes. No simultaneous submissions. Reports in 1–2 months.

Payment and Policies

First North American serial rights. Pays on acceptance. $.20–$.25 per word. Authors receive at least 1 copy of the issue.

Writer's Guidelines

Susan Salaki, Editor
Box 608
Pittsburg, MO 65724
417-993-5544

AT A GLANCE:
WRITER'S GUIDELINES

- Writers, Inspirational
- 99% freelance
- 100% new writers
- Bimonthly
- Circ: 500
- Receives 30 queries, 60 mss each month.
- Pays: $25 per piece on acceptance.

From the Editor:
"I look for sincere and useful information written in a straight-forward, relaxed style."

Best Bet: Readily usable information for writers and philosophical articles describing the writing process.

Avoid: Pretension and paranoid treatise.

Sample copy: $4.98
Send #10 SASE for guidelines.

Profile
A bimonthly publication for writers. 8x10; self cover; 10 pages.

Focus and Audience
Useful, inspirational, and insightful articles for writers.

Interests and Word Lengths
- *Nonfiction:* Features, essays, and personal-experience pieces useful to writers. 800–1,000 words. Accepts poetry.
- *Departments:* Roundtable Discussions, forum for writers; Where to Sell Your Work, the writers market; Friendly Feedback, manuscript exchange.
- *Cartoons:* Non-political satirical cartoons.

How to Submit
Send complete ms with cover letter. Include SASE. Accepts photocopies, computer printouts, 3.5- and 5.25-inch IBM disks, and fax submissions. No simultaneous submissions. Reports in 2 weeks.

Payment and Policies
First North American serial rights. Pays on acceptance. $25 for features. Authors receive 1 copy of the issue.

Writers Information Network

Elaine Wright Colvin, Director
P.O. Box 11337
Bainbridge Island, WA 98110
206-842-9103

Profile

A bimonthly newsletter published by the Association
for Christian Writers to provide a link between writers
and publishers/editors. Est.: 1983; 8.5x11; newsletter; 16
pages.

Focus and Audience

Aims to help Christian writers further develop their writing and marketing skills. Provides a meeting ground of
encouragement for writers and public speakers. Keeps
writers abreast of industry news and market information.

Interests and Word Lengths

- *Nonfiction:* Religious market information; industry
  news and trends; practical how-to advice on writing
  and marketing; news and events of interest to Christian writers; devotional and inspirational material;
  book reviews. 50–300 words.

How to Submit

Send ms with cover letter and resume. Include SASE.
Accepts photocopies and computer printouts. No simultaneous submissions. Reports in 1–2 months.

Payment and Policies

First North American serial rights. Payment varies.
Often in the form of free one-year subscription or books.
Authors receive copies of the issue.

Year One

Elizabeth McAlister, Editor
1933 Park Avenue
Baltimore, MD 21217
410-669-6265

AT A GLANCE:

YEAR ONE

- Politics, Bible Study
- 50% freelance
- Quarterly
- Circ: 2,200
- Receives 2–4 mss each month.
- No payment. Offers contributor's copies.

From the Editor:
"We publish biblical and political reflections and news of communities committed to nonviolent resistance."

Sample copy: Free. No guidelines.

Profile

A quarterly newspaper that promotes nonviolent resistance. 11x17; 8–12 pages.

Focus and Audience

Offers biblical and political reflections on nonviolent activism and resistance based in the Judeo-Christian tradition.

Interests and Word Lengths

- *Nonfiction:* Analysis of and Bible studies applicable to current social and political realities. Reflection pieces and news. No word-length restrictions.
- *Poetry:* Accepts protest poetry.
- *Artwork:* B/W and color photos and illustrations.

How to Submit

Send complete ms with cover letter. Include SASE. Accepts photocopies, computer printouts, and Macintosh or MS-DOS disks. Simultaneous submissions okay. Report time varies.

Payment and Policies

All rights; authors retain reprint rights. No payment. Authors receive as many copies of the issue as requested.

You!

Tom Ehart, Managing Editor
29800 Agoura Road, No. 102
Agoura Hills, CA 91301
818-991-1813

AT A GLANCE:
You!

- Catholic, Teen
- 50% freelance
- 20% new writers
- 10 issues a year
- Circ: 100,000
- Receives 15 queries,
  15 mss each month.
- Payment negotiable.

From the Editor:
"Write upbeat, humorous articles in the language of teens. Give positive alternatives and solutions to teen issues, especially moral and social."

Best Bet: Articles that are upbeat, and humorous, but sincere and unafraid to speak the truth and point out negative things and wrongs.

Avoid: Fiction and dry, wordy, or textbookish articles.

Sample copy: $2 with 10x12 SAE and $1.44 postage. Send #10 SASE for guidelines.

Profile

A Catholic teen magazine that views popular culture through the eyes of faith and in light of Catholic beliefs. 10x12; glossy cover; newsprint; 28 pages.

Focus and Audience

Uses a contemporary format that challenges teens and young adults to have an optimistic view of life, a generous spirit, a disciplined and confident personality, and a desire to serve God, the Church, and humanity.

Interests and Word Lengths

- *Nonfiction:* Conversion experiences, radical experiences of faith, teens doing great and positive social work; features on tough social and moral problems. 200–1,000 words.
- *Departments:* Faith, conversion experiences. Makeover, before and after stories. Issues, timely topics. Fashion, Family, and Friends. 200–750 words.
- *Photos:* 4x6 or 3x7 B/W or color prints. Color slides.

How to Submit

Send complete ms with cover letter and clips. Include SASE. Accepts photocopies, computer printouts, Macintosh double density disks, and faxes. Simultaneous submissions okay. Reports in 2 months.

Payment and Policies

First International rights. Payment is negotiable; most writers are not paid. Authors receive up to 5 copies of the issue.

Young & Alive

Richard J. Kaiser, Editor-in-Chief
444 South 52nd Street
P.O. Box 6097
Lincoln, NE 68516
402-488-0981

AT A GLANCE:
YOUNG & ALIVE

- Christian, Visually-impaired Young Adults
- 90% freelance
- 5–10% new writers
- Quarterly
- Circ: 26,000
- Receives varied number of queries and mss each month.
- Pays: $.03–$.05 per word on acceptance.

From the Editor:
"Follow guidelines. Use timely topics and a conversational style. Keep in mind that you are writing for the sight-impaired."

Best Bet: Material that specifically meets the need of visually-impaired young adults.

Avoid: Highly controversial subjects.

Sample copy: Free with 9x12 SAE and $1.45 postage. Send #10 SASE for guidelines.

Profile

A quarterly Christian magazine for blind and visually - impaired young adults. Published in Braille and large print for an interdenominational Christian audience. 6.5x9.25; glossy cover; Braille or large print; 65–70 pages.

Focus and Audience

Provides wholesome, entertaining material that stimulates the thinking, feelings, and activities of sight-impaired young adults, ages 16–20. Assists readers in testing new ideas, forming relationships, and developing values in a positive way.

Interests and Word Lengths

- *Fiction:* Does not accept fiction per se. Serials, satire, and parables must at least be based on a true or actual incident or happening. 800–1,400 words.
- *Nonfiction:* Devotional and inspirational articles. Adventure, biography, camping, careers, handicapped experiences, health, history, hobbies, holidays, marriage, nature, practical Christianity, sports, and travel. Although visually impaired young adults have the same interests as their sighted counterparts, material should meet the needs of the visually impaired, specifically. 800–1,400 words. Accepts puzzles and quizzes.
- *Photos:* B/W glossy preferred. Accepts color transparencies.

How to Submit

Prefers query with outline. Will accept complete ms with cover letter. Include SASE. Accepts photocopies and computer printouts. Simultaneous submissions okay. Reports in 2–3 months.

Payment and Policies

One-time rights. Pays on acceptance. $.03–$.05 per word. Authors receive 2 copies of the issue.

Young Salvationist

Captain Lesa Salyer, Youth Editor
615 Slaters Lane
P.O. Box 269
Alexandria, VA 22313
703-684-5500

AT A GLANCE:
YOUNG SALVATIONIST

- Salvationist, Young Adult
- 80% freelance
- 10–20% new writers
- 10 issues a year
- Circ: 50,000
- Receives 10–20 queries, 30–50 mss each month.
- Pays: $.10 per word on acceptance.

From the Editor:
"We encourage submissions from new writers as well as accomplished authors. Write clearly and concisely. Don't talk down to young people. Send for a sample copy and theme list."

Best Bet: Believable stories and real-life articles that offer Christian truths from a Salvationist perspective.

Avoid: Sermonizing; tacked-on morals.

Sample copy: Free with 9x12 SAE and 3 first-class stamps. Send #10 SASE for guidelines and theme list.

Profile
A magazine for Salvationist youth. Published 10 times a year by The Salvation Army in the U.S. 8.5x11; 16 pages.

Focus and Audience
Presents a Christian perspective of issues affecting high school and college-age young adults. Wesleyan in theology and politically non-partisan.

Interests and Word Lengths
- *Fiction:* Short stories on any topic from a distinctly Christian perspective. Wants convincing plots with believable conflicts solvable by the main character. Use realistic characters and natural dialog. 500–1,000 words.
- *Nonfiction:* Feature articles on and interviews with Christian musicians and athletes. Address real-life issues faced by teenagers and offer Christian truths without sermonizing. Conclusions or solutions should be consistent with biblical principles. 500–1,000 words.

How to Submit
Query with outline or send complete ms with cover letter. Include SASE. Accepts photocopies and computer printouts. Simultaneous submissions okay. Reports in 1 month.

Payment and Policies
First North American serial or one-time rights. Pays on acceptance. $.10 per word. Authors receive 4 copies of the issue.

Your Church

James D. Berkley, Editor
465 Gundersen Drive
Carol Stream, IL 60188
708-260-6200

AT A GLANCE:
YOUR CHURCH

- Christian, Church Business
- 90% freelance
- 10% new writers
- Bimonthly
- Circ: 150,000
- Receives 5 queries, 2 mss each month.
- Pays: $.10 per word on acceptance.

From the Editor:
"Query first showing your understanding of *Your Church*'s editorial slant and subject matter."

Best Bet: Practical, concise, and pastor friendly articles on church business management.

Avoid: Negative or patronizing attitudes toward clergy or churches; flowery prose; general religious articles.

Sample copy: Free with 9x12 SAE and $1.67 postage. Send #10 SASE for guidelines.

Profile

A controlled-circulation trade journal focusing solely on church business administration. Published by Christianity Today, Inc. 8x11; 50 pages.

Focus and Audience

Designed to help churches with the business of ministry—administration, facilities management, and purchasing. No general religious fare. Written for pastors and church business administrators.

Interests and Word Lengths

- *Nonfiction:* Practical articles on church computing, finance, law, music, audio-visual resources, office equipment and systems, facilities management, construction and renovation, church furnishing, and general church management. 900–1,200 words.
- *Departments:* Original research on church statistics. 900–1,000 words.
- *Illustrations:* Cartoons about church business from an insider's perspective.

How to Submit

Query with outline. Include SASE. Accepts photocopies, computer printouts, 5.25-inch IBM-compatible disks, and fax submissions. No simultaneous submissions. Reports in 2 months.

Payment and Policies

First rights plus anthology rights. Pays on acceptance. $.10 per word. Authors receive 2 copies of the issue.

Youth and Christian Education Leadership

Lance Colkmire, Editor
1080 Montgomery Avenue
P.O. Box 2250
Cleveland, TN 37323

AT A GLANCE:

YOUTH AND CHRISTIAN EDUCATION LEADERSHIP

- Church of God, Education
- 80% freelance
- 5% new writers
- Quarterly
- Circ: 12,000
- Pays: $30–$50 on acceptance.

From the Editor:
"Let your writing show you have done your research. Do not theorize; instead, be very practical. Explore what works, what doesn't, and why."

Best Bet: Personal-experience articles from Christian education workers, especially teachers.

Avoid: Generic how-to's; articles that require no research.

Sample copy: $1 with 8.5x11 SASE. Send #10 SASE for guidelines.

Profile

A quarterly publication for Church of God educators. 8x11; 32 pages.

Focus and Audience

Provides practical information, inspiration, and direction for Christian education teachers and workers in Pentecostal congregations.

Interests and Word Lengths

- *Nonfiction:* Personal testimonies and feature articles concerning trends in Christian education; interviews with noted Christian educators; well-researched how-to articles on successful Christian education ministries. Quote recognized Christian educators and offer statistics. 400–1,000 words.
- *Departments:* Outreach, Senior Adult Ministry, Children's Ministry, and Youth Ministry. Offers specific ways in which churches are ministering in these areas. 200–400 words.
- *Photos:* B/W photos of individuals and groups.

How to Submit

Send complete ms with cover letter and resume. Include SASE. Accepts photocopies and computer printouts. Simultaneous submissions okay. Reports in 3 months.

Payment and Policies

First North American serial or one-time rights. Pays on acceptance. $30–$50 per piece. Authors receive 3–5 copies of the issue.

Youth Update

Carol Ann Morrow, Editor
1615 Republic Street
Cincinnati, OH 45210-1298
513-241-5615

AT A GLANCE:
YOUTH UPDATE

- Catholic, Teen
- 90% freelance
- Monthly
- Circ: 30,000
- Receives 12 queries, 12 mss each month.
- Pays: $.14 per word on acceptance.

From the Editor:
"Query first, after requesting guidelines and sample and studying them."

Best Bet: Articles for Catholic teens that address timely topics.

Avoid: Cuteness; glib phrases and clichés; academic or erudite approaches; preachiness.

Sample copy: Free with guidelines for a #10 SASE.

Profile
A monthly publication for Catholic teenagers. Published by St. Anthony Messenger Press. 8.5x11; 2-color; folded; 4 pages.

Focus and Audience
Aims to support the growth of teenagers in faith through application of Catholic principles to topics of timely interest. Readers are high school-age teens who vary both in religious education and reading ability.

Interests and Word Lengths
- *Nonfiction:* Articles on prayer, spirituality, and timely topics relevant to teenagers. Include as sidebar a quiz, checklist, inventory, or table related to article topic. Use examples, anecdotes, references to the real world, inclusive language, and a casual, conversational tone. Past topics include African-American values, parents, money, confession, anger, TV, divorce, breaking up, time management, St. Francis of Assisi, alcoholism, and the Beatitudes. 2,300 words.

How to Submit
Query with outline. Include SASE. After acceptance, authors are required to answer follow-up questions presented by the editor. Answers are published with the article. No simultaneous submissions. Reports in 6–8 weeks.

Payment and Policies
First North American serial rights. Pays on acceptance. $.14 per word. Authors receive copies of the issue.

GLOSSARY

All rights: Ownership rights contracted to a publisher. Allows use of manuscript anywhere and in any form without consent of the author.

Assignment: Commissioning a manuscript by an editor for a predetermined fee.

B/W: Black and white; refers to photographs, slides, and illustrations.

Bibliography: A list of the books, articles, and other sources referred to in a text or consulted by the author in its production.

Bimonthly: Published every two months.

Byline: A line at the beginning of an article crediting the author.

Circulation: Average number of copies of a publication sold per printing.

Clips: Samples of a writer's published work.

Contributor's copies: Copies of the issue in which the writer's work appears.

Copyedit: Closely editing a manuscript for grammar, punctuation, style, and mechanics.

Copyright: The exclusive legal right to copy, publish, and sell written works, music, photographs, and illustrations.

Cover letter: A brief business letter accompanying a complete manuscript. (see *How to Write a Cover Letter,* p. 7)

Deadline: Due date for the submission of a complete manuscript.

Denomination: A religious organization uniting a number of congregations in a single legal and administrative body.

Doctrine: The position of and principles in a specific system of belief.

Disk submissions: Manuscripts submitted on computer diskette.

Dot-matrix printout: Computer printout where the individual characters are composed of a pattern of dots.

Essay: Analytic or interpretive article written from a limited or personal point of view.

Feature: Often a lead article of human interest rather than news.

Fiction: An invented story of the imagination.

Filler: Short items used to fill a page: jokes, puzzles, short facts.

First North American serial rights: The right to publish an article or story for the first time in North America.

Genre: A category of fiction characterized by a specific format, style, or content such as romance, mystery, or fantasy.

Glossy prints: Photographs printed on a shiny finish as opposed to a matte finish.

In-house: Material written by a publication's staff, usually departments or columns.

Interfaith: Involving people of different religious faiths.

International Reply Coupon (IRC): Coupon exchangeable in any foreign country for postage on a single-rate, surface-mailed letter.

Kill fee: Percentage of an agreed upon fee that is paid to a writer for a completed assigned article that has been canceled.

Lead: The beginning of an article.

Lead time: Time between the acquisition of a manuscript and its publication.

Letter-quality printout: A computer printout that looks typewritten.

Manuscript: A handwritten or typewritten document.

Ms/mss: Manuscript/manuscripts.

Nonfiction: Literature based in fact not invention.

Novella: A work of fiction falling in length between a short story and a novel.

One-time rights: The right to publish a piece one time.

Outline: A summary covering the main points of an article under headings and subheadings.

Parable: A short fictitious story that illustrates a moral or religious principle.

Payment on acceptance: Payment for an article or story is made upon the editor's decision to publish it.

Payment on publication: Payment for an article or story is made on or following its publication.

Personal-experience piece: An article based on the author's experience.

Proofread: The reading and correction of a manuscript's errors, usually spelling, punctuation, and typographical.

Quarterly: Published four times a year in regular intervals.

Query: A business letter written to interest an editor in an article idea. (see *How to Write a Query Letter,* p. 5)

Reprint: A subsequent printing of an article in a different publication or format.

Reprint rights: The right to publish an article or story that has previously appeared in another publication. Also called Second rights.

Resume: A short account of one's professional and educational qualifications and publishing credits.

SAE: Self-addressed envelope.

SASE: Self-addressed, stamped, envelope.

Self cover: A publication that uses the same interior and exterior paper.

Semi-annual: Published twice a year.

Serial: A story published in parts at intervals.

Simultaneous submission: Submitting the same article or story to more than one publication at a time.

Slant: A particular approach to an article that will appeal to a specific readership.

Slush pile: Describes a back log of unsolicited manuscripts.

Solicited manuscript: A manuscript specifically requested by an editor.

Staff written: Written by the publication's staff; usually columns or departments.

Synopsis: A brief summary of a fictional piece.

Tabloid: A style of newspaper that is half the size of an ordinary newspaper and contains news in a condensed fashion.

Theology: The study of religious faith, practice, and experience.

Transparencies: Color slides.

Trim size: The height and width of a publication.

Unsolicited manuscript: Any manuscript not specifically assigned by an editor.

Word count: Refers to the approximate number of words in manuscript.

World rights: The right to publish a manuscript anywhere in the world.

Writer's guidelines: Editorial objectives and specifications provided by editors for writers.

Writing samples: Examples of a writer's unpublished work often sent with a query.

INDEX OF PUBLICATIONS